CITY OF CHAMPIONS

Also by Stefan Szymanski

Money and Soccer

Soccernomics

Playbooks and Checkbooks

Fans of the World Unite!

National Pastime

Also by Silke-Maria Weineck

*The Tragedy of Fatherhood: King Laius and the
Politics of Paternity in the West*

*The Abyss Above: Philosophy and Poetic Madness
in Plato, Hölderlin, and Nietzsche*

CITY OF CHAMPIONS

A HISTORY OF TRIUMPH AND DEFEAT IN DETROIT

STEFAN SZYMANSKI AND
SILKE-MARIA WEINECK

THE
NEW
PRESS

NEW YORK
LONDON

Requests for permission to reproduce selections from this book should be made through our website: https://thenewpress.com/contact.

Published in the United States by The New Press, New York, 2020
Distributed by Two Rivers Distribution

ISBN 978-1-62097-442-1 (hc)
ISBN 978-1-62097-443-8 (ebook)
CIP data is available

The New Press publishes books that promote and enrich public discussion and understanding of the issues vital to our democracy and to a more equitable world. These books are made possible by the enthusiasm of our readers; the support of a committed group of donors, large and small; the collaboration of our many partners in the independent media and the not-for-profit sector; booksellers, who often hand-sell New Press books; librarians; and above all by our authors.

www.thenewpress.com

Book design and composition by Bookbright Media
This book was set in Sabon and Alternate Gothic 2

Printed in the United States of America

10 9 8 7 6 5 4 3 2 1

CONTENTS

INTRODUCTION: JANUARY 1, 2020

The Paris of New France, then the Motor City. The Arsenal of Democracy, later Motown. New Fallujah, the Murder Capital, the Comeback City. Detroit has gone by so many names since its founder, Antoine Laumet de la Mothe Cadillac, declared in the early eighteenth century that "all nations will come to settle there." They did, and they built what we believe is the most American of American cities, embodying the country's glory and agony alike.

This book is about Detroit as the City of Champions and its many triumphs and defeats, athletic and otherwise. Sports have a unique power to unify those who have nothing in common—they are the last mass ritual in a fractured world. Athletic events mark city life and city time. By now, they are the only venues in which a city routinely expresses itself *as* a city. The Tigers, the Lions, the Red Wings, and the Pistons belong to Detroit before they belong to their owners, and it is not by chance that Joe Louis's fist has become the most recognizable symbol of the city, eclipsing the giant monument known as *The Spirit of Detroit*.

Sports not only have the power to create community in the moment, to bind people in fleeting experiences of shared pride, exuberant joy, bottomless rage, or crushing disappointment—be that in Tiger Stadium or the Masonic Temple, where the Detroit Roller Derby league plays. Sports create stories and images that endure long past the event, often centered on legendary figures: Ty Cobb, Charlie Gehringer, Hank Greenberg, Joe Louis, Sugar Ray Robinson, Gordie Howe, Bobby Layne, Dave Bing, Tommy Hearns, Isiah Thomas. This book tells many of these stories, but it is not a book about famous athletes so much as a book about the city that watched them win and lose, and so it tells the city's stories alongside theirs. Our accounts are not meant to be exhaustive—they build on the work of countless historians, journalists, novelists, and other keen observers, and anybody who wants to delve deeper will find references to their books and articles in the notes.

Sports are and have always been a site of struggles that seemingly exceed them. The fact that they bring people together who would otherwise have nothing to say to each other does not mean that they erase the fault lines that run through American public life. No matter how loudly major league owners clamor for political neutrality—which is simply a particular kind of politics, anyway—sports are about race, sports are about money, sports are about gender, infrastructure, violence, aesthetics, class, history, and identity. Sometimes, you can forget about all of that during the game or the fight or the race, but it always comes back: in a city's Olympic bids and the global political forces that doom them, in the anti-Semitic jeers hurled at Hank Greenberg, in Joe Louis's fight against Hitler's favorite boxer, in a city budget that can find money for a stadium but not for heated classrooms, in a women's baseball league that forces its players to wear make-up and slide into base wearing miniskirts.

"All cities are mad: but the madness is gallant," the American journalist and novelist Christopher Morley wrote. "All cities are beautiful, but the beauty is grim."[1] Detroit can be very grim and very beautiful, quite mad, and so gallant. Just as it rose higher than most cities in the first half of the twentieth century, it fell harder than most in the second half. The times when the Tigers, the Red Wings, and the Lions could nab all the major league championships in a single year are long gone, as are the years when Detroit was one of the richest cities in America. The city that changed the country and the world when it began churning out millions upon millions of cars, the city that made the weapons of war that defeated the Axis powers in 1945 was abandoned after the war, first in a trickle, then a stream—abandoned by those who wanted to leave or had no choice in the matter, then abandoned by the country that did little to stem, let alone reverse, its economic decline. Few American cities survived the rise of the suburbs intact, but few were hollowed out as dramatically as Detroit, the first major American city to go into bankruptcy.

And yet, Detroit is still beautiful, still gallant, still ever-changing—a city that pulls on your heartstrings, not least because it is a border town, and those always carry a certain ambiguity of belonging. Even Chrysler, in marking its cars "imported from Detroit," signaled they were foreign in a way. Of course, there is something of a cliché in two Europeans falling in love with the city, picking their favorite team (Detroit City Football Club!), and deciding to write a book about it. Detroit has seen its share of white tourists who marvel and shudder at the industrial ruins and the abandoned homes, grab a fancy meal at Selden Standard, catch a show at the Fox Theatre, pose with *The Fist*, take a quick ride on the People Mover, and take off again. We have tried very hard not to be those people but to immerse ourselves in the rich, troubling, glorious, multi-layered history of the city, from its earliest days to its ongoing rebirth as "the most exciting city in America," to quote the *New York Times*.

Our chapters are anchored in iconic moments in Detroit sports, but they fan out, as it were, into the life of the city and its people that surrounds these moments and gives them deeper meaning. Sometimes the stories of the sports and stories of the city emerge as closely intertwined, sometimes they run in parallel. Some of the stories speak about victory and conquest, others about defeat and humiliation. Still others are ambivalent—sports create community, but they create intense conflict as well—conflict is, after all, the beating heart of competitive sports, and the unbridled emotion they authorize can turn ugly in a heartbeat.

We have chosen to tell these stories in reverse chronological order, so our readers can go back in time, uncovering layer after layer; see patterns emerge; see the city rise and fall and rise again as it hurtles through American history, and as this history hurtles through it in turn. In this regard, the book functions like a palimpsest, where you encounter the most recent and the most familiar stratum of meaning first, going back in time as you discover the older events that shaped what came after—like an archaeology project that uncovers buried layers of Detroit's history, unfamiliar and yet intrinsically linked to the present.

In today's Detroit, the major league teams, whose layered history we touch on again and again, may be struggling a bit—but all over town, smaller enterprises have sprung up, clubs and leagues that belong to their players and their fans and the neighborhoods, not the billionaires. The Detroit Roller Derby league, for instance, and the Detroit City Football Club are not just good fun to watch; they are building community, and they command intense loyalty in return.

Spanning more than a hundred years, this account is not, needless to say, a complete history of either Detroit or its sports. We do believe, however, that much of the city's past is mirrored in the exploits of its major league teams, its legendary athletes, their fans, and the spaces in which they played and fought, cheered and suffered. Calling the book "City of Champions," a term coined in that golden season of 1935–36, may seem a bit wistful, seeing that Detroit has not seen a major league trophy in more than a decade. But the Motor City remains one of the top five cities in the United States when it comes to major league championships, and it remains one of America's preeminent sports cities, one of its many sources of pride. To our regret, this book largely neglects the history of Detroit's women—the culture and history of the city's sports have been dominated by men, and our book could not but reflect this state of affairs.

Contemporary accounts of Detroit often talk of a "wasteland," conjuring the notion of a barren emptiness. There are indeed large tracts of the city today resembling the prairies and woodlands that once covered the land before the city was built, even though new buildings are springing up in many of them as we write this. Beneath today's urban meadows, however, lies the archaeology of a city that has existed for over three hundred years, an archaeology as interesting as that of ancient Rome or the Inca ruins of Machu Picchu. Detroit, too, has its ruins, and these ruins carry multiple meanings, infused with complex histories—whether it is the crumbling old Ford plant in Highland Park, the first facility to build cars on an assembly line, or derelict Michigan Central Station, the stunning Beaux-Arts building now owned by the Ford Motor Company, which has promised to redevelop it.

Detroit is the crucible of modern America. It is the place where generations of immigrants and of migrants from the South joined together, under intense pressure, to shape a social and an economic system that from its core disgorged in unprecedented volumes that quintessential American product, the motor car. As the nineteenth-century transcendentalist Theodore Parker put it, "Cities have always been the fireplaces of civilization, whence light and heat radiated out into the dark"[2]—though the heat of the factories created its own darknesses in turn. The social system in Detroit shaped Americans' fears and aspirations in their struggle to build their lives, their families, and their nation, producing both extraordinary success and catastrophic failure—most brutally, the failure to grant African American Detroiters a full and equal share in the life of the city, which remains the most segregated in the nation. At every stage along the way, narratives of those struggles have relied on metaphors of competition, of winning and losing, of teams and opponents. Over and over again, the city has turned to sports to unite a fragile community and to pitch Detroit and Detroiters against their rivals. Major league teams, in particular, represent their cities in a way their elected representatives never quite manage, and they are rewarded with a fierce loyalty that few politicians ever command.

This book is a labor of love, a love we hope our readers will share and spread.

ONE

SEPTEMBER 5, 2017

Little Caesars Arena opens, and Detroit is once more a four-sports city. The stadium's owners promised that the stadium, financed partially with public money, would anchor a thriving neighborhood development, but so far, only parking lots have proliferated. A cautionary tale about sports development, and a lesson Detroit should have learned decades earlier. The Detroit City Football Club models a different relationship to the community that surrounds and sustains it.

Start on the spot on the Detroit River where Antoine de la Mothe Cadillac made landfall in 1701. A short stroll takes you past the International Memorial to the Underground Railroad to *The Fist*, the memorial to Joe Louis, planted in the middle of eight-lane Jefferson Avenue. Walking on up Woodward Avenue, you pass the Coleman A. Young building, named after the city's first black mayor. The building houses much of the city's administration, and outside is the peculiar sculpture *The Spirit of Detroit*, which vies with *The Fist* for the honor of symbolizing the City of Champions. On your left now is the terminus of the QLine, whose trams first started rolling three miles up Woodward in the summer of 2017, reminiscent of the streetcars of a bygone era. Less than one hundred yards further, you enter Campus Martius, the point where the radial spokes that form the principal avenues of Detroit meet: Michigan, Gratiot, Lafayette, and Woodward itself. Remodeled often, the center of Campus Martius now boasts a restaurant, tables where deceptively relaxed chess players hustle for a few dollars, an urban beach that doubles as a huge sandbox for children, a sound stage, and an outdoor bar. Staying on Woodward, you will pass on your right a

Brazilian steakhouse, a Mexican restaurant, and the site where Shinola, the city's fashionable retailer of bicycles, watches, and leather goods, will soon open a new luxury hotel. As you reach the Whitney Building on your left, the view opens onto Grand Circus Park, where in the summertime, you can watch an amateur production of *Othello*, or perhaps *Romeo and Juliet*.

Some of the city's most important public spaces can be found here. If the southern end of Woodward is six o'clock on the dial of Grand Circus, the Detroit Opera House is at five o'clock, and at four o'clock stands the Detroit Athletic Club, for more than a century one of the finest meeting places in the city for the well connected. At three o'clock, surrounded by twenty-foot plaster models of angry tigers, stands Comerica Park, home of the Detroit Major League Baseball team. Right behind it is Ford Field, the modestly adorned but vast indoor stadium where the Detroit Lions play. The two stadiums are so close that any decent quarterback could throw a Hail Mary pass from one to the other, and any decent batter could hit a fly ball back.

Crossing Grand Circus, still continuing along Woodward, you can stop to admire the magnificent Fox Theatre and the Detroit Hockeytown bar on your left. A bridge will take you across the eight-lane Fisher Freeway, a noisy barrier between downtown and midtown, but one which people are more willing to cross these days. On the other side of the freeway there is a row of townhouses on the right, while on the left looms District Detroit, the brand new development that is opening on this day, September 5, 2017.

District Detroit is the brainchild of Mike Ilitch, whose mark is to be found everywhere in contemporary Detroit. Ilitch was born in Detroit in 1929 to parents who had immigrated from Macedonia. After serving in the marines during the Korean War—he didn't see combat because they wanted him to play for a military baseball team in Pearl Harbor instead—he played minor league baseball for a few years before using all his savings to start a small company: Little Caesars Pizza.[1] As Little Caesars grew, so did Ilitch's involvement in the life of the city. He invested in real estate, funded city charities, and ultimately became one of the major players in Detroit's sports teams, owning first the Detroit Red Wings, then the Detroit Tigers. In a city increasingly abandoned by the white population, Ilitch became a hero to many of its citizens because he stayed, and with him, his money. In 2009, when GM was forced to suspend its sponsorship at Comerica Park, he used the space to advertise the three struggling automakers, free of charge.[2] District Detroit was his last great project—a shopping mall and business center surrounding an arena built to house the Red Wings. Ilitch passed away in February 2017, before the official opening, but construction must have been far enough along for him to know that he could rest secure in his legacy.

At the time of Mike Ilitch's death, only one piece was missing before the city would once again be a four-sports town. In the summer of 2017, negotiations to bring the final team home from the suburbs proved a success when an agreement was reached in July: the Pistons were returning to the city, joining the Red Wings at District Detroit. Four major league franchises would now operate within one mile of each other, a feat only Philadelphia had managed so far.

The opening ceremony, as described in the *Detroit Free Press*, kicks off with a performance by the Cass Tech High School Band. More than a thousand people are there, and dozens of construction workers watch, still wearing their hard hats. News cameras line the risers. Christopher Ilitch, CEO of Ilitch Holdings, declares that his family has "put our heart and soul into something truly spectacular for the people of this city, state and region." The grand opening, he says, "launches a new era in Detroit professional sports where four teams, including the Tigers and Lions, play within four blocks of each other in downtown, a claim no other city in the U.S. can make." His father, the late Mike Ilitch, "would be doing his signature double fist pump showing his excitement if he was still here."[3] Michigan governor Rick Snyder, Detroit mayor Mike Duggan, City Council president Brenda Jones, and Detroit Pistons owner Tom Gores join Ilitch on the stage. "As far as Detroit goes, this is a huge win," Gores tells the crowd. "I think this could complete our comeback."[4]

Allan Lengel of the property magazine *Urban Land* breathlessly reports on the scope of the project in April 2018, calling Ilitch's announcement of the project a "public bombshell" and noting that the "urban sports/entertainment district in Detroit is not the first in the country. But the District Detroit . . . is being billed as one of the largest of its type in the nation, with eight world-class theaters, five mixed-use neighborhoods, a 250- to 300-room hotel, restaurants, bars, and three professional sports venues to host the aforementioned baseball, hockey, and football teams, plus the National Basketball Association's Detroit Pistons. . . . The company's website boasts that the project will link 'downtown and Midtown into one contiguous, walkable area, where families, sports fans, entrepreneurs, job seekers, entertainment lovers, and others who crave a vibrant urban setting can connect with each other and the city they love.'" The reporter continues:

> Data from the University of Michigan project that the District Detroit will account for an economic impact of more than $2 billion by 2020, plus create more than 20,000 construction and construction-related jobs and 3,000 permanent jobs. It has already generated more than $700 million in contracts for Michigan companies and created 836 apprentice jobs.
>
> Among the developments under construction are the Mike Ilitch School of Business, for which Mike Ilitch and his wife Marian contributed $40 million toward the $50 million total cost.
>
> In addition, Google will take up nearly 30,000 square feet (2,800 sq m) on the second and third floors of a new mixed-use structure being built next to the Little Caesars Arena, and a new nine-story, 234,000-square-foot (22,000 sq m) headquarters building for Little Caesars Pizza is being built at a cost of $150 million. Little Caesars will be moving to the new building from Fox Office Center, which is connected to the Fox Theatre, a grand entertainment venue. That building will continue to be used for employees of Ilitch Holdings and Olympia Development [the property development arm of Ilitch Holdings], and others.[5]

Thus, the District Detroit joined a slew of stories about the renaissance of the city, emblematic of a narrative of renewal that people have told about the city ever since it exited Chapter 9 bankruptcy in November 2014—and as so often happens in the history of Detroit, this grand plan comes stamped with the name of a billionaire. Just one year after the opening, however, the headlines change. A particularly brutal one appears in *The Guardian* on October 8, 2018: "Big Promises for a Thriving Urban Core in Detroit Vanish in a Swath of Parking Lots." Here is a further taste from that article:

In recent years, Ilitch companies in and around The District leveled at least 30 buildings and currently maintain nearly 40 blighted or vacant structures. On blocks where historic buildings once stood, they have laid dozens of surface parking lots. Those are controversial because the Ilitches charge up to $50 per spot, and a vast stretch of once-dense downtown real estate is now a sea of Ilitch-owned parking spaces.

The article notes that a website has sprung up, called "Terrible Ilitches," which tracks demolished and neglected lots, barren parking lots, and lots the family bought from the city for $1 apiece.[6] The chair of a neighborhood council that advises the Ilitches' Olympia Development on community benefits believes that the project has led to a "net deficit" and is "not even at zero" yet. The reporter also quotes sports economist Victor Matheson, who dryly notes that it's pretty common for new stadium-centered developments to be slow to deliver and not live up to the hype, but adds, "It is extremely rare to see a stadium cause a neighborhood to go backwards— that is very rare."[7]

In November 2018, the *Detroit News* follows suit with an article titled "Cass Corridor Neighbors See Unfilled Promises in Little Caesars Arena District." The paper reports that neighbors "were promised five new walkable neighborhoods filled with shops, restaurants and housing. What they've gotten so far, they say, has been traffic gridlock, twenty-seven parking facilities—some taking up entire blocks—and fewer places to live."[8] In March 2019, *Crain's Detroit Business* hammers the point home, in a piece titled "Is District Detroit Delivering?"—by now, that reads like a rhetorical question. Quoting Cristopher Ilitch again ("the District Detroit will be one of the most unique and exciting places in the country to live"!) the article points out that there were "no shovels in the ground" with regard to the promised 687 new apartments, and that "the lack of progress on housing is among the things that feed into a growing narrative that Olympia makes big development plans but are only truly committed to delivering on the pieces tied directly to their existing businesses, such as Little Caesars Arena, the new Little Caesars pizza headquarters, along with parking garages and lots." In the meantime, the Ilitches and Olympia insist that the projects are in the pipeline, that all will be well.

The story encapsulates many of the themes that will surface throughout this book—the outsized role of major league team owners, the complicated and often troubled relationship between sports and city development, the repeated failure of municipal incentive schemes, the many ways in which glitzy prestige projects have left behind those who were meant to benefit from them the most—in Detroit, this has predominantly meant African Americans, but also immigrants and the poor of all races and ethnicities. The disappointment that is the District Detroit is all the more notable since the areas surrounding the development have been thriving, complete with all the losses and sacrifices gentrification entails. While the Ilitches built parking lots around what's now known as "the Pizzarena," neighboring Brush Park, midtown's Cass Corridor, and the downtown have evolved into bustling and highly desirable neighborhoods. The entire area of greater downtown Detroit now goes by "the 7.2 Square Miles," a sobering reminder that the city's revival is largely limited to just a fraction of its 138-square-mile territory—as always, gentrification has attracted mostly white, affluent, and well-educated newcomers who can afford real estate that has already priced out most of the city's population. It is 2017, the fiftieth anniversary of the Uprising, the Rebellion, the Riot.

Those who present ballparks and stadiums as a silver bullet for all that ails struggling cities—a crowd that mostly consists of developers and owners and politicians who depends on their largesse—are clearly and demonstrably wrong.[9] Those who dismiss the meaning and power of sports out of hand, we believe, are wrong as well—"to ignore sport is to ignore a significant aspect of any society and its culture," as Tim Delaney and Tim Madigan write.[10] The history of American sports mirrors the history of the country, and sports have always been political—particularly with regard to America's ongoing legacy of slavery, segregation, and discrimination, an entanglement we will trace again and again in subsequent chapters. Their economic benefit to the cities that host them may frequently be marginal, but at their best, major league sports have an almost unparalleled capacity to create community and pride. Ideally, the teams belong to their city; their triumphs are the city's triumphs, their defeats create rituals of collective mourning. They are their hometown's ambassadors, they spread the city's name, and in troubling times—of which Detroit has seen many—they can be one of the few remaining sources of good news and good cheer.

It is probably too early to tell how the District Detroit will play out. While early signs have been discouraging, to put it gently, it is still possible that there will be a suitable payoff from the city's considerable investment of public funds—$324 million in taxpayer money (not counting the value of sweetheart land deals), with few strings attached, despite misleading early rhetoric that the cost to the city would be $0. Surprisingly, the deal was finalized as the city was finally going broke. Detroit has been the largest American city by far to ever declare itself insolvent, and in some accounts, the city's bankruptcy is the nadir of its history. But actually, significant if localized improvements had already emerged when the financial crisis ended and Congress bailed out the motor industry. In *The Metropolitan Revolution*, Bruce Katz and Jennifer Bradley highlighted changes in Detroit over recent years to illustrate how seemingly broken cities are making a comeback.[11] Published in 2013, just before the city entered Chapter 9, the book declared the city center an "innovation district," thanks largely to the investment of Quicken Loans billionaire Dan Gilbert, who now owns the majority of skyscrapers in the downtown. His commitment to the revival of his hometown, which included moving almost all his employees there, helped to spark an investment boom, as other businesses have followed Gilbert's lead. Bradley and Katz point out that these developments have created powerful synergy with the huge Detroit medical system and with Wayne State University, connected now by a new streetcar system that unites downtown and midtown—though far from everybody in Detroit is a Gilbert fan, as we shall see in the next chapter.

There are many dimensions to this still-fragile Detroit revival. Out on the East Side is the fabulously eccentric Heidelberg Project, which has turned two streets of decaying housing into an enchanting art installation. In springtime, the Movement Electronic Music Festival draws fans from all over the world—techno, after all, was born in metro Detroit. Craft breweries are springing up everywhere, while the riverfront walk for the first time exploits the leisure potential of the city's waterfront, where you can also keep an eye on the Canadians. New cycle paths such as the Dequindre Cut link the riverfront to the Eastern Market's thriving flower and food stalls—Detroit now has a vibrant cycling community with over seventy miles of pathways. Artists and young people in search of a city that is both hip and affordable have been steadily colonizing corners of the city where houses can still, in some cases, be bought for as little as $100, though one-bedroom apartments in "the 7.2" go for hundreds of thousands of dollars now. The Detroit Institute of Arts, which houses an impressive collection of European art alongside the iconic Diego Rivera murals of industrial Detroit, remains one of the finest museums in the country, but there are smaller ones as well, such as the Motown Museum including Hitsville U.S.A., which celebrates the history of Motown records. The Fox Theatre still attracts national and international acts, the three major casinos offer nightlife along with an opportunity to lose your life's savings, there is an expanding club scene, and any number of fantastic restaurants have opened up, and appear to be thriving.

In the end, though, Americans love no leisure activity more than they love sports, and Detroit's pro teams are called upon to represent the city to the nation. With around 170 regular season home games across the four sports, chances are there is a major league game on tonight, and if not, there is one tomorrow or there was one just yesterday. Of course, as with all things Detroit, the teams have a ways to go. It has been more than a decade since anyone won a championship, and there is no sign that this is about to change anytime soon. To be sure, the Tigers did mount a credible effort to win the World Series, with standout pitching from Justin Verlander and a batting lineup led by Miguel "Miggy" Cabrera. In fact, much of this effort could be read as a last homage to Mike Ilitch, as the family realized that his time was running out—a World Series victory would have been an astonishing capstone to a lifetime of business success and undying devotion to Detroit's sports. But it was not to be—we will tell that story in the next chapter, along with the story of the city's bankruptcy and its causes. Suffice it to say that in August 2017, less than six months after Mike Ilitch died, Verlander was traded; the road to Major League Baseball success began to look like a very long one indeed; and the District Detroit began to falter.

Certainly, the Lions could be said to have raised their game—they are now back to a level where we may comfortably call them mediocre. At least, in this decade, they've had as many regular seasons over .500 as under, and they twice made it to a wild-card playoff game. While there are cities where such records would be cause for despair, here, they count as better than nothing, though the contrast with the college football teams in Ann Arbor and Lansing has been a source of bitterness. As for the Pistons or the Red Wings? Those two used to be a source of wild pride in the D, but they have been treading water, and sometimes underwater, for a decade. The stage is set, but the actors capable of filling that stage have yet to step up.

It is fair, then, to ask whether the major league teams are really the city's best hope. The city is host to an abundance of sporting activities that do not require billionaire owners or large public subsidies. Just around the corner from the District Detroit on Temple Street, you'll find the Masonic Temple, where the Detroit Roller Derby league holds its games, fielding teams like the Pistoffs, the Devil's Night Dames, and the Grand Prix Madonnas.[12] Similarly, Detroit City Football Club—DCFC, or simply "City," as it is known—is prospering on the basis of an entirely different model. Unlike major league teams, whose fortunes are dictated almost entirely by the whims of their super-rich owners, DCFC is a true community endeavor, and the club has made it its mission to have an impact in the community, organizing youth programs, fielding a women's team that started competing in 2020, and partnering with local charities. DCFC was the first American team to sport a uniform featuring rainbow colors in support of the LGBTQ community. While its new stadium in Hamtramck has a modest capacity of 7,933, City has earned fierce loyalty not so much for its soccer performance—which is a work in progress—as for its multifaceted commitment to the people who live, work, and cheer in their neighborhood.

TWO

OCTOBER 24, 2012

In 2012, the Tigers, favorites to win the World Series, flounder against the Giants. Roughly two months later, Republican governor Rick Snyder signs a slightly revised version of the emergency manager law that voters had soundly rejected in a statewide referendum, and half a year after that, Detroit enters Chapter 9 bankruptcy. Dan Gilbert begins buying up iconic downtown property, but his plans to bring a Major League Soccer team to Detroit, so far, have failed—leaving the field to the homegrown DCFC, which is soaring.

Game 1 in the 2012 World Series. The score is tied at 0–0. The count is 0-2, with two outs at the bottom of the first. Justin Verlander, winner of the previous year's Cy Young award and the most revered player on the Detroit Tigers, will surely close out the inning easily. He throws a high fastball. Not the kind of pitch on which Pablo Sandoval thrives, but it's over the middle of the plate, so he swings anyway. Home run, 1–0 Giants. These things happen.

In the second inning, honors are even: three up and three down for both the Tigers and the Giants. At the top of the third, Austin Jackson gets a single, but no one else gets on base; the score is still 1–0. At the bottom of the third, Verlander disposes of the first two batters and has two strikes against Ángel Pagán. Pagán fouls off three of the next four pitches and leaves one for a ball. Verlander throws a pitch far outside—you'd expect that to be a swing and a miss, or at worst a ball. But, somehow, Pagán connects and doubles to left field. Next up is Marco Scutaro, who fouls off a couple of fast balls after reaching full count. Verlander then throws a slider, not a bad pitch under the circumstances and well executed, only Scutaro gets hold of it and singles to center field, allowing Pagán to score. 2–0 Giants. Sandoval is up to bat again. Verlander throws a couple of changeups to draw a swing, but Sandoval is not tempted, and the count is 2–0. So he throws a fastball right on the outside edge of the plate—a near-impossible pitch—and Sandoval hits it out of the park. 4–0 Giants.

Verlander gives up a single to Buster Posey, but then Hunter Pence grounds out to end the inning. In the top of the fourth, it's three up and three down again for the Tigers, and in the bottom, Verlander has another tough inning. Brandon Belt is first up and gets a walk. A strikeout and groundout brings Barry Zito, the Giants' pitcher, to the plate. The man has a lifetime batting average of .102, but tonight he gets a hit into left field, and Belt scores. 5–0 Giants, after four innings.

This had not been the script that everyone had been working off. Verlander was Detroit's ace, their best card and their highest hope, and now, they have to take him out of the game after four innings. Zito is not a bad pitcher, either—he also has a Cy Young award, only his is ten years old. Verlander is in his prime, and he had been one of the reasons that Detroit was the favorite to win the World Series.

After the game, Verlander talks about "being out of sync," and journalists said he had too much pent-up energy going into the World Series, but in truth there was nothing much wrong with his pitching.[1] On another day, the score could easily have been 0–0 after five innings. This night, though, was one for the record books. The game ended 8–3 to the Giants after Sandoval hit another home run in his next appearance at the plate, making him the first player to hit three home runs in his first three at bats in a World Series game. Only three other players have ever hit three home runs in a World Series game: Babe Ruth, Reggie Jackson, and Albert Pujols. Not bad company.

The other reason the Tigers had been favored to win the series was their offense.[2] The biggest star in the lineup was Miguel Cabrera. Cabrera had won the baseball Triple Crown that season, leading the American League in batting average, home runs, and RBIs—the first person to achieve this feat since 1967, and only the fifth person to do so since 1945. Only one other Tigers player had ever managed it: the legendary Ty Cobb, in 1909 (later in the book we will tell his story).

And then, there was Prince Fielder, whom Detroit had signed as a free agent at the end of January 2012; his $214 million contract was the most expensive in the team's history.[3] In 2007, when he was twenty-three years old, he had become the youngest player to hit fifty home runs in a season. His regular season batting average in 2012 was a career best, and he also led the American League in "hit by pitch," a rather painful way to command respect. Indeed, Fielder had helped Cabrera win the Triple Crown, since opposing teams were far less inclined to give him intentional walks knowing that Fielder was on deck behind him.

On paper, the Tigers looked a sure thing. They had been widely tipped before the season started, and although they struggled a little in midseason, they finished strongly to win their division by three games over the White Sox. In the American League Championship Series, they swept the New York Yankees. But the Giants did to the Tigers what the Tigers had done to the Yankees. Once they started to slide, the Tigers could not find a way to stop. After managing two runs in the ninth inning of Game 1, they went another nineteen innings without scoring a single run, and in the process, they lost the next two games without ever getting close. The San Francisco Giants swept the World Series 4–0. With only four hits between them in twenty-seven plate appearances, Cabrera and Fielder ended the World Series with a combined batting average of .148. The audience did not appear to enjoy the experience much, either: as of 2019, it remained the lowest-rated World Series in history, with an average TV viewership of 12.6 million, a mere 12 percent of U.S. TV households. By contrast, when the Tigers won the 1968 World Series, 57 percent of U.S. households were watching. Times had changed, and so had Detroit—the city's financial troubles were coming to a head. Detroit was nine months away from declaring itself broke.

In 1970, the authorized strength of the Detroit Police Department was 5,065, serving a population of just over 1.5 million.[4] By 2012, the population of the city had fallen to around 707,000, and the police department employed around 2,570 officers—broadly similar to the ratio of officers per citizen in 1970.[5] Nonetheless, this statistic spelled bankruptcy, and here is why: as the population fell, so did the revenues that the city generated, be it from property taxes or parking tickets. If revenues had fallen in proportion to the population decrease, adjusting the number of active police officers would not, in itself, have created a financial crisis. But police officers, like firemen, retire at the age of fifty-five after a career of roughly thirty years, and they can expect to live for another twenty to twenty-five years. The problem was not the number of the men and women on active duty, but the number of those who had turned in their uniforms. By 2012, more than 32,000 people in Detroit were entitled to a monthly pension payment, more than three times as many as the city still employed.[6]

As is the case for most public employee pension schemes in the United States, the pensions were partially funded by employee contributions and partially by the city. How is an employer's contribution to a pension fund calculated? It is not an easy question to answer. Generally, pension contracts promise to provide a fixed percentage of the pensioner's final salary, say 50 percent. But it is not always easy to predict what an employee's final salary will be and for how many years she will draw her pension. Historically, the actuaries who do this kind of math have consistently underestimated lifespan—Americans live longer now than they did fifty years ago, and the projections had failed to take that fact into account. But a contract is a contract, and the city had no choice but to try and pay up. In other words, Detroit now found itself having to fund liabilities it had accrued at a time when it was twice its current size and had more than twice the revenues: adjusted for inflation, Detroit's 1970 revenues of $384 million would have been worth $2.3 billion in 2012, and yet that year, the city took in only $1.1 billion.[7]

Detroit's enemies and detractors like to talk about corruption and mismanagement, but this was a demographic catastrophe that no administration could have overcome. Unsurprisingly, those who favored blaming the city's leadership were Republican candidates running for Michigan office, either statewide or locally. It is, of course, more attractive to blame Detroit itself rather than to think of the city's hardships as largely the end result of complex forces beyond its control, as if the city had been struck by a hurricane in slow motion. In an alternate scenario, the state and its many municipalities—including the counties ringing Detroit like a band of wealth and privilege around a slowly suffocating urban center—might have felt duty bound to come to the city's aid, sharing treasure and other resources. But if they could convince themselves that all of Detroit's woes were of its own making, then they could wash their hands of it. And that is what they did: in their best moments they muttered piously about thrift and good government; in their worst—and this they did frequently—they blew racist dog whistles loud enough to lure a hundred packs of Rottweilers to your door.

Behold, for example, the recently deceased notorious troll L. Brooks Patterson, who, for a quarter of a century, served as CEO for Oakland County, an exceedingly wealthy suburban county just outside of Detroit. He liked to quote a line he considered, it appears, a fine bon mot: "What we're gonna do is turn Detroit into an Indian reservation, where we herd all the Indians into the city, build a fence around it, and then throw in blankets and corn."[8] Not all conservative Michiganders indulge in fantasies of genocide when they talk about Detroit, but Mr. Patterson's general sentiment is far from rare.

To be fair, Detroit *did* have some governance issues as well, some of them serious. No one, for instance, was sure just how large the city's debt was—$20 billion was commonly bandied about, but it was at best a ballpark figure. Record keeping was abysmal—70 percent of accounting entries on the city's books were still performed manually, and 85 percent of city computers used a version of Microsoft Windows that Microsoft no longer supported.[9] A series of budget cuts had rendered hard- and software updates impossible.

When Republican governor Rick Snyder took office in early 2011, one of the first bills he signed turbocharged the Michigan emergency manager law, which enabled the governor to appoint an outside official to take control of a city's finances after declaring a fiscal emergency. Michigan voters rejected the law in a statewide referendum a year later, only to see it reborn and re-signed a month later, with some cosmetic changes—and a provision stipulating that it could not be overturned by the people.[10] Now, any number of events could trigger a declaration of financial emergency: inadequate funds to cover public workers' salaries, for instance, or a request by a city's creditors. Once appointed, the emergency manager was empowered to take steps to deal with the short-term effects of the crisis, by cutting spending, including spending on public services. If such measures were likely to make matters worse in the long run, that didn't matter: quick financial results were the priority.

For a while, Snyder sought to negotiate with Dave Bing, Detroit's mayor in 2012—he would have preferred Bing himself take responsibility for draconian public service cuts that would balance the budget and forestall the appointment of an emergency manager. After all, the law was demonstrably unpopular, and even Republicans were not crazy about the optics of a white governor dictating solutions to an African American mayor. But the negotiations failed, and after the legislature passed the revised version of the emergency manager law, Snyder appointed Kevyn Orr in April 2013. In July of that year, Orr recommended that the city file for Chapter 9 bankruptcy.[11]

Who, then, was to shoulder the burden of restoring the city's finances? Should it be its creditors or its people? The city still owned some valuable properties that it could, in theory, sell—most notably the Detroit Institute of Arts (DIA). The DIA, located on Woodward Avenue in midtown, is the city's cultural crown jewel. Founded in 1885, it accumulated an extraordinary collection, mostly during the first few decades of the twentieth century as the auto industry made the city one of the wealthiest on earth. Among the DIA's treasures are works by Rembrandt, Picasso, Van Gogh, and Matisse, but its centerpiece is the vast and beloved set of 1933 murals by Diego Rivera, the *Detroit Industrial Murals* depicting the production lines of the Ford Motor Company. Some argued—almost certainly mistakenly—that a sale of the art collection could raise up to $5 billion.[12]

The choice that allegedly faced the city was heartbreaking: sell its most prized possession to fund pensions, or keep the art and accept pension cuts as high as 50 percent. Those who argued against selling the DIA were accused of snobbery: "The comfortable people who object so strenuously to the sale of a few works of art are not brave defenders of artistic values. They are defenders of elitism," Hamilton Nolan argued in the now defunct *Gawker*, in a piece entitled, with great pathos, "Sell Detroit's Art, Save Detroit's People."[13] The piece did not consider whether it might not be the greater snobbery to assume that a city down on its luck would be willing to sacrifice its art. And as the piece noted, the city likely had no right to sell any of the holdings that the city had not paid for in the first place—which would have made possibly as little as 5 percent of the collection fit for the auction house.[14] And yet, Christie's appraisers began making regular visits to the museum.[15] The debate grew heated quickly: accusations that some cared more about privileged museum patrons than the city's pensioners, who had worked hard and in good faith only to find themselves impoverished in old age were countered by a sense that the city had to fend off those who know "the worth of everything and the value of nothing."[16]

Fortunately, the bankruptcy court's judge, who asserted that to sell off the art would "forfeit the city's future," managed to find a solution that became known as the "Grand Bargain." Private foundations would contribute to the pension liabilities in exchange for leaving the DIA untouched, and the State of Michigan contributed a significant sum. The group included the Ford Foundation, which, at Henry Ford's death, had been endowed with a large slice of his fortune. The foundation wanted to acknowledge and honor its commitment to Ford's legacy in Michigan. The pensioners did not escape unscathed, but saw their incomes cut by less than 5 percent on average, although they also lost future cost-of-living increases.

Detroit emerged from Chapter 9 in November 2014, but some companies had started investing in the city before the bankruptcy ended.[17] In 2016, the *Detroit News* estimated that Quicken Loans founder Dan Gilbert had spent over $450 million buying sixty-two downtown properties[18], many of them iconic Detroit landmarks such as One Woodward (designed by architect Minoru Yamasaki), the First National Building (Albert Kahn), Book Tower (Louis Kamper), and the David Stott Building (John Donaldson). In 2017, work began on an eight-hundred-foot skyscraper intended to be the city's tallest building, located on the site of the old Hudson's department store, one of Detroit's most famous landmarks.[19] The fact that Gilbert clearly believes in the future of Detroit has led some to see him as that future's emblematic figure, another rich savior. To others, he is associated with a rapidly gentrifying downtown—so much of which he now owns—that is leaving much of greater Detroit behind.[20] Nothing encapsulated the Janus face of Gilbert's development investments as much as the sign his real estate company Bedrock hoisted in a window of the Vinton Building, at the corner of Woodward Avenue and Congress Street. Featuring a busy throng of young and overwhelmingly white people, its tagline read: "See Detroit Like We Do." The message seemed clear: Detroit, a city with an 85 percent African American population, belonged to affluent whites now, and they get to determine the image of the city.

Hurt and outrage followed instantaneously.[21] Gilbert pointed out that the offensive ad was only one of a series, with the other installments depicting a far more diverse population, but the damage was done and he was forced to issue a statement admitting that the slogan was in poor taste and pledged to "kill" the campaign.

Set against this background, it is hardly surprising that Gilbert's plans to bring a Major League Soccer franchise to Detroit have met with mixed reactions. As we will see, the city has a checkered history with billionaires who want to add a sports team to their already bulging portfolios. But in this case, the resistance is not only fueled by skepticism about fat-cat motives, but by the rabidly loyal fan base of the Detroit City Football Club. The community-based club, founded in 2012 by five Detroiters, bears little resemblance to MLS teams. Rather than relying on the American model of closed leagues controlled by billionaire owners, the founders of DCFC envisaged a local team operating much closer to the European model, where clubs are frequently member associations controlled by the fans. Most of the founders had a background in community organizing, and they saw DCFC as providing more than just on-field entertainment. The club joined the National Premier Soccer League, a growing organization of amateur clubs, and they played their first games at the home field of Cass Tech, one of the city's great educational institutions located a few blocks away from The District Detroit.[22]

Then something remarkable happened. In the same year, two brothers decided to form a group known as the Northern Guard Supporters(NGS), and they took it upon themselves to turn DCFC games into a sporting spectacle few clubs can match. They brought drums, flags, flares, and smoke machines, and they instituted a series of hymns and chants that amount to a full-fledged liturgy of taunt and celebration.[23] They developed the NGS Tetris, a dance enacted on the terrace during the game to the melody of the venerable video game's theme song.[24] NGS is probably best described as a state of mind. These are defiant Detroiters, proud of their city, and not remotely interested in corporate solutions imported from elsewhere. They embrace the extraordinary diversity of the city, celebrating white, black, Hispanic, Arab, and every conceivable identity that Detroit has to offer—there is always at least one rainbow flag flying at the game, and "F*CK MLS" T-shirts, protesting what is widely seen as a potential corporate takeover that would erase the club's community culture and values, are a common sight.

NGS works with the owners of DCFC to make sure that the enterprise is a success, but the "Rouge Rovers," as their traveling bands of fans are also known, are not controlled by them. The owners see their job as laying the foundations that allow groups like NGS to thrive in their ambition to turn soccer game attendance into a *Gesamtkunstwerk*, the German term for a work of art that appeals to all senses simultaneously.

By the end of 2014, DCFC had outgrown its Cass Tech location and decided on an ambitious plan to renovate Keyworth Stadium in Hamtramck, an independent city curiously located in the center of the Detroit. Hamtramck is an important element of Detroit's history, sporting and otherwise, and we will return to it in later chapters. Keyworth is itself a storied location: the old high school football field was originally opened by Franklin Delano Roosevelt in 1936, and John F. Kennedy gave a speech at the stadium during the 1960 presidential election campaign. The owners, the city of Hamtramck, agreed to lease it to the club provided it could come up with the money to renovate it. The club used a crowdfunding site, MichiganFunders .com, and succeeded in raising $750,000—the largest amount ever raised in Michigan by this method.[25]

The first game at the stadium was played on May 20, 2016, and since then, the club has regularly played to capacity crowds of adoring fans, despite playing soccer at the amateur level. Establishing ties with like-minded community-based teams, it has invited clubs such as FC United of Manchester in England, and Bundesliga 2 club FC St. Pauli from Hamburg in Germany to play friendly games.[26] In a sign of the club's growing reputation, in 2018 it hosted a friendly with Necaxa, a team from Mexico's Liga MX, which draws more viewership on TV in the United States than Major League Soccer.[27] Also in 2018, the club opened the Detroit City Fieldhouse on Lafayette, two miles east of the downtown. The Fieldhouse is a community center: indoor soccer pitches are designed to promote the game in the city, and a bar and restaurant serves as a meeting space.[28] A small attached store sells popular DCFC gear. The club and its supporters have all sorts of ambitions, but they are united in the one thing they do not want: to join MLS, or to see Detroit soccer fall into the clutches of a corporate, Disney-fied organization. Instead, they want to promote participation in all forms of soccer, and other sports (such as wiffle ball and dodgeball) for all ages

and for all the different communities of Detroit. It's not a business trying to make money by selling sports to the community, it's an organization whose business is making sports available to build the community of Detroiters. Its model has been a resounding success: in 2019, the club announced it was joining the National Independent Soccer Association (NISA), which was provisionally sanctioned by the U.S. Soccer Federation as a third-tier professional league earlier in the year.

Before the 2012 World Series debacle, a writer for *The Guardian*, predicting and rooting for a Tigers triumph, wrote: "Hey if there's any city that could use a redemptive sports win right now, it's Detroit."[29] But redemption, be it in sports or in other matters, may well take a shape that is uniquely Detroit.

THREE

DECEMBER 28, 2008

2008 is a terrible year all around. The Lions have the most abysmal season in the history of the NFL, Detroit mayor Kwame Kilpatrick resigns in the midst of a corruption scandal, and, in the wake of the subprime mortgage collapse, the country as a whole enters a catastrophic recession. Detroit, reliant on the car industry that had failed to read the writing on the wall for decades, is hit particularly hard.

Green Bay Packers 31, Detroit Lions 21. Lions coach Rod Marinelli, the *Washington Post* noted dryly, "declined to discuss his future with the team. 'This is not fun to go through, obviously. But there's people going through a lot worse than this.'"[1] People—to be sure. Football teams? Not so much. Marinelli's future was revealed the next day: he was fired. Not for losing this game—but for losing all sixteen. Every single one. The Packers' victory had been the last loss of the season and the last straw.

Sure, you could argue that this was no worse than the Tampa Bay Buccaneers' 1976 season, when the team went 0-14, but that had been the Buccaneers' very first NFL season, and back then the regular season lasted only fourteen games. Detroit, by contrast, was a team founded in 1930, and they had somehow managed to beat the rookies' disaster record.[2] The media was merciless. The friendly liberals at NPR led with "Detroit Lions, Worst NFL Team Ever"; *USA Today* went with "0-16 Lions Enter Hall of Shame." The *Washington Post* was marginally more charitable with "Zero-Sum Game for Lions," while the *New York Times*, deciding that there was no analogy wretched enough in the history of the NFL, went beyond football and compared the Lions to Zippy Chippy, a New York racehorse that did not win a single one of the one hundred races it ran. The *Detroit News* summed it up with laconic clarity: "Perfectly Awful."[3]

Throughout the season, the team hardly ever came close to a win. The average margin of defeat was sixteen points, and on only three occasions was it less than seven points. The closest game of the season was a two-point defeat at the Minnesota Vikings, courtesy of a safety that saw Lions quarterback Dan Orlovsky run out of the back of the end zone—during his first game of the season. But even that game was not nearly as close as the score would suggest: Minnesota's total yards for the game were almost double those of Detroit. The most humiliating result of the season came in week 13, when the Tennessee Titans overwhelmed them 47–10. Tennessee had racked up 41 of those points before the fourth quarter started.

With a nice touch of irony, offensive tackle Jeff Backus declared in the press conference following the Packers game that "it was one of those years where it just all kind of came together."[4] And indeed, there were many factors that contributed to the catastrophe. To begin with, the players on the team were simply not great. The previous two years, the quarterback had been Jon Kitna, who had amassed consecutive 4,000 passing yards seasons, becoming only the second player in franchise history to achieve that mark. But he was injured in the fourth game of the season, and Orlovsky, the backup quarterback, was not in the same class. In the game-by-game quarterback ratings—based on a formula that accounts for passes, touchdowns, interceptions, and so on—Detroit was near the bottom, but not the very worst in the league. That honor they earned with their defense: the combined average rating for quarterbacks playing *against* the Lions that year was 109.3, a rating that no single quarterback achieved for that entire season. The defense was so dreadful that it made the other guys' offense look fantastic.[5]

Marinelli was not a terrific coach, either. His record of 10-38 over three seasons is one of the worst in NFL history when we look at coaches with equivalent experience. A talented defensive coach, he was a fine team player who froze in the headlights when handed the leadership mantle. A decent man, he took responsibility for the failure that duly got him fired the day after the Packers game. But he also complained about the attitude at the franchise. "You know what surprises me?" Marinelli said. "It's that everybody seems to look at everything very negative. I think it just can wear people out—'This can't work,' 'This won't do it.' Now that part is a fight, I have to admit."[6]

While it's hard not to feel for Marinelli, it is also true that the Lions had actually benefited hugely from the draft system of the NFL that hands the highest draft picks to the worst-performing teams. Even before Detroit hit absolute rock bottom, they had done badly enough to qualify for two second-overall picks, one third, a seventh, a ninth, and a tenth. If you are good at picking the best talent coming out of college football, that should be enough to build the core of a winning team. And in fairness, they did choose Calvin Johnson in 2007, who turned out to be one of the greatest wide receivers of all time. But while several of the other picks were decent enough players, they were unable to function effectively as a team.

Marinelli had to take some of the blame here, but there is enough to go around for the senior management to take its share. Even before the 2008 season, the CEO Matt Millen was so widely hated that Lions fans campaigned to have him fired, while fans of competing teams campaigned to keep him in the job. John U. Bacon, the celebrated chronicler of Michigan football, claims that in his interviews, he could not find a single insider willing to say a good word about Millen, who was both a bully and deeply stupid.[7] His pronouncements were legendary for their incoherence as well as for their casual reversal of positions he had previously espoused. This one is especially fine for its pure absurdity: "When you think of Detroit, you're not thinking of wine and cheese. You're closer to the brat market up here. Regardless of who comes in here, Detroit is Detroit. This is a tough town, a blue-collar town. This is about making a real living. This isn't about dodging things. There's enough white-collar stuff up here, but even the white collars have dirt under their collars. That's the way it's supposed to be."[8]

To be fair, Millen himself had warned them. He had been a celebrated NFL linebacker between 1980 and 1991, playing on Super Bowl–winning teams no less than four times (twice with the Raiders and once each with the 49ers and the Redskins), and after retirement, he made a career in TV and radio commentary. But when William Clay Ford Sr., the Lions' owner, asked him to take over as CEO in 2001, Millen told him, "Mr. Ford, I really appreciate this, but I'm not qualified." Ford responded, "You're smart. You'll figure it out."[9]

Millen would prove himself right. Bill Ford, as everybody called him, Henry Ford's grandson, was an intelligent man, with a degree in engineering from Yale. He had earned a reputation for creativity when in 1954 he took over the Continental Division, tasked with creating the second generation of the Ford Continental, originally his father Edsel's baby. The company, however, would come to be run by his elder brother Henry II, who refused to grant Bill a real say. The Continental turned into a debacle, and Bill Ford withdrew from the company almost completely. For about ten years, he succumbed to alcoholism, but in 1964, he pulled himself together, devoted himself to his family, and bought the Detroit Lions—an enterprise that he could fully control. He remained the owner until he died fifty years later.[10] That half-century was a monument to mediocrity, culminating in the calamitous 2008 season—the memorial of his tenure.

Why Ford was such a poor owner has long been a matter of keen debate. Many argued he was too distant and patrician—for example, he did not fire Marinelli personally but had Millen do the deed. John Bacon, however, argues that this is the verdict of people who did not know him. On the contrary, Bacon says, this man of extraordinary talent who bore one of the most prestigious names in American history was in fact quite shy and would have much preferred to be treated as an ordinary Joe. Deeply competitive himself, he was quite willing to spend large sums of money to construct a successful team—but he had lousy judgment when it came to hiring senior management. He trusted Millen for no good reason, and he held on to him long after Millen's flaws had become too glaring to ignore. When Ford finally let Millen go, after the first four defeats of 2008, it was too late to save the team from ignominy.

Talking of things everybody could have seen coming, the year 2008, needless to say, evokes calamities far more severe than the sorry fate of a football team. In that very year, the subprime mortgage lending scam nearly brought down the global economy, triggering the worst recession since the Great Depression of the 1930s.

The carmakers of Detroit, Ford, General Motors, and Chrysler, were badly hit by crisis. Despite being the home of the modern auto industry,

Detroit's pre-eminence in the market had peaked somewhere at the end of the 1950s—and, of course, most of the manufacturing itself had left the city. As the postwar economic miracle created serious competition from companies such as Volkswagen, BMW, Mercedes, Honda, and Toyota, the Detroit firms struggled to keep up. For a long time, they had considered themselves immune from foreign competition, but by the 1980s, their market share was clearly falling, as foreign producers started to build plants in the United States.[11]

The car industry is a lightning rod for political arguments about economic decline and the role of the state, more often than not characterized by posturing rather than by appeal to the relevant facts. People on the left accuse CEOs of inefficient management and failure to invest, while those on the right point their finger at the uncompetitive costs meant to result from powerful union influence. The truth is more complex. It is true that management was slow to adapt, and it is also true that unions had won significant and expensive privileges. But to a certain extent, the decline was inevitable: the employment legacy of the Big Three goes back to a time when you needed far more workers to build a car than you do now. While new competitors could start from scratch, Detroit was slow to figure out how to respond and transition. Much of their cost burden stemmed not from current employees but from retirees as well as their dependents, for whom the unions had negotiated benefits packages that included health coverage—an expenditure that would balloon more quickly than anybody had foreseen. To that extent, the financial troubles of the industry mirrored those of the city. And not only had the unions won those concessions in better times, U.S. manufacturers now had to compete with companies from Germany and Japan, both of which heavily subsidize health care costs out of general taxation, giving them a clear advantage.

In 2008, the Big Three directly or indirectly employed around 1.6 million people, counting component suppliers and related businesses. At the time, the population of the city of Detroit was around nine hundred thousand, and only a fraction of these citizens worked in auto-related businesses. So while we often use "Detroit" as a metonym for "Ford, GM, and Chrysler," the city itself is not necessarily that important to their businesses. Henry Ford, who never wanted to be in Detroit, located his original assembly line first in Highland Park, a self-governing enclave within the city, and then in Dearborn, a town that borders the city on its southwestern side. From the 1950s onward, car plants in Detroit were steadily shut down, and now only two remain, the GM Hamtramck plant adjacent to Detroit City FC's Keyworth Stadium and the Chrysler plant off Jefferson Avenue, way out on the eastern side of the city.[12] Still, many of the city's residents commuted to work at car plants outside the city, and metro Detroit, which includes the adjacent counties and has a population of 4 million, is highly dependent on the motor industry.

By the second half of 2008, it seemed likely that the crisis would push the Big Three over the edge. When the government decided to bail out the banks, the auto companies seized on the opportunity to argue that they, too, needed and deserved support in a crisis that was not of their own making. Toward the end of the year, negotiations started with Congress, and the outgoing Bush administration agreed on financial aid. Not everybody was pleased—on November 18, Mitt Romney, the son of Michigan's popular former governor George Romney, wrote an infamous op-ed in the *New York Times*, titled "Let Detroit Go Bankrupt."[13] A day later, at a U.S. Senate hearing on November 19, the carmakers asked for $25 billion of support. In the following weeks, a bailout package was negotiated and announced on December 10, only to be voted down by the Senate on December 11. George W. Bush intervened, and on December 19, by executive order, committed over $17 billion in financial aid to the Detroit car companies—Ford turned down the funds, but Chrysler and GM accepted. At the time, the move was unpopular: according to one opinion poll in March 2009, only 37 percent of Americans supported the bailout.[14]

In the end, the financial commitment proved to be far greater than the $17 billion. In 2009, both Chrysler and GM entered Chapter 11 bankruptcy, and support from the government to facilitate the companies' survival brought the total support to around $80 billion, according to government figures. The investment, however, turned out to be a fairly good one: most of this money was repaid, with interest. In 2014 the government announced that the bailout was officially over. Chrysler had repaid all of the money owed ahead of time, whereas GM ended up $10 billion short—about one-twentieth of one percent of Federal government revenues over the period.

Whether or not you think the car companies were worth saving, the cost of saving them turned out to be negligible.[15]

While the bailouts averted the collapse of the car industry, the recession nonetheless had catastrophic consequences for Detroit. Estimates of job losses vary, but some suggest that between 2008 and 2009, around half a million manufacturing jobs were lost in the auto industry. Detroit was devastated: in 2008, the unemployment rate in the city was below 10 percent, by 2009 it had officially risen to 30 percent—and according to Mayor Dave Bing, the true figure was closer to 50 percent.[16] Recessions tend to hit the poor the hardest, and they tend to be the first to lose their jobs.

Bing himself was mayor as a result of yet another crisis. A Hall of Fame basketball player who had played for the Pistons from 1966 to 1975, Bing became mayor of Detroit in May 2009, after Kwame Kilpatrick's resignation in September 2008 had triggered a special election. For many of Detroit's detractors, Mayor Kilpatrick embodies Detroit's failure to govern itself. First elected in 2002 at the age of thirty-one, he was the youngest mayor in the city's history. His mother represented Detroit in the U.S. House of Representatives at the time, and his father was an active politician as well. With impeccable political connections, he also reveled in the title "America's first hip-hop mayor," bestowed by the press. Kilpatrick sought to speak for a city with an 80 percent African American population surrounded by counties that were about 90 percent white. Supported by ample evidence, the sense that the city was the target of racial animus emanating from its white neighbors ran strong in Detroit, and Kilpatrick promised to remedy the situation with aggressive, city-driven policies of investment: "We can do this on our own."[17]

Soon, however, rumors began to spread in the press that the hip-hop mayor spent much of his time and the city's treasure on extensive parties at the grand Manoogian Mansion, tucked away off Jefferson Avenue on the riverfront opposite Belle Isle. At first, they were hotly denied. Soon, however, Freedom of Information Act requests yielded confirmation. The courts became involved, and charges included misuse of public funds, perjury, obstruction of justice, and conspiracy. Scandal followed scandal—Kilpatrick's Wikipedia page has a fairly flabbergasting list of them.[18] Many Americans, including some Detroiters, concluded what they were already committed to believe: that a majority-black city was incapable of running itself, even though the animus was often couched in terms of "the Democrats' failure," which is itself frequently, if not always, a dog whistle.[19] Alongside sober analyses of corruption, racist commentary ran rampant, a fact Kilpatrick's allies noted frequently: "You talk about race, come on man, that's what it is," his brother-in-law Daniel Ferguson claimed. "If Kwame Kilpatrick was white and his name was Kent Masters Kensington, he would not be on trial."[20]

Be that as it may, not many would argue that Kilpatrick was innocent. Legal proceedings continued long after Kilpatrick resigned, and in 2013 he was found guilty of participating in numerous fraudulent schemes to award contracts for the city's Department of Water and Sewerage in exchange for kickbacks. For crimes including racketeering, extortion, mail fraud, and tax evasion, he was sentenced to twenty-eight years in prison—a shockingly harsh sentence if you compare it to that of Illinois governor Rod Blagojevich, who got fourteen years.[21] As Mike Riggs wrote in *CityLab* in October 2013, "There's no question Kilpatrick broke the law, disgraced his office, and screwed over Detroit. But locking him up for 28 years is a ludicrous solution."[22]

No doubt, leadership matters in city government as it does in sports management, and neither Detroit nor the Lions were well-served in 2008. But while the Lions doomed themselves, Detroit's problems neither begin nor end with Kilpatrick. He was preceded in office by Dennis Archer and succeeded by Dave Bing, both of whom have reputations as honorable men, and they couldn't save the city, either—and it is difficult to see how they could have, seeing that the fundamental reason for Detroit's decline is crystal clear. Between 1950 and 2000, the city's population declined from 1.8 million to 0.9 million. To lose almost one million people, half of the population, cannot but lead to an economic catastrophe, particularly if it is predominantly the wealthy or the comfortable who leave. As we noted in the previous chapter, public employees provide essential contributions to any city, and they deserve reasonable pensions for a life of service, pensions that are funded by city tax revenues. If half the population leaves, you likely lose more than half of your tax revenues, but your pension obligations remain the same. In the end, money runs out to fund anything else—including roads, current services, schools, and streetlights. So even more people leave. As we mentioned before, in the face of this population collapse, most of which was overseen and frequently furthered by white politicians, even an administrative genius would have struggled to make an impact. The brutal truth is that the economic collapse of Detroit was not caused by the people who stayed, but by the people who left.

FOUR

NOVEMBER 19, 2004

In Auburn Hills, white Pistons fans provoke an Indiana Pacers player who leaps into the stands and starts throwing punches. The "Malice at the Palace" changes the sport forever, but it also fits in neatly with an image of black Detroit, which had contributed exactly nothing to the notorious brawl. In the days of the rise of "ruin porn," nuanced takes on Detroit make way for either aestheticized images of suffering or right-wing caricatures of a once-proud city in free fall—in the meantime, the Pistons and the city see themselves as simply "goin' to work," the proud team of a blue-collar city.

A foul, a shove, a scuffle; an athlete lies down, a drink flies through the air, and the NBA would never be the same again. What happened? An eyewitness recalls the scene as a series of unfortunate events:

> If Ron Artest doesn't make that hard foul on Ben Wallace, it doesn't happen. If Ben Wallace doesn't react the way he did, it doesn't happen. If the referees control the situation, it doesn't happen. If Artest doesn't go lay down on that scorers' table, it doesn't happen. If the fan doesn't throw the beverage, it doesn't happen. . . . You take away any one of them and the whole thing doesn't happen.[1]

But it did happen, and the reactions came in fast and furious. David Stern, who had been NBA commissioner at the time, would later recall the "Malice at the Palace," as these events would come to be known, as the biggest crisis of his career. He placed much of the blame on the media for reacting with rehearsed outrage: "The brawl . . . provided [sic] much of the media in the course of that weekend to use the words 'thugs' and 'punks' with respect to all of our players which to me is freighted with respect to what they're really saying and brought up visions of the way the media treated us a decade or more earlier." Was he saying the coverage was racist? "Yeah, mildly, let's say."[2] Of course, he himself had called the events of the game "shocking, repulsive, and inexcusable—a humiliation for everyone associated with the NBA."[3]

The brawl, involving the Indiana Pacers, the Detroit Pistons, and a number of Pistons fans, had a history. Both teams play in the Central Division of the NBA's Eastern Conference, and in 2004, they were among the league's best defensive outfits. In spring earlier that year, they had met in the 2003–04 Eastern Conference finals. The rivalry between the two Midwestern teams ratcheted up a notch when the Pacers hired Rick Carlisle, the very coach whom the Pistons had just fired and replaced with Hall of Fame coach Larry Brown.

In the conference finals, after losing game 1 in Indianapolis, Detroit's newly signed Rasheed Wallace predicted that his team would win the next one, another home game for the Pacers: "You can write it."[4] And so it was written. In fact, the Pistons went on to win four of the next five games, largely thanks to their defensive play. It was not pretty, and often violent. In game 6, with the scores tied at 59 and 3:57 remaining, Ron Artest floored Rip Hamilton, the Pistons' leading scorer, with a right forearm to his nose, drawing blood. Hamilton took it sportingly, so to speak. "I'm happy I got hit," he declared afterward. "Sometimes it takes getting hit like that to get you right, ready and focused." While Artest claimed he'd been hit first, the Pistons got the free throws, took the lead, and never gave it up. In one of the lowest-scoring playoff games in NBA history, the Detroit Pistons advanced to the finals and took the NBA trophy.

Such was the background when the Pacers returned to the Palace of Auburn Hills, home of the Pistons since 1988 (more about that move in chapter 10). The Pistons were eight games into the season. That night, the Pacers were determined to prove themselves the better team, and they took a scorched-earth approach. Having overwhelmed the Pistons, they led 97–82, with 45.9 seconds left in the game. If your opponent's defeat is guaranteed, you're generally expected to ease up, play out time, and coast to the win. But that night the Pacers decide they have a point to prove. After an Indiana free throw, the Pistons bring the ball up court and pass it to center Ben Wallace in the paint. As Wallace goes up for the shot, Ron Artest smacks him on the head from behind.

Wallace retaliates by shoving Artest, and a slew of players come off the bench to stave off a full-blown brawl. Between security staff and players from both teams holding onto the two men, much of the action is purely performative at this point, more vigorous taunting than actual scuffle, and not terribly unusual. But just as things start to settle down, Artest climbs on top of the scorers' table and lies down. This curious gesture proves to be the match that lights the tinder. The scorers' table and the chairs that surround the court form an effective barrier between the players and the fans that is meant to be sacrosanct—and now Artest is on his back in no-man's land. Maybe it is nothing more than an innocent attempt to calm himself down, and maybe it is intended to provoke, but given the volatile atmosphere inside the arena, and with the benefit of hindsight, it is not surprising that at least one Pistons fan sees the enemy prone and decides that he's a target impossible to resist. A plastic cup of diet coke—or perhaps beer, as competing accounts claim—flies through the air and hits Artest on the chest.

In a split second, Artest leaps up into the stand and starts in on the fan—the wrong one, it turns out, though it hardly makes a difference at this point—it's quickly becoming a general brawl. Some fans recoil in dismay, but plenty of others are eager to join in, and more players run into the stands in support of their men—Pacers as well as at least one Piston, Ben Wallace himself. Punches fly and connect. "Holy shit!" David Stern, who is watching on TV, exclaims.[5] After about ten minutes, it is over, and they manage to stop the fighting, though getting the Pacers off the court, into the safety of their locker room, and out of the stadium is a bit of a challenge, given the ire of the Pistons fans who rain drinks and objects on them from the stands.

Later, Pacer Stephen Jackson would remember that Artest turned to him in the locker room: "[Artest] looked at me like, 'Jack, you think we going to get in trouble?' Jamaal Tinsley fell about laughing. I said, 'Are you serious, bro? Trouble? Ron, we'll be lucky if we have a freaking job.'"[6]

But even before they are hustled out of the arena, much of the country has already decided who was to blame.[7] John Saunders of ESPN calls the Detroit fans "a bunch of punks" and says, "I don't blame the players for going into the stands."[8] Comedian Bill Burr will declare later that he thoroughly enjoyed watching "out-of-shape civilians get the shit kicked out of them by professional athletes."[9] Tim Legler, a former NBA player, echoes the sentiment: "The blame should be put on the Detroit Pistons fans."[10] Both the league and the justice system take a more even-handed approach, however. The NBA comes down hard on both teams, but harder on the Pacers: they suspend Artest for the remainder of the season, the harshest penalty for an on-court violation in the history of the NBA, which will cost him $5 million in salary. Ben Wallace is suspended for six games, costing him $400,000 in salary. Four more Pacers and three more Pistons players receive suspensions of varying lengths.[11]

On December 8, Oakland County prosecutors charge five Indiana players (Artest, Jermaine O'Neal, Jackson, David Harrison, and Anthony Johnson) and five fans (John Green, William Paulson, Bryant Jackson, John Ackerman, and David Wallace) with assault and battery.[12] Months of legal haggling follow. The players eventually plead no contest, and only Green ended up serving jail time—thirty days. Everyone else gets away with fines, probation, and community-service sentences, and all five fans are banned from attending Pistons games for life.

The incident would emerge as a watershed moment; ten years later, *Men's Journal* would title a commemorative article, "How the 'Malice at the Palace' Changed Basketball Forever," a sentiment widely echoed in the sports media, and the author of the piece declares wistfully that "we knew that this was the last day of the NBA we grew up with."[13] And indeed, the NBA introduced a number of reforms. It enhanced security arrangements at games, limited the sale of alcoholic beverages, and introduced various rules of conduct regulating things such as "emotional expression." One of the more controversial moves was the mandatory dress code David Stern established for all players who were representing the team off the court, be it at events or during media appearances. Stern denied that the new "business casual" decree had anything to do with the brawl at Auburn Hills, but few if any are willing to believe him on that count. Instead, the dress code was widely seen as a thinly veiled attempt to censor hip-hop culture, which wide swaths of the country crudely associated with criminality and a lack of respect for dominant white culture. The code prohibited, with few carve-outs, sleeveless shirts, shorts, T-shirts, jerseys, or sports apparel as well as headphones, sunglasses while indoors, headgear of any kind, chains, pendants, or medallions worn over the player's clothes.

Clearly, the code was targeting a particular look, and just as clearly, this look was associated mainly with black players.[14] As a piece in *Rolling Stone* recounts, Philadelphia 76er Allen Iverson thought it was "targeting my generation—the hip-hop generation." Jason Richardson, of the Golden State Warriors, was yet more explicit, calling it "kind of racist" and said that it "targeted blacks." Over time, however, many of the players reacted to the mandate in creative ways that both honored and subtly mocked the league's respectability politics. In the end, the NBA emerged as "the most stylish league around, and NBA superstars are the most stylish group of athletes of all time," declared *GQ* style expert Mark Anthony Green.[15] And no matter how much the bosses may have wished otherwise, the sport's hip-hop image would be there to stay, along with NBA players' reputation as perhaps the most outspoken and politically eloquent of American athletes.[16]

As Yago Colás puts it with not a small amount of sarcasm in *Ball Don't Lie*, "The so-called Malice at the Palace became a popular touchstone, a symbol for media commentators and league officials of the catastrophes to which, in effect, insufficiently regulated blackness could lead."[17] These reactions to the Malice fit in seamlessly with an image of Detroit as a black, and hence lawless, city. Rush Limbaugh's commentary, as transcribed by Media Matters, is a particularly striking example:

LIMBAUGH: I don't think anybody ought to be surprised, folks. I really don't think anybody ought to be surprised. This is the hip-hop culture on parade. This is gang behavior on parade minus the guns. That's the culture that the NBA has become. So if anybody will be honest with you about it in the NBA, and a very few will have the courage to, because saying what I just said is going to be tagged as racist, but I, my friends, am fearless when it comes to this because the truth will out, and that's what's happening here, and part and parcel of this gang culture, this hip-hop culture, is: "I'm not going to tolerate being dissed. I'm not going to be disrespected," and "disrespected" is now so broad that it includes somebody looking at you the wrong way. . . .

CALLER: This is not a new thing with the Piston fans.

LIMBAUGH: I know. That's why I say call it "New Fallujah, Michigan."[18]

All this happened during the Iraq War, and, as Derek L. John noted, "as the graphic NBA fight footage was sucked into cable television's spin cycle it butted up against the latest carnage from the war in Iraq, and the violent images played endlessly until they appeared as two sides of the same coin."[19] And indeed, Detroit has already been coded as foreign, as we will see in chapter 6, and with the "War on Terror" in full swing, what would come more naturally to Detroit haters than conjoining the new Islamophobic and the old racist discourse? The talk of urban "war zones" had already been normalized, complete with a certain nonchalance when it comes to the suffering of civilians.

In tones of a more refined and ambivalent distaste for "the N.B.A.'s hiphop milieu," Harvey Araton commented in the *New York Times* that the brief brawl had been "the most frightening eruption of sustained violence in an American sports arena." While Araton is clearly and explicitly aware of the double standard for NBA players that made "race . . . the elephant in the arena," he nonetheless sees fit to claim that "the sight of large black men rushing off the bench to throw punches at one another tended to evoke outcries in the media and from fans about the end of sports civilization as we know it." This is a baffling misrepresentation of the actual events, given that "large black men" rushed off the benches to contain the fight. And, of course, such narratives erase the fact that not a single one of the Pistons fans involved was black.[20]

There is a chain of associations in play in much of the contemporary coverage that links the blackness of the NBA to the blackness of Detroit, even though the game was played in white Auburn Hills, a city in Oakland County, and Ron Artest, the man who rushed the stands and would later take the name Metta World Peace, played for the Pacers, not the Pistons.[21] Of course, the link between basketball and African American culture is real, across the United States and in Detroit. Nielsen's market research tool, Scarborough, has broken down the Detroit teams' fan base by race, and unsurprisingly, the Pistons have more black fans than the Lions (about even), the Tigers (mostly white), and the Red Wings (mostly white). And the fact that the Pistons played at the Palace, on the white side of Eight Mile Road, often rankled with black Detroiters. But black Detroit didn't start the brawl.

Eight Mile Road, the border between black and white Detroit, had been made famous in the days of the Malice by white hip-hop artist Eminem, who was easily the most recognizable Detroiter worldwide at the time, not least because of his autobiographical film *8 Mile*, which had been a sound success. The movie portrayed a white rapper's struggle for recognition on the Detroit music scene in the mid-90s, and many of its scenes appeared to portray the city as a site of decay and mindless destruction. Eminem was taken to task for this, and in his autobiography, *The Way I Am*, he reacts to his critics:

> The house burning scene caused some drama in Detroit. Some folks protested. When I was coming up, there was this thing called Devil's Night, which used to go down the night before Halloween. Basically, kids would burn down abandoned houses, which were easy to come by in my hometown. The city of Detroit finally cracked down on it, but Devil's Night was definitely still poppin' during the time *8 Mile* is set, so it had to be part of the flick. What we were trying to portray in the scene was something most of us can relate to: we all do stupid things as kids, and these kids are just fucking around. In the scene, I pick up a photograph—proof that a family once lived in this pit of a house. The scene shows how fucked up poverty can be and points to the positive message of the movie: that no matter where you come from, whether it's the north side or the south side of 8 Mile, you can break out of it if your mentality and drive are right. Breaking out is the point of the film.[22]

At the time, images of a decaying Detroit had been spreading rapidly via the internet, often to an audience that not so secretly delighted, with a frisson, in the gritty images of destruction and despair. A case in point is the website The Fabulous Ruins of Detroit, which appeared in 1997 and spawned a genre now critically dubbed "ruin porn."[23] To be sure, vast areas of crumbling factories and burnt-out houses offered plenty to choose from. While many of the photographers may have sought to bring attention to the plight of Detroit, they ended up both aestheticizing suffering and reinforcing stereotypes of Detroit as the emblem of hopelessness, giving fodder, in turn, to those who have long detested Detroit for frequently sinister reasons. Some of the most famous images of the genre feature Detroit's Michigan Theater, built in the grand French Renaissance style and opened in 1926. Located around the corner from Comerica Park, the venue, in its heyday, saw performances by the Marx Brothers, Frank Sinatra, Louis Armstrong, Glenn Miller, Bob Hope, Benny Goodman, and Bette Davis, but by the 1950s, it had been converted into a movie theater. In 1971, as the population of the city declined, it went out of business.[24] For a short period it operated as a rock venue, but vandalism put a stop to that, and later in the decade, the formerly grand and storied place was gutted and turned into a 160-space parking deck. Images of cars parked in this once glorious palace went around the world and would inscribe a particular image of Detroit in the global imagination. Thomas Morton, writing for *Vice* magazine, summed the trend up in a sarcastic headline: "Something, Something, Something Detroit: Lazy Journalists Love Pictures of Abandoned Stuff."[25]

Nobody would dispute that Detroit had a notable and troubling amount of decaying buildings, and anybody who has been to the city lately will recognize the impulse to document the most stunning sights of decay—but the voyeuristic focus on the ruins of Detroit was not just lazy, it also missed the beauty and vitality of Detroit that co-exist with the melancholy scenes of destruction. Similarly, the fascination with the Malice drowned out all that went well for the Pistons that year, setting them apart from less-than-stellar seasons in the city's other sports. The 2003 Tigers had produced the worst performance in the history of the American League and had come within one loss of the worst ever season in Major League Baseball. The Tigers were slightly better 2004, but still produced a losing season. The Lions were not quite as epically terrible in 2003 and 2004 as they would be in 2008, but they still only managed to win 11 out of 32 games over the two seasons. The

Red Wings had dominated the regular season in 2003–04, but flamed out to Calgary in the conference semifinals. The 2003–04 Pistons, however, got the job done. They had not only beaten the Pacers in the conference finals, as we mentioned earlier, but, against all odds, defeated the LA Lakers to become NBA champions for only the third time in franchise history. 2004 was a *great year* for the Detroit Pistons.

That year's team was the creation of Joe Dumars, one of the all-time greats who played for the Pistons between 1985 and 1999. He was appointed general manager in 2000 and set about building a team he liked to call the "Goin-to-Work Pistons"—a tagline that turned into a marketing slogan over the years. This is how the *Detroit Free Press* portrayed the new image:

> Hardworking guys, no whiners, no knuckleheads. But "Goin' to Work" is also a calculated articulation of that persona, an ethic that permeates the Pistons organization, from the work shirts worn by Palace staff to the PERC cards (for Palace Employees Really Care) issued to Palace workers caught in the act of doing good deeds for customers.

By the end of the 2003–04 season, Dumars had signed every single player on the team.[26] He himself had always been a quiet player on the hardwood. A powerful shooting guard who played very strong defense, he had been, above all, a team player, and that's what Dumars looked for in the players he brought on board. While coach Rick Carlisle had taken the team to the Eastern Conference finals in the previous season, disputes with the management had led to his dismissal. Larry Brown, the new coach, brought with him thirty years of experience in the NBA and NCAA, including an NCAA Championship with Kansas. If ever a coach fitted in the with going-to-work theme, it was Brown, a man with a reputation as a teacher who could turn losers into winners.

As highly respected as he was, he had never won an NBA championship. Hopeful preseason forecasts saw him perhaps beating the New Jersey Nets for the Eastern Conference, but that's as far as expectations went. Since Michael Jordan had abandoned the Chicago Bulls, the Western Conference teams had bossed the finals. Between 2000 and 2002, the LA Lakers, starring Shaquille O'Neal and Kobe Bryant and coached by Phil Jackson, had won three championships in a row, while the San Antonio Spurs had taken the title in 2003. The best odds in Vegas on an Eastern Conference team were for the Nets, at 12–1 against. Even if the Pistons could vanquish them, any further spoils seemed out of reach.[27]

Chauncey Billups, Richard Hamilton, Ben Wallace, and Tayshaun Prince made up the core of the team; Billups at point guard and Hamilton at shooting guard were the leading scorers. Without question, though, it was the defense that made the Pistons stand out that year. In the previous four seasons, the champions had averaged between 96 and 101 points per game; in 2003–04, the Pistons managed a mere 90, the sixth worst in the league that season. But the Pistons conceded only 84 points per game, compared with a range of 90–97 for the previous four champions. The defensive leader of the team was Ben Wallace, who had been named defensive player of the year by the NBA the previous two seasons. But pretty much everyone excelled at defense—including players coming off the bench like Lindsey Hunter and Mike James, whom Rasheed Wallace nicknamed "the pit bulls."[28]

Rasheed himself was the last piece in the jigsaw that season. The Pistons acquired him in a trade on February 20, when most of the regular season was already over. He had broken records for the most number of technical fouls, which generally meant "unsportsmanlike conduct," and he was an accomplished trash-talker. He would later become famous for his signature line, "ball don't lie," a taunt he would offer every time an opposing player missed a free throw—implying that the foul had been awarded in error, and that said error had now been corrected.[29] His exuberant defiance made him popular in a city where on any given day, you could probably pass at least one person wearing a "Detroit Against the World" T-shirt. To Joe Dumars, Rasheed meant the difference between a respectable performance and victory: "I thought we were a contender to go deep into the playoffs without him. I thought he could be the piece that gets us over the hump and win this thing."[30]

Arguably, being in the weaker Eastern Conference made the path to the finals easier. Their 54-28 record in the regular season ranked only sixth overall in the league, and they made relatively easy work of disposing of the Milwaukee Bucks in the first round of the playoffs. They rushed to a 2–0 lead over the Nets in the next round, only to lose the next three games. In game 6 in New Jersey, Detroit were a mere two points ahead with just over a minute to play, and managed to block four shots to win out in a close game. After that close call, game 7 at Auburn Hills was almost an anticlimax. The Pistons won easily. Then came the Pacers and Rasheed Wallace's game 2 prophecy.

Facing Shaq and Kobe's Lakers in the finals was a completely different proposition. The Vegas bookies had the Lakers' chances to win it at 80 percent. But then the Pistons won game 1 in LA, holding the Western Champions to only 75 points. Detroit's defense forced 15 turnovers and kept the Lakers below 40 percent shooting. It was a revelation. The Pistons narrowly lost game 2, blowing a six-point lead in the final minute before losing in overtime, and the series moved to Detroit for the next three games. In game 3, the Lakers managed a paltry 68 points, and the Pistons won convincingly. A pattern was established: the Pistons could not stop Shaq and Kobe, but they could make them work hard for their points while shutting out every other Lakers player. At the end of the series, the two top scorers were the Lakers stars, but no one else on their team got close to the Pistons' starting five. In game 6, Bryant and O'Neal started bickering, and Phil Jackson looked at a loss as to how to coach his team. The TV commentators, whose working assumption had been the Lakers cruising to triumph, had to revise the narrative: "We're making it an LA story. In fact it's also a Detroit story," admitted Mike Tirico, somewhat apologetically.[31]

A Detroit story indeed: game 5 was a rout, and the Pistons clinched the series 4–1 with a 100–87 victory at Auburn Hills. The Goin' to Work Pistons achieved one of the all-time upsets over a team of LA superstars. It was all about defense, and it was all about teamwork. As the *Detroit News* wrote, "We beat I."[32]

A couple of days after the final game, William Rhoden wrote in the *New York Times*: "These Pistons are likable, and Detroit, led by the energetic [Kwame] Kilpatrick, 34, is rejuvenated. Kilpatrick said there are 17 new restaurants downtown and six new hotels and riverfront developments. 'The city hasn't been this happy and filled with this much glee since 1989–90. I've been a Pistons fan all my life, I went to Pistons basketball every year. The resurgence of the city and of this new, young energetic team, is also part of what we're doing on the basketball court as well.'"[33] Just over a year later Kilpatrick was elected for a second term as mayor.

"Goin' to Work" is how Detroiters see themselves, no matter what the rest of the world thinks. They are proud of their auto-industry heritage and the hard, backbreaking work that built it. It's a feeling that crosses the racial divide, not least because the industry's workforce always included a large percentage of African Americans. From its earliest days, black Americans could get work in car plants—not, perhaps needless to say, on an equal footing with white workers, but often enough union jobs that paid decent wages. They were routinely allocated the hardest, most dangerous jobs, such as foundry work where massive forges pressing hot metal made for often lethal working conditions. And pay rates for black workers were usually among the lowest in the industry. But even in the face of these discriminations, making cars was the shared work of the Motor City, and a source of shared pride. The Goin' to Work Pistons also shared that pride, which stood in stark contrast to the national image of a crumbling, dangerous, abandoned Detroit, as foreign as Fallujah, and hardly worth saving.

FIVE

SEPTEMBER 27, 1999

The Tigers play their last game at "The Corner," the stadium that was their home for over a century. The Tiger Stadium Fan Club had failed in its long quest to save the structure, and it is the end of an era. We look back at Tigers History, meet Mike Ilitch again, and have things to say about other Tigers owners and team owners in general. Mayor Dennis Archer does not merely build a new stadium for the Tigers, he also brings the Lions home. Downtown Detroit slowly begins to ascend again, while still mourning the demolition of the iconic Hudson's department store.

The last game in the place that was your home for more than a century. The place where you won four World Series. The stadium that had been one of the best-attended ballparks in the country for most of that time. You gotta win that one. And the Detroit Tigers were in luck: the last visiting team they played that season were the Kansas City Royals, incidentally the only team against which the Tigers had a winning record that season.[1]

At the bottom of the eighth, the Tigers lead 4–2, probably good enough—but given their season, they can still blow it. Dean Palmer doubles on a line drive, and then Damion Easley singles. With two on, relief pitcher Jeff Montgomery intentionally walks Karim Garcia, so the bases are loaded, and remain loaded after Gabe Kapler grounds out. Then rookie Robert Fick walks up and strikes the next pitch straight out of right field. The Royals fail to answer in the top of the ninth, and the game ends 8–2.

That grand slam was the last home run hit at "The Corner." Fick would leave the Tigers in 2002 and play for four other teams, playing in the majors until 2007. But to this day, he gets asked about that moment. "I don't get tired of talking about it," he said in 2015, "it's my claim to fame."[2]

"The Corner" was shorthand for Tiger Stadium, located at the corner of Michigan and Trumbull Avenues. It had been built in many layers, and by the 1990s, it resembled a fortress with high walls roughly trapezoid in shape, mounted with floodlights rather than turrets. It was an intimate place, the two tiers of the stands almost leaning over the field. It had a peak capacity of 52,416.

Whether you consider a ballpark a thing of beauty or not really depends on how much you like baseball. If you don't care much about it, you might think that all the attention is on the game itself, so the surroundings are largely irrelevant to the experience. But most stadiums are referred to as the "home" of the team, and by extension, they are the home of the fans. And people care about their homes.

Objectively speaking, Tiger Stadium had little to offer by way of architectural beauty. Its lines were not elegant, its materials were not of the finest, and by the 1990s, you wouldn't have been wrong if you called it old and dilapidated. But after all is said and done, it was the home of the Detroit Tigers, who had played at The Corner since 1896.

In was in this park that Ty Cobb, one of baseball's legends, had stolen bases and hustled runs for more than two decades. This park had been home to four World Series championship teams, and they said goodbye to it in style. After the last game, the closing ceremony paraded the former greats, introduced one by one to the crowd. Almost no one remained from the World Series of 1935 and 1945, but the respective stars of the 1968 and 1984 Tigers were there: Al Kaline and Willie Horton; Alan Trammell and Lou Whitaker, who had played together at Tiger Stadium for nineteen seasons. Elden Auker, who pitched six innings in game 3 of the 1935 World Series, where Detroit won 6–5 at Wrigley Field, gave a farewell speech: "We live on by those who carry on the Tiger tradition and who so proudly wear the Old English D."[3]

The National Register of Historic Places was created in 1966 to indicate places deemed worthy of preservation because of their historic significance. There are around eighty thousand specific structures included on the list, and Tiger Stadium was once one of them, listed in 1991, thanks to the Tiger Stadium Fan Club. The club sprang up in 1987 in response to owner Tom Monaghan, who had announced plans to build a new stadium. Monaghan made his fortunes in pizza: in 1960, he had founded Domino's Pizza in nearby Ann Arbor and turned it into one of the nation's largest food chains. As basic as his product may have been, his own consumption was anything but: he was known for his ostentatious lifestyle, which included an $8 million Bugatti and a collection of Frank Lloyd Wright buildings. He had bought the team at the end of 1983 from longtime owner John Fetzer and was instantly rewarded with a World Series win in the following season. But after that the team struggled to make an impact, and in the following eight years, the Tigers made it to the postseason only once.[4]

Fetzer had started complaining about the state of the ballpark toward the end of his tenure, and in 1977, he sold it to the City of Detroit for $1 in exchange for a thirty-year lease to the ball club and an agreement that the city would commit a $5 million federal grant for the park's refurbishment.[5] The city also contributed to the refurbishment of the stadium through an $8.5 million bond issue, repaid out of ticket revenue and the rent that Fetzer paid the city. After the renovations were completed, Monaghan at first declared that he had no plans to leave. But as the 1980s progressed, his views shifted. It wasn't only that he, like most owners, saw an opportunity to get the public to fund a more lavish structure, complete with luxury boxes and other amenities to generate revenue. He also had the public support of the mayor, Coleman Young, who observed in 1988, with his usual bluntness, that "it's obvious the damn thing is falling down."[6] Young was a passionate advocate of investments meant to revive the city, and he believed in the power of sporting venues to achieve that end. It is also possible that there were other reasons he didn't share the sentimentality regarding Tiger Stadium: the park had long been an iconic place to the white fans, but for an equally long time, The Corner had a reputation for being unwelcoming to the black population.[7] The Tigers had been famously slow to integrate black players into the team. After Jackie Robinson was the first player to break the color bar in 1947, the Detroit ball club took more than a decade to hire their first black player, Ozzie Virgil, who joined the team in 1958. Only the Boston Red Sox were slower to integrate. Walter Briggs, owner of the Tigers between 1936 and 1952, refused to sell tickets for the boxes in the stadium to African Americans. His own great-grandson, Harvey Briggs, said it bluntly: "He was a racist."[8]

The Tiger Stadium Fan Club, however, was deeply attached to the place, and their message was simple: the stadium is a historic monument, and for the relatively small outlay of $26 million, it can be transformed to provide all the modern facilities the owners might want. They had a plan, named for Mickey Cochrane, the player-manager who led the Tigers to their first World Series in 1935. It was credible enough, drawn up in 1990 by professional architects and supported by many of the architectural community's leading lights.[9] To back up its negotiating position, the Fan Club, which by now had several thousand members, organized "stadium hugs" where fans linked arms around the entire stadium.[10] They also managed to get a measure onto the city ballot in 1992, prohibiting the public financing of a new stadium. The measure passed.[11]

Monaghan, however, refused to have anything to do with the Cochrane plan and instead started a PR battle, which included hiring the legendary University of Michigan football coach Bo Schembechler as president of the club. This backfired spectacularly when Schembechler fired the equally legendary Tigers broadcaster Ernie Harwell, refused to listen to anyone who argued that the stadium was not obsolete, and generally put the club owner and management in a bad light by acting like a bully. After Monaghan saw himself forced to fire Schembechler in turn, he decided he'd had enough of worldly possessions such as sports teams and devoted his fortune to promoting the Catholic faith. As part of this process of letting go, he sold the Tigers that year to his pizza rival, Mike Ilitch. Round one to the Tiger Stadium Fan Club.[12]

Ilitch, as a former minor league ballplayer, looked like a much more promising owner. It was plain that owning a major league club was the fulfillment of a lifelong dream, and he had shown himself willing to invest in his other Detroit team, the Red Wings. Add to that his well-documented emotional commitment to the City of Detroit, and it's easy see that the Tiger Stadium Fan Club had reason for optimism. The Ilitch ownership era started out with a burst excitement: players were bought, innovations at the ballpark were introduced to raise revenues, there was goodwill all around. In 1993, the team rallied, and attendance jumped to almost 2 million.

Alas, the peace turned out to have been nothing but a cease-fire. Ilitch quickly decided he wasn't getting his money's worth from the stadium, and he abruptly set out his stall to get a new one.[13] The 1994 season was interrupted by a strike that started in August, causing the World Series to be canceled for the first time since 1904. When play eventually resumed in April 1995, fans, furious about the strike, protested at various ballparks, including the homes of the Mets, Cincinnati, Pittsburgh, and the Yankees. But Detroit garnered the most attention when unhappy fans started throwing objects such as cigarette lighters, coins, batteries, beer and whiskey bottles at the players. As the players fled, some fans ran onto the field, in a style previously seen only with soccer hooligans. This was the hundredth year that baseball had been played at The Corner, and it started out with thirty-four arrests.[14]

At the same time, public opinion about new ballparks was shifting. Many of the new builds of earlier years had been deeply unpopular, considered soulless and characterless. But in 1992, Camden Yards in Baltimore opened as the new home of the Orioles, and people were impressed by the quality of both the architecture and the experience. The new Rangers stadium at Arlington Park in Texas made a favorable impression as well, and people started to think that a new stadium might not be such a bad idea after all.

Coleman Young had left office at the beginning of 1994, but his successor, Dennis Archer, proved just as enthusiastic, if a little less outspoken, in his support of the new stadium plan. Ilitch promised to contribute the lion's share of the cost, but he nonetheless demanded a substantial public contribution. Archer was focused primarily on revitalizing the downtown area—getting companies such as Compuware to settle there and persuading GM to purchase the Renaissance Center and move its headquarters to the downtown. For him, a new sports facility was just another symbol to create confidence in the city, and he was more than happy to work with the likes of Mike Ilitch, who had proven his commitment to Detroit. Archer started working on plans soon after being elected, and in October 1995, an agreement in principle was reached with the Tigers, the State of Michigan, and the City of Detroit to spend $235 million on a new stadium. Sixty-two percent would come from Ilitch, 23 percent from the state, and 15 percent from the city. A site was identified west of Woodward Avenue, and the City Council set about reversing the ordinance banning stadium subsidies.[15]

The Tiger Stadium Fan Club flexed its muscles again, and they were able to force a referendum on whether to endorse the City Council's decision, scheduled for March 1996. In an acrimonious campaign, Archer and Ilitch proved much better advocates than Young and Monaghan had been. They portrayed the Tiger Stadium Fan Club as a group of out-of-town obstructionists who were more invested in their own nostalgia than in the Tigers or the City of Detroit. Players, old and new, were wheeled out in support of the new park, while Archer and Ilitch gave joint presentations at churches across the city, a pivotal constituency in Detroit. It wasn't even close: the referendum approved the stadium subsidy plan with 83 percent of the votes—on that day, Tiger Stadium got its death sentence.[16]

Dennis Archer, in his autobiography, wrote that his "vision to transform downtown Detroit into a world-renowned destination for sports and entertainment hinged on building new stadiums for our professional sports teams."[17] And at this stage, he pulled off a major coup: his agenda included not just building a new stadium for the Tigers, but bringing the Detroit Lions home as well. They, too, had played at Tiger Stadium, before moving to the Pontiac Silverdome in 1975. He expanded the plan to incorporate a domed stadium for the football team, which would go up side by side with the new ballpark—not on the west side of Woodward, but on the east side, right in the heart of the downtown. Back then, David Axelrod, who went on to become a key adviser to President Obama, worked for Mayor Archer as a researcher on redevelopment. Axelrod later recalled, "I remember doing interviews with Detroiters about what Detroit was like in the past. We wanted to find out what it was like to come downtown to the stores and theaters. And I realized that Dennis' vision was very much about rekindling that sense of community with a downtown hub."[18]

On August 20, 1996, Mayor Archer, Mike Ilitch, William Clay Ford, and Wayne County executive Ed McNamara called a press conference to announce the deal. They would build the two facilities at a cost of $505 million. The funding package for the Tigers was unchanged, but the new Lions dome would receive a subsidy of around $150 million from the city as well as from county and tourism taxes. This new package required a further referendum in the November election, but the war had already been won, and the resolution passed without any problems.[19] Mayor Archer had taken a significant step toward fulfilling his ambition to reshape the downtown.

The 1996 season turned out to be a remarkable one for the Tigers on the field as well, but not in a good way. They lost 109 games, at that point a record for the club dating back to its establishment in 1901. At one point, it looked like they might even beat the all-time record of 120 losses, set by the New York Mets in their first season. In one game alone, the Tigers gave up 24 runs, also a record. This abysmal performance was one of the nastier aspects of the political game played for public dollars: Mike Ilitch *wanted* the Tigers to be bad. The worse they played, the clearer the message to the city: without a new stadium, their team would always be in the basement. In order to achieve defeat, the owner cut spending on team payroll to the absolute minimum. A few years earlier, in 1993, Ilitch's payroll had almost matched the New York Yankees—by 1996, he had cut that number in half, placing them nearly last in Major League Baseball in terms of team salary.

Those shenanigans expose an unpleasant truth about major league sports in the United States. Whose team is it? The fans will say "our team," but of course, the owner who pulls the strings will always be some rich guy— or very occasionally a rich woman—who bought it. It's an odd situation where the control of the national pastime falls into the hands of whoever has amassed a large enough fortune to take control of it, but that's the American way. Effectively the fans are hostages to the owners' whims, and there's nothing they can do about it.[20]

Even after the deal had been made, it did not get better. In 1997, Detroit posted the second-lowest payroll in baseball, and while things started to pick up a little in 1999, the club was staffed largely by veterans with nowhere else to go, and by rookies who had yet to deliver on their promise.[21] It's therefore not surprising that Detroit did not have a winning season in their three remaining years of Tiger Stadium's life. Pictures of the ballpark in the last few years are melancholic.[22] Between 1994 and 1998 attendance fell to levels that hadn't been seen since the early 1960s. On some days, there appeared to be more players on the field than fans in the stands. It was as if they had doomed the team along with its ballpark.

A mile away, another era ended in demolition in 1998. At 1206 Woodward Avenue, a few hundred yards away from the site of the new ballpark, stood the glorious J.L. Hudson building, the department store originally built in 1911 and significantly expanded as the city grew. Over the years, the building turned into a huge edifice, and in its day it was among the largest department stores in the world. Hudson's was hugely popular, not least because it accepted returns at any time, no matter how long ago the purchase—a costly investment, but it bought tremendous customer loyalty. Hudson's was not just a store but an institution—it played a significant role in the community, staging an annual Thanksgiving Parade and organizing a brilliant firework display as part of the International Freedom Festival.[23] From 1923 onward, the store was known for flying what was claimed to be the world's largest flag.[24]

But as Detroiters moved to the suburbs, Hudson's started to decline, and the store became increasingly empty. As the downtown hollowed out, Hudson's was eventually driven to close the store in January 1983. Nobody could find a business interested in renting the space, and Hudson's fell to the wrecking ball.[25] The demolition required the removal of 200,000 tons of concrete and produced 35,000 tons of scrap metal.[26] It was a sorrowful affair. Many Detroiters mourned Hudson's demise as they would the death of a person, despite its history as an exclusive place that had for a long time not been hospitable to black customers. In the words of local activist Sandra Hines: "There was no need for Hudson's anymore. But . . . in terms of it being a landmark people did feel when they tore Hudson's down that it was something being taken out of downtown Detroit that could never be replaced. But they didn't have a need for it once we had white flight."[27]

The demolition of Tiger Stadium a year later was on a smaller scale, but emotions ran just as high. After 6,873 games there would be no more baseball at The Corner. As a symbol of what stood there, the one thing they left behind was the flagpole. After the last out of the game, Ernie Harwell, the veteran commentator, simply said: "Thank you, old friend."[28]

SIX

OCTOBER 27, 1995

The "Russian Five" burst onto the hockey scene after the Red Wings outsmart the KGB in a series of hair-raising recruiting adventures. Mike Ilitch writes the checks for the necessary bribes, and the "Red Reign" begins, yielding the city's first Stanley Cup in decades. Detroit may be the most American of cities, but it is also, in more ways than one, a border town. This chapter delves into the meaning of the Canadian border, a famous commercial, and the deeply ambivalent image of Detroit as foreign territory.

A few minutes into the game at Calgary's Olympic Saddledome, Red Wings coach Scotty Bowman sends in five skaters whose names you might sooner expect in a Tolstoy novel than on the roster of a team from Detroit: Sergei Fedorov, Vladimir Konstantinov, Slava Kozlov, Slava Fetisov, and Igor Larionov. Kozlov scores in the tenth minute, and the game ends 3–0 to Detroit.[1] Though the Calgary Flames were not particularly hard to beat at that point, the rout made the rest of the NHL sit up. The experiment that would become known as the "Russian Five" had begun.

At first, conventional wisdom reacted with skepticism. Certainly, the Soviet Red Army teams of the 1980s had dominated international hockey, but in a league where prowess in boxing was valued as highly as the ability to control the puck, Red Army tough might not cut it. And nobody had known what to expect: Larionov had been signed only three days before the game, and while Coach Bowman had hastily explained to the players how they would line up on the ice, he had neglected to mention one thing: when the five Russians were on the ice, they themselves would decide how to play. It took them ten minutes of huddling before they figured out their plan, but when the time came, it quickly became clear that they knew what they were doing. The Flames were not the only ones taken by surprise; the Red Wings players on the bench also marveled at the sheer artistry of their play. That night, Keith Gave of the *Detroit Free Press* reported, "Detroit Red Wings television broadcaster David Strader . . . carefully tucked away two copies of the final score sheet"—he knew that he had just witnessed a historic moment.[2]

Drafting Russians in the early 1990s was no simple matter. During the Cold War, it had been out of the question altogether, but in 1985, Mikhail Gorbachev was elected general secretary of the Communist Party, ringing in a new era of *perestroika* (reform and restructuring) and *glasnost* (openness) that would eventually lead to the end of the Cold War. NHL teams realized that there might be opportunities to draft some Russian talent. The first player to be officially released to play in the United States was Sergei Pryakhin; the Calgary Flames picked him last overall in the 1988 draft, on the assumption that it would be easier to persuade the Russians to release their lesser players first.

But Jim Devellano, the Red Wings' general manager, and Jim Lites, the executive vice president, developed a different strategy—they wanted to go after the stars, and the story of how they went about it may well be the wildest story in sports recruiting. After considering a few different players, they eventually grabbed Sergei Fedorov in the 1989 draft, arguably the best forward in the world at that time. Drafting him was one thing, getting him to Detroit was another. It's fair to say that Russian hockey was not the most pressing concern to the architects of glasnost. All the top players were army officers, and the military essentially ran the sport. By Russian standards, they lived luxuriously. Defection was no longer the big deal it had once been, but desertion remained a criminal offense, and most Russian players were wary of leaving without a military discharge.

Curiously, then, nobody was actually able to tell Fedorov about his good fortune until a month after the 1989 draft. Keith Gave offered to act as go-between, on the condition he would be allowed to break the story one day. He managed to catch Fedorov in Helsinki, where the Russian team was playing a match. Gave conveyed the offer, and negotiations commenced. Whenever the Russian team was on tour, Lites wrangled an opportunity

to set up a meeting. At the time, Russian citizens were not yet free to move abroad at will, and whenever the team traveled abroad, a KGB minder was there to keep an eye on them. As we mentioned above, he could have defected without too much trouble, but deserting from the army was a different matter for Fedorov. His military service was set to end the following year, and he promised to make a move then. Even though he remained anxious about possible repercussions for his family, he finally took the plunge in Portland, on another tour. Lites was waiting in a car outside the team hotel, engine running, and Fedorov simply walked out the door, jumped into the car, and was gone.

Next came defenseman Vladimir Konstantinov. He, too, had been selected in the 1989 draft, and he, too, was an army captain who did not want to desert. As Gave recounts, getting him out proved more complicated. He had signed a twenty-five-year contract with the army, so he needed an honorable discharge to get out. Ever inventive, Lites and Devellano bribed Russian doctors to produce a cancer diagnosis that would do the trick, but the Red Army commander who managed the national hockey team was suspicious and banned Konstantinov from flying abroad. As if that wasn't trouble enough, blackmailers stole all of Konstantinov's documents and demanded a ransom of equipment and autographs. It was at this point that the Soviet old guard mounted a coup against the Gorbachev regime, and, as luck would have it, it failed, and the old system finally collapsed. Russians were ready to start their own version of democratic capitalism, and while general confusion reigned, the Detroit fixers managed to get Konstantinov on a train to Budapest in Hungary; there, he was picked up by Mike Ilitch's private jet, which flew him to the U.S.A. and the Red Wings.

Third on the shopping list was the left-winger Slava Kozlov. Detroit drafted him in 1990, and once again, the sticking point was military service. For a while, all negotiations ended in vague promises and murmurs of "not yet." When he signed a lucrative contract with the Red Army team in the fall of 1991, the opportunity seemed to have faded. Eleven weeks later, Kozlov crashed his car, killing one teammate and putting himself on life support in a coma. To the Red Wings, the calamity was just another opportunity: this honorable discharge didn't have to be faked, they thought. They promised Kozlov that they could arrange for the best medical treatment if only he came to Detroit—and if their man recovered, all the better. And indeed, Kozlov got better, but once again, the Red Army smelled a rat and sought to have their doctors revise the diagnosis. So once again, the Red Wings took their wallet out, bribed the physicians, and Kozlov was on his way. He arrived in Detroit in February and made his debut for the Red Wings on March 12, 1992.

By now the Cold War was well and truly over, and after the dissolution of the Soviet Union in 1991, players were free to move. So the last two players of the five, Slava Fetisov and Igor Larionov, were easier to sign but altogether riskier bets. In 1995, both players had been already signed to other NHL teams; Fetisov was traded to the Red Wings in April, Larionov in October. While the first three were all in their early twenties when they joined the Red Wings, Fetisov was thirty-seven and Larionov thirty-four. Both were members of the legendary "Green Line" of the Soviet hockey team of the 1980s that dominated the international game. But weren't they too old now? The answer came on October 27, 1995. Less than two years later, the Red Wings swept the Stanley Cup in four games, thanks in large part to the Russian Five.

The Stanley Cup victory of 1997 was Detroit's first since 1955. The team had struggled badly in the 1960s and 1970s, a period commonly referred to as the "Dead Wings" era.[3] In 1982, Mike Ilitch bought the team, and he was determined to see them succeed. No matter how much they spent on talent, it would take fifteen years for the investments to pay off. Ilitch's open checkbook paid the bribes to get the Russians out, and in the end, it was the decision to import talent that turned things around. Once again, migration led to triumph—it's the story of Detroit, you might say, and indeed the story of the United States. Under Ilitch, the team thrived, winning the Stanley Cup in the season following the Russian Five's signings, and again in 2002 and 2008. From 1991 until 2017, the Red Wings had made it to every post-season, but then the streak ended in April of that year, two months after Ilitch's death.

But that, too, is the story of Detroit. Each sports team, and the city itself, has always depended on the generosity and vision of wealthy businessmen—giving them tremendous power over the city's fate in the process. Whether it is Henry Ford or Dan Gilbert, William Clay Ford or Mike

Ilitch, without the backing of the super-rich, Detroit is stranded. It is a risky way to live: the city's mayors have had ample occasion to learn that the tycoons were just as prone to walking away as they were to stepping up.

There is wonderful serendipity in the fact that five former Red Army players signed for the Detroit Red Wings: it is hard to tell if the exuberant title page of the *Detroit Free Press* proclaiming "Red Reign" after the 1997 Stanley Cup victory was a conscious pun. But there is also reason to think that no other team in the NHL would have even considered the gambit. Detroit and hockey have been close for more than a hundred years, and the Red Wings are one of the Original Six teams that made up the NHL between 1942 and the expansion that started in 1967.[4] Of the other five teams in the group, three are in the United States (Boston, Chicago, and New York), and only two are in Canada (Montreal and Toronto). Even so, hockey is without question a predominantly Canadian sport, as TV ratings bear out. Hockey Night in Canada—a venerable weekly broadcast on Canadian TV showing NHL games—typically garners a viewing audience of 2 million from a population of 36 million. By contrast, regular season NHL games typically get an audience below 500,000 in the United States, out of a population of 325 million.[5] Hockey is truly popular only in pockets of the country, one of those being the region containing the northern border states of Michigan, Wisconsin, and Minnesota.

Detroit, of course, is a border town. In fact, along with Buffalo and El Paso, it is one of a small handful of U.S. cities of any size that has been located right on the border throughout its history—San Diego, by contrast, has now expanded to reach the Mexican border, but the Gaslight District that makes up the original downtown is located fifteen miles away from it. The Detroit River, which would become the border between the United States and Canada, is only half a mile wide at the point where Cadillac established his settlement. Detroit and Windsor grew up together on opposite sides of the river, and local lore claims that they were connected by a secret underwater pipeline that moved illicit beer across the border during Prohibition. To this day, the bridge and the tunnel are the site of more cross-border traffic than almost any other location in the country, generating a yearly revenue currently estimated at around $100 billion.[6]

In most people's minds, Detroit conjures up a number of images, be they positive (the home of the motor car, the home of Motown Records, or the Arsenal of Democracy during World War II) or negative (a city of ruins, a murder capital, or a den of drug addicts). The fact that Detroit is a border town, however, hardly ever figures in the popular imagination—even Detroiters themselves don't speak of it much these days. And yet, it is an important aspect of the city's culture and history, and nothing illustrates that better than the story of the Detroit Red Wings who, today, feature a left-winger named Justin Abdelkader, one of the few Arab American athletes competing at the major league level, whose name commentators habitually mispronounce as "abdicator."

You could almost call the Red Wings a Canadian team, although that might make some Detroiters mad. Scotty Bowman is a Canadian, as was every single one of his predecessors. As of 2019, the Red Wings have hired only two U.S.-born coaches, including the current one. Before 1995, a full 89 percent of the 746 players who had appeared for the Red Wings were Canadians, and less than 7 percent were U.S. born (with a smattering of other nationalities making up the total). True, in recent years the percentage of U.S. American players has increased a bit, but the composition of the teams remains overwhelmingly Canadian. The Russian Five simply replaced one type of foreigner on the team with another—ironically so, since the fiercest rivalry in international hockey had always been between Canada and the Russians.

Even the franchise's original name comes by way of Canada—when Canadian-born businessman James Norris bought the team in 1932, they were called the Detroit Cougars—a name that reflected that at their founding in 1926 the ownership had bought all of the players from the folding Victoria Cougars.[7] Norris re-christened the team the Red Wings, and brought the franchise back from the verge of bankruptcy. He remained the owner until he died in 1952, and the Norris family retained control of the franchise until 1982, when Mike Ilitch bought the team. Heck, the team even played its first season in Windsor, Ontario, because there was no stadium in Detroit to house them. For years after they moved to Detroit, management was irritated to see that whenever the Montreal Canadiens or Toronto Maple Leafs came to town, the visitors had more support in the stands than the home team.

Even now, Canadian fans make up a good chunk of the audience: Windsor does not have an NHL team of its own, and according to club figures, about 10 percent of season ticket holders are Canadian. Stricter border controls have cut into that number—before 2007, you did not even need a passport to travel between the two countries. The Canadian support may also be a reason that the Red Wings never left the downtown, as the Lions and Pistons did. The Joe Louis Arena is just a short trip across the bridge, and busloads of Canadian fans regularly cross the border for home games.

Detroit, like all American cities, is an international community, but the element of the "foreign" plays a particular role here that is not exhausted by the city's Russian players, its Canadian fans, or the 126 languages spoken in metro Detroit.[8] There is a famous Chrysler ad featuring Eminem, produced for the 2011 Super Bowl, called "Imported from Detroit." In it we see the artist drive through the city in a black Chrysler 200, past factories and skyscrapers and ruins. It lingers lovingly on *The Fist*, passes by *The Spirit of Detroit*, moves past a black doorman, a black businessman, a black gospel choir practicing in the Fox Theatre, past a white figure skater whirling by a woman in a Muslim head dress. The script is proudly defiant, and worth quoting in full, not least for the way it reprises the Pistons' "goin' to work" ethic:

> I got a question for you.
> What does this city know about luxury, huh?
> What does a town that's been to hell and back know about the
>   finer things in life?
> Well I'll tell you.
> More than most.
> You see, it's the hottest fires that make the hardest steel.
> Add hard work and conviction.
> And a know-how that runs generations deep in every last one
>   of us.
> That's who we are.
> That's our story.
> Now it's probably not the one you've been reading in the
>   papers.

The one being written by folks who have never even been here.

Don't know what we're capable of.

Because when it comes to luxury, it's as much about where it's
from as who it's for.

Now we're from America—but this isn't New York City, or the
Windy City, or Sin City, and we're certainly no one's Emerald City.

This is the Motor City—and this is what we do.

———

You can read the ad's title, "Imported from Detroit," in several ways. It
plays on the notion that Americans think of luxury cars as foreign cars, but
in a way, it also marks Detroit itself as foreign territory—at least foreign to
those "who have never even been here." It speaks to the sense that Detroit
has been betrayed by the rest of America: it built the nation's biggest industry, and now no one ever seems to miss an opportunity to malign or ridicule
the city. But there is a third interpretation, even though Chrysler probably
did not intend that one. As a border town, Detroit always has been half-
foreign anyway. The flag of the city includes the fleur-de-lys, a symbol of its
French roots, and the three lions of England, a symbol of its British roots. It
is an American city, not just a city in the United States.

To its credit, "Imported from Detroit," even though it features a white
star, accurately portrays the city as majority black—in contrast, say, to the
Gilbert ad we mentioned in chapter 2. And it is fitting that the Red Wings
logo flashes by only briefly. Hockey is generally a white sport, and according
to reliable consumer survey data from Nielsen, the Red Wings are the least
popular of Detroit's major sports teams in the African American community. This may be less a result of intentional discrimination than a byproduct
of geographical factors—hockey is a bit of a rural sport—and of structural
inequality: in the United States, racial barriers are supported and maintained by economic barriers.[9] Hockey—beyond the stage of pond hockey, at
least—is an expensive sport to play, reducing access for African Americans,
who are more likely to be poor. At the same time, hockey is perceived to
have a racism problem, which it has not yet been able to solve. When Coleman Young, the legendary first black mayor of the city, got the Joe Louis

Arena built to keep the Red Wings in Detroit, he joked, with gentle sarcasm, that he did so for that famous African American hockey player, Joe Louis.[10]

You might think, then, that the hockey team would be little beloved here, but you would be wrong. If you bring up the history of the Canadization of the Red Wings, Detroiters generally are nonplussed. Whatever the demographics of the fan base, they think of the Red Wings as their team. Among the black population, you generally elicit nothing but warmth when you mention the Wings: many black people may not follow them closely, but they are proud of them nonetheless. In some ways, it is a testament to the sense of unity that is so typical of Detroit—where outsiders see strife and trouble, Detroiters' loyalty to the city is boundless—they are, after all, the ones who stayed when so many left. And in a place where good news is sometimes hard to come by, all success is worth celebrating.

More importantly, perhaps, the relationship between Canada and Detroit and Canadians and Detroiters is largely peaceful, though some Detroiters remember a good deal of tension. A friend of ours who grew up in working-class Detroit in the 1970s tells us:

> I remember *lots* of anti-Canadian hostility when I was a kid. And Detroiters who crossed the border told all kinds of cautionary tales about anti-American hostility on the other side of the border. You could still spend American money in Canada then, and that, or American plates on your car, or pronouncing "house" the wrong way or asking for the check instead of the bill, guaranteed that the Canadians would look for a way to screw you over. And they were notorious for their racism, since Windsor was overwhelmingly white. When I lived in Toronto in the nineties, the anti-American sentiment was breathtaking. America-bashing was literally taken for granted. And needless to say, we were every bit as anti-Canadian as they were anti-American!

Even if Canada does often fail to live up to its reputation as a liberal paradise, in Detroit, Canada's importance transcends its reputation as a hockey mecca. There is a more somber history to consider than the history of hockey, and a hospitality more vitally important than the welcome extended to

hockey fans who cross the Ambassador Bridge. Detroit was the terminus of
the Underground Railroad, and only a few feet away from the plaque that
commemorates Cadillac's landing on Hart Plaza, you find the "Gateway
to Freedom International Memorial to the Underground Railroad." Before
the U.S. Fugitive Slave Act of 1850, that shameful compromise between the
South and the North, enslaved men and women who managed to escape to
the North often stayed in Detroit. After the act passed, the enslaved who
fled were not safe from capture and re-enslavement anywhere in the United
States, and by 1860, 4 million enslaved men, women, and children could
find safe harbor only beyond the border. The Underground Railroad, a network of hiding places along routes from the South to the North, was run,
often at great risk, by freed African Americans and white abolitionists. The
final stop on the journey was "Midnight," a codename for Detroit. From
there, you could cross the river to Canada, where slavery had been abol-
ished.[11] This memory runs deep in the city.

The memorial is a sculpture that consists of nine figures. Seven are facing the river, looking toward Canada. A well-dressed man points across the
water, and following his gaze are an older man carrying a sack and a woman
carrying a baby. A stooped old man, behind them, also with a sack on his
back, is squinting in the same direction. Next to them a young woman stares
at the ground with her hand on the shoulder of a boy—they look exhausted.
A girl and boy look back toward Woodward Avenue, the boy beckoning to
follow them to freedom. Bordertowns are vectors of escape.

SEVEN

JUNE 19, 1988

A heartbreaking defeat rings in the era of the Bad Boys—a team whose swagger seems tailor-made for Detroit. But the crime rate is skyrocketing, and while the city itself embraces the polarizing team's defiance, complete with a skull and crossbones logo, the rest of the country sees one more reason to write off Detroit as a city of thugs. A throwaway remark in a locker-room interview ignites a media firestorm.

"Enough already," Mitch Albom wrote the next day. "Can't we go to court? Can't we plead that the Pistons have endured all that must be endured to win an NBA championship, that they have tasted frustration, tasted agony, tasted weird calls and weird bounces and angry crowds that wanted them dead? And they came back again and again, back from the coffin, and they did it again Sunday, and it still wasn't enough."[1] Albom would later become famous as the author of *Tuesdays with Morrie* and *The Five People You Meet in Heaven*, and you can certainly sense that this prose wants to break free of sports.

But in fairness, the game had been a heartbreaker. Originally, few people had given them much of a chance in the finals—they were up against the Lakers, and the Lakers had Magic Johnson, Kareem Abdul-Jabbar, and James Worthy. But in the first game, in Inglewood, the Pistons had shocked the Lakers—and everybody else—by winning. Then the Lakers won the second and the third, and the writing was on the wall, it seemed. The Pistons, however, refused to co-operate with expectations, and they got the next two. It was 3–2 now, with two games remaining in California. They only needed to win one.

It is the third quarter of game 6, on June 19. They are behind by six points when Isiah Thomas takes off: he just starts scoring, and he goes on a 14-point run before rolling his ankle so badly he can barely walk. With five minutes left, he hobbles off the court—only to be back a minute later. He limps whenever he doesn't have the ball, and he scores whenever he does. By the end of the quarter, he has amassed 25 points, the record for a single quarter in the NBA finals. And now the Pistons have a two-point lead. He stays on for the fourth quarter, still limping, still going strong. There are 27 seconds left, and the Pistons have a one-point lead. The NBA title is within touching distance.[2]

And then it all goes away. As Kareem Abdul-Jabbar tries to make a sky-hook, the ref calls a foul on Bill Laimbeer. If you look at the video, it is plain that Laimbeer did not touch him—to this day, the call is known as the "phantom foul."[3] But Abdul-Jabbar scores with two free throws, and it's 103–102. "For the final 14 seconds," Jim Finkelstein and David McHugh write, "A determined city held its breath, its team behind by a single point, on the brink of its first championship in 31 years." But it wasn't meant to be. Sure, game 7 was close as well, but Thomas, still injured, could only play half of that one, and while at times the Pistons were able to run them close, the Lakers never really looked like losing. In the end, the result turned out as first scripted, with a final score of 108–105. The defending champions had won the NBA title for the fifth time since 1980. All the pundits who had never given Detroit a chance could feel vindicated—though they would have to eat crow soon enough.

We could have anchored this chapter in 1989, when they do win the title, or in 1990, when they win it again. Or in 1987, when Isiah Thomas sets off a media firestorm—more on that later. But there is something about playing gloriously on a bum ankle, about the grim grit of it, the sheer determination in the face of a tremendous handicap, and the fact that it isn't enough, though it ought to have been, that is very Detroit.

Moreover, this is the season when the Pistons become the Bad Boys. It builds over the winter. In January 1988, the *LA Times* calls them "the reigning bad boys of the National Basketball Assn." Mitch Albom writes a column titled, "Bad Boys? These Pistons Are Pussycats," whose first line is, "You wake up one morning, and everybody hates you."[4] He goes on to note that "people are suddenly comparing them with the Los Angeles Raiders. They say a game against the Pistons is like a blind date with Freddy Krueger. One WTBS announcer even introduces them as 'the team people love to hate.'" The Raiders, of similar reputation, take notice, decide they are seeing kindred souls, and Al Davis, their owner, sends a care package full of Raiders gear. He explains, the *New York Times* reports, that "he got the idea after watching a CBS television feature on 'The Bad Boys of Basketball.'"[5] Isiah Thomas is up for it. "Loved it," guard Isiah Thomas said. Later, he would write: "The way I saw it, we would be like the old Oakland Raiders. . . . That's the same portrait that had been painted of our team: a bunch of crazies all assembled on one basketball team. The implication was that none of us really belonged, that our locker room was a padded cell, and that Chuck Daly was coaching in an insane asylum."[6]

So far, it's just a description, though an increasingly popular one. Then the Pistons' annual team video of the 1987–88 season, produced by the NBA entertainment department, is released, titled "Bad Boys." Isiah Thomas happily embraces the name: "We adopted a line from the movie *Scarface*, because I love Al Pacino. . . . For the first few games, we'd walk onto the court and get into our huddle, and we'd all say, 'Say hello to the Bad Boys, because you ain't never going to see Bad Boys like us again.'"[7]

A delighted Coach Daly pretends to be reluctant about the tag, and native Detroiter Bill Berris works with graphic artist Robin Brant to create a new unofficial team logo: the skull and crossbones borrowed from the Raiders, but with a crack in the skull, superimposed on a stylized basketball, DETROIT in black and silver caps above, and "Bad Boys" in ragged brush script below. It's not exactly subtle. The logo and the merchandise emblazoned with it quickly become insanely popular in Detroit, which adores the defiance the logo embodies.[8] Apparently Jalen Rose, of Fab Five fame, loved the brand as a Detroit teenager, and you can easily imagine how it would have inspired the later team, known for their joyous trash-talk, their impeccable hip-hop fashion sense, their fast and fantastic game.[9] Everybody else hates the Bad Boys, which makes it all the sweeter when they finally triumph.

Back in the 1980s, it had been hard to find anyone who actually wanted to be drafted by Detroit. Violent crime was at an all-time high during those years, and the city's reputation was so terrible that players went out of their way to look unappealing. Those were the Reagan years, and a cold wind was blowing toward the poor. Isiah Thomas, the leader of the Bad Boys, though not the baddest of them, had been no different. He wanted to go to Chicago. In the 1981 draft, he told the Dallas Mavericks that he wouldn't wear a cowboy hat, which wiped out his chances of signing with them—they took his best friend Mark Aguirre instead. But Detroit wasn't as easily fooled. He tried hard to scare them off during the interviews, but they didn't care. It turned out to be an excellent fit—they built an entire team around him, and Thomas would lead them to two trophies, back to back.

Thomas was no stranger to mean streets. He had grown up in the roughest of neighborhoods on Chicago's West Side, and he often recounted that his main memory of childhood was hunger. "My mother, two sisters, six brothers, and I were a true ghetto family," he wrote in *The Fundamentals*. "We fought and scraped—and occasionally begged—for every bit of food, every piece of clothing. We must have lived on every corner of the West Side at one time or another on the run from one landlord, one bill collector, or another."[10] His mother, Mary, had fought hard to keep her sons away from street gangs, even confronting gang members with a shotgun on her doorstep, but she still lost two sons to drugs and alcohol. Mary got Isiah into a private school, St. Joseph's in Westchester, Illinois, and upon graduation, he won a scholarship to Indiana, where he led the Hoosiers to an NCAA championship in only his second year. He left college to play in the NBA, but not before his mother insisted he sign a legal contract with her, promising to complete his degree. On May 11, 1987, the *New York Times* headline reads, "Thomas Keeps Promise to Mom." He graduated after years of summer courses, correspondence courses, and a night class at Wayne State—unbeknownst to his mother. He couldn't make it to the ceremony—they were in the playoffs—but Mary Thomas sure could, and on Mother's Day, she received his cap, gown, and tassel at the door of Assembly Hall.[11] In *The Fundamentals*, he calls her "my greatest role model and the most important figure in my life."[12]

It's a sweet story, and Thomas was meant to be a sweet young man, a "cherubic-faced sophomore" trained by Bobby Knight, the authoritarian taskmaster who was finally fired after one too many violent altercations.

Thomas, however, grew up with the sense that "you were predator or potential prey,"[13] and that must have limited his capacity for compliance. After he left Indiana, "the Thomas who led the Bad Boys," basketball-culture scholar Yago Colás writes,

> seemed transformed, regressed even—at least through the lens of the myth of blackness—to his raw urban roots. Adherents of the myth of blackness might imagine that Thomas had been contaminated by the city in which he now played; for Detroit, with its postindustrial detritus and Devil's Night incendiary mayhem, had itself become an offense to white America, which vastly preferred nostalgic images of Detroit of the 1950s, symbolizing America's ingenuity, industrial might, and class cooperation. In this sense, the Bad Boys and Thomas became the perfect repositories for the anxieties and resentments of the white basketball unconscious.[14]

Others, too, made the connection between the Bad Boys and their city. In early 1988, Albom quotes Bob Neal, the WTBS announcer, "who said that yes, he has been calling Detroit 'the team people love to hate' on national broadcasts since last season. 'It's the image they have around the country now,' he said. 'I think people relate to Detroit as a tough, blue-collar, hardball town—and now Detroit basketball fits the mold literally.'"[15]

Thomas's Pistons certainly played rough, but it is hard not to see how "tough, blue-collar, hardball" shades into "poor, black and angry," to quote a long *New York Times* feature on Detroit by Ze'ev Chafets, published in 1990 but largely set in 1988.[16] It's roughly twenty years after the city's uprising, the so-called "riots" we will discuss in chapter 12, violent crime is at an all-time high, Reagan had run (and won) on demonizing "welfare queens," and in 1988, the Bush campaign broadcast its infamous "Willie Horton" ad, designed to exploit the widespread fear of black men. Coleman Young, Detroit's first black mayor, has become a figure conservative America loves to hate in the same way people love to hate the Pistons. We quote Chafets again: "Under him, Detroit has become not merely an American city that happens to have a black majority, but a black metropolis, with all the trappings of a third-world city." That is hair-raising prose, quite possibly inspired partially by anti-Arab sentiment, and it comes from a supporter of sorts, a native son who wants to see Detroit revive, and revive *as* a black city. And yet—in case the message isn't clear, the *Times* inserts a subheading: "The battle lines are clear and dangerous: the white suburbs vs. the black city."

In the late 1980s, the Pistons are symbolically drafted into this larger battle. Their story prefigures, to a certain extent at least, the way the "Malice at the Palace" would be covered in 2004, and it explains why a Pacers player getting into a brawl with white fans in Auburn Hills would somehow become a story about Detroit, at least to the Rush Limbaughs of America. Sure, the NBA is majority black, vastly so in the 1980s, but there are still something like white teams, and a team's symbolic blackness is not necessarily measured by its number of African American players. Jeffrey Lane writes: "At the televised level, basketball is a black sport and cultural institution. Thus when a team fields a notable number of white ballplayers—and this number can be as small as five or six on a fourteen-man professional roster—fans and sportswriters immediately take notice. These 'white' teams, of course, still have black members—perhaps even a black majority—yet the blackness of the ball club is often negated by the conspicuous white presence. The Celtics of the 1980s are considered a white team, and, indeed, they were whiter than the rest of the NBA."[17] And for years, the Celtics are the Pistons' nemesis.

This is the background of a media frenzy swirling around Isiah Thomas and Pistons forward Dennis Rodman in 1987, about a year before Thomas's heroic performance in game 6 of the finals. It was the third year in a row that the Pistons had lost to the Celtics in the playoffs, in a series characterized by great play and serious fouls on both sides. The animosity between the teams was palpable, and in the locker room interviews, the Pistons didn't hold back. Thomas bitterly declared that the better team lost, but it was Dennis Rodman, then a rookie, who lit the fuse when he called Celtics star Larry Bird "very overrated." Bird, he allegedly added, had won three MVP awards in a row only "because he was white." Thomas probably should have left it alone, but he doubled down: "I think Larry is a very, very good basketball player, but I have to agree with Rodman. If he were black he'd be just another good guy." There was also talk of referee bias.

The moment was a gift to the media who were itching to exploit tensions that had long been bubbling under the surface. The *Los Angeles Times*, representative of most of the national coverage, wrote: "You can dismiss Rodman's comments as the blatherings of an excitable rookie, even though he's 26. But Isiah is a mature man, a veteran, a hero and a spokesman. When he accuses the refs of homerism, the media (writers and broadcasters vote for the MVP) of racism, and Bird of whiteism, he embarrasses us all."[18] Perhaps so, but the same piece claimed, with jarring condescension, that Thomas needed both "a history lesson" and "a brush-up in current events."

Larry Bird did not deserve the slam—but Thomas didn't need the history lesson, either. He had lived the history that was at stake here—and it wasn't about how good Bird was but about how Bird was marketed, about the image of Bird. As Jeffrey Lane writes, if "Bird were black, he would still have been a phenomenal basketball player; his gifts were undeniable. However, he would not have meant the same thing to white hoops fans nationwide, to a desperate NBA, and to the legacy of the Celtics organization."[19] Yago Colás points out that the Pistons players had "expressed a belief, by no means theirs alone, that Bird—like the white stars Pete Maravich, Bill Bradley, and Jerry West before him, and with due acknowledgment of his 'exceptional talent'—was nonetheless the beneficiary of the . . . desire for a great white hope who could single-handedly turn back the tide of black dominance of basketball at the sport's highest levels." In fact, when you search for the term "great white hope" online, the name Larry Bird pops up reliably, even though the term was first coined with regard to boxing—as we'll discuss in chapter 16.

Lane argues that Bird's popularity was at least in part the effect of an "impulse that is probably inside all white fans. It is simultaneously a frantic desire to be included and a patronizing belief that the white athlete can restore the sanctity that has been traditional to sports and reverse the damage caused by black irreverence."[20] And he has a striking example:

> A television piece entitled *History of the NBA*, which aired in
> 1990, opens with a montage that matches images of hoops in

different environments with shots of the NBA's all-time best in action. Produced by HBO Sports and NBA Entertainment, the documentary's voiceover informs us that while the game has grown and changed over time, it retains a "simple purity." With these words, the film cuts to a shot of two horses passing a basket mounted on a grass field (presumably on a farm) and then goes to a slow-motion sequence of Larry Bird pulling up for a three on Charles Barkley. Like horses and farmland, Larry Bird represents what is still untainted in America.[21]

It is important to note that Bird himself, who grew up in a dirt-poor town in Indiana, where his mother Georgia worked two low-wage jobs to support her six kids while his father Joe slowly drank himself toward suicide, is unlikely to have shared in this nostalgia for the rural white heartland. But Bird did not control his image, and neither did Thomas. After the locker room remarks, the American press, as always eager to give every social conflict the "both sides" treatment, did not simply take Bird's side; they loved the larger storyline of what they now call "reverse racism," and they hounded Thomas to expand on his views. Eventually, he and Bird agreed to hold a joint press conference to clear the air. Thomas was distraught: "I'm hurt, my family is hurt, my mother's crying, and I can't believe this is happening."[22]

The press conference did not go over too well.[23] It's rarely a good idea to stress your own pain in an apology, but what infuriated people more was that Thomas stood by his larger point: "Larry definitely had to work hard to get where he is at, but so many times it's been said about black athletes that their talent is 'God-given' or that it's 'natural ability.' I had to work just as hard to get where I am. It's not God-given or instinctive. Basketball is a game where you do things over and over again. When someone makes a great play it's not a matter of instinct, but how quickly you can recall."[24]

Just a few years later, Charles Murray and Richard Herrnstein published *The Bell Curve: Intelligence and Class Structure in American Life*, a book arguing that inequality in America was to a large extent the product of genetic inheritance—"natural," in other words.[25] Even though Herrnstein and Murray denied that this had been their intended message, people believed the controversial book gave credence to the idea that black Americans might be athletically or musically gifted, but not intellectually equipped to take on more responsible roles. Such theories, without basis in respected science, fundamentally ignore the role of environment, culture, and, in particular, history, but they are widely shared—the idea of the "naturally gifted" black athlete, whose talent is inborn and whose accomplishments are hence less worthy of respect, remains popular to this day.

In an ideal world, Thomas would have given a one-hour lecture on racial discrimination, be it in sports coverage or in the criminal justice system, followed by a brief and sincere apology to Larry Bird—he would have been more than capable of it. But the moment wasn't one that called for nuance and context, and his comments were not deemed sufficiently contrite. To his credit, Larry Bird himself was gracious: "The main thing is that if the statement doesn't bother me, it shouldn't bother anybody," he said. "If Isiah tells me it was a joking matter, it should be left at that. . . . I've answered a lot of questions about it, and talked about it to my family and they still love Isiah Thomas."[26] And afterward, at practice, he added, disarmingly: "I knew what he said wasn't coming from the heart; it was coming from his mouth."[27]

That particular event had primed the country to disdain the Bad Boys, but they made it work for them—facing the hostility of an entire nation, they embraced their image and decided to win. And win they did. It was not exactly pretty. And yet, the "Bad Boys" tag often disguises how exceptional they were as athletes—it erases their athletic prowess under a stereotype that fitted the country's contempt for Detroit and often merged with it. The key to their success was the defense, and in blocking and rebounding, the Pistons were without parallel—they were a true "94 feet defense" team. The MVP of the 1989 finals, where the Pistons took out the Lakers 4–0, was Joe Dumars, the player least suited to the label "Bad Boy." And, of course, sweeping the Lakers was a tremendous feat. In retrospect, however, defeating the Bulls in the conference finals—as they would again in the following season—was an even greater triumph. These were, after all, the same Jordan Bulls who would go on to win the following three championships and six of the next eight. How did the Pistons manage to pull that off? By playing to the Pistons' now legendary "Jordan Rules," which dictated that any player on Jordan's team who got the ball would get no peace and no quarter, by fair means or foul.[28] Bad boy stuff, in short, and effective.

After they won the 1989 finals in an away game, the champions returned to Detroit in triumph. The city organized a parade along Woodward Avenue, leading from the Fox Theatre, newly renovated by the Ilitches, through Campus Martius and down to Larned Street. The parade ended at the Joe Louis monument, the giant sculpture of the boxer's fist that had been erected less than three years earlier.[29] The newspapers covered exuberant celebrations all across the city, some involving gunfire and some vandalism. For the most part, however, the police reported that the crowds were merely rowdy, wielding nothing more offensive than a broom to symbolize the sweep over the Lakers—in other words, nothing even close to Philadelphia after an Eagles win (or an Eagles loss, for that matter). "A little violence," the modest *Free Press* headline read.[30]

"A little violence" was not what Americans expected from Detroit in the 1980s—the city had become synonymous with guns and homicide. Detroit was labeled "murder capital of the United States"—homicides had increased more than almost sixfold in a decade. For much of America, the equation was simple: Detroit became the murder capital when and because it became a majority-black city. Make no mistake, the violence was, indeed, awful and traumatic, but Detroit—as so often—was an enlarged mirror image of the country as a whole. Lethal violence was sweeping the nation in the 1980s, peaking in the early 1990s. While Detroit was indeed hit particularly hard, singling out the city as exceptional appears a projection, a phantasmic attempt to segregate (in more senses than one) violence from the country that has always fostered it. Gun death is as American as apple pie—or rather *more* American, because lots of countries like apple pie, but few can rival the mayhem that visits America year after year. When it comes to the murder rate in developed countries, the United States ranks fourth, after Mexico, Turkey, and Estonia. No Western European country even comes close.

Of course, many Americans are aware of this unenviable record and would dearly like to see action to change it. Surely, however, those same Americans would bristle if the United States as a whole were dismissed as a nation of violent thugs by the world at large. And yet, that is precisely how many Americans used to talk about Detroit—and often enough still do. In

2014, Paul Kersey, a white supremacist blogger, self-published a book about Detroit baldly claiming that the decline of the city was causally linked to the rising share of the black population.[31] Kersey is a fringe figure, to be sure, but at how many dinner tables around the country will you hear the same argument? And how many comment sections, Twitter feeds, and Facebook walls will push it along?

Violent crime is not, despite common misperception, an urban problem: when it comes to victimization rates, there is little difference between metropolitan, suburban, and rural areas, and you are, in fact, more likely to be the victim of aggravated assault in the countryside than in the city.[32] But that does not mean that Detroit does not have a problem. By the 1980s, Detroit was flooded with weapons, the result of a decades-long trend, and a study published in 1991 showed that the incidence of homicides in Detroit was closely linked to the availability of guns in the city over the previous three decades.[33] But more than anything, violent crime is linked to poverty, and a 1993 meta-analysis that looked at the crime wave of the 1970s and 1980s concluded that homicide and assault were robustly correlated with poverty and income inequality.[34]

It is true, then, that Detroit became more murderous as it became more black—because it became more *impoverished* as it became more black. This is not to suggest that being poor makes you a criminal—there is actually evidence that theft is more common in better-off communities. Rather, it is well established that the conditions that cause poverty also cause crime: the absence of public services, poor-quality schools, limited employment opportunities, and systematic discrimination are prime examples. The decades of white flight did not merely change the racial demographics of the city, they radically changed the city's economy. As we discussed earlier, any city that loses more than half its citizens will fall into dire financial straits, but the economic catastrophe was heightened by a history that had systematically destroyed black wealth or had prevented it from accumulating in the first place.

To document the extent of the ways in which black economic mobility was actively undermined is beyond the scope of this book, but Ta-Nehisi Coates's 2014 *Atlantic* essay, "The Case for Reparations," lays much of it out in excruciating detail.[35] It is worth remembering, Coates argues, that many of the New Deal policies were crafted to exclude most African Americans from the benefits that lifted countless white Americans out of poverty. We now think of Social Security as a universal program, but when "President Roosevelt signed Social Security into law in 1935, 65 percent of African Americans nationally and between 70 and 80 percent in the South were ineligible."[36] Similarly for the GI Bill: "The historian Kathleen J. Frydl observes in her 2009 book, *The GI Bill*, that so many blacks were disqualified from receiving Title III benefits 'that it is more accurate simply to say that blacks could not use this particular title.'" Mortgage lending practices were infamously racist, and black home buyers, if they could find a loan at all, were hit with higher interest rates and brutally unfavorable conditions. Segregation and discrimination in housing were rampant, and practiced openly: "The American real-estate industry believed segregation to be a moral principle. As late as 1950, the National Association of Real Estate Boards' code of ethics warned that 'a Realtor should never be instrumental in introducing into a neighborhood . . . any race or nationality, or any individuals whose presence will clearly be detrimental to property values.' A 1943 brochure specified that such potential undesirables might include madams, bootleggers, gangsters—and 'a colored man of means who was giving his children a college education and thought they were entitled to live among whites.'" This history matters because most capital in the United States is inherited—overwhelmingly, you do well because your parents did well, and real estate, in particular, is the middle classes' dominant asset.

We can put concrete numbers to the effects of these policies. A recent study of real estate records in Chicago during the 1950s and 1960s concluded that, owing to predatory lending practices that specifically targeted black families who were barred from conventional mortgages, "the amount of wealth land sales contracts expropriated from Chicago's black community was *between 3.2 and 4.0 billion dollars* [emphasis added]."[37] The practice, known as home contract sales,

> offered black buyers the illusion of a mortgage without the protections of a mortgage. Buyers scraped together excessive down payments and made monthly installments at high interest rates toward inflated purchase prices, but never gained ownership—

if at all—until the contract was paid in full and all conditions met. . . . Unlike those who enjoyed mortgages, contract buyers accumulated no equity in their homes. Should a buyer want to sell before the contract concluded, they would lose their entire investment. Should they miss even one payment, there were no laws or regulations to protect them against eviction, and the loss of every dollar they invested in their home.

While no similar study has been conducted for Detroit, contract sales were common practice in that city as well, and, more shockingly, they have recently made a comeback.[38]

Black Detroit, in other words, was not poor because it was lazy, or uneducated, or criminally inclined—black Detroit was poor because for decades on end, the country had made it its mission to keep it poor. And it is this kind of poverty that surrounded a young Isiah Thomas who never forgot, even though he improbably, miraculously, escaped it—as many elite black athletes escaped it, though it goes without saying that not all black athletes come from a background of deprivation, and not all black athletes think, act, talk, or play alike.

The Pistons intentionally cultivated a particular style and a particular image that merged with the decade's image of Detroit, an image that was deeply and inextricably tied to race—though it's easy to oversimplify these matters. Bill Laimbeer, the most hated of the Bad Boys, was white, and black superstars like Magic Johnson or Michael Jordan, who didn't cultivate the Bad Boys' irreverent, unapologetic style were almost universally beloved. The Pistons' in-your-face strategy served them well for a while, but perhaps not in the long run: Isiah Thomas did not speak for all of black America or for all of black basketball. In fact, one of his most bitter defeats came at the very hands of Michael Jordan and Magic Johnson, who made sure he was excluded from the famous Dream Team, the U.S.A.'s 1992 Olympic Team that all but strolled to gold. His post-Pistons career was marked by failure and scandal. And when Joe Dumars, former Bad Boy, became the Pistons' general manager in 2000, he settled on a team that, rather than resurrect the flamboyance and turmoil of the late 1980s, would simply be "goin' to work."

In a coda to the era of the Bad Boys, Detroit's women ballers staged their own interlude on July 21, 2008, with what is known as the "Sparks-Shock Brawl." As Lindsay Gibbs writes in her wonderful recap, "one of the most memorable nights in WNBA history" resulted in six ejections and five suspensions. A fight that broke out between the Detroit Shocks' Plenette Pierson and the Los Angeles Sparks' Candace Parker "escalated to involve the majority of the players and coaches on both teams, including Lisa Leslie, Katie Smith, Deanna Nolan, Cheryl Ford, Delisha Milton-Jones, . . . Cheryl Reeve, Michael Cooper, Rick Mahorn, and Marianne Stanley"—and aging Bad Boy Bill Laimbeer, now the Shocks' coach.[39] In contrast to the hysterical coverage that followed the "Malice at the Palace," the press took this one in stride. The *Wall Street Journal* wrote: "It was, in the classic sense, one of those things that occasionally happens when highly competitive people want the same thing and one can't have it."[40]

EIGHT

APRIL 15, 1985

Tommy Hearns loses to Marvin Hagler, but Detroit remains America's preeminent boxing city in the 1980s, thanks to the legendary entrepreneur Emanuel Steward and his storied Kronk Gym—a beacon of success in an otherwise grim economic landscape. In the aftermath of a nasty post-game riot, the Tigers lose their luster.

As the fight started, "Marvelous Marvin" Hagler strode straight up to Tommy "Hit Man" Hearns and lashed out with a huge right hook. From that point on, it was clear that the fight would live up to the hype—even Muhammad Ali and Bo Derek were in the audience. As usual, the promoters had let everybody know that the two men hated each other passionately, but they always do, after all. This time, it might have been true. For three minutes straight, they stood toe-to-toe and traded punches with furious abandon. Here is how the *Detroit Free Press* opened its description of the first round: "From the opening bell he [Hearns] and Hagler began to tear at each other as if each blow, each breath, might be their last."[1]

The second round was less ferocious, as Hearns tried to box rather than slug. Hagler, though, continued with the full-frontal approach, and by the end of the round, he had Hearns backed up against the ropes. The judges' scorecards showed a small lead for Hagler, as they did after the first round. About a minute into the third round, a Hearns punch enlarged the cut on Hagler's forehead, and the blood flowed so copiously that the referee temporarily halted the fight to allow Hagler's doctor to inspect him. Hagler insisted he was ready to fight on, the doctor said "the cut's not bothering his sight," and so the referee let them go at it again—Hagler later said he found the injury motivating. But he also knew that time was running out.

If this went on much longer, the cut would start gushing again, and the blood loss would make it impossible to fight. He advanced toward Hearns and punched and punched and punched until he had pummeled Hearns onto the ropes. Another swing with his right, and Hearns began to lose his balance. As the man tried to right himself, Hagler ran up to catch him and hit him hard, three times in a row. Unable to defend himself, Hearns rolled off the ropes and onto the floor of the ring. As the referee counted, Hearns struggled up once more, but he was clearly out on his feet.

The Boxer of the Year 1984 was defeated, and the fight, also known as "The War," was over. Afterward, Richard Steele, the referee, said the opening round had "the most action of any first round in any fight I have seen."[2] *The Ring* declared it the fight of the year, and some even consider it the greatest fight ever.[3] When it was over, it emerged that Hearns had broken a bone in his hand in the flurry of exchanges in the first round; to his credit, he never tried to use this as an excuse. Emanuel Steward, his trainer and manager, said that "it was a more physical fight than we wanted and before the first round had ended I sensed trouble ahead."[4] Others were more critical of Hearns's strategy, and one wrote: "Tommy fought the wrong fight. He should have started cautiously, lose the first couple of rounds. Don't get into a dogfight, but that's what he did. He got into a dogfight with Marvin and he lost."[5]

Tommy Hearns was born in Tennessee. His mother moved the family to Detroit when he was ten years old, at a time when the city's industrial future still held promise. By the end of the 1960s, optimism had turned to despair. Living on Helen Street and attending school on the East Side of Detroit, Hearns had to navigate gangs, drugs, and rising gun violence. But from early on, the young Hearns believed he had what it took to make it to the top of a sport for which Detroit was famous: boxing.[6]

When the era of Muhammad Ali ended, some feared that boxing was dying out, particularly since the media were expanding their coverage of the NFL and the NBA dramatically. In addition, the dangers of boxing were becoming all too clear; the old idea that boxing was a fine sport to build young men's character was fading fast. In the 1980s, however, four fighters arrived on the scene to prompt a boxing renaissance: Roberto Duran, Sugar Ray Leonard, Marvin Hagler, and Thomas Hearns. These four, boxing in the welterweight and middleweight divisions, fought with such ferocity that they attracted larger and larger audiences. A series of fights between 1980 and 1989 demonstrated how well matched they were. Duran, the eldest of the quartet, defeated Leonard in their first fight in 1980, but he lost the two rematches and also lost to Hagler and Hearns. Leonard, arguably the greatest of the four, beat Hagler and Hearns, but a rematch with Hearns resulted in a draw, while Hagler beat Hearns in their only match in 1985. Most of these matches were close, and many are remembered as among the greatest fights in history. Once they became crowd-pleasers, they also made more money than any boxers had made before them.

It's not easy to place Hearns in the hierarchy of boxing. His defeats usually came in close fights, which are widely considered classics. In an era of multiple world titles, he held five over his career, a record at the time. Yet he never overcame Leonard or Hagler. To his Detroit fans, he was without question among the all-time greats, and throughout his career he was a loyal Detroiter: twenty-seven of his sixty-three professional fights were hosted in the city. He did not much like his nickname "The Hitman," which all too uncomfortably evoked Detroit's sky-high murder rate at the time. Understandably, Mayor Coleman Young, who took a close interest in Detroit's boxing success, was not crazy about that image, either. Hearns himself preferred his alternative nom de guerre, the "Motor City Cobra."[7]

Once Hearns became rich, he followed what is by now the well-established trend among the well-to-do and moved out to the suburbs, into a luxury home in Southfield, a city on the northwest corner of Detroit that borders Eight Mile Road. When he got grief about leaving the city behind, he revealed, in 1984, that he had been working in Detroit as a police reserve officer, going out on patrol as often as three nights per week. His partner praised his ability to defuse conflicts by telling tales from the ring.[8] Without question, Hearns was a hero in the tough black neighborhoods of the city, but his fortunes fell. He ended up in trouble with the IRS—an event so common in his line of work it almost goes without saying. Faced with a tax bill of $448,000 in 2010, he was forced to sell off many of his personal possessions, including a 1957 Chevy, three boats, and all his boxing memorabilia.[9] As of 2019, he still lives in Detroit, though his street patrols days may be over.

For many years, Tommy Hearns was the most important boxer trained and managed by Emanuel Steward, who saw himself both as the father figure Hearns never had as a kid and as Hearns's most important asset. At times, Steward would claim, modestly, that "I am blessed with Tommy," and at other times, less modestly, that "I made Tommy Hearns."[10] The question of who made whom would one day bring their partnership to an end, but by that time they had both risen to be acknowledged masters of the fight game.

Emanuel Steward emerged from the gyms of the city to make Detroit the preeminent boxing city in the United States in the 1980s. Born in West Virginia, he came to Detroit in 1955.[11] Trained at the Brewster Recreation Center, where Joe Louis once boxed, he was an outstanding amateur boxer and actually won a national Golden Gloves award in 1963 at bantamweight. He thought about going pro but decided he could better provide for his family by learning a trade as an electrical engineer.

Coaching part-time for a while, he eventually started working at the Kronk Gym. The Kronk was located on the West Side, at 5555 McGraw Avenue, in what had once been a Polish enclave. Named for the Polish councilman who had lobbied for it, the gym was built in 1922 to provide the opportunity for physical exercise and to help keep young Detroiters out of trouble. In 1971, Steward trained a team of seven boxers—and when they won every bout in the Detroit Golden Gloves tournament, people started to sit up and take notice. The following year, he resigned his engineering job with Detroit Edison to become a full-time boxing trainer. By 1974, he had two amateur national champions.

Hearns is probably the greatest of all the boxers Steward nurtured from amateur to pro, but the list of successful Kronk boxers is a very long one indeed. By the end of the 1980s, the gym had produced two Olympic gold medalists and five world champions. First came Hilmer Kenty from Ohio, who won the World Boxing Association's lightweight title in February 1980. Next, Steve McCrory and Frank Tate, both born in Detroit, who won gold medals at the 1984 Olympics in Los Angeles (in, respectively, the flyweight and light middleweight classes). Then came Milton McCrory, younger brother of Steve, who was the World Boxing Council's welterweight champion between 1983 and 1985. Last, two more Detroiters: Jimmy Paul

(International Boxing Federation lightweight champion from 1985 to 1986) and Duane Thomas (WBC light middleweight champion, 1986–87).

By the 1980s stories about the Kronk Gym had turned into veritable legends. Steward tried to maintain a stable of thirty to sixty boxers at any one time, and he often bragged that there were more contenders for world titles in his gym than in the rest of the world combined. Training sessions were intense, located in a cramped basement where the temperature was maintained at a stifling 80–90 degrees. Stuart Kirschenbaum, who served as Michigan's boxing commissioner between 1981 and 1992, marvels that Steward "turned boxing into a team sport" in Detroit. Wearing one of the colorful Kronk jackets marked you as a serious contender, he remembers, but Steward was more than a local celebrity—he was a world figure, Kirschenbaum stresses.

Kirschenbaum, an amateur boxer from New York, came to Detroit at the end of the 1960s. He became a major player in the Detroit boxing scene, all while maintaining a podiatry practice. He still practices in a building next door to the iconic Fisher Building in midtown Detroit, where we visited him to listen to his stories: how he found Joe Louis's widow, Martha Louis, in a nursing home in a Detroit suburb, penniless, and became her guardian. About his friend Muhammad Ali, who owned a house on the western side of the state and was frequently seen at Detroit boxing venues. The saddest of his stories is a story of death, fire, and destruction: in April 2013, a former maintenance worker showed up at the Park Medical Centers where Kirschenbaum's practice was located. Myron Williams was looking for Sharita Williams, who had broken off their relationship. A few hours later, Sharita and Myron Williams were dead in a murder suicide, and the building was engulfed in flames.

The heartache over the young woman's death eclipses another loss from the fire: a vast collection of Joe Louis memorabilia Kirschenbaum had built over more than a decade. In his office, Kirschenbaum walks to a sideboard and pulls out a plastic bag. Inside is one of the few things that survived the fire: one of Joe Louis's gloves, bronzed. It is in bad shape, and as he pulls it out to show it to us, it crumbles some more. Kirschenbaum flinches, then shrugs, like a man who has lost his trust in conservation. "When Emanuel Steward died, boxing died in Detroit," he says.

For all his love of boxing, Steward was a businessman. His key inspiration was the motivational speaker Glenn Turner, who exhorted his clients to "dare to be great."[12] Steward had run a cosmetics distributorship named "House of Escot," which was operated by Glenn Turner's company, Koscot Interplanetary Inc. In 1977, Turner went to prison for seven years, guilty of running a pyramid scheme. Steward had moved on to boxing, but he never forgot to "dare to be great." He was a generous man, too, who frequently helped out his boxers financially when they got into trouble. Even though Steward's record as a businessman is mixed—he had a tendency to overextend himself in his ambition to create a sprawling organization—pretty much every product of the Kronk Gym testified to Steward's extraordinary motivational skills. And it was his genius as a trainer that that made him a fortune.

As the fame of the Kronk spread, the ever-entrepreneurial Steward expanded, setting up Kronk Gyms in Tucson, California, London, and Belfast. By the early 1990s, he and Hearns had fallen out over money, and many other Kronk boxers deserted him. He went on to become a hired gun, selected by boxers such as Lennox Lewis and Naseem Hamed to act as their personal trainer. By the 2000s, he was also working as a commentator for boxing matches on TV. All the while, he kept the original Kronk Gym in Detroit running.

In a city that had fallen on hard times, the success of the Kronk meant a lot. Having risen to the very top of his game, Steward became a symbol of what black businessmen could achieve in the 1980s, despite the tremendous odds against them. To this day, the entrenched myth that African Americans lack entrepreneurial drive or skills harms black businesses in the United States.[13] In 2018, a group of researchers published the results of a "mystery shopper" experiment that sent six African American and five white men to seventeen banks, ostensibly to seek small business loans—all wore a blue collared shirt and khakis, all presented near-identical business profiles—although the black testers were made to seem a bit better off than the white ones—and all asked for $60,000–$70,000 to expand their operations. The result? Banks were twice as likely to offer the white testers help with loan applications, and three times as likely to invite follow-up appointments with the white entrepreneurs than with the better-situated black ones.

They asked the black ones for more documentation, presented them with intrusive questions about their private lives, and were less likely to thank them for making an appointment.[14]

Such practices shed light on the divergence between the immense success of black athletes and their too-frequent failure to subsequently move into senior management. Athletic talent is beyond dispute—LeBron James can demonstrate his superiority in five minutes on the court, to everybody's assured satisfaction. Nobody becomes an elite athlete without tremendous ability, discipline, and willpower, but success in management or business depends not just on performance, but on perceptions, expectations, prejudices, stereotypes, fears. Prowess on the field or in the ring can be objectively measured; quality performance in business and management is not just hard to measure, it is often difficult even to observe. Emanuel Steward's product, however, *was* athletes—and nobody could argue with the stable of talent he produced.

Steward was deeply beloved in Detroit. In his autobiography the Irish boxer Andy Lee, whom Steward lured to Kronk Gym in 2003, recounts both the generosity of his mentor and his universal acclaim in the city. Lee himself became one of the preeminent boxers at the Kronk in that decade, and he speaks with awe about Steward, the gym, and Detroit: "I love this city, love its proud people, but it has always been a place of extremes . . . but I never feel unwelcome or unsafe in Detroit." Of Steward he writes, "He is incredibly generous, with his time and with his knowledge. I watch him for days on end dealing with top promoters and high-powered lawyers, in person and on the phone, and then the next day he's every bit as comfortable stopping and chatting to a homeless person back in Detroit, giving them as much of his time if not more. Generous too, often to a fault, with his money."[15]

At the time of the Hagler-Hearns fight, the Tigers were 5-0 for the season. They were also World Champions, having won their fourth World Series in 1984. That season would be remembered for the team's extraordinary start, racing to 35-5, the best start to the first quarter of the season in the history of Major League Baseball. With pitching ace Jack Morris backed up by Dan Petry, and the local batting tyro Kirk Gibson already in place, the Tigers had shrewdly traded for pitcher Guillerme "Willie" Hernández during the season. A team historically known for its power batting and lame pitching had one of its strongest-ever pitching line-ups. In the postseason they swept the Kansas City Royals, and in the World Series disposed of the San Diego Padres in five games.

There is a sense that the 1984 Tigers who won the fourth World Series for Detroit were not celebrated as joyously as the 1968 Tigers who won the third. Individuals on the 1984 team may have been much beloved—notably Alan Trammell and Lou Whitaker, who played together on the Tigers for nineteen seasons, the longest double-play partnership in the history of baseball. But the win itself, while of course a source of pride and joy, did not inspire the same enthusiasm. The historical context is probably a part of that: the 1968 team pulled the city together after the harrowing events of 1967, even if just for a few days. However much Detroit enjoyed the success of the 1984 Tigers, the team did not create the same sense of community. By 1984 the city was black and the suburbs were white—Whitaker (black) and Trammell (white) might show what teamwork could do, but political cooperation at the city and county level was much harder to come by.

The subsequent behavior of Tom Monaghan didn't help either. After winning a World Series in his first full season in charge, he waged an aggressive campaign to ditch Tiger Stadium and build a new one at public expense. When this plan failed, he claimed to have had enough with material things and offloaded the team to the next pizza mogul.

The aftermath of the final game of the 1984 World Series was an embarrassment to the city. As fans left Tiger Stadium and mingled with the crowds that had gathered outside, a police car was overturned. By the end of the evening, one man was dead and one hundred injured. Three rapes were reported. Headlines such as "Motown Madness" and "World Series Rampage" added to the lawless image of Detroit. The most famous photograph of that World Series did not involve a home run or strikeout, but a drunk seventeen-year-old kid dancing for the TV cameras in front of a burning car. Three years later saw the release of the film *Robocop*, which portrayed Detroit as a violent, dystopian sinkhole.

Emanuel Steward passed away from cancer in 2012. Aretha Franklin sang at the funeral, Tommy Hearns broke down crying. Sugar Ray Leonard, Wladimir Klitschko, Lennox Lewis, Evander Holyfield were among the mourners.[16] His family tried to keep the gym going and maintain his legacy, but vandalism caused the original Kronk site to be closed in 2006. A new site was opened a few years later, at 9520 Mettetal, about six miles further west, and is still in operation as of this writing. Various plans were developed to rebuild the gym on its old site, and some funds were even raised. But at the end of 2017 it was mysteriously burned to the ground and was finally demolished at the end of 2018.

Kirschenbaum says the sport is finished.[17] He speaks with the authority of a man who has spoken funeral orations at the graveside of too many fighters who have died young because of too many blows to the head. All his life he has loved the sport, but now he sees that it is coming to an end, and he is not sorry. Of all sports, this is the one evoking the most conflicted emotions— its violence is repulsive, its management exceptionally corrupt. But there is a purity in the personal duel of the boxing match. It is not a game for fools, and chess champions have often expressed a sense of shared struggle with boxers. Like chess, it is hard to blame defeat on luck, and so victory, when it comes, is total—but so, of course, is defeat. Detroit, which has seen its share of both, has always had an affinity with boxing, and earlier this decade, there's been talk of reviving Detroit as a "production line of great fighters," in keeping with its history as one of the sport's premier U.S. sites.[18] But the time when Detroit boxers were household names is over. Boxing itself is dying, largely surpassed by mixed martial arts, or MMA. It's hard not to conclude that the demolition of the Kronk marked the last rites of one of Detroit's most successful sports.

NINE

JUNE 6, 1982

*The Motor City hosts its first Formula One race. As with all schemes
to boost Detroit's image and economy in the 1980s, the results are
mixed—or downright tragic, as in the case of the erasure of the Poletown neighborhood. Suddenly, the country wants fuel-efficient cars,
the Big Three are not prepared, and the city suffers the consequences. On Devil's Night, six hundred houses go up in flames—a dark
ritual that will come to define the image of Detroit in the 1980s.*

"Most of the horror stories leading up to the Detroit Grand Prix proved
largely unfounded," said the mealy-mouthed correspondent of the *LA
Times*, without specifying what exact horrors had been announced.[1] But in
the 1980s, any journalist could dunk on the city by rote. "Detroit, a city of
problems, became a city of promise Sunday when a crowd estimated at more
than 100,000 paid blue-chip prices to watch John Watson, a 36-year-old
Briton, win the inaugural Detroit Grand Prix," opined the more fair-minded
Chicago Tribune.[2] Intended to do for Detroit what the prestigious Monaco
Grand Prix had done for that principality, this was the first grand prix in the
United States to be raced on a street course.

The event had been organized by Detroit Renaissance Inc., a consortium
of major businesses connected to the city, under the leadership of the Big
Four automakers.[3] Founded in 1971, its purpose was to encourage business investment in the city—this was the time when Ford made its enormous investment in the Renaissance Center.[4] These seven interconnected
skyscrapers on the Detroit River waterfront visually dominated the race.
Historically, the riverfront had been a maze of docks for freight traffic, railyards, and warehouses. When the docks and railway lines closed as industry

in the city declined, the planners started to think about redeveloping the riverfront as a public amenity.[5] In chapter 11, we will tell the strange story behind the RenCen's creation.

The starting line of the race was right on the riverfront, which is now the Milliken State Park wetlands demonstration area. A sharp 180-degree turn took the drivers along Atwater Street and right up Antoine as far as Jefferson, where they negotiated their way around the I-375 intersection, along Congress, to Larned and then onto Jefferson again in a straight-ish line. At Washington Boulevard, facing the Cobo Center, the driver had to make another sharp 180-degree turn to follow the line of the river, past Hart Plaza and the site of the Cadillac and Underground Railroad monuments, back to the starting line to complete the 2.6-mile course. The huge international television audience for Formula One Grand Prix racing was treated to excellent views of the Renaissance Center, the Detroit River, and the border between the United States and Canada.[6]

The president of Detroit Renaissance, Robert McCabe, had promised that the event would not just advertise the city but would turn a significant profit for it as well. Staging the race was expensive. Detroit Renaissance provided about $2.5 million, while the city contributed another $800,000 for the repaving of the streets to make them suitable for Formula One cars.[7] Anyone who has ever lived in Michigan, infamous for some of the worst roads in the country, knows that you need a very good reason to take money out of the road-building budget for a comparatively frivolous purpose such as this one. But international coverage was meant to lure investors to Detroit, and in addition to the fees that broadcasters and sponsors paid for the rights related to the event, McCabe argued, local businesses would see increased revenue as well. Alas, a survey of local businesses a few days after the event revealed a mixed picture. Bars and restaurants located inside the RenCen reported big increases in sales relative to a typical weekend, but businesses based just on the other side of Jefferson Avenue fared less well. Joe Portalski, who co-owned a restaurant on the corner of Larned and Brush, reported that business had actually been down: the barricades for the course ran right past his door. "The place just wasn't visible," he said.[8]

The race was troubled by other teething pains. A day of practice was lost when race officials required the re-laying of the entire track to meet safety standards.[9] Another practice day was spoiled by rain, so few spectators turned up. Like good Michiganders, the drivers grumbled about the quality of the road, and Alain Prost, then world champion, complained that the course made for "a very dangerous race" that was "much too bumpy."[10] When the day of the race arrived, it was sunny, and the event was pronounced a success. The Detroit public, however, was a little bemused. A let's-hear-from-the-people feature in the *Detroit Free Press* was split between enthusiasts who welcomed the attempt to raise the city's profile and puzzled motor sport aficionados who, like most Americans, preferred NASCAR and drag racing to this foreign import.[11]

At the time of the Grand Prix, the country was in the grip of the Reagan Recession. The worst downturn in the U.S. economy since the Great Depression had started in July 1981, and the recovery would not set in until November 1982.[12] Even before the downturn, the *New York Times* had reported that seven of the cities with the highest unemployment rates in the country were in Michigan, and Detroit, at 13 percent, was not even the worst.[13] The state's unemployment rate would peak at 17 percent, with Detroit officially hitting 18 percent, although Mayor Young claimed that in reality it was closer to 25 percent.[14] Michigan's economy, in other words, was in dire need, and 1982 saw a number of events designed to show Detroit in its best light. Detroit Renaissance hosted the Montreux-Detroit Kool Jazz Festival in August, and Super Bowl XVI, between Joe Montana's San Francisco 49ers and the Cincinnati Bengals, was played in the Pontiac Silverdome, then home of the Detroit Lions.

The decision to host a grand prix was probably driven by Ford, whose UK subsidiary produced a large fraction of the engines that powered the Formula One cars.[15] The recession of the early 1980s was a turning point for the U.S. motor industry, on which the Detroit area deeply depended. Car production in the United States had hit its all-time peak with over 10 million units in 1973, and in 1979, there were still over 9 million cars rolling off the assembly lines. By 1982, however, production had fallen to 5 million, and though it recovered somewhat in the following years, domestic production soon resumed its downward trend again.[16] Ever since the 1960s, imports from Germany and Japan had nibbled away at Detroit's market share, but between 1978 and 1981, imports surged from 18 percent to 27 percent of total sales in the United States.[17] Large increases in the oil price caused by the Iranian Revolution in 1979 drove rising demand for fuel-efficient small cars, in which foreign producers excelled.

The failings of the Detroit car manufacturers have been a subject of extended discussion since the 1960s. After World War II, Detroit was responsible for something like three-quarters of the global car manufacturing capacity. That share has declined ever since, but the standard of 1945 or 1950 was never realistically sustainable. After all, the motor car was invented in Germany, and the industry has thrived in Europe when the continent has not been at war. Inevitably, the long peacetime dividend made European producers increasingly competitive. At the same time, Japan had worked to amass a wealth of engineering skills, which were put to good use in their postwar auto industry.

Exporting cars had always been a marginal activity—exporters really rely on a strong domestic market to drive their business. The Europeans and Japanese, accordingly, had honed their skills at producing fine small cars, ideally suited to the narrow roads and relatively short distances their citizens are likely to travel. By contrast, U.S. consumers wanted large, comfortable vehicles that don't cramp you during long-distance travels. As far as Detroit could see, the market for small cars was a niche one, and as long as oil prices were low, they were right. The two oil price shocks that hit in the 1970s took the Detroit auto producers by surprise—but to be fair, nobody had really seen them coming.

High oil prices and the recession in 1979 nearly destroyed Chrysler, and the company only survived thanks to a U.S. government bailout of $1.5 billon.[18] The car companies looked to the government to save them in other ways, notably by throttling imports—in 1981, Japanese producers agreed to "voluntary" import restrictions. To cut long-term production costs further and keep prices competitive against the cheaper imports, the carmakers invested in machinery. Automation worked out for the car companies, but it contributed to rising unemployment in Detroit. According to one study, annual investment in U.S. transport equipment tripled between 1976 and 1980, while manufacturing employment in Detroit fell from 609,000 in 1978 to 422,000 in 1982. Unemployment skyrocketed to 16 percent, and black unemployment rose more sharply still, to 27 percent.[19] By Christmas

1982, Mayor Young had declared a "hunger emergency." In the following months, Germans, who followed dramatic TV coverage of the crisis, started sending CARE packages to Detroit, in fond memory of the ones concerned Americans had sent to Germany after World War II via the Cooperative for American Remittances to Europe.[20] Helmut Schmidt, the German chancellor, publicly expressed his concern for Detroit.[21]

The recession and the accompanying loss of jobs exacerbated the flight from the city that had begun decades earlier and accelerated after 1967. The vicious circle of flight, tax revenue loss, service cuts, and worsening conditions leading to more flight continued to revolve slowly but inexorably. Between 1970 and 1980, the city population fell from 1.5 million to 1.2 million. Education, police, and the firefighting services all had to be cut back in the face of the budgetary crisis. In the late 1970s almost 30 percent of firefighters were laid off.[22] This in turn contributed to one of the worst problems the city was facing at the time. As people left the city for the suburbs, the irony was that many of these houses could have been taken over by those who remained, had they had the means to do so. In the aftermath of 1967, the federal government had for a while supported policies to promote home ownership for the less well off. The Department of Housing and Urban Development was created by President Johnson in 1968 with the purpose of addressing the housing crisis, with a view to enabling low-income families in urban areas to obtain mortgages at low interest rates and with small down payments. After Richard Nixon became president in 1969, George Romney, former governor of Michigan who had firsthand experience of Detroit's housing problems, enthusiastically promoted a policy of cheap housing. However, following his 1972 re-election Nixon felt obliged to cut spending in the light of growing economic problems, and policies that primarily benefited African Americans in urban areas were seen as disposable. He declared a moratorium on the loans program.[23] In Detroit, one consequence was that growing numbers of properties were left empty, often dilapidated, sometimes vandalized by the departing Detroiters who knew they would never be able to sell their property. The fire hazard created by these predominantly wooden structures helped cement an image of Detroit for a generation.

Devil's Night, the night before Halloween, had been a local tradition in

Detroit for many decades, but it had largely been little more than hijinks: ringing doorbells, soaping windows, and toilet-papering the neighbors' trees. Low-level trouble. The abandoned houses, however, seemed to invite mayhem instead. As the empty buildings became playgrounds for Detroit's youth, on Devil's Night some of them started to go up in flames. By the 1980s, the problem was getting out of hand—on October 30, 1983, almost six hundred fires broke out, and the strapped fire department was only able to respond to the biggest ones. With so much of the city ablaze, people didn't know whom to blame. Some said it was local hooligans; others, thrill seekers from the suburbs; yet others, absentee owners seeking to claim on their fire insurance.[24]

To a national audience, the excesses of Detroit's Devil's Night confirmed that the city had become hell. In 1990 Ze'ev Chafets's *Devil's Night: And Other True Tales of Detroit* came out, and the *New York Times* published a previously cited long feature essay drawn from the same material.[25] Both works start with these ominous lines: "It was in the Fall of 1986 that I first saw the devil on the streets of Detroit."[26] Chafets, who had grown up in Pontiac, emigrated to Israel in 1967. He came back and lived in Detroit in 1988 and 1989. His book is hard-nosed, and the account it provides of the political tension caused by an all-black city surrounded by all-white suburbs is well worth reading. Chafets grew up a liberal, and he understood the nature of segregation and discrimination that African Americans faced. Later in life, he lurched to the right and became a fervent supporter of Rush Limbaugh. Limbaugh himself, of course, has often made it his mission to demean Detroit, even though he doesn't appear to command the most basic facts about its history; in 2013, Detroit's public radio station WDET lost patience and took him to task for some the most ludicrous of his assertions, such as the claim that the blame for the city's 1967 uprising rests on the election of Mayor Young, which occurred six years later, in 1973.[27]

Such ideologically motivated fictions grabbed onto whatever facts were available, and the destruction of Devil's Night was certainly a fact. But what leads to a climate where six hundred houses burn in one night? Undoubtedly, the root cause was the economic collapse of Detroit, in particular the job losses for its citizens. Two hundred thousand manufacturing jobs, one-third of the total, had been lost between 1978 and 1982.[28] There had been a time where almost anyone willing to work could find a job in a car plant, but by the end of the 1970s, the factories were disappearing from the city. Mayor Coleman Young, like many others, believed that maintaining manufacturing jobs was essential to the survival of the city, but the rules of the game were changing. As the near full employment of the 1950s and 1960s gave way to chronic unemployment in the 1970s, companies started to demand incentives to invest in a location. This practice, popular with major league team owners, is alive and well with corporations, as the somewhat obscene beauty parade of U.S. cities begging to become Amazon's second HQ, orchestrated by the company in 2017–18, amply demonstrated. Local governments are expected to provide companies tax breaks, investment subsidies, and expedited planning processes; companies, meanwhile, develop a veritable shopping list of perks and favors from their potential domiciles, playing cities against each other.

This incentive game would eventually destroy Poletown, a neighborhood located more or less in the dead center of Detroit. The Grand Boulevard, inspired by Paris and conceived in the nineteenth century as a spacious, tree-lined avenue to encircle the city as it then stood, ran along the northern edge of Poletown and then turned south to form its eastern border, on the way to Belle Isle. North of Grand Boulevard was the city of Hamtramck, which would come to be entirely surrounded by the city of Detroit in the first half of the twentieth century. Polish settlers started arriving in the Detroit area in the 1860s, and by the 1880s, 22,000 or more Polish-speaking immigrants had made it their home—most settling in these two neighborhoods. In 1910, the Dodge Brothers opened a factory in Hamtramck to build engines for Henry Ford, before starting to produce their own cars in the factory that became known as Dodge Main.[29]

Between 1910 and 1940, Dodge Main was one of the biggest plants in a thriving industrial region, but signs of decline were already becoming visible by the start of World War II. New factories designed for military production were increasingly built outside the city, and workers started to move to where the new jobs were to be found. By the 1950s, deindustrialization was in full swing, and in 1955, the construction of Interstate 94 cut Poletown in half, diminishing the community's coherence.[30] Poletown had been ethnically homogeneous until then, but soon, new groups started to move in and the area became both more diverse and increasingly depopulated. In January 1980, Dodge Main, now owned by the near bankrupt Chrysler Corporation, was abruptly shut down and three thousand workers were laid off.

At the time, all the car companies were making major investments in new plants, and GM approached the city with an offer. It would commit to building a new Cadillac assembly plant inside the city, generating six thousand permanent jobs, provided the city gave the company a five-hundred-acre rectangular tract of land on which to build. Coleman Young and the city were eager to accommodate, but GM turned down all the sites the city offered. It turned out that the company had set its sights on a parcel of land that included the old Dodge Main plant but extended all the way down to I-94, consuming the northern portion of what remained of Poletown. This would require action under eminent domain—the government's right to forced acquisition of people's homes. To be sure, homeowners would have to be compensated, but Coleman Young used his good connections to get a federal government loan to pay the cost of land acquisition up front, while the city was only required to pay back half of it. The plan had the support of the United Automobile Workers (UAW) and the Roman Catholic Archdiocese of Detroit, but it required the demolition of about 1,400 houses, homes to roughly 3,500 residents.[31]

Resistance proved futile, even though some of the residents formed the Poletown Neighborhood Council to organize the community against its destruction. Not everybody in Poletown opposed GM's plans, however, and as the demolition of Dodge Main progressed at the beginning of 1981, around 80 percent of residents were successfully persuaded to accept the compensation they were offered and moved out. Many of the fiercest opponents were elderly residents who did not want to leave their neighborhood. In the spring, the struggle turned ugly, and several empty houses were destroyed by arson—possibly to signal to those who remained that the next houses to burn might not be empty. By the end of 1981, it was over, all the residents had been evicted, and GM had its new plant—supported by a tidy government subsidy.[32]

The fight over Poletown had been a difficult one. Many people sympathized with the city government and respected its efforts to bring jobs to the city. By that time, everyone recognized that the Detroit auto companies were fragile, and no one wanted them to disappear. On the other hand, many felt deep sympathy for the elderly residents being torn from their homes. The mayor's insistence that Hamtramck—another Polish enclave—was the true Polish neighborhood particularly rankled with the opponents. One Poletown resident commented that it would have been bearable had the City simply said that Poletown must be sacrificed so that Detroit might live. What really hurt was the City's insulting self-justification that declared the area a blighted urban wasteland not worth preserving.[33]

It is easy to understand why the city government, faced with a collapsing industrial base, acted the way it did. As far as it was concerned, it was promoting the wider public interest. Sure, a market economy usually leaves decisions about what and when to buy and sell to the individual, and the rise of Detroit itself used to be a prime exhibit in the defense of the capitalist system, before it became a prime example of its cruelty. Detroit had grown into an industrial powerhouse without much interference from government, but toward the end of the twentieth century, the system that had sustained Detroit—though not all its citizens—left the city behind. The industry chose other locations to build its cars, automation cost jobs, sustained attacks made the unions that had fought for decent wages and conditions ever weaker, and those workers who could still find jobs in the new factories moved away with them. Coleman Young was the mayor responsible for those left behind, even though the exodus was in full swing long before he came into office.

In aggregate, the United States is a very rich country, but as everybody knows, the wealth is unevenly distributed, ever more so as time goes on. A large fraction of the population is drawn into cycles of poverty—poor neighborhoods have poor schools, poor living conditions lead to poor health, and the poor get "nickel-and-dimed"—as Barbara Ehrenreich documents in her book by the same title—at every turn.[34] Escape is possible in theory, but exceedingly difficult and rare in practice. In Detroit, those left behind were predominantly black residents who, as we detailed in the last chapter, had faced systematic segregation and discrimination in the North ever since they had left the Jim Crow South in hopes of finding a better place. But many Northern cities with predominantly white populations faced similar problems, driven by a decline in traditional manufacturing industries such as steel, coal, and textiles. Even though the impact of that decline fell disproportionately on the black population, the racial demographics of the city were certainly not the cause of its decline.

According to sunny economic theory, capitalism will eventually eradicate discrimination, since the labor of disfavored minorities is cheaper and hence ought to be more attractive in the labor market—thereby driving wages back up. So far, this clearly has not happened. But in the long run, you say? Well, as a famous economist once said, "in the long run we are all dead."[35] In the meantime, discrimination persists mostly unabated, and the nonchalant exhortation to "leave it to the market," ever popular with those who own the marketplace, has not worked in practice. Local governments in the Rust Belt were not inclined to sacrifice their cities to the "creative destruction" that is the hallmark of capitalism, and instead chose to intervene, in the attempt to address the economic crises that hit them. But those interventions came at significant costs to countless individuals, including—perhaps especially—those they were meant to help.

There is a widespread cynical assumption that all politicians are corrupt, that nobody works for the public interest, that everybody is out for themselves. And to be sure, examples abound, and appear to be proliferating at the most alarming rate. But corruption is likely not what drove the destruction of Poletown. Coleman Young, who was accused of supporting business over community, wrote that "the irony of being on the big-guy side was not lost on me. But I wasn't inclined to compromise, considering the stakes. Without intending to be flip, I commented that you had to crack some eggs to make an omelette—or starve. My city was figuratively starving, and I'd crack eggs until the hen keeled over if I had to."[36] You might sympathize with his broader rationale, but this is not the language someone uses to heal the wounds of people driven from their homes, and the demise of Poletown—a kind of government-sanctioned, fully legal Devil's Night of its own—created a climate of mistrust among Detroiters who saw themselves faced with an impossible choice between keeping jobs in the city or keeping their communities intact.[37]

An even greater and more bitter irony emerged once the cost-benefit studies totted up the economic impact of the new plant that had been built at such heavy cost. They found that the financial return to the city, including the benefits that come with the creation of jobs, was not even enough to cover the cost of the public subsidy.[38] The city might have done better to hold on to the money, and Poletown might have been demolished for nothing. But politicians are loath to be seen "doing nothing," even if that is, at least in hindsight, the best available option. They need to be seen to be doing *something*.[39] And they have a tendency to double down: once a path of action seems politically feasible, repetition compulsion sets in, and politicians will find themselves going down that same path over and over again, no matter the results.[40]

In that sense, Poletown might be seen as a precursor to a different kind of development that has become characteristic for Detroit, and, of course, elsewhere. As potential industrial investors demanded more and more incentives to locate in the city, sports organizations caught on. We have seen how the Tigers, Lions, Red Wings, and Pistons have all benefited from the theory that their presence will generate an economic dividend for the city as a whole. Economic research has found little evidence that such benefits exist, despite the surfeit of such public investments across America over the last thirty years.[41] But data-based arguments tend to lose out to the desire to do something, anything, to address an urban crisis—and perhaps the simple optimism that accompanies breaking ground plays a role as well.

In the twenty-first century, the GM plant at Poletown, the historic Dodge Main site, became one of only two car plants left within city borders. Technically speaking, half of the plant was actually located in the city of Hamtramck, the small city surrounded by Detroit. Soccer fans attending Detroit City FC games at Keyworth Stadium can see trains shunting back and forth from the plant, often tooting their horns to the delight of the crowd.

As for the Detroit Grand Prix, it continued as a Formula One event until 1988, and the drivers never stopped grumbling about the shoddy quality of the roads—not without reason, since the track kept breaking up. The event became known as the Formula One race that was hardest on drivers and cars alike. In the end, the sport's governing body, FISA, declared the temporary pit area unfit, and the city didn't have the money to build a proper one. To the relief of the drivers, that was the end of it. It's unclear if the event ever made a profit or if it ever did anything to boost the image of the city. After all, if you're interested in Formula One, you're watching the race, not the city, and if you're interested in investing in Detroit, it's going to take a lot more than a couple of hours of very fast cars navigating potholes to convince you that it's a good idea. With the international competition gone, the Detroit Grand Prix turned into an IndyCar race series, which still runs on beautiful Belle Isle—popular enough, but no longer expected to revive either the image of Detroit or its finances.

TEN

APRIL 1, 1977

The Red Wings, justly known as the "Dead Wings" at the time, announce they will move to Pontiac, along with the Pistons—team flight merges with white flight. The announcement comes as a major blow to Mayor Coleman Young, who is mounting his re-election campaign. After extorting major incentives and concessions, the Wings decide to stay, Young gets re-elected with 60 percent of the vote, but the Pistons depart. Detroit almost acquires a second NBA team.

Not for nothing were they called the Dead Wings. Over the previous twenty seasons, the average win percentage for the hockey team had been a dismal 47 percent. At 43 percent, the Pathetic Pistons were even worse off.[1] In the same period, the Red Wings had had a mere seven winning seasons, the Pistons three. By 1977, the Red Wings had not made it to the playoffs in the previous seven seasons. Since moving to Detroit from Fort Wayne, Indiana, in 1957, the Pistons had made the playoffs barely half the time, and won only two playoff series, one in 1962, and the other in 1976.

By April 1, 1977, the Red Wings had won a mere sixteen games that season, with two left to play. This was, far and away, the worst record in the league and the team's worst showing since its founding in 1926. So on April 1, as if to make a point, the Red Wings, or rather their owners, announced that they would move their franchise to Pontiac, thirty miles north of the city.[2] And Bill Davidson, owner of the Pistons, told journalists he might join the Wings and leave Detroit behind.[3]

In July that year, the *Detroit Free Press* ran a feature asking if "our pro teams" make money. Owners (no!) and players' unions (yes!) pointed fingers at each other, and the writer wryly concluded: "There's a paradox in this capitalistic society of ours when it comes to owning a sports franchise: no one will admit they're in it for the money. Without exception, general managers and front office personnel agree that the man who pays the bills is in it for the love of the game and not for his love of money."[4] But, as baseball player union leader Marvin Miller pointed out, "you can't have it both ways, complaining about the salaries and then saying you're not in it for the money because you are a fan." To which owners, who blame high salaries for high ticket prices, respond that they're simply acting as trustees of the team on behalf of the fans. And so on and so on.

It is exactly that claim, to "represent fan interest," which rings hollow. When the Brooklyn Dodgers moved to Los Angeles in 1958, no one could begrudge the West Coast its first team. Up to that point, no Major League Baseball team had located further west than Kansas or further south than Washington, DC. But how could the owner claim to care about fans in Brooklyn, where the team had played for seventy-three years? The feelings of three generations of supporters, many of whom developed an intense love affair with the team, counted for nothing when it came to the potential revenue of a more profitable location. That may be the logic of a capitalist society, but it is most certainly not the logic of "love of the game."

In the second half of the twentieth century, in an era when TV money actually made professional sports a more profitable business than ever, fans had to get used to losing their teams. Every franchise sold since the 1950s has yielded significant capital gains for the owners.[5] Moreover, franchises were increasingly acquired by the super-rich, who could shield their profits in other businesses against losses incurred by the franchise. For most of these owners, the team properly functions as a pension plan, much like a 401(k). You pay in money now, you get a tax deduction—the amendment to the tax code that allowed pension plans to write off assets such as sports franchises was passed in 1978—and then you sell your asset at a healthy profit or pass it on to the kids at the end of your life. But if you're a sports fan, as most owners are, controlling a team is also far more fun than overseeing a 401(k). So, in fact, the owners do get to have it both ways, reaping profit and glory.

Until 1977, the home of the Red Wings had been Olympia Stadium.

Olympia was located at 5920 Grand River Avenue, at the northwestern corner of the Grand Boulevard where it turned south toward the Detroit River. The Grand River is Michigan's longest stream, rising near the state's southern border, about seventy-five miles west of Detroit. Grand River Avenue (U.S. 16) runs east from Grand Rapids, following the river's course, and then continues southeast from Lansing all the way to Campus Martius in Detroit.[6] Olympia was only three miles along Grand River Avenue from Campus Martius. The Red Wings, or the Detroit Cougars as they were then known, played their first game at Olympia Stadium on November 22, 1927, barely a month after it had been built at a cost of $2.5 million, equivalent to about $36 million in 2019 dollars. With a capacity of sixteen thousand, it had hosted a great many iconic events in the city apart from the hockey team. Before it closed down in 1980, it saw, in chronological order, appearances by Nat King Cole, Duke Ellington, Ella Fitzgerald, Count Basie, Chuck Berry, Fats Domino, Elvis Presley, Louis Armstrong, Hank Williams, Johnny Cash, The Rolling Stones, The Beatles, The Beach Boys, Cream, Led Zeppelin, The Jacksons, Pink Floyd, Frank Sinatra, Stevie Wonder, Elton John, David Bowie, The Eagles, Bob Dylan, and Earth, Wind & Fire.[7] The Old Red Barn, as it came to be known, also regularly hosted boxing events. Some of Joe Louis's earliest fights took place there, as well as fights between other great boxers of the day, such as Sugar Ray Robinson and Jake LaMotta.

The rumor that the Red Wings were thinking about leaving Olympia had first surfaced in May of the previous year, as management made clear that they thought the capacity was no longer sufficient for the team.[8] This was a bit of a surprising conclusion seeing that the team had been averaging gates in the range of ten thousand to thirteen thousand for many years—with thousands of seats to spare, in other words. Management argued, however implausibly, that if the Red Wings were to make a run at the playoffs, they needed more space. During this period, NHL teams were under pressure from the rival World Hockey Association to compete for talent. The competition drove up salaries, making it more expensive to field a winning team. In October 1976, the Red Wings' general manager, Lincoln Cavalieri, told reporters that they, together with the Pistons, were thinking about finding a new arena. Many different locations were in the mix, they said, and sure, the city was one of them, but "the thing that's gotta happen is that someone has to come up with $15 million."[9] And thus, the legal extortion commenced.

The threatened departure of two more teams—the Detroit Lions had already left town—reflected a larger flight from the city. The teams, some argued, were simply following the fans to their new homes. White flight merged with team flight, and unsurprisingly, narratives of race were the common undercurrent. In the *Detroit Free Press*, Joe Falls openly frames the case for relocating the Pistons in racial terms:

> Right now they're averaging about 7,400 (in the 11,000-plus Cobo Arena) and this isn't enough to make money. Except for the playoffs. It's hard to see how they're ever going to get more than they've been getting this season. Right now the Pistons crowd is about 50-50 black and white. This means about 3,700 blacks, which is about all the blacks who are interested in supporting the team. It also means 3,700 whites, which isn't much in a metropolitan area of more than three million whites. What I'm saying is this: The Pistons can't get enough white fans to come downtown to support them in a profitable style and there aren't enough inner city black fans with the interest or affluence to do the same. So, by moving to Pontiac they will take their black fans with them because people are very dedicated to the team and sport but they will also pick up a lot of white fans who will be willing to venture forth into the night into the suburbs.[10]

The case for leaving was, no doubt, aided by the sense, and often the reality, that the city was not a safe place to be. On November 8, a thirty-one-year old corporate executive from Farmington Hills was gunned down in a parking lot outside Olympia after attending an exhibition tennis match between Bjorn Borg and Rod Laver. His wife said that he had not been afraid of being robbed because he only had four dollars in his wallet, and when he was found, his car keys were still in his hands. They had regularly attended sports events at Olympia and other Detroit venues, she said.[11] Horrific stories like this made the rounds.

But even without them, it didn't matter much what the fans or the pundits thought; in keeping with the American way, the owner would decide where the team would play. Unlike Red Wings owner Bruce Norris, whose father had bought the team in 1932, Bill Davidson was a newcomer to franchise ownership. He had bought the Pistons in 1974 from Fred Zollner, who founded the Fort Wayne Pistons in 1941 and moved the team to Detroit in 1957. Zollner in turn had sold it to Davidson in 1974 for $8.1 million, a nice pension for the seventy-three-year-old.[12] Davidson could easily afford it—he was an extremely rich man by then. He had graduated from the University of Michigan and Wayne State Law School after the war, taking over the family business, Guardian Industries, which he managed to turn around. Back then there was plenty of business in Detroit for a manufacturer of automotive glass. Later, he branched out into pharmaceutical distribution, another fine business choice in a nation with the world's most expensive health care.

Davidson had played football in the army during the war, and he had originally wanted to buy into that sport, but, in the end, he settled for basketball.[13] By all accounts, he was a fun guy who liked to party—Isiah Thomas once said that even if Davidson wasn't the owner, "he'd still be someone I'd want to hang out with. Put it this way: we'd get into a lot of trouble."[14] Thomas also spoke highly of Davidson's regular-guy ways—apparently, he refused to wear a tie throughout his career, long before that became acceptable in business circles. He was both generous in explaining how business works and generous with his fortune. Throughout his life, he made substantial charitable donations, not just to his beloved Israel but to a wide range of good causes, including charitable projects in Detroit.

When Davidson died in 2009, the Pistons he had bought for $8 million were worth $430 million. This represents an annualized rate of return of 12 percent, compared to the 11 percent he would have gotten had he put his money in the stock market. And that doesn't even include all the fun he had with his team. Like other team owners, it seems, he had had his cake and eaten it too.

But without question, he had a difficult relationship with the city, and in particular with Mayor Coleman Young. He was, at times, accused of racism. Jim Lites of the Red Wings once claimed that the Pistons made a "conscious" decision "not to market to blacks." Davidson dismissed this allegation as "hogwash," and added, hardly reassuringly, that "people act like they're giving something to you; really it's the other way around." As he saw it, the team belonged to him, not to the fans or the players or the city. In addition, Detroit had long been a union town, and Davidson was a successful union buster. His later comments on Coleman Young's attempt to keep the Pistons in the city reek of contempt: "It's not that the city of Detroit doesn't have needs, it's just that one of them wasn't the Detroit Pistons."[15]

By the time the Red Wings and Pistons were openly stating their plans to leave, Coleman Young was nearing the end of his first term and thinking about re-election. Young's tenure had been controversial. He had shut down STRESS, a police unit created by his predecessor that was associated with the deaths of twenty-four suspects, twenty-two of whom were African American.[16] Young had pursued a vigorous policy of diversifying the city's institutions, particularly the police department, which had a broad reputation for racism.[17] It was a policy that wasn't to everybody's liking, particularly since Young also chose to expand the police presence in Detroit rather than forcefully address the underlying causes of the city's crime problem. Heather Ann Thompson's book *Whose Detroit? Politics, Labor, and Race in a Modern American City* is one of the best accounts of the tensions that developed. She writes: "Notably Detroit's first black mayor chose to deal with [the] brewing public safety crisis by beefing up law enforcement rather than by addressing its economic roots, in no small part because, after 1965, federal dollars flowed much more freely if they were to be used to get tough on crime, not if they were earmarked for things such as more jobs and better schools."[18]

While the number of homicides in Detroit fell quite significantly during Young's first term in office, there was a general perception that the city's collapse was, if anything, accelerating. This caused a lot of people to blame the mayor, who faced a tough challenge from principal rival Ernest Browne Jr. in the 1977 election. Browne had been one of the celebrated Tuskegee pilots during World War II, and he had founded the Black Historic Sites Committee in 1971 to promote greater appreciation of African Americans' contributions to Detroit's development.[19] He had defeated a number of white

candidates in the non-partisan primary, and so for the first time Detroit
would choose between two black candidates. Browne presented himself as
a unifier, in contrast to Young's image as a divisive leader, and he wooed
the white vote by winning the support of police and firefighter unions.[20] At
the time, the Detroit electorate was split roughly evenly between black and
white voters, and the *Washington Post* found Browne's success worthy of
this comment: "This city's white voters, who traditionally have supported
white candidates, demonstrated in Tuesday's mayoral primary that they can
pull the lever for a black."[21]

In the midst of this challenge, losing the Red Wings and the Pistons would
not have helped Young's re-election chances. His focus was on building a
downtown arena in the west riverfront area, part of his strategy to halt the
drift to the suburbs.[22] After the railroads had closed down, this area had
been designated for redevelopment, but progress was slow. Arguments about
building a major new sports facility had raged in the city administration for
many years, with options for new locations including the riverside, midtown
by Wayne State, and the State Fairgrounds site at the intersection of Woodward and Eight Mile Road, on the city's northern border. The factions were
hopelessly divided. Since the 1930s, the city had had an influential planning
department, which had been trying to develop policies of urban renewal,
but with little success.[23] Young largely stripped this department of its power
and centralized decision making under his authority. His choice of location
was the riverfront, where he decided to build a new twenty-thousand-seat
sports facility. Browne led the opposition.[24]

Meanwhile, between the summer of 1976 and spring of 1977, the Pistons
and the Red Wings solicited potential bidders for a new facility and played
them off against each other. In addition to Pontiac and Detroit, other nearby
townships, such as Westland (just west of Detroit), expressed interest.[25] The
Detroit plans got gummed up when the Pontiac people helped some Detroiters mount a legal challenge to Young's plan to issue new municipal bonds,
on the grounds that the mayor had not made enough information public.[26]
Young, however, did have one ace up his sleeve. During the presidential election of 1975, he had played a key role in organizing the black vote in support
of Jimmy Carter, which Carter had dire need of after the white Southerner
made some dubious comments about "ethnic purity." Carter owed Young,

and he promised $5 million of federal funding to contribute to the arena project.[27]

But when the Red Wings announcement came on April 1, the city was still stuck in the courts, and it looked as if Coleman Young had lost the battle. Rather than concede, though, the mayor stubbornly insisted that the project would go ahead.[28] He argued that the arena didn't need the Wings: the downtown could host plenty of other events, sporting and otherwise. He relied on projections showing that the arena could be in use on 127 days of the year, although he was still hoping that the Pistons would stay. The city finally won its court case on May 20, and they broke ground on the $24 million project on the following day.[29] It had come down to the wire: the federal funds would have been canceled unless work started by May 22.[30]

While construction continued over the summer, it seemed that Coleman Young might be investing in a white elephant. But triumphal vindication came on August 3 when the Red Wings announced that they had signed a thirty-year deal to play at the new arena. They would be staying in the city after all.[31] The general manager later explained that the key to the deal was the parking garage the city had agreed to build—the team would not just get a new facility but would also gain parking for an annual rent of $450,000, a much better deal than Pontiac had been able to offer. The city even threw in the Cobo Arena concession, ensuring the Red Wings owners would face no competition from the adjacent facility. At the time, the Pistons played at the Cobo, which meant that if scheduling issues arose in the largely parallel basketball and hockey seasons, the Red Wings would decide. "There's no question Norris got a helluva deal," said George Matish, a lawyer for the city of Detroit.[32] Coleman Young was re-elected in November with almost 60 percent of the vote.

In the end, amid acrimony, it was the Pistons that left for Pontiac. On September 26, they signed a deal to move to the Pontiac Silverdome, adapting the vast football stadium to a 22,500-seat arena, using a fraction of its capacity.[33] Coleman Young took it personally and made no secret of his disdain for Davidson. Davidson reciprocated.

Years later, in 1985, when the Pistons were planning to leave the Silverdome to return to Detroit, a small drama played out. By that time, the Pistons were doing better, thanks to their bright young star Isiah Thomas. A

2013 biography of Dave Bing, the former basketball star who was now a steel company owner and would one day become mayor himself, tells it like this:

> Young was madder than a hornet. It still angered him eight years later that the Pistons had bolted from Cobo Arena downtown for a shared residence with the Detroit Lions at the Pontiac Silverdome. . . . Basketball was the city game, in other words, the "black game.". . . As far as Young was concerned the city didn't have an NBA basketball team any longer. The Pistons were now suburbia. He wanted the "city game" back in the city.[34]

At first, then, Young supported a plan to bring the Pistons back to Detroit. Secret negotiations broke down when Davidson got wind of the plan and shut it down. It then emerged that the owner of Milwaukee Bucks wanted to sell, so Young and Bing hatched a plan to bring that team to the city, with Bing taking a 10 percent stake as managing partner. After retiring from the NBA, Bing had started his own steel business in Detroit, and he was doing very well. Negotiations really heated up when Mike Ilitch, the new owner of the Red Wings, offered to join the consortium and rent out the Joe Louis Arena for games. Other credible wealthy backers joined the scheme, including Alfred Taubman and Peter Stroh from the famous Detroit brewing company bearing Stroh's name. The deal would have made Bing the first African American owner of an NBA team, and it would have given the Detroit metro area two NBA franchises.[35] Realistically, it seemed unlikely that the metro area could sustain two basketball teams, and in the end, the deal fell through.

After forty years in the suburbs, the Pistons finally returned to the downtown with the opening of Little Caesars Arena in 2017. By this time the combatants Young and Davidson had long passed. Dave Bing, at least, got to see his Pistons back, playing a short walk away from where they had been during his own heyday.

ELEVEN

DECEMBER 26, 1970

The Lions have the first chance in decades to make it to the Super Bowl, but they sputter out in the lowest-scoring postseason game in NFL history. Detroit once again tries to build a downtown stadium and once again fails—this time, because Detroit's downtown is deemed too black and hence not safe enough. Instead, Detroit gets treated to the Renaissance Center, a now iconic part of the skyline, yet all but cut off from the city it is meant to serve. Detroit elects Coleman Young, its first black mayor.

The last time the Lions had been any good was 1957. For thirteen seasons in a row, the team had failed to make the playoffs. From 1958 to 1968, the team had played 148 games and won only 64 (43 percent). In this period they had only four winning seasons to their name. It was as if someone had locked them in the basement. Then, in 1969, everything changed: suddenly, the team was back in business, and in the 1970 season, the Lions went 10-4, with only one home defeat.

It was around this time that football was superseding baseball as the dominant national sport. 1970 was the year that the NFL, following the merger with the AFL, adopted the league structure that has largely remained in intact to the present day. The four divisions of the old NFL were expanded to six, giving the league twenty-six teams in total. Since then, the only significant change has been the addition of six more teams.

Football had always been big in the Midwest, and Detroit's main rivals within their division have remained the same: the Chicago Bears, the Green Bay Packers, and the Minnesota Vikings. The expansion of the playoff system, however, opened new opportunities. Until 1970, you had to win your division to advance, but with six divisions, the creation of an elite eight allowed for two extra teams to make the cut, selected from the six teams that placed second place in their division. In 1970, Detroit's runner-up record was good enough to get them there.

The revival of the Lions had a lot to do with quarterback Greg Landry, whom they had drafted two years earlier. He was growing into the role. The 1970 season was the first in which he threw for more than one thousand yards, to which he added a very respectable 350 rushing yards. In the divisional playoff, Detroit was matched against the Dallas Cowboys, who had topped the NFC East, also with a 10-4 record. The *Detroit Free Press* led with the optimistic headline, "Super Bowl–Starved Lions Roar Today."[1] If the players went on to win the next three games and took the Super Bowl, they were in line for a bonus of $25,000 each. The bookmakers made the Lions three-point favorites against Dallas, a small advantage, but an advantage nonetheless.

On December 26, disappointment struck. Both teams had very strong defenses, and the result was the lowest-scoring postseason game in history, a record which stands at this writing. Only twice in the game did the Lions make two consecutive first downs, and the team failed to score even once. The Cowboys managed a field goal in the first quarter, and neither team scored at all in the next two quarters. In the fourth quarter, Dallas drove to the Lions goal line and, rather than take the field goal, went for it on fourth down. The defense held them off, but when the Lions' offense took over, the Cowboys forced a safety. 5–0. The Cowboys restricted Greg Landry to only 48 passing yards and 15 rushing yards. Near the end of the game, the Lions managed a drive that took them deep into Dallas territory, but it was not to be.

The Monday-morning quarterback at the *Detroit Free Press* complained that if only they had had more faith in Landry's passing game, they might have won![2] But Detroit, playing away from home, was facing one of the all-time great coaches, Tom Landry (unrelated to Greg). The Cowboys ended up losing to the Colts in Super Bowl V, but they went on to win Super Bowl VI the next year and Super Bowl XII in 1977. For two decades, Tom Landry's Cowboys were a constant fixture in the postseason, while it would be another twelve years before the Detroit Lions made it to the playoffs again.[3]

Once the season was over, one of the longest-running sagas in Detroit's history garnered attention again—the construction of a downtown stadium. Depending on how you count, this debate had raged since 1921, when the *Detroit Free Press* reported on whether "to build one gigantic stadium to seat 50,000 or to build two," the larger structure being favored as a potential Olympic Stadium for the 1928 games.[4] The Lions had started playing at Tiger Stadium in 1938, and they were still there when William Clay Ford acquired the team in 1964. Almost immediately, Ford started lobbying the mayor, the City Council, and anyone else who would listen to build him a stadium.[5] After all, playing football in a baseball stadium, where many of the fans find themselves a long way from the sidelines, is far from ideal. In addition, Tiger Stadium could accommodate just over fifty thousand, and as the NFL's popularity rose, demand for tickets far exceeded capacity. With only seven home games guaranteed, owners were understandably keen to maximize opportunity for ticket revenue. Equally unsurprisingly, they were keen to get other people to pay for it.

The city's officials were, in fact, very eager to please, but they couldn't agree as to the best site. There were two main contenders, the State Fairgrounds located at Woodward and Eight Mile, and downtown on the west riverfront where the railway yards were closing and redevelopment land was becoming available. Unrelated strategic interests informed preferences. George Romney, governor of Michigan from 1963 to 1969, and a crucial ally if state funds were to be tapped, wanted the Fairgrounds site, which would be more convenient for out-of-town visitors. Jerome Cavanagh, Detroit's mayor from 1962 to 1970 and the poster child for progressive policies in the 1960s, initially favored the Fairgrounds site as well.[6] Most city planners, who, at that point, held considerable sway over land use in the city, supported the mayor and the governor, although a minority held out for a riverfront development.[7] The idea of transforming the riverfront from an industrial graveyard into a vibrant city amenity was seductive to anyone interested in preserving the downtown. By the mid-1960s, Cavanagh had switched sides.[8] Meetings were held, reports issued, costs estimated, but few concrete steps were taken.

By 1970, William Clay Ford was becoming impatient. Truth be told, he was skeptical about a downtown stadium. The terms of the debate anticipated the hard-fought negotiations we described in chapter 10, developments that kept the Red Wings in town but took the Pistons to the suburbs. First,

Ford worried that a central location would create congestion in the downtown, making it difficult to get fans into and out of the stadium while also alienating the surrounding businesses. Second, none of the plans provided for enough parking, further complicating the logistics. Third, he thought the estimated cost of $125 million was too high to be realistic, and if he signed up for the plan, it would only be scaled down later, to his disadvantage.[9] But, perhaps above all, he worried about safety in the downtown. As far as he was concerned, most of his season ticket holders lived in the suburbs and he was fine with the idea of moving closer to them.[10]

Suburban authorities quickly jumped into the planning vacuum. First, the city of Southfield offered to build a facility.[11] When its offer didn't suit, Pontiac, thirteen miles further north, entered the fray.[12] The Detroit politicians and planners were shocked when, in October 1970, the Lions announced they had signed an agreement to move to Pontiac, though it was only an agreement in principle. They had still thought that Ford was bluffing.[13]

Early in 1970, a group of business leaders in Detroit had gotten together to work on redevelopment plans in the city. The idea was credited to Joseph Hudson, president of the department store, and its proponents included representatives of the city's banks and major businesses. Most importantly, it included the chiefs of Ford, General Motors, and Chrysler. Over the coming years, Henry Ford II, chairman of the board of Ford Motor Company, older brother of William Clay, became the driving force of the organization Detroit Renaissance, whose contribution to the Detroit Grand Prix we mentioned in chapter 9.[14] Between 1970 and 1972, Detroit Renaissance dedicated itself to supporting plans for the downtown stadium, which it continued to promote even when William Clay announced the move to Pontiac.[15] The organization did not give up until the plan finally collapsed in 1972, in the wake of a series of legal disputes.

From that point forward, the main project of Detroit Renaissance would become the construction of the Renaissance Center. Popularly known as the RenCen, it was supported by fifty-two corporate partners and a consortium of twenty-eight banks ready to fund loans, making it the largest urban real estate project ever assembled in the United States.[16] And the biggest underwriter of the project was Ford, both the chairman and the motor company. They identified the land for the development on the riverfront east of the Cobo Center and south of Jefferson Avenue. John Portman, an archi-

tect whose reputation rested largely on the construction of shopping malls
and hotels, appears to have been given free rein. The city's administration,
delighted to be the beneficiary of such a high level of corporate concern,
moved to curtail the powers of the influential planning commission, which
had expressed concerns about the design.[17]

The outcome remains today one of the most iconic landmarks in Detroit.
RenCen consists of seven interconnected skyscrapers; the central tower, and
the tallest one, is shaped like a cylinder, an homage to the city's automobile
engineering heritage. It was designed as a city within a city, if not a fortress.
As Portman saw it, the Detroit downtown was dangerous, so the RenCen
had to project an image of safety, an island of security in a dangerous sea: "a
self-contained citadel," commentators called it.[18] And that is exactly what
he achieved. It is hardly surprising, then, that RenCen has done very little
to improve the downtown, precisely because it is an island that may as well
have a moat around it. By and large, you get there by car, not on foot: you
can drive in and out from the suburbs, park next to RenCen, and never set
foot into the rest of Detroit. Pedestrians seeking to reach RenCen have to
cross East Jefferson—that is, eight lanes of speeding cars. It can be done, but
it's an ordeal, and you certainly don't feel invited to make the crossing.[19] To
make matters worse, the compound became a financial millstone for Ford in
the years after it opened. Other businesses, expected to lease space, passed,
and to prevent the prestige project from standing empty, the company ended
up relocating a large fraction of its executives into the building. Eventually
Ford allowed RenCen to go bankrupt, and it was sold off to property specu-
lators.[20] In a final irony, it was General Motors who took over in 1996, and
GM is still headquartered in RenCen today.[21]

Seeing his tremendous commitment to riverfront development, how was it
possible that Henry Ford II could not get the downtown stadium built? All
he needed was to overcome his younger brother's skepticism and enter into
a family partnership. A large stadium would have been the perfect comple-
ment to the RenCen. Henry had even been involved in the refinancing of the
Houston Astrodome, a large downtown stadium. Was it sour grapes on the
part of William Clay, who still resented the way that Henry had excluded
him from the family business? Was it that Henry had no desire to share the
glory of rebuilding the downtown with his brother, whom he had squeezed
out of the family business?

As usual when it comes to postwar Detroit, the failure to build a down-town stadium, the departure of the Lions, and the subsequent departure of the Pistons cannot be disentangled from the politics of race. No matter how committed the—almost exclusively white—politicians were, no matter how meticulously they planned, after the city's 1967 uprising, there was one narrative that dominated all others: the downtown was a scary place, and fans would stay away. An article in the *Detroit Free Press* from March 28, 1969, spelled it out with exemplary clarity:

> Put simply, the case for putting the new stadium anywhere else than downtown Detroit rests on fear. People are reluctant of going into Detroit to see a ball game for fear of getting beaten up, or having their car stolen, or being robbed. By whom? By Negroes, of course. So people argue that the solution to the problem is to put the new stadium out in the clean white suburbs. I don't agree. For what it's worth, I think the stadium should be built downtown, along the riverfront site advocated by Mayor Cavanagh. For one thing, Negroes are as scared of coming out into the suburbs as white people are of going downtown. Perhaps more. So what is the racial composition of the crowd rooting for the Lions and Tigers? I don't know. But once you start putting up a stadium in one place or another for racial reasons (veiled racial reasons, but racial reasons all the same) you start breaking down your fans into blacks and whites. Baseball's got enough trouble right now without having to try to handle that one. If the big problem is fear of people going downtown, let's design an anti-fear stadium. Then publicize it. Make the parking lot well lighted and put a fence around it. Hire a lot of guards to stand inside and outside the stadium. Do any number of things the police might suggest.[22]

A few years after the uprising, it was becoming clear to everyone: the suburbs were white and the city was majority black, a demographic fact that would dictate the terms of Detroit's fate for decades to come. After years of supporting and electing progressive whites, who they hoped would recognize and address their struggles, black residents, including black politicians, were finally coming to the fore in Detroit.

Coleman Young was born in Alabama in 1918; his family moved to Detroit along with the large number of black Southerners who joined the Great Migration that continued until the 1970s. He graduated from Eastern High School in Detroit, on Grand Boulevard on the East Side. The school was later renamed the Martin Luther King High School, and it has always been known for sports. When Coleman Young was a student in the 1930s, he played fullback for the football team. "I wasn't very big and got beat up on every play," he later recalled ruefully. He also remembered running cross-country, on a route that started at the school, took him to Belle Isle, and around the island before heading back to the school. His fitness would have stood him in good stead earlier in his childhood, when he competed for a backbreaking summer job at the age of ten or eleven: for fifty cents a day— a fortune, as far as he was concerned—the job required carrying fifty-pound blocks of ice to households at a time where private refrigerators where still an unheard-of luxury. The trouble was that most of the other kids in his neighborhood wanted the job as well, and Young lost out to an older kid with a lot more muscle: Joe Louis.[23]

As a young man, he worked at Ford, which had a policy of welcoming black workers, and at the U.S. Post Office. During the war, he served as a bombardier and navigator in the celebrated Tuskegee Airmen group, and in 1945, he was arrested for refusing to accept segregation at a base in Indiana.[24] We recount the story behind this incident in chapter 16.

From his days at Ford, where he joined the UAW, Young had a reputation as a communist sympathizer. In 1952, he was subpoenaed to testify before Senator Joseph McCarthy's House Un-American Activities Committee (HUAC). "I am not here to fight in any un-American activities," he said at the hearing, "because I consider the denial of the right to vote to large numbers of people all over the South un-American."[25] He refused to answer any questions, and his testimony included the following testy exchange:

Mr. [Frank] Tavenner [HUAC's counsel]: You told us you were the executive secretary of the National Negro Congress.

Mr. Young: That word is "Negro," not "Niggra."

Mr. Tavenner: I said, "Negro." I think you are mistaken.

Mr. Young: I hope I am. Speak more clearly.

Mr. [John] Wood [representative from Georgia]: I will appreciate it if you
    will not argue with counsel.

Mr. Young: It isn't my purpose to argue. As a Negro, I resent the slurring
    of the name of my race.

Mr. Wood: You are here for the purpose of answering questions.

Mr. Young: In some sections of the country they slur.[26]

His political career developed, and throughout the 1950s and 1960s,
Young was an active political organizer on Detroit's East Side. In 1960, he
was elected as a delegate to help draft a new state constitution for Michigan
and in 1964 was elected to the Michigan State Senate. In 1973, he ran for
mayor of Detroit.

Young was not the first black candidate for mayor—that had been Richard Austin, who ran against Mary Beck in the 1969 primaries. Beck, a
Democrat, was a powerful advocate of women's rights and a pioneer for
women in politics in Detroit. She was the first woman to be elected the city's
Common Council and the first to become president of that body.[27] After
losing the primary, she said: "There was much more discrimination than
I thought against a woman holding an executive position."[28] That may be
so, but her views on law and order may have played a more significant role.
The *Detroit Free Press* observed that her platform consisted of a "strident
'law and order' theme, tinged by some of her supporters and by publicity
with racial overtones."[29] While she was carefully restrained in her public
pronouncements on race, her supporters were crystal clear. One respondent
to a *Detroit Free Press* survey said, "We need a mayor who will stand up
for the white people. We don't owe the n——s a goddamn dime; we've fed
them since the Civil War." Another commented, "We can't possibly live
with blacks; they want to take over."[30]

By 1969, about 44 percent of the city was black, and voting was highly polarized by race. Many white people said they simply weren't prepared to see a black man become mayor. Black voters, who had supported white politicians in every election up until then, were beginning to demand and expect representation. Beck lost the primary to Roman Gribbs, another Democrat who became the leading white candidate. Gribbs had started his campaign as a moderate, but then tacked sharply to the right and made crime his main campaign issue in order to pick up Beck supporters. In the election itself, Gribbs won by 6,194 votes out of more than half a million votes cast. In an election dominated by the issue of race, the white man had won.[31]

This was an era of radical politics in the African American community. Any progress in securing civil rights had been bought at a heavy price, and Detroit was a hive of revolutionary thought and activism.[32] In response, Gribbs sanctioned the creation of a special unit within the Detroit Police Department: Stop The Robberies, Enjoy Safe Streets (STRESS). STRESS targeted black communities and used highly questionable tactics to do so. A favorite ploy was the "decoy operation," where a police officer tried to entrap potential criminals in an undercover sting.[33] It was also brutal. During its existence, it's worth mentioning again, STRESS shot and killed twenty-four men, twenty-two of whom were African American.[34] Even after a Wayne County sheriff deputy, who happened to be black, was gunned down in his apartment by STRESS, white conservatives continued to support the crackdown. Many people thought of the city as a war zone, where brute and lethal force had to be tolerated.[35]

However much some whites supported Gribbs, it was widely understood that he was "a 'transitional' mayor, preparing Detroit for black rule."[36] It was no great surprise when he decided not to stand for a second term. Richard Austin had been as moderate as they come, but Coleman Young was no moderate. In 1973, he campaigned against the tactics of STRESS and its impact on black communities, which now commanded a majority in the city. To polarize things even further, his opponent, John Nichols, was the police commissioner who had implemented STRESS. Coleman Young won handily, taking 56 percent of the vote, which was mostly black but benefited from a significant minority contribution from liberal whites.

Heather Ann Thompson described the aftermath of the election thus:

As Young prepared to take office on January 6, 1973, he publicly issued "a warning to all dope pushers, rip-off artists and
muggers [that] it's time to leave Detroit. Hit the road! . . . I
don't give a damn if they're black or white, if they wear super
fly suits or blue suits with silver badges." Ironically, however,
the city's criminal element did not take Young's victory as its
cue to abandon the city, but the city's white population did—
at least those whites with the economic means to flee. For the
whites financially unable to participate in the post-1973 exodus,
"There remain[ed] a virulent racial bias that many believe [to be
Young's] biggest challenge." Coleman Young had, indeed, won
the mayoralty, but his victory was qualified. For Detroit blacks,
who had fought so hard first inside, then outside, and finally
back inside of the system, the city now held promise. For Detroit
whites, however, the events of 1967 to 1973, culminating in the
election of Young, sent them flying out of the city and into the
Republican fold.[37]

TWELVE

OCTOBER 10, 1968

A year after the uprising, the Tigers' World Series win briefly unites a traumatized city.

Showers of confetti burst out of the windows and floated through the streets, strangers kissed and boogied on the sidewalks, bikers shared their beers with cops, and the entire city reverberated with the sound of thousands of honking cars, with jubilant teenagers sitting on the roofs and jumping on and off the hoods.[1] Thirty thousand fans set off to the Metropolitan Airport to welcome home the victorious Tigers. The traffic jam was ten miles long, and lots of fans simply abandoned their cars and walked on. They jumped over fences and barriers, littered the runway with broken bottles, and a bunch of them climbed onto the fuselage of a plane—doing enough damage to force air traffic control to close the runways. Fourteen outgoing flights were canceled. Governor Romney flew in on his private jet, but he couldn't persuade the crowd to go home. It was almost 10 p.m. by the time services were restored, and the team had been diverted to land at Willow Run Airport in Ypsilanti, twenty-five miles west.[2] Thousands of savvy fans had sussed out the detour and welcomed the winners, along with Mayor Jerome Cavanagh and Governor Romney, who described the chaotic scene as "just fantastic."[3]

At Tiger Stadium that night, the impatient crowd got rowdy and threw beer cans at the police, who retaliated by beating the fans with night sticks.[4] The city went crazy, but with only some exceptions, in the most joyous way.[5] "City officials reported no damage during the spontaneous downtown carnival and only 11 arrests, for public drunkenness," Billy McGraw recalled in 2018, though there must have been some fudging involved.[6] It could have been any celebration of a spectacular win in any city in America. But the 1968 celebrations were hailed as more than that. Reportedly, team owner John Fetzer told its manager, Mayo Smith, "You've not only won the pennant and the series, you might have saved the city."[7] Even earlier, after Detroit secured the pennant, the *Detroit Free Press* proclaimed that "for one brief, shining moment after Detroit won the American League pennant, blacks and whites mingled in color-blind joy, thousands strong, on the streets of downtown Detroit," and asked, rather hyperbolically, "why, 13 months after the costliest riot in American history, did blacks and whites love one another without reservation?"[8]

Needless to say, no sports event, however glorious, will ever be able to shoulder the burden of healing a city in that much pain. The jubilant coverage does underscore sports' unique capacity to elicit raw emotion, frequently for worse but often for better as well, and while it is beyond its power to create "love without reservation," one evening filled with a sense of togetherness is not nothing. The city needed a win as badly as ever a city did. It was not in good shape. That same night, a teenager was shot below the right eye and killed at the corner of Clifford and Woodward, about five hundred yards away from Campus Martius. Another man was shot and killed as he walked to his car parked on Sibley Street, where Little Caesars Arena now stands. In Capitol Park, two people were critically injured by stab wounds, one in the abdomen, the other to the throat. On Kercheval, passing cars were stoned. Looting broke out on Woodward, with the window display of a hosiery store emptied and broken windows reported by numerous store owners. Twenty-five-year old Larry Adkins was robbed of $17 by three thugs who then stabbed him in the back.[9] If those events weren't mentioned much—the *Free Press* relegates them to page B-4—then it's because they didn't really stand out.

It's too bad that the Tigers hadn't made it in 1967. That season, the team was formidable. The typically strong batting lineup was led by Al Kaline, an obvious Hall of Famer at the peak of his career. Willie Horton, the local lad, was starting to make a big impact. For once, the Tigers had strong pitching too. Youngsters Mickey Lolich, Joe Sparma, and Denny McLain were boasting ERAs of under 4, while veteran Earl Wilson was having one of the best seasons of his career. By September 1967, Chicago, Minnesota,

Detroit, and Boston were in a four-way tie for the pennant. By the end of the month, the Tigers were still in it, but doubts were creeping in: the team had blown four games after leading in the eighth inning or later. So now it all came down to the last weekend of the regular season. Minnesota, the leaders, would play two games in Boston, who were one game behind, while Detroit, also one game behind and delayed by rain cancelations, had to play two doubleheaders against the California Angels at Tiger Stadium.

On Saturday, the Tigers won the first game thanks to the pitching of Mickey Lolich and then blew a four-run lead in the second game. Meanwhile Boston beat Minnesota, and so these two were now level. Whoever won in Boston on Sunday would have 92 wins for the season. Detroit, with 90, therefore needed to win both Sunday games, which would get them into a one-game playoff for the pennant.[10]

They did win the first one, but the second would be their undoing. Detroit went out to a 2–1 lead, but quickly fell behind, and by the bottom of the ninth, they were trailing 8–5. With runners on first and second, Dick McAuliffe (who had 22 homers for the season) went to the plate as the tying run. It was not to be. McAuliffe hit a grounder straight to second base, who threw to first, and with the double play the Tigers' season was over.[11]

Even with the season on the line, one-third of the seats in Tiger Stadium that day were empty.[12] When the game ended, the fans who had attended vented their disappointment by throwing their seats—about five hundred of them—onto the field. Home plate was stolen, others tried to dig up the pitcher's mound. The visiting team dugout was vandalized, the lightbulbs on the scoreboard were taken, telephones were broken. One fan was arrested for attacking a policeman. Watching from the owner's box, John Fetzer wrote a letter to himself, which later became public. "They destroyed scores of stadium seats and piled the rubble in the dugouts. Still others clawed at home plate and the pitcher's mound, while a bedlam of confusion turned many more hundreds into a near mob scene with the elements of combat everywhere on the playing field." He then ended on an odd note: "John Fetzer has just died, this is his ghost speaking."[13]

As we know from countless examples, vandalism is not a monopoly of the losers. In Boston, the Red Sox won their last game and took the pennant. In the ensuing celebrations, fans invaded the field at Fenway Park and refused to leave until the staff turned on the sprinklers. Several kids tried to climb into the broadcast booth, and an injured fan was found collapsed in the Minnesota dugout that had been ripped apart by other fans. The wild scenes of celebration across Boston were near indistinguishable from the scenes of riotous despair in Detroit.[14]

Even if Detroit was hit particularly hard, the 1960s were an exceptionally violent decade across the United States as a whole. All forms of crime increased dramatically. Between 1960 and 1970, across the country total reported crime rate per 100,000 people doubled, as did the rate of property crimes and aggravated assault. Violent crimes and vehicle theft more than doubled. The homicide rate actually increased more slowly than any other crime category, but still increased by more than 50 percent.[15] In this regard, the scenes at baseball games mirrored general phenomena in the big cities. Criminologists have found that urban crime rates rose faster than elsewhere, and the larger the city, the faster the rate of increase, at least with regard to robberies and homicide.[16]

There was no single cause of the rise in crime. The period was one of growing instability and social conflict, driven in part by resistance to the civil rights movement on the right, and to protests against the war in Vietnam on the left. As social barriers that had stabilized an unjust order slowly and painfully broke down, factors such as relative and absolute deprivation, poverty and racial inequality, the breakdown of social control via traditional patriarchal family structures, and disorganization due to urban decline have all been found to correlate positively with higher crime rates.[17] While both dog whistles and foghorns increasingly began to blame African Americans, a growing propensity for violence was an all-American affair. Look at photographs from the era, and you will see that the intermittent mayhem at the baseball stadiums of the 1960s is instigated and enjoyed by a predominantly white audience. That was certainly true for Tiger Stadium.

The 1960s was a roller-coaster decade for African Americans. There were the unquestionably great strides of the civil rights era, with the Jim Crow laws of the South ruled unconstitutional at last. Legal segregation officially ended, and the civil rights acts passed—even if it had taken a shockingly long time to get politicians and the courts to uphold the most basic promises of the U.S. Constitution. While much of the New Deal legislation had originally excluded African Americans in large numbers—Social Security, for instance, did not include agricultural and domestic workers—benefits were beginning to be a little more equitably distributed, and the War on Poverty provided gains for the poorest in society, among whom the black population was disproportionately represented.

At the same time, 1960s Detroit was also the city of Motown, the most successful black-owned business in the country at the time. Founded on a shoe-string budget by native Detroiter Berry Gordy, a former featherweight boxer, Motown began churning out No. 1 hits starting in 1961, and it was "becoming bigger than music," as Kelley L. Carter writes for *The Undefeated*.[18] The record label was fundamentally shifting the industry, desegregating pop music. Motown has been criticized "for what some believed was a disgraceful practice of making black singers palatable to a white audience," in David Nantais's telling, but there is no dispute that Diana Ross & the Supremes, Marvin Gaye, Smokey Robinson, The Marvelettes, The Temptations, Stevie Wonder, and so many others revolutionized the music scene and made Detroit the center of that revolution.[19]

Motown is often understood to have developed a deliberately political identity characterized by socially conscious lyrics and a strong anti–Vietnam War stance only after it left the city in the wake of the uprising. But Marvin Gaye's anti-war album *What's Going On* (1971) was still recorded in Detroit, and as early as 1964, Martha and the Vandellas' "Dancing in the Street" was an exuberant celebration of black cities: "Philadelphia, PA (Dancing in the street) / Baltimore and D.C. now (Dancing in the street) / Can't forget the Motor City (Dancing in the street)." There is reason to be skeptical of the "usual tale of Motown's politics—a story that dramatically locates Motown's political breakthrough in Gaye's 1971 artistic triumph."[20] While the company did by and large seek to have its records seen "as music" rather than "as black music," as Motown songwriter and producer William "Mickey" Stevenson stresses, Motown recorded Martin Luther King's "I Have a Dream" speech as early as 1963, and Motown's "Black Forum" label, a series of civil rights recordings, debuted with a 1967 recording of another King speech, "Why I Oppose the War in Vietnam."[21] Music and politics were intimately connected in civil rights–era America, and Detroit was no exception.[22]

The victories, however, had come at a very steep price. The struggle had been protracted and often bloody, and it took near endless campaigns and protests to draw the country's attention to the gross injustice committed daily in its midst—a task in which the new medium of television helped quite a bit. Titans of the movement, Martin Luther King Jr. and Malcolm X, were assassinated, along with allies such as Bobby Kennedy. The rising homicide rate mostly affected black families—much of inner-city violence was black on black, just as most white homicide was and remains white on white. The police force remained overwhelmingly white and largely hostile to the black community—abuse, beatings, and worse were an everyday experience for many black people. White supremacists weren't giving up, and not even lynchings had stopped entirely.

In 1966, one year before the Detroit uprising, James Baldwin wrote for *The Nation* an essay he called "A Report from Occupied Territory," where he describes the horrifying police regime that ruled over African Americans:

> I have witnessed and endured the brutality of the police many more times than once—but, of course, I cannot prove it. I cannot prove it because the Police Department investigates itself, quite as though it were answerable only to itself. But it cannot be allowed to be answerable only to itself. It must be made to answer to the community which pays it, and which it is legally sworn to protect, and if American Negroes are not a part of the American community, then all of the American professions are a fraud. This arrogant autonomy, which is guaranteed the police, not only in New York, *by the most powerful forces in American life*—otherwise, they would not dare to claim it, would indeed be unable to claim it—creates a situation which is as close to anarchy as it already, visibly, is close to martial law.[23]

In the same essay, he points out that "what I have said about Harlem is true of Chicago, Detroit, Washington, Boston, Philadelphia, Los Angeles and San Francisco—is true of every Northern city with a large Negro population. And the police are simply the hired enemies of this population."

The same point emerges from Chris Hayes's book *A Colony in a Nation*: the rise of organized protests in the era along with the rise of violent crime (which wouldn't reach its zenith until 1992) led to a new form of segregation, a bifurcated system of justice and policing that equated disorder with unlawfulness—at least for the black population. Hayes writes:

> The American criminal justice isn't one system with massive racial disparities but two distinct regimes. One (the Nation) is the kind of policing regime you expect in a democracy; the other (the Colony) is the kind you expect in an occupied land. Policing is a uniquely important and uniquely dangerous function of the state. Dictatorships and totalitarian regimes use the police in horrifying ways; we call them "police states" for a reason. But the terrifying truth is that we as a people have created the Colony through democratic means. We have voted to subdue our fellow citizens; we have rushed to the polls to elect people promising to bar others from enjoying the fruits of liberty. A majority of Americans have put a minority under lock and key. In her masterful 2010 chronicle of American mass incarceration, *The New Jim Crow*, Michelle Alexander argues convincingly that our current era represents not a shift from previous eras of white supremacy and black oppression but continuity with them. After the 1960s, she contends, when Jim Crow was dismantled as a legal entity, it was reconceived and reborn through mass incarceration.[24]

It is important to keep in mind that the black minority of the 1960s was not united in its reaction to the developments of the decade. As Hubert Locke put it, a "common assumption in the white community appears to have bordered on the belief that at birth every Negro receives a life-time membership of the NAACP, which in turn speaks ex-cathedra for all Negroes."[25] Black opinions about the best strategies to pursue varied considerably, even within the civil rights movement. But both Martin Luther King Jr, who advocated nonviolent means, and Malcolm X, who favored armed resistance, were bitterly resented and eventually killed by those who did not want equality, whether pursued by peaceful or by violent means. In these times of turmoil, upheaval broke out in cities across the country.

In the popular discourse of white America, these events are usually called "race riots." The word "riot" is meant to evoke an angry mob engaged in indiscriminate destruction of property and violence against persons, especially the representatives of law and order—and in post-60s America, it is safe to say that most people will think of Harlem in 1964, Watts in 1965, or Detroit in 1967. Originally, however, the term referred to white attacks on communities of color, such as the horrific destruction of the prosperous black Greenwood district in Tulsa in 1921, which cost the lives of at least three hundred people and left more than a thousand homes in ruins. In an excellent blog post for the *Los Angeles Book Review*, Steve Light asks why we did not call these attacks pogroms, or massacres. He continues:

> The killing of African-Americans and the destruction of their homes and commercial and institutional buildings and structures in Greenwood was an officially sanctioned event. . . . Certainly the event could be called a "riot," but it was a riot by whites. . . . But, then, "riot" is rather imprecise since it blurs the willful, the organized nature of such events. Riot? Well, certainly it is a question of a pogrom against the African-American community.[26]

It should come as no surprise that Detroit has seen its share of these pogroms, along with many other battles such as an uprising of Polish workers in 1894 and the Battle of the Overpass, to which we will return later.

In Detroit an altercation between police and black youths erupted on August 9, 1966, at the corner of Kercheval and Pennsylvania on the East Side.[27] Riot police were immediately sent to the scene; community leaders who were working with the police, under the liberal regime of Mayor Cavanagh, identified revolutionary black activists; a car carrying weapons was intercepted. Tensions remained high the following day and trouble was expected in the evening, but a heavy rain appeared to cool down tempers, and there was no further violence. Cavanagh's administration touted the peaceful resolution as proof that its progressive policies were working, and were helping the city avoid the extremes witnessed across the rest of the country. To others, the spin hid the truth about the origins of the unrest: it happened right next to Lafayette Park and the old Black Bottom neighbor-

hoods, where successive administrations had perpetrated their urban renewal schemes—we will return to those stories later. Many black Detroiters saw
it as James Baldwin did: "Urban renewal means black removal."[28]

A year later, it would become abundantly clear that the tensions could not
be contained—and in retrospect, both contemporary witnesses and historians of urban America would argue that it had always been a question of not
of "if" but "when." What would commonly be known as "the Detroit Riots"
broke out after a police raid on an illegal after-hours drinking club, locally
known as a "blind pig." It was around 3:45 a.m. on Sunday, July 23, on the
corner of Twelfth Street and Clairmount, six blocks west of Woodward in
midtown. Here, there was a dense strip of stores centered around a growing
black community that had been pushed out by the urban renewal machina-
tions, moving into neighborhoods abandoned by white Detroiters who had
left for the suburbs. All summer long, tension had simmered between the
police and neighborhood groups who suspected that the widespread prostitution in the area—catering to white male clients from the suburbs—was
sanctioned and protected by the police, who did not, so the accusations
went, act on neighborhood complaints and demands for action.[29]

After the raid, eighty-two people were arrested and driven off, but in
the process, a large crowd started to gather and some bottles began to fly.
The discontent gathered momentum into the early morning as the police
mobilized and community leaders sought to restore calm. By 11 a.m. it
became apparent that the angry crowd would not go home, as the police
demanded, and while the area around the blind pig was under police control, more crowds were starting to gather at the edges. By late afternoon,
reports of looting and arson along Grand River Avenue, Woodward, and
Gratiot emerged, extending across larger and larger parts of the city. By the
end of that night, three hundred fires had been recorded, and forty were still
blazing, involving over ten thousand Detroiters and one thousand police.
There were reports of sniper fire aimed at firefighters. Just after midnight
on the following day, the first reported death occurred—a white male loot-
er was shot by a white store owner. A few hours later, a guardsman shot
a white male coming down from a roof, believing him to be a sniper. As
the night wore on, Governor Romney and Mayor Cavanagh requested first
state troopers, then National Guard troops, then federal troops. A series of

political, legal, and strategic disagreements meant that the soldiers were not deployed for almost twenty-four hours.

By Monday evening, a running battle started between the police and snipers, pinning down the firefighters and allowing the fires to spread. By midnight, five police stations were under attack. On the third day, with the deployment of troops, the authorities seemed to be bringing the disturbance under control, but sniper fire continued again that evening. By day four, the battle was becoming increasingly intense with more and more reports of atrocities. This included the shocking Algiers Motel incident, where police killed three unarmed African Americans in their custody and assaulted and abused several more—the subject of Kathryn Bigelow's controversial film *Detroit*. The murderers were indicted, but eventually went free—a pattern that would repeat in twentieth- and twenty-first-century America over and over again. By Thursday, concerns were growing about the welfare of trapped residents and their access to food and water; there was also evidence that out-of-towners were coming to the city, either to observe or to seek trouble: police identified the license plates of cars from Alabama, California, Illinois, Kentucky, New York, and Ohio. Occupants were typically armed white males primed for mayhem.

By Friday the disturbances were starting to peter out. While there were sporadic reports of incidents over the weekend, by Monday it was over. Forty-three people were dead, seven hundred injured, and property to the value of around $50 million had been destroyed.[30] According to the testimony of many white witnesses, the black people on the streets expressed no particular hostility to white residents—their fight was predominantly with the police. Events did not unfold in a simple way along rigid racial lines, and many black Detroiters implored the military to act more aggressively toward looters, a good number of whom were white. But even if the disturbances became something of a free-for-all, it was nonetheless clear that police overreach and police brutality, along with a history of severely strained race relations in general, were at the root of the escalating protests. The uprising, however chaotic, was driven by a demand for change and for recognition of the civil rights of the black population—and at least in some ways, it can be said to have succeeded.

Media coverage often focuses on the destruction and theft of property to lament the lawlessness of such rebellions, but if those meant to enforce the law are themselves the problem, the status of "the law" becomes more complicated. Some activists have pointed out that vandalism and looting can also be understood as a symbolic attack on the very economic structures that create and maintain inequality. Albert Cleage Jr., for instance, an influential black writer, preacher, and activist from Detroit, speculated that "we live in a materialist society. . . . Perhaps those who loot and burn don't have any real revolutionary philosophy, but they know one simple thing: tear up the white man's property, and you hurt him where it hurts the most."[31]

The mainstream U.S. press, unsurprisingly, had a different take. Here is a fairly representative account in *Time* magazine from August 4, 1967:

> Here was the most sensational expression of an ugly mood of nihilism and anarchy that has ever gripped a small but significant segment of America's Negro minority. Typically enough, Detroit's upheaval started with a routine police action. Seven weeks ago, in the Virginia Park section of the West Side, a "blind pig" (after-hours club) opened for business on Twelfth street, styling itself the "United Community League for Civic Action." Along with the after-hours booze that it offered to minors, the "League" served up black-power harangues and curses against Whitey's exploitation. It was at the blind pig, on a sleazy strip of pawnshops and bars, rats and pimps, junkies and gamblers, that the agony began.[32]

The passage drips with contempt and mockery for the neighborhood and its people, associating black political action with underage drinking, "rats and pimps." While acknowledging some history of oppression ("the wrongs and disabilities have, in fact, been significantly reduced"), most of the piece focuses on looting and arson rather than the abominable conditions and legitimate grievances that found a violent outlet during those five days.

One conflict that came to a head here was, as noted above, the tensions between different camps within the black communities, roughly represented by the strategies and convictions of Martin Luther King versus those of Malcolm X. Moderate black leaders, such as Hubert Locke, aide to Detroit's police commissioner during the uprising, were torn between the desire to have their voice of protest heard and a desire to prevent power in the community falling into the hands of black revolutionaries.

Needless to say, this brief chapter cannot even begin to do justice to the complexity of the uprising, its many origins and aftermaths. It is fair to say, however, that the series of urban rebellions in the 1960s served notice to America with regard to the enormous tensions between black and white communities in the era of "the new Jim Crow," to use Michelle Alexander's well-considered term. The disparities had been long in the making, as Thomas Sugrue's indispensable book *The Origins of the Urban Crisis* demonstrates.

A simple table in Sugrue's book illustrates why Detroit has a special place in American race history.[33] It lists a measure of "dissimilarity," capturing the extent of segregation in sixteen of the largest northern U.S. cities for each decade between 1940 and 1990. Generally speaking, the typical northern city in 1940 had a dissimilarity index of 90 on a scale between zero (no segregation) and 100 (complete segregation). By 1990, in three-quarters of these cities this index fell to a range between 68 and 83, marking a significant (though hardly praiseworthy) rise in integration. For Detroit, the needle did not move in that half-century: it was stuck between 85 and 90 throughout. Detroit was segregated, stayed segregated, and remains segregated—not by law, but by persistent economic, political, cultural, and historical forces that have taken over the role of openly discriminatory policies.[34]

Such was the history that no World Series triumph could erase it nor heal its deep wounds. For the span of one rowdy and joyous evening, it may have been out of mind at least, allowing a glimpse of what a unified city might be like. Perhaps that was what Willie Horton meant when he said, "I believe the '68 Tigers were put here by God to heal this city."[35] It was a good thing, to be sure, that the 1968 Tigers, largely unchanged from the previous year, were an integrated team, and wildly popular in the city. Willie Horton, the first black Tigers player to achieve stardom, was a Detroiter through and through, and a favorite in the stadium and the city.

By May 10, the team topped the league, and they never gave up the lead after that—by the end of September they were twelve games ahead of the field. The Tigers had bettered their season win percentage, to .636, which had been surpassed only three times before—in 1909, 1915, and 1934. Denny McLain in particular had a magical season, ending with an ERA of

1.96, which earned him the Cy Young and AL MVP award, all at the preco-
cious age of twenty-four. In September, he won baseball fans' hearts during
a special game in which Mickey Mantle, in his farewell season, played for
the last time at The Corner. McLain threw him a soft pitch so the legendary
Mantle could record one final home run in Tiger Stadium. The entire stadium rose to its feet to applaud as the great man circled the bases, although
the Commissioner of Baseball later threatened McLain with an investigation for "compromising the integrity of the game."[36]

In the World Series, Detroit faced St. Louis, who had dominated the
National League in similar fashion. 1968 had been the year of the pitcher;
for St. Louis, Bob Gibson had been setting records with an extraordinary
ERA of only 1.12, throwing thirteen shutouts along the way. In game 1,
Gibson brought the Tigers down to earth by striking out 17 batters, a World
Series record. The Cardinals won the game 4–0. In the second game, pitcher
Mickey Lolich hit a home run for the Tigers (the only one of his career), and
they won comfortably 8–1. The next three games were at Tiger Stadium.
The first two went to St. Louis, with Gibson once again overpowering the
Detroit batting lineup in game 4. Down 3–1, Detroit now had to sweep the
final three games, a feat achieved only twice before in major league history.
Game 4 started disastrously when Lolich gave up three runs in the first
inning, but the Tigers clawed their way to victory, scoring two in the fourth
and three in the seventh, with Lolich regaining control and not allowing St.
Louis to score again.[37]

The teams now returned to Busch Memorial Stadium for the last two
games. In game 6, McLain gave up a single run while the Detroit batting
went wild, scoring ten in the third inning, including a grand slam, while the
Cardinals desperately tried to staunch the flow with three different pitchers.
So it all came down to the last game, with Mickey Lolich facing Bob Gibson
on October 10—surely St. Louis were still the favorite? After six innings,
the scores were tied at zero. Then at the top of the seventh, with two men
on, Curt Flood, one of the best fielders in the game, committed an error
that yielded two runs to Detroit. An additional run in that inning more or
less settled it. Both teams added one run in the ninth, and then the Detroit
celebrations began.

Tiger Stadium features statues commemorating the exploits of five Hall
of Famers: Ty Cobb, Hank Greenberg, Charlie Gehringer, Hal Newhouser,

and Al Kaline. But there is a sixth statue: Willie Horton. He's had an impressive career, but he will likely never make it into the Hall of Fame, which admits very few players each season. There are other reasons why Willie Horton enjoys monumental and monument-worthy status in the city. Born in Virginia in 1942, the youngest of fourteen children, his family moved to Detroit in 1947. He attended Northwestern High School in midtown, and grew up not far from Briggs Stadium, as it was then known. He hit his first home run there during a high school championship game, signed with the Tigers organization in 1961, and, after playing in the minors, made his debut in the majors in 1963.[38]

During the 1969 season, the pitcher of the Seattle Pilots, Jim Bouton, kept a no-holds-barred diary that exposed the seamy side of the game—the drinking, drug taking, gambling, and womanizing of the national pastime. Published in 1970, the book was an instant bestseller that also got Bouton ostracized by his peers. The entry for August 15 observes, "The situation of the Negro in baseball is not as equitable as it seems. He still has to be better than his white counterparts to do as well." After telling a story about a player whose stats would have given him a shot at the majors, Bouton continues: "There are a lot of Negro stars in the game. There aren't too many average Negro players. The obvious conclusion is that there is some kind of quota system. It stands to reason that if 19 of the top 30 hitters in the major leagues are black, as they were in 1968, then almost two thirds of all the hitters should be black. Obviously, it's not that way. In the case of the Tigers the fact that only three of their players are black is no less astonishing."[39]

On the first Sunday of the 1967 uprising, the Tigers were playing a doubleheader against the Yankees. Most of the players had no idea what was happening while Mickey Lolich gave up the win in the first game and Willie Horton hit a home run to help win the second. During the game, smoke started to drift over left field, but the commentators had been told not to mention the uproar in the city, and once the second game was over, the players were ordered to go home—except for Lolich, a member of the National Guard, who was told to report for duty, and spent the next week in uniform patrolling the city with a rifle in his hand.

Willie Horton, however, did not go home, either. As the *Detroit News* reported years later:

The players had been urged to leave in a hurry, to head straight home, to stay far from the smoke and searing tempers that had turned a town into a cauldron.

Horton could do no such thing. He was a Detroit resident. He knew these neighborhoods. These people. These issues of poverty and justice that few could appreciate unless you, too, had been affected by the loss in only a few years of 156,000 manufacturing jobs, which later devolved into the flight of 246,000 jobs from a town that 10 and 20 years before had been a shrine to America's might.

He, too, understood race's ugly consequences, how they could bore into a man or woman, not daily, but hourly, moment to moment. Horton pulled his Ford to an intersection as thick with simmering people and surrounding cops as with black smoke that could be seen for miles.

"I got there, by myself, around 7 p.m.," Horton remembers of that evening of July 23, 1967. "It was scaring me. There were people on all sides of me. It was like a war. But a war isn't supposed to be in your community.

"I got on top of the hood of my car. I had my uniform on. I had my street clothes in a duffel bag."

Everyone knew Horton. Everyone knew he needed to be elsewhere.

"Go home, Willie, we don't want you to get hurt," Horton remembers hearing, continually.

Horton's car already had been scorched by fire in an area where fire, more than any sense of order or law, increasingly ruled.

"Don't defeat this purpose!" Horton pleaded. "This isn't about looting."[40]

His words fell on deaf ears that night, but Horton, who played for the Tigers until 1977, became a symbol of peace and goodwill, and he devoted himself to the city. In 2004, the governor declared his birthday, October 18, to be Willie Horton Day in the state of Michigan.

THIRTEEN

OCTOBER 18, 1963

Eager to host the 1968 Summer Olympic Games, Detroit presents its case to the International Olympic Committee in Baden-Baden, Germany. Despite a personal appeal from President John F. Kennedy and a united front presented by Mayor Jerome Cavanagh and Michigan governor George Romney, Detroit loses out to Mexico City—the eighth time the city fails in its quest to attract the Games.

Detroit rolled up in style. Mayor Cavanagh led the delegation, and he had much to say about Detroit as the quintessentially American city—a kaleidoscope of cultures, ethnicities, and nationalities. Governor Romney emphasized the state's fiscal strengths. They had brought interpreters and fancy equipment, so their speeches were simultaneously translated into French. They screened a film in which President John F. Kennedy himself expressed his enthusiastic support for the Detroit bid, along with images of a broad array of sporting facilities at the city's disposal—Detroit TV broadcast the film that very same evening.[1] The audience in Baden-Baden's palatial Kurhaus was so impressed that it interrupted the presentation with applause no fewer than twelve times—a good sign for the Motor City.

And then it got weird. The Argentinians had gone first, reading their humdrum pitch in French, followed by translators who repeated it in English. Seeing Detroit's elegant presentation, they asked if they might repeat their presentation—using Detroit's equipment! Gracious to a fault, the Detroiters agreed, and naturally, the French and the Mexican delegations requested the same favor. The Michigan team, which never managed to realize that this competition was a cutthroat affair, granted it. France, playing to type, extolled the beauty of Lyon and the world-class skills of its chefs. Finally, the Mexican delegation spent a good deal of its time denying that altitude would be a problem and, rather scandalously, offered to pay board and lodging for any Olympic athletes who wanted to come two weeks early in order to adapt to said "no problem" altitude.

There was a Q&A, and the representatives of the international sports federations proceeded to a vote. The result was as shocking to the Motor City as it was unambiguous: with two votes for Buenos Aires, twelve for Lyon, and fourteen votes for Detroit, the International Olympic Committee (IOC) had awarded the 1968 Olympic Games, with thirty votes, to Mexico City. This was the eighth time Detroit had thrown its hat into the ring, and the eighth time the city was spurned.

The bid's chairman, Fred Matthaei, declared himself to be "surprised, disappointed, shocked." Douglas Roby, a U.S. member of the IOC who was strongly connected to both Detroit and the bid, blamed the decision on anti-American resentment: "I really thought we had it. But I am convinced now the members simply do not think the games should come to the United States, even though they haven't come here since 1932. They think the United States has everything. We are a 'have' nation. This is an era of 'have-nots.'"[2] IOC president Avery Brundage, an American born in Detroit, thought that "Detroit definitely would have picked up support on later ballots"—but there were no later ballots.[3] Mexico lucked out by a single vote. Thirty was exactly the number of votes needed to constitute an outright majority of the fifty-eight IOC members. Had Mexico City received twenty-nine, Buenos Aires would have been eliminated in a new round of votes, and perhaps, just perhaps, Mexico would have just fallen short again, and there would have been a runoff between the two top cities. Who knew which horses could have been traded in that world of topline sports politics?

One vote, then. And that is where it becomes so particularly galling: it appeared quite likely that this single vote that put Mexico City over the line came from a representative of the United States.[4] John Garland was the son of William Garland, responsible for bringing the 1932 Olympic Games to Los Angeles and an IOC member from 1922 until his death in 1948. The younger Garland had "inherited" his father's seat, and by all accounts, he simply detested Detroit. He had a long record of opposing Detroit's Olympic aspirations at every turn, denigrating the city's fitness in none too subtle

public statements.[5] These days, quite sensibly, IOC members from the bidder nation are not allowed to vote precisely because they'd be assumed to
favor their own nation. John Garland's nation, however, appears to have
been Southern California.

You would think Brundage, the native Detroiter, would have reined him
in, but Brundage had been a close friend of the elder Garland, and he held
John in quasi-paternal esteem. By all accounts, every time the Detroit Olympic Committee complained about Garland's malicious shenanigans, Brundage would smile indulgently and tell them not to worry.[6] Brundage, in any
case, was no champion of the city—one of a long line of Detroiters who left
and never looked back.

To be fair, the defeat of Detroit's Olympic aspirations can hardly be laid
just at the feet of John Garland or Avery Brundage. It had been widely
reported earlier in the week that Cold War politics were hampering the
city's chances.[7] After Tokyo 1964, Rome 1960, and Melbourne 1956, it was
certainly the turn of the Americas, but Mexico is part of the Americas too.
Additionally, the Soviet Union controlled a significant bloc of votes supporting Mexico City over the rival superpower. And then there were financial
considerations: surprising as it may seem by today's standards, the athletes
were expected to pay their own room and board, for the Olympics were still
rigidly amateur. Without much doubt, each of the competing cities would
have happily absorbed the expenses involved, but appearances had to be
upheld, and each city had to put a price tag on athlete accommodations:
Detroit had figured $3 per day and got undercut, however minimally, by
Mexico City's charge of $2.80 per day.[8] But more importantly, the founda-
tion of the Non-Aligned Movement—representing countries that sided with
neither the U.S.S.R. nor the U.S., many of which had just emerged from
colonial rule—decided that it was a time for the torch to finally travel to one
of the developing nations.

There were many reasons Detroit lost out that year, then, some of them
good ones. And still, it was a shame, for the 1968 Detroit bid was, by any
objective criteria, a strong one—and honed over decades and decades of
trying. By February of 1963, the Detroit Olympic Committee had established fifteen subcommittees, including Executive, Finance, Accounting,
Athletic Facilities, Catering, Ethnic Group Participation, Housing, Legal,

Medical, Public Relations, and Transportation.[9] They had Cavanagh's and Romney's full support, but they had also enlisted many of the city's big hitters, including Henry Ford II as well as senior executives of all the Detroit auto companies, along with other industrialists, bankers, politicians, lawyers, academics, and press and TV representatives. Al Kaline, the Tigers batter, was on board. Detroit's African American community was less well represented, although the NAACP's Edward Turner served on the Games Programming Committee, and Richard Austin, who would later run for mayor, on the Accounting Committee.[10]

Detroit has always been well endowed with sports facilities that could be used for Olympic events—a fact that remains true today. In 1963, Detroit proposed indoor venues such as Olympia Stadium, the University of Detroit's Memorial Arena, and the Light Guard Armory, and outdoor facilities such as the University of Detroit Stadium, Tiger Stadium, the Brennan Pools, and the University of Michigan's football stadium in Ann Arbor (aka "the Big House"). Belle Isle would provide a fabulous setting for equestrian events; the sailors and the rowers would have the Detroit River and Lake St. Clair for their competitions. Last but not least, there was the riverfront Cobo Arena of Auto Show fame, completed in 1960 as part of the Civic Center, and a fine illustration of Detroit's dynamism.[11]

The bid's slogan was "A City on the Move," and it had only one glaring weakness: Detroit had no Olympic Stadium and would have to build one. But where? The question of site divided opinion, as it would for another decade. The frontrunner was always the State Fairgrounds just off Woodward and Eight Mile, at the northern edge of the city.[12] However, the owner of the Tigers, John Fetzer, had his eye on that site for a future baseball facility. William Clay Ford, on the other hand, right then in the process of acquiring the Lions, favored the Fairgrounds for the Olympic Stadium, as did Cavanagh and Romney, who were working well together despite belonging to different political parties. The city planning department, however, historically a strong voice in the development of the city, was more interested in boosting redevelopment in the downtown riverfront area. Yet a third option under discussion was Wayne State University's stadium in midtown, which could have been enlarged. That alternative had an added advantage: the university could repurpose any newly built Olympic Village facilities as student accommodations. The bickering and the back-and-forth lasted too long for the choice to settle, a lack of resolve that undermined the bid's credibility. The IOC was understandably reluctant to rely on promises of resolutions to come and essential facilities to emerge—who knows, Detroit might have done better in Baden-Baden had they made up their mind and broken ground.

In retrospect, the Olympic bid may also testify to the overreach of white progressives of the 1960s such as Jerome Cavanagh. No doubt, Cavanagh was a force for progress and a strong supporter of civil rights, a stance which earned him solid electoral support from African American voters—more than 30 percent of Detroit's population, at a time when the white flight to the suburbs was well underway. To be sure, there was at least some African American representation on the Olympic committees, and two African Americans accompanied the delegation to Baden-Baden—including Rafer Johnson, a truly inspirational figure who had taken Decathlon gold during the 1960 games.[13] Including a few African Americans in your most visible endeavors, however, does not mean you have taken the temperature of the affected communities when it comes to city politics, and Cavanagh was taken by surprise when the energy and resources devoted to Olympic bid created resentment among a significant portion of African American Detroit. The growing tensions boiled over when Olympic politics and housing politics spectacularly clashed, turning what was meant to be a glorious PR event into a humiliating spectacle.

The publicity stunt had been cleverly conceived: on September 27, they would light a torch in Los Angeles, the site of the last Olympic Games in the United States, and carry it across the country to Detroit, along legendary Route 66. The final torchbearer, Hayes Jones, arrived in Detroit on the evening of the 12th of October, a Saturday. In front of the City-County Building downtown, Cavanagh was waiting to receive the torch in a ceremony meant to create a brilliant photo opportunity, garnering broad public support for the bid. Instead, a significant number of black Detroiters showed up to loudly boo both Cavanagh and Detroit's Common Council, decisively defeating the purpose.[14] Rumor has it that John Garland took not a little delight in informing the IOC of the publicity disaster that had unfolded just six days before the IOC vote.

Cavanagh, furious, called the protesters "rowdy and disgraceful," but they, in turn, saw a bigger disgrace in a Common Council vote that had taken place only four days earlier.[15] One factor that had rendered Detroit one of the most segregated cities in the country were the blatantly discriminatory practices of bankers and real estate agents when it came to home sales and loans. They had instituted a point system for ranking applicants, which was based not just on income but also on occupation and race. A version of blatantly illegal practices known, in aggregate, as "redlining," the point system effectively excluded black Detroiters from white neighborhoods.

Up for a vote at the council was an "open occupancy" ordinance that would have banned such practices. Cavanagh, like Romney, supported the measure and actively campaigned for it, and yet, shockingly, the council, still dominated by white power brokers, voted it down. It wasn't even close: 7 to 2.[16] Who could possibly blame black Detroit for taking institutionalized and blatantly sanctioned racism to be a more urgent concern than yet another bid for the Olympics? A bid that, furthermore, might well lead to more urban renewal (read: black removal) if it were to succeed.

Cavanagh's and Romney's civil rights bona fides were real. At a major conference on "open occupancy" organized the year before, Romney had said that he was "personally convinced that racial, religious and ethnic discrimination is our most serious domestic problem."[17] On coming into office in 1961, having won 85 percent of the black vote, Cavanagh appointed African Americans as city controller, head of the Mayor's Commission on Children and Youth, secretary to the Department of Public Works and, most importantly of all given the history of police misconduct, commissioner of police.[18] The unions, not always a force for racial justice, supported progressive policies at the time, and the most notable expression of that support came from Walter Reuther, the powerful head of the UAW. While race relations in Detroit had a long way to go, under Cavanagh many had come to see the city as a beacon of hope with regard to social justice and integration. Famously, in June 1963, Martin Luther King Jr. himself led the Walk to Freedom along Woodward Avenue, from Adelaide Street to Cobo Hall, culminating in an early version of one of the most stirring speeches in U.S. history, "I Have a Dream." According to estimates, 125,000 citizens marched with Dr. King, among them many of Detroit's politically active religious leaders. Cavanagh and Reuther were there, and Romney, he said, was missing only because his religious beliefs did not allow him to march on a Sunday—but he did send a representative in his place.[19] And just a few years later, Cavanagh would be the only elected politician to serve on President Johnson's "Model Cities" task force, an ambitious but ultimately unsuccessful national endeavor to reimagine urban renewal and fund an array of projects and services (the program was terminated in 1974, after an increasingly conservative America turned against its largest cities).[20]

But in 1963, the optics of racial unity were largely an illusion, in Detroit as elsewhere—the council vote exposed the raw hypocrisy. To be sure, quite a few white residents were committed to increased social and racial justice, and willing to vote for candidates committed to change—but many more were not, and Detroit remained divided, segregated, and troubled. After having been asked to display "patience" for decade after decade, more and more African Americans were tired of the political dictates of the "white moderates" whom MLK excoriates in his famous "Letter from Birmingham Jail."

Detroit in this era was a hotbed of black political thought, much of it supported and developed by a powerful network of churches. King brought the Walk to Freedom to Detroit in no small part because of his admiration for the Reverend C.L. Franklin, pastor of the New Bethel Baptist Church, located less than a mile north of the Olympia Stadium on Linwood Street.[21] Franklin, born in Mississippi in 1915, came to Detroit in the 1940s, where his celebrated lyrical sermons soon attracted a devoted following.[22] In the early 1960s, he founded the Detroit Council for Human Rights (DCHR), aiming to take leadership away from the NAACP, which he perceived to be out of touch with everyday black experience. The Walk to Freedom launched the DCHR to prominence, but its success would be short-lived: a month later, the DCHR's attempt to stage a regional leadership conference floundered when Franklin refused to allow members of more radical black organizations to participate.

One of the most influential of the figures Franklin sought to exclude was Reverend Albert Cleage Jr., mentioned in the previous chapter. Cleage had created his own church just four blocks south of New Bethel on Linwood, which would eventually become the Shrine of the Black Madonna. In the early 1960s, Cleage's ministry was focused on helping the poor while demanding greater recognition of black leadership in the civil rights movement. He scorned the idea that white politicians such as Jerome Cavanagh and Walter Reuther could assume the mantle of leadership in black communities, and he promoted the proliferation of new black political thought— the same kind of thought that would be practiced at a certain speakeasy establishment on Twelfth Street in 1967.

By 1968, when he published *The Black Messiah*, Cleage's philosophy had been transformed into a fully separatist theology focusing on the reinterpretation of the Bible in ways that centered African and African American consciousness, subjectivity, and spirituality. Cleage had split from the DCHR soon after the Walk to Freedom, and in early November, he organized a rival conference that is remembered primarily for another famous speech, this one entitled "A Message to the Grass Roots." The speaker was Malcolm X, who had close ties to Detroit and frequently lectured in the city on the need for revolutionary action, not necessarily of the nonviolent kind. "Who," he asked, "ever heard of a revolution where they lock arms, as Rev. Cleage was pointing out beautifully, and sing 'We Shall Overcome'?"[23]

For these activists, the Olympics were at best a distraction, at worst another plot to preserve the status quo. Over the course of the next few years, historical events would overwhelm all of these actors. In November 1963, President Kennedy was assassinated. In the aftermath of the national grief, Lyndon B. Johnson forced the passage of the Civil Rights Act, which had languished under a Senate filibuster. In 1965, Malcolm X died in a hail of bullets in the Audubon Ballroom in Manhattan, and in April 1968, Martin Luther King Jr. was fatally shot on the balcony of the Lorraine Motel in Memphis, Tennessee. The high hopes that had, for a brief time, united black and white leaders died with them, as segregation continued and police forces across the country found new ways to uphold white power and privilege and to subject black America to its own separate regime of mass incarceration. By comparison, the careers of white liberals such as Cavanagh and Romney were minor casualties.[24]

It may be a frivolous thought experiment to wonder if a successful Olympic bid would have changed the course of Detroit's history. We can be reasonably certain that the construction of an Olympic Stadium and other facilities, even if they had created some jobs for a while, would have done little to address the root causes of poverty and injustice in the city. In fact, if previous urban renewal projects are anything to go by, they are more likely to have added to them. At the same time, one should not entirely discount the psychological effects of a large-scale international event of such prominence and prestige as the Olympics. In addition, there is the simple fact that, for a few years at least, the word "Detroit" would have evoked the Games—a global feel-good affair that could have put Detroit on international maps in a new way. It might just have changed the atmosphere for a while. Then again, it is as likely that any protest such as the ones of 1967 would have been met with even more brutal and crushing force, leading to more rather than less bloodshed—the 1932 Olympics, after all, had done nothing for Watts.

One of the saddest memorials to the failed bid of 1963 can be found in the dusty boxes of the Detroit Olympics Archive in the Detroit Public Library. To build support for the bid, the Detroit Olympic Committee organized a local petition drive, and the bundles of signed petitions have been preserved. There must be tens of thousands of signatures, from schoolkids across the city and from all neighborhoods in metro Detroit. For a moment, then, the Detroit Olympics might have brought the city together, in the same way the Tigers would by winning the World Series in 1968. Everything bad and sad would have re-emerged soon thereafter, there is little doubt. But history is timing, and it is not impossible to think that the bread and circuses of the Olympic Games might have nudged the city away from the conflagration of 1967—who knows with what results?

It is fitting to the memory of Detroit's failed bid that the iconic moment of the 1968 Olympic Games was not a singular athletic feat but two raised fists: the black power salutes of Tommie Smith and John Carlos.

FOURTEEN

DECEMBER 29, 1957

In the championship game, Tobin Rote leads the Detroit Lions to an astonishing 56–10 win over Cleveland, securing the third NFL title in six years for the Motor City. In the same year, Ford launches its most ambitious car, the Ford Edsel, billed as the car of the future. Detroit is at the top of its game. But the Lions will never win another title, and the Edsel—overambitious, overpriced, and under-researched—becomes a symbol of the car industry's miscalculations. The city enters its long economic decline.

"Can These Be OUR Lions?" the incredulous headline asked.[1] Detroit is at its apex, and so is its football team. Fourteen minutes into the first quarter, the lead was 17–0; by the end of the half, it was 31–7. Being accustomed to nail-biters, the crowd of 55,000 at Briggs Stadium was stunned. Detroit hadn't scored more than thirty-one points in an entire game that season (although, by coincidence, they had scored exactly 31 points four times, one of those to lose the game). But this was the championship game, and the opponents were Cleveland, natural rivals. The same team that had humiliated Detroit in the 1954 championship game, 56–10. In their growing exuberance, the Lions even scored a touchdown on a fourth-down trick play, switching from a field goal attempt to a run into the end zone.[2]

The Detroit team didn't let up in the second half, either. After a Cleveland touchdown midway through the third quarter narrowed the score, the Lions got 28 more points, unanswered. The final 59–14 score pleasingly reversed the result of the 1954 debacle, and the Detroit Lions were NFL champions for the third time in six years. The result was all the sweeter for being something of a surprise. The team had started with low expectations and went

8-4 in the regular season, tied with the 49ers at the top of the Western Conference. The required playoff in San Francisco on December 22 didn't start out well: at halftime Detroit was down 24–7. But by the end of the third quarter, the lead had narrowed to six points, and with ten more points and solid defense in the fourth quarter, it was the Lions who scored the conference title and went on to the championship game.

By 1957, viewing the game was no longer reserved exclusively for those in the stadium. The TV had reached almost 80 percent of all U.S. households, up from only 9 percent in 1950. This was a change at least as dramatic as the internet revolution of the 1990s, possibly more so.[3] To be sure, most games still went out to regional markets, with only three games nationally televised—but one of those was Detroit's traditional Thanksgiving game.

And then there was the TV blackout rule—in 1957, games could not be broadcast within seventy-five miles of the home stadium, so the championship games at Briggs Stadium would not be shown in Detroit—officially.[4] Detroiters love their sports, they are inventive, and they're not overly subservient to the rules. Briggs Stadium was sold out, so a lot of them just moved to the suburbs for the day, where TVs could pick up signals from other towers; the out-of-town bars welcomed the increased trade. Others, however, looked for solutions closer to home; one particularly enterprising homeowner in the city rigged up a long lead wire on a tree outside his house to act as an antenna long enough to allow him to catch the signal coming from outside the seventy-five-mile limit. In Wyandotte, fans borrowed chairs from a funeral home and repaired to the garage of a gas station, whose owner had kindly shelled out for a fifty-five-foot antenna.[5]

The shining star of the 1957 team was quarterback Tobin Rote. In the championship game, he threw for 280 yards with four touchdowns and no interceptions. His triumphal performance included one 78-yard pass as well the first rushing touchdown of the day. Rote had been acquired in a trade in the summer of 1957 after a spectacular 1956 season for the Green Bay Packers, when he led the league in passing yards and passing touchdowns and was second in the league in rushing touchdowns. In 1956, his 29 touchdowns had set a new record.

It might seem odd that the Lions traded for a star quarterback that season, since they already had their own: Bobby Layne, the future Hall of

Famer. At the beginning of the season, Layne and Rote alternated, but in the penultimate game of the regular season, Layne broke his leg in three places. Hence it was either because of extraordinary foresight or a pure stroke of luck that the team had someone of Rote's caliber to finish the season.[6]

Bobby Layne, aka The Blond Bomber, was the champion of the team, a larger-than-life Texan. As a college player for the Texas Longhorns, he set several records that stood into the twenty-first century, including accounting for all 40 points in their Cotton Bowl win over Missouri in 1946. He also played baseball in college, as one of the best pitchers in Longhorn history. In 1948, he had been drafted by the Steelers, but the team wasn't to his liking, and after a series of trades, he ended up with the Lions in 1950. Layne led the team to consecutive championships in 1952 and 1953, and would have added a third were it not for that blowout defeat in the championship game of 1954.

In the 1950s, Bobby Layne was not just the face of the Lions, he was the face of the NFL. Notoriously tough, he eschewed the pads and protection other players wore. He ran the team as much as the coach did, taking part in designing plays before games and calling his own plays on the field. He helped to develop several innovations such as the two-minute drill, used to squeeze more plays out at the end of a game.

He was what people call a natural leader—and a hard drinker. Rumor had it that he partied six nights a week and played football on Sundays. He used barroom sessions to forge team cohesion, and under his guidance, the Lions were thought to be the most tight-knit team in the league, on and off the field. Harley Sewell, who played guard for them, recalls that "when I was a rookie, I went with Layne to get a tube of toothpaste, and didn't get back for three days." Layne's competitiveness was legendary, and the team that was shaped around him was the most successful in the history of the Detroit Lions. By the time he retired, he held the league record for total passing yards, total completions, and total touchdown passes.[7]

It wasn't just the Lions. In the 1950s, the city had reached its zenith—on a per capita basis, Detroit was one of the richest big cities in America, making it one of the richest in the world. Its population peaked during that decade, reaching 1.8 million people. Motown Records launched at the end of that decade. But it is also the time when the city entered its economic decline—slowly at first, then rapidly. If there is a single symbol of what went wrong, it might be the Edsel, a car Ford Motor Company launched at the beginning of the 1957 football season.[8] Named in memory of Henry Ford's beloved son, the Edsel had been under development since 1955. It was meant to take a mid-market position, somewhere between models such as the Galaxie, in the price range of $2,000–$2,500 (for reference, the median income of a woman in full-time employment in the United States in 1955 was $2,100), and the Lincoln, which started at around $4,500 (the median income of a man in full-time employment in the U.S. in 1955 was $3,900).[9]

Edsel Ford had worked closely with his father on the development of the company from the 1920s, and he was largely responsible for the company's conversion into wartime production, which would prove so essential to the Allied victory. In 1943, at the age of forty-nine, he had suddenly died of cancer. Edsel's sons, Henry II and William Clay, took leadership positions in the company, but the move to commemorate Edsel by naming the new car after him may have been connected to the broadening ownership as well. In 1956, following a stock flotation, the family had given up overall control of the Ford Motor Company. Even if they no longer owned the whole company, however, they still wanted its products to represent the family and its values. Edsel's two sons were divided on the issue: Henry II loved the idea, but Bill, who pointed out that cars named after people did not have a good track record, hated it.[10] Henry won out.

The Edsel included several innovative features, such as a push-button transmission located on the steering wheel. The styling included a distinctive vertical grille as well as features that were, allegedly, created in response to extensive market research. And yet, the Edsel is remembered as a historic failure, "ugly, overpriced, overhyped, poorly made and poorly timed."[11] In the end, the hype might have been the biggest mistake. Ford had teased the release for a year—"E-Day" was meant to reveal nothing less than the car of the future. But the Edsel didn't live up to the expectations the company had unwisely created—not nearly impressive enough to earn its advance laurels, the car turned out to be unreliable as well. Ford usually built its models in a dedicated plant, but the Edsel was produced across a range of them. As a consequence, the assembly lines never got used to the construction, and errors were frequent. The car of the future was a lemon.[12]

At the time, your car was the dominant means to signal your social status, and if you were moving up in the world, you needed your ride to show that. The Edsel—relatively expensive both to own and to maintain—competed with Ford's other mid-market brand name, the lower-priced Mercury range, which possessed broadly similar features. It did not convey the kind of prestige that would have justified its price. When even the most intense marketing failed to produce sales, it turned out that the vaunted market research either had not delivered or had not been heeded. As soon as Ford realized that consumers weren't going to take to the Edsel, Robert McNamara, who had rapidly risen to senior executive positions in the company, took action to kill the thing, and it disappeared in 1960.[13]

Today, the Edsel is often associated with an excess of style over substance. The name conjures up an era of tailfins and engines far more powerful than they needed to be. In fact, it was in many ways representative of the types of car produced in Detroit during these years, and many of its rivals, such as those made by DeSoto and Oldsmobile, looked similar and sold well. Detroit still dominated the production of cars globally, and its companies held a full 95 percent of the domestic market. The industry, in which there had been roughly twenty significant producers ten years earlier, was gradually consolidating into what would become the Big Three: Ford, General Motors, and Chrysler. Over the years, the car companies had learned that it was more profitable to compete on style rather than on price, as the car was transformed from simply an efficient means of transport to a lifestyle statement. Above all, they emphasized speed, comfort, and looks, with powerful engines and plush interiors. To a certain extent, they were quite the success—the cars of this era remain recognizable today as some of the most stylish ones ever produced, and it's hard not to smile when you encounter one on the road.

In the 1970s, James Flink would argue that there were three eras of "American automobile consciousness." During the first, people became used to the idea of owning a car; during the second, lasting from 1920 through the 1950s, Americans idolized them. In the third era, however, starting at the end of the 1950s, the public imagination slowly began to see the car less as a progressive force than a social problem, related to safety concerns, worries about the environment, and the impact on urban life—such as the demise of public transportation, the compromised safety of pedestrians and children playing in the streets, pollution.[14] The Edsel arrived just as attitudes were changing.

Nonetheless, in the 1950s, Detroit was still booming. As the car companies shifted from wartime production back to peacetime manufacture, car output rose from just over 2 million in 1946 to over 7 million 1955. No wonder there was confidence in the future and a willingness to innovate. The optimism has also infected city planning, which had identified significant gaps to fill. Detroit had grown in higgledy-piggledy fashion as the car industry developed between 1900 and 1930, while the challenges of the Great Depression and wartime production in the 1930s and 1940s had not done much to beautify the city. Housing, in particular, was a tremendous problem for the city's workers, whether they had arrived at the end of the nineteenth century or during any other wave of migration and immigration. City planners got ambitious: they wanted to improve the quality of housing, rationalize the zoning of districts, and create an urban space that would be both practical and comfortable.[15] In the background of these laudable aims lurked a long-standing policy of racial zoning that had squeezed almost the entire black population of the city into the Black Bottom area, located on the downtown's east side.

Despite appalling housing conditions, Black Bottom was a thriving neighborhood, bordering on Paradise Valley, the legendary entertainment district celebrated for its music and notorious for its vice: there you could catch performances by Duke Ellington and Count Basie, Billie Holiday, Sarah Vaughan, Charlie Parker, and Miles Davis.

Widely sanctioned and ruthlessly enforced, housing segregation ensured that there were not many other places to go if you were black; the shortage in public housing was acute, and worse for African Americans. As Thomas Sugrue notes, during the war, 14,446 black Detroiters had applied for public housing; 1,731 found a place. The situation didn't improve after the war ended: between 1947 and 1952, 37,383 black families and 56,758 white families sought public housing—the city could accommodate 41 percent of the white families, and a bare 24 percent of the black ones.[16] The slum landlords knew the black population had few alternatives, enabling them to charge monopoly rents well above those a white person would pay for an equivalent property. In the wake of the New Deal, pretty much everybody agreed that any policy of urban renewal had to improve the quality of housing, and in the 1940s, representatives of the African American community had supported the relevant initiatives. But it soon transpired, rather shockingly, that while Black Bottom would indeed be razed, the site would not be used to build integrated public or affordable housing. Rather, Black Bottom would be replaced with upscale housing units, under the aegis of private enterprise. And there would be a highway, of course.

In January 1946, Mayor Edward Jeffries's housing commission asked the city's Common Council to condemn the crowded neighborhood. Market ideology won out, and Black Bottom was losing the peace. In April of that year, Jeffries suggested that "this area be acquired by the city and completely cleared of all buildings thereon, that the area then be re-planned, with the object in mind of disposing of as much as possible to private enterprise for redevelopment for housing and incidental commercial purposes after providing sufficient space for parks, playgrounds, schools and other public uses."[17]

In the early 1950s, using funding provided by the Federal Housing Act, the destruction of Black Bottom began, and black families were driven out of the area—it would be one of the first neighborhoods razed in the name of mid-century urban renewal whose cost would be borne by the poor. Unsurprisingly, the African American community came to despise the process and the ideology that displaced so many families.[18] Using census data to map demographic data, you can see how dramatic a shift it was: a 1950 graphic shows a strong concentration of African American Detroiters in the east-central areas, bordering downtown. Just ten years later, most of the area is white, and black Detroit has been pushed northeast.

The result is still evident: in some regards, Lafayette Park stands as one of the finest pieces of urban redevelopment in the United States, with stylish townhouses, apartment buildings, and green spaces representing an oasis near the city's center. The redevelopment was designed by Ludwig Mies van der Rohe, a leader of the Bauhaus movement and one of the most influential architects of the twentieth century. Mayor Albert Cobo, who oversaw the plans, led the city from 1950 to 1957; his election had depended significantly on his commitment to maintaining segregated housing in Detroit, and he also made sure that the city would invest little in the construction of public housing.[19] According to 1970s census figures, Lafayette Park, built on the grounds of Black Bottom, was 70 percent white. The Burton Historical Collection, part of the Detroit Public Library, holds more than two thousand photographs of the vanished neighborhood, and in 2019, Emily Kutil curated a stunning exhibition titled "Black Bottom Street View" that allowed visitors to walk past these photos to get a house-by-house view what was now a spectral neighborhood.[20]

It is important to keep in mind that the 1950s, often idealized as America's golden age, were not golden for everybody, and sports were no exception. In the South, of course, Jim Crow still reigned, but the North had found its own, no less effective roads to segregation. The Lions saw the systems clash after they signed their first black player in 1948: Bob Mann. Mann, whom they later traded for Bobby Layne, was soon joined by Mel Groomes and Wally Triplett. The integration of the major leagues was there to stay, but the transitional years were rough. Mann was from Virginia, and he had played football at the University of Michigan in Ann Arbor, one of only two African Americans playing for the Wolverines at that time. Back then, Michigan still dominated college football, and in the 1948 Rose Bowl, Mann's team thrashed the University of Southern California, 49–0. The Lions had been poor in 1948 and were actually not much better in 1949, but Mann had an excellent first season with the team, leading the NFL with over 1,000 yards receiving. Mann was thus a valuable player—but not valuable enough for the coach to stick his neck out. At one point, when the Lions were to play an exhibition game against the Philadelphia Eagles in New Orleans—a city that, like most Southern cities, strictly enforced segregation—Mann asked his coach, Bo McMillin, to stand up for the black players, and to let them play against their segregationist opponents. McMillin refused, telling the players they couldn't stay with the white teammates at the hotel, and during the game offered them a place on the bench. Decades later, in 2005, Mann would recall this incident with bitterness: "I said if I can't play in the game I don't want to sit on the bench. . . . Bo could've ended all that. He was supposed to be Mr. Great Liberal. But he didn't do it. He just passed it by. He could've been a big guy, a big fellow, but he didn't do it. I've never forgotten that. Don't tell me how liberal Bo was; he wasn't. He had a chance to be a hero, step up to the plate, but he didn't do it."[21]

Adding insult to injury, the team asked Mann to take a pay cut at the end of the season. He turned them down and moved to the Green Bay Packers; the Lions then traded for Layne.[22]

It was only a year before Bob Mann joined the Lions that Jackie Robinson had broken the color barrier in baseball when he signed with the Brooklyn Dodgers. Over the following decade, more and more baseball teams integrated, but by 1957, the Detroit Tigers stood out, along with the Boston Red Sox, as one of the two teams that had remained all-white. This was almost certainly a result of the policies of Walter Briggs, who was the sole owner of the Tigers from 1935 to his death in 1952. Briggs was devoted to the Detroit Tigers, but, certainly in the eyes of contemporary African Americans, he was also a stone-cold racist—and at the time it showed in his managing of the ball club.[23] Briggs had started his working life as a laborer in the railyards of Detroit in the 1870s, and became an upholsterer of railway carriages. His experience transferred to the newly developing automobile industry of the 1900s, and he ended up running his own firm. In close collaboration with Ford, he became one of the largest builder of auto bodies in Detroit. His factories were known for their dangerous conditions and low wages, and Briggs was famous for his fierce opposition to unionization. He did employ African Americans, just as he was prepared to rent out his stadium to teams from the Negro Leagues in the 1920s and 1930s, but he was less receptive to African Americans attending Tigers Games and certainly to African Americans actually playing for the club. It wasn't until August 1953, a year and a half after Briggs died, that the club hired the first African American to its minor league affiliate, and not until July 1958 that Ozzie Virgil, a player from the Dominican Republic, became the first black player to represent the Tigers.[24]

1958 turned out to be a terrible year for the Detroit auto industry. The failure of the Edsel was mirrored in poor sales of new cars, particularly in the mid-price ranges. Since the 1940s, cars had become wider and longer in order to provide more comfort, while more aerodynamic designs also made them lower. Cost-conscious consumers were more interested in low-cost, entry-level cars. The Detroit companies found themselves unable to build such cars at a significantly lower price than the mid-range cars, and they gambled on the assumption that, given the sheer size of the country and the distances people traveled, there would always be a demand for spacious, comfortable rides. From the mid-1950s on, however, Detroit started to face competition from companies who built exclusively for shorter-distance markets and urban conditions, where smaller size was a real advantage on narrow streets. In 1958, the Volkswagen Beetle became one of the best-selling cars in the United States. Imported cars rose from around 3 percent of the U.S. market in 1957 to over 10 percent by 1959.[25]

Car production in Detroit fell to just under 4.2 million in 1958, down by more than 2 million from the previous year. The decline in sales was enough to trigger a recession in the U.S. economy as a whole, which shrank by 0.7 percent, causing a sharp rise in layoffs and unemployment. It was a warning to the industry, but the economy rebounded in 1959, and Detroit recovered much of its market share by the early 1960s. The respite would prove temporary, and foreign competition would soon return to torment the automakers.

1958 was also the year the Lions lost Bobby Layne—traded to the Pittsburgh Steelers, the team he had sought to avoid joining years earlier. The Lions coach confessed that the system of having two star quarterbacks was impractical, and he decided to go with Rote. The next couple seasons were not kind, and Rote was unable to prop up an aging team; he in turn was released at the end of the 1959 season. By the same token, Layne did not go on to win any championships with Pittsburgh. Joe Schmidt, a linebacker who played alongside Layne for the Lions and went on to coach the team from 1967 to 72, would later claim that "to this day I believe we would have won three more championships if Layne hadn't been traded."[26]

As the years of failure would mount, the legend of the curse of Bobby Layne grew. Reports that he cursed the Lions so that they would not win a championship for fifty years are probably unfounded.[27] Then again, Detroit has been waiting for another title ever since.

FIFTEEN

APRIL 15, 1952

*The Red Wings win the Stanley Cup, the first team ever to achieve
a clean sweep of the postseason. The team is dominated by the core
group of players known as "The Production Line," but sputters to
a halt when the team trades Ted Lindsay in retaliation for his efforts
to establish a players union. Since Detroit is one of America's preeminent union towns, the defeat is particularly bitter.*

It was the opening day of the baseball season, and the *Detroit Free Press*
devoted an entire page to the Tigers' prospects. Tucked away on the following page was a small story about game 4 of the Stanley Cup, to be played
that evening at Olympia. The hockey match turned out to be the more memorable event by far. Metro Prystai, a Canadian with Ukrainian ancestry,
scored the first goal after six minutes and fifty seconds. Glen Skov, a Canadian of Danish ancestry, scored again in the second period, and Prystai
completed the win with a third goal in the third period. The Red Wings had
swept the Montreal Canadiens, winning all four games. Having done the
same to the Toronto Maple Leafs in the semifinals, the Red Wings became
the first team to sweep the postseason, a feat only ever repeated by the Montreal Canadiens in 1960.[1]

Hockey is played by teams of six players, one goaltender, two defense-
men, and three forwards. The three forwards, playing at center, left wing,
and right wing, form "the line," and the Red Wings' most famous one consisted of Sid Abel at center, Ted Lindsay on the left, and Gordie Howe on the
right. In an homage to Detroit's industrial identity, the three, who had started to play together in 1947–48, were christened "The Production Line," and
even though they did not score in game 4—the team rotated through three

different lines—no one doubted that those three were the source of the Red Wings' dominance.[2]

Sid Abel was the team captain, though Lindsay was the guy who made it his business to keep the team together. Gordie Howe was the star and, without a doubt, the greatest Red Wings player in history. His name is big enough for major infrastructure: the new bridge to Canada, paid for entirely by the Canadian government, will be called the "Gordie Howe International Bridge." Construction began in 2018, and the bridge will lead to Canada from the spot where the River Rouge empties into the Detroit River, about five miles from the downtown on I-75. It will compete with the Ambassador Bridge a couple of miles upstream, completed in 1929 when Gordie Howe was one year old.

Howe was born near Saskatoon, Saskatchewan, a small city about 1,600 miles northwest of Detroit. Set up by teetotalers trying the escape the liquor trade, it was a struggling community that depended largely on the quality of the harvest in any given year. Howe grew up in a poor family, and his early life was not easy. But in a world where every kid played hockey, his extraordinary talent stood out—and he was ambidextrous. Roy MacSkimming, to whose account of Howe's life much of this chapter is indebted, says that the scouts came to watch Howe when he was still a kid.[3]

In 1943, the New York Rangers invited him to their training camp, but he didn't think the team was right for him—advantage Red Wings, who persuaded him to sign at their own camp in Windsor the next year. He put in one season for the Omaha Knights farm team before he debuted in Detroit in 1946. In the early days, having forgotten to arrange for a place to stay, he slept on the benches at Olympia, along with a number of other players. He didn't find it all that uncomfortable, he'd later recall, but he did mind the rats scurrying up close to borrow some body warmth. In retaliation, they would use any rat they could catch for pucks in pick-up games.[4]

He soon started to break records—between 1950–51 and 1954–55, he led the league in scoring, and even though that was an era of relatively low scores in the NHL, he still ranks as one of the most prolific players in history. But he didn't just score—he was just as happy to create assists so his teammates could share in the glory, and unlike many goal scorers, he was a fighter to boot.

Violence, often of a quite spectacular nature, has always been part and parcel of hockey, especially Canadian hockey, and Gordie Howe was happy to mix it up. The fans coined the idea of a "Gordie Howe hat trick"—a goal, an assist, and a fight.[5] In 1950, one of those brawls almost cost him his life: seeking to hit another player on the boards, he instead collided with a railing, fracturing his nose and cheekbone and lacerating his eyeball, which caused him to hemorrhage from the brain. The surgeon saved his life by drilling a hole in his skull to release the fluid.[6]

Those injuries happened in game 1 of the Stanley Cup semifinals in March 1950. Even without Howe, Detroit went on to beat the Toronto Maple Leafs four games to three; more spectacularly, the finals saw them come back from 3–0 down to win the cup 4–3, with the last two games played at Olympia. This was the team's fourth Stanley Cup victory in twenty-four years.[7] After recovering from his near-death experience, Howe was in the starting lineup in the first game of the following season, on October 11.[8] The Red Wings would go on to win four more Stanley Cups in the next six seasons, with Gordie Howe leading the team in scoring.[9]

In those years, the Production Line truly came into its own. In the early years, Howe and Lindsay were the rookies, and it was the experienced Abel who had held things together. In 1950–51, the team led the league in regular-season points but fell to Montreal in the semifinal of the Stanley Cup. In 1951–52, the Red Wings closed the regular season on top again and then finished the job to win their fifth Stanley Cup.

That summer, Sid Abel was traded to the Chicago Black Hawks, but by the 1952–53 season, Alex Delvecchio had taken his place on the Production Line, where he would play for another twenty-three years. Those who were there during those golden years often attributed their success to the team's extraordinary cohesion. Many of them roomed together at boarding houses close to Olympia. Between 1930 and the end of the 1950s, Minnie "Ma" Shaw ran one of the most famous of those, and it's estimated that 175 Red Wings lived at Ma Shaw's at one time or another, including Gordie Howe and Ted Lindsay.[10] When not practicing, the players hung out together in the evenings, catching movies, drinking, and even attending ballroom dances. On Monday evenings, the team rented out an entire Italian restaurant, so they could bond in peace. MacSkimming sums it up thus: "Living together at home as well as on the road, they bonded by doing practically everything together, from playing cards and drinking beer to dating women and worshipping God."[11] It's always hard to judge whether cohesive teams lead to success of whether success leads to cohesive teams, but the 1950s Red Wings clearly excelled on both fronts. Ted Lindsay was at the heart of those bonds, and his relationship with Gordie Howe was particularly strong. After they left Ma Shaw's, they bought a house together and formally agreed to share bonuses—each believing that his game was crucially enhanced by the other.

After the back-to-back Stanley Cup wins in 53–54 and 54–55, nobody could have imagined that the Cup would not be theirs again for almost half a century. The team did not collapse immediately, but in retrospect, the 1956–57 season was something of a swan song. In the semifinals at the end of March, the Bruins eliminated the Red Wings in five games. It was to be Ted Lindsay's last series for Detroit.

During that winter, Lindsay had started to take an interest in player pensions—the league ran the pension scheme in such a secretive fashion that the players themselves could not get any details on it. Lindsay, sensibly, wanted more information, and moreover, he planned to establish a players' association that would represent the players in this and other matters, such as standard contract negotiation. Other sports had paved the way: the Major League Baseball Players Association (MLBPA) had been formed in 1953, the National Basketball Players Association in 1954, and in 1957, the NFL players were beginning the process of starting theirs. Lindsay sought advice from the lawyers representing the MLBPA, and in February of 1957, he announced not only that the players would form the National Hockey League Players' Association (NHLPA) but that all but one of the 112 players in the NHL had agreed to join. Well aware of the distrust of "unionism" among both owners and significant numbers of players, the association, Lindsay said, would not seek conflict with the owners but partner with them. They were not a "trade union," he stressed, and their goal was not to negotiate individual salaries—the focus would be on general issues of shared interest.[12]

His carefully conciliatory approach did not save him from the owners' wrath. This was the era of McCarthyism, and some owners quickly started wondering aloud if they had communists in their midst—a most convenient storyline at the time. Jack Adams, the Red Wings' general manager, confronted the team and demanded that they denounce the Association. He smeared Lindsay to journalists, describing him as "a cancer" and "the ruination of the team."[13] It may beggar belief that in 1950s Detroit, of all places, you could disparage what was not even a full-fledged union in those terms, but by summer, Lindsay had been traded to the Black Hawks.

The owners refused to recognize the Association, and in September, the NHLPA filed a grievance against the NHL with the National Labor Relations Board (NLRB), for unfair labor practices. However, once Lindsay, the driving force behind the endeavor, had left Detroit, Adams managed to persuade the remaining Red Wings players to withdraw from the Association. The Montreal players soon followed suit. The owners agreed to meet with player representatives at the NHL winter meetings in Palm Beach, Florida, but, crucially, they insisted that there could be no lawyers present. After thirteen hours of talks, Lindsay and the players agreed to dissolve the Association in exchange for some minor concessions by the owners. They agreed to set up an owner-player council to hear grievances, but its findings were not binding upon the owners. It was a bitter defeat.

It would take the players another decade of watching the experience of the other professional leagues to fully grasp the benefits of a players' union and to revive the NHLPA. Collective bargaining would pay off: when Lindsay had first tried to organize them, the players were paid about 37 percent of the revenues generated by the league. By the end of the millennium, the figure was 57 percent, largely thanks to collective bargaining.[14] Suffice it to say that unionization did not, in fact, destroy the NHL, as the owners, like bosses everywhere, had proclaimed it would.

It should not have taken this long—Detroit had been a union town since the 1930s, a victory won in bloody battles, some of which we will describe in chapter 21. Although, by now, most of the union jobs had since left the city, Detroit's allegiance to unions, which was instrumental in creating the American middle class, was still going strong. This is the city where an eighteen-year-old Jimmy Hoffa organized a strike on the loading docks of a food warehouse, starting a career that would catapult him to the presidency of the Teamsters—and would get him killed. It's the city of Walter Reuther, whose organization forced the car industry to accept the UAW—they called him "the most dangerous man in Detroit" in turn. It is hardly surprising, then, that the idea of the NHLPA was born in Detroit—but it stings that it was defeated there at first. In a way, the NHL owners' victory foreshadowed future defeats: today, the narrative that unions are ruinous for business, a narrative always popular with owners of teams and of factories, has taken hold across the country.

The 1950s were a turbulent decade in Detroit labor politics. The Great Migration had brought large numbers of black workers and their families from the South over the previous four decades, and the city, while still predominantly white, had become a biracial metropolis. In the 1950 census, African Americans counted for 16 percent of the population—by 1960, the number had reached 29 percent. Heather Thompson points out that "as a result of this massive migration, African Americans fundamentally altered the city's geography, dramatically recomposed its working class, and unwittingly unsettled both the civic and labor order." The city had taken a turn to the political right after the war, and in the UAW a rift between left-liberal forces and a reformist center had opened up—in part driven by the African American workers' demand for greater representation and power.[15] The memory of the horrific 1943 riot was still alive; Detroit was bursting at the seams, leading to severe housing shortages; and conflicts between various political factions were common. The commitment to unions ran strong, but not everybody agreed that black workers were entitled to equal protection. A 1951 survey found that a mere 18 percent of CIO members in Detroit were "in favor of full racial equality," with 65 percent opposed.[16] Those numbers, shocking as they are, were still better than those in the AFL and other unions, where 8 percent favored full equality, with 58 percent opposed—figures suggesting, perhaps, that the CIO members were more polarized and had a stronger civil rights wing than other unions. As the author of the survey notes, these results came after the unions, at least officially, had persistently opposed discrimination and had protected black workers from retaliation.

While many Americans now associate the protests of the 1950s and 1960s with the deep South, the North looked just as grim. In the South segregation was supported by the law; in the North it was simply the everyday reality. As Detroiter Clyde Cleveland would later recall, "The North was just as segregated as the South when I was growing up, particularly in terms of housing. . . . The experiences that I had of not being served at a restaurant were not in Georgia or Alabama or Mississippi—they were right here in the City of Detroit."[17] The abysmal relationship between the police and the community added further tensions. Yet despite all this, the Detroit civil rights movement made important strides in the 1950s, often side by side with the unions.

While union membership may have had a long way to go to accept integration, union leadership was largely supportive, though its efforts at times tended to be lukewarm. David M. Lewis-Colman notes that in 1952, the UAW "launched a bold-sounding 'four-pronged attack on discrimination at the hiring gate' in Detroit and Michigan." Reuther and his men, however, refused to frame those demands in terms of racial equity, and black civil rights leaders were underwhelmed with the effort—even if it led to some positive results. At the same time, the UAW had not managed to force the Big Three to include its model non-discrimination clause in all contracts. Lewis-Colman writes, "The union took a cautious and conciliatory approach to bargaining with the Big Three and resisted attempts by black workers to launch a more vigorous campaign to secure a non-discrimination clause." Nonetheless, the union did lobby for fair employment legislation throughout the 1950s, worked closely with the NAACP, and managed to see fair practice laws enacted in twelve states, including Michigan.[18] While their commitment, under Reuther's centrist leadership, may have struck black civil rights leaders as lacking, the unions' partnership with the civil rights movement, even if uneasy at times, is certain to have contributed to the anti-union sentiment that doomed the players' union.

Gordie Howe will get his bridge, but Ted Lindsay, the failed unionizer, has been largely forgotten, along with the rest of the Production Line and the fabulously successful team of the 1950s. Today, only sports historians, statisticians, and the most committed Red Wings fans remember them, and they have left few traces. Olympia is long gone, without even a plaque to commemorate the site, and most of the players have passed away. Nonetheless, one Red Wings ritual remains: in the final game of the 1952 Stanley Cup, when the team had thoroughly vanquished the Canadiens, Pete and Jerry Cusimano, brothers and storeowners in Detroit's Eastern Market, hurled an octopus onto the ice, its eight arms symbolizing the number of victories required to win the Stanley Cup. To this day, during each home game of the playoffs, at least one octopus, and as many as thirty-six, will sail through the air to commemorate the glory and inspire its return.

SIXTEEN

OCTOBER 26, 1951

Joe Louis's last fight. The champion bows out with a defeat, but his legacy will endure. The longest-reigning heavyweight champion, known as both "the Brown Bomber" and "the black Moses," and Detroit's most famous athlete, Louis shouldered the heavy burden of representing the African American community. During World War II he gave tireless support to the U.S. war effort and used whatever influence he had to combat discrimination in the armed services—while frequently being its target himself.

"Louis, greatest ring idol of our generation, apparently came to the end of the comeback trail as he lay on his back with his head sticking out over the working press seats," the *Detroit Free Press* reported. "He shook his bruised face from side to side and blinked again and again. He tried vainly to bend up and get his legs off the rope so he could rise."[1] But he could not, and so ended the boxing career of Detroit's Joe Louis, the greatest heavyweight champion of them all, at the fists of Rocky Marciano, who would in the following year take the heavyweight title himself and become the only heavyweight champion to retire undefeated.

When Joe Louis died in 1982, the entire city of Detroit mourned. In a pure coincidence, the Detroit chapter of the NAACP held its "Fight for Freedom" dinner at Cobo Hall that night, where Governor William Milliken declared that Joe Louis "symbolized greatness, especially for Detroit and especially for Michigan." Mayor Coleman Young, who grew up in the same neighborhood, reminisced about the time Joe beat him out of a job on a horse-drawn ice-wagon. U.S. senator Don Riegle added, "I think Joe Louis symbolized the whole struggle of black people in our society."[2] Today, the giant sculpture of his powerful black fist, Robert Graham's four-ton *Monument to Joe Louis*, is easily the most recognizable symbol of the city.

Just moments before it was all over, Louis had gotten up one last time. A left hook to the chin had taken him down, but "like a big cat he rolled over immediately and took a count of eight on one knee." He got up only to take hook after hook until the final right "landed on the Bomber's bruised and puffed left cheek," and that was it.[3] The conclusions of many, maybe most, great boxers' careers have followed this course: first retirement (which, in Joe Louis's case, happened in 1949), an ill-advised comeback (1950), some defeats, some wins against opponents they would not have considered worthy a few years earlier, then the final knockout.

What was unusual about Joe Louis's career was not its end, but what it had all meant. When he left the ring for good, his status surpassed that of any boxer who had come before him. Not only did he hold the championship for twelve years, longer than any heavyweight before or since, he had become a national icon, "the first universally embraced black American hero."[4] To many black Americans, he was a source of pride and of a heightened sense of self-worth; to many white Americans, particularly during the war years, he was both a great boxer and a patriot, allowing them to imagine themselves color-blind. "Under the stress of a national emergency, for a brief period," Howard Bryant writes, "Joe Louis succeeded in erasing the color line."[5] For a while, then, he came to embody the height of what it could mean to be a black American—propelled in part by the political and economic forces that would ultimately lead to the achievements of the civil rights era.

Joe Louis might have been the first great athlete who fully shouldered the responsibility to represent "his race," a burden never placed on white athletes. "Musicians were never proof that America was fair, because Lena Horne and John Coltrane didn't have a scoreboard, a final buzzer that told you coldly and definitively if you won," Bryant writes with regard to black ballplayers. "America liked that. Ballplayers were the Ones Who Made It. And being the Ones Who Made It soon came with the responsibility to speak for the people who had not made it, for whom the road was still blocked. The responsibility became a tradition so ingrained that it hung over every player."[6] Joe Louis, who inaugurated that tradition, was fully aware of its implications and yet accepted it with clear eyes and few illusions. To Sugar

Ray Leonard, the undisputed welterweight champion, he was simply "the perfect example of the perfect man,"[7] and to those who called him "a credit to his race," sportswriter Jimmy Cannon responded that he was a credit "to the human race."[8]

To appreciate the extraordinary developments that made Joe Louis, in his friend Frank Sinatra's words, the man who exemplified "our national character and the ideals that motivate us," we need to go back in time: to 1940, when Louis had already been champion for three years, and further back to 1908, when Jack Johnson became the first black world heavyweight champion.[9] At the beginning of the twentieth century, most white boxers simply refused to fight black boxers for championship titles—certainly one way to avoid defeat. But Tommy Burns, a Canadian who lived in Detroit and won the title in 1906, had a different take on these matters, and he agreed to fight Johnson in Sydney, Australia, in 1908. To the dismay of white America, Johnson won and would go on to defend the title against a series of white challengers—a procession to which we owe the coinage of "the great white hope."

Johnson was an outrage to white supremacist society not simply because he defeated white fighters but because he openly dated and married white women—at a time when black men could die for just looking at one. He was charged twice for violating the Mann Act, a federal law that made it a felony to transport across state lines "any woman or girl for the purpose of prostitution or debauchery, or for any other immoral purpose." The first woman he had allegedly "trafficked" was Lucille Cameron, his second wife—she refused to testify against him, and the case fell apart. He wasn't so lucky the second time around, just a month later. Even though his affair with Belle Schreiber pre-dated the Mann Act, he was convicted by an all-white jury and sentenced to a year and a day in prison after she testified against him. Incidentally, the judge who presided over the trial was Kenesaw Mountain Landis, the future commissioner of baseball who would make it his business to enforce the color line until the day he died.

Johnson skipped bail and, together with Cameron, he fled the country—first to Canada, then to Europe, South America, and Mexico. But the celebrity-exile life eventually got old, and in 1920, he surrendered at the Mexican border to serve his sentence. Johnson died in 1946; in 2018, he was posthumously pardoned by President Trump, apparently at the prompting of Sylvester Stallone, whose eponymous hero in the *Rocky* franchise bore some resemblance to Rocky Marciano, the boxer who ended Joe Louis's career.[10]

Johnson's preference for white women and his general refusal to conform to the moral standards of the day had certainly not endeared him to the white population, but he was not particularly popular with much of the black one, either. Hence, when Louis emerged as the leading black boxer of the 1930s, his trainer and manager set out to craft a very different image, one designed to prove that Louis was nothing like Johnson.[11] Not that this was a difficult task: Louis was a quiet-spoken, restrained man, fond of some affectations that would not have sounded out of place in an English country gentleman—for most of his career, for instance, he and his trainer referred to each other as "chappie." Fond of fine clothes and attractive women, he quickly became a hero to the African American population—in no small part the result of his sovereign victory over the German boxer Max Schmeling in 1938, a fight so crucial to the history of sports and race that we have devoted its own chapter to it (chapter 20).

During the years of the Great Depression, when the economic collapse intensified the hardships of Jim Crow and Northern segregation alike, African Americans were in dire need of a champion. Joe Louis fought his first professional fight in 1934, and his name turns up over and over again in blues songs of the era: in 2001, the *New York Times* declared that, in fact, "Only One Athlete Has Ever Inspired This Many Songs."[12] One heartbreaking story describes a black prisoner being led to the gas chamber in a Southern state, crying out, as he dies, "Save me, Joe Louis! Save me!"[13] The novelist Richard Wright writes: "From the symbol of Joe's strength they took strength, and in that moment all fear, all obstacles were wiped out."[14] In 1941, Joe Louis appeared on the cover of *Time* magazine, which tried to explain his significance to a white audience: "He was a living legend to his people: a black Moses leading the children of Ham out of bondage."[15] In the 1940 general election, both the Republican candidate, Wendell Willkie, and the Democratic candidate, Franklin Roosevelt, courted Joe Louis's support to win over the black vote. Louis was persuaded to stump for the Republican, in part because of Willkie's support for civil rights.[16]

Since he had won the title in 1937, white attitudes to Louis had gradually changed—the careful marketing, which included rules such as "never be photographed next to a white woman," was paying off: "Only the soft-spoken and polite Louis, whose black managers drilled into him the importance of appearing even more polite, unthreatening and self-effacing than he naturally was, could have pulled it off. Louis thus became the only black man in America licensed to slug a white man and get rich doing it," the *New York Times* wrote.[17]

As a heavyweight champion, he was clearly a powerful figure, but unlike Johnson, he did not openly mock racialized societal rules and expectations, and thus defied the pervasive stereotypes that declared black men to be either submissive fools or dangerous savages. While cartoons and caricatures of their days portrayed Louis and Johnson in similar racist ways, Louis's demeanor and his steady rise as a supremely gifted athlete chipped away at the narrative about black boxers that had been established around Johnson.[18] To be sure, plenty of whites watched Louis's ascent with worry and suspicion. Along with his many admirers, Father Charles Coughlin, Detroit's notorious anti-Semitic and white supremacist radio host, was ecstatic when Louis lost his first fight to Max Schmeling, in 1936, the German boxer who was the darling of Hitler and the Nazis. Coughlin declared the outcome a "wonder, appealing to all."[19] But the tide was slowly turning, and more and more people embraced Louis as an American champion.

Louis himself took his position as "the black Moses" very seriously: "If I ever do anything to disgrace my race, I hope to die," he declared, and he worked hard throughout his life to oppose the very racism that had forced him into his role.[20] In 1941, while lobbying for increased funding for work on race relations, he told Roosevelt that "the hardest fight I ever had was against prejudice and discrimination." His activism was not only a matter of principle, but also a concrete fight to improve the material conditions of millions of black Americans living in a state of poverty made more abject by discrimination: "We were protesting the rats and the rat bites that the babies got because the houses were so rundown and the landlords wouldn't make repairs. You know, I was a grown man, but I'd get tears in my eyes when I'd see those babies with rat bites all over them. I'd cry even more about the babies I didn't see because they were dead."[21] While he is talking generally here, he may well have been thinking about Detroit and the conditions in Black Bottom, which he would have known well.

Joe Louis did speak for his race, but he also saw himself as a proud American. It was this combination that, along with his stunning prowess in the ring, helped him to gain acceptance and admiration across much of white America. It is important to note, particularly in light of those who now view him as a sellout or a dupe, that he wasn't under any illusions as a patriot:

> I think about America often. I know how beautiful it is, how rich it is. I know because I've been through practically all of it. I even know better because I've been all over the world. Don't like to take unnecessary pride in myself, but I've seen it all. And because I've seen it all, I get sick sometimes way deep down inside myself. There is so much here. Can't there be a way we can share it? It makes me sick to see people, because they're black, catching so much hell. Something is wrong with that. I know I caught hell all during my career because I was black. . . . The people would all be there looking at me, expecting much of me. I felt weak and disappointed in myself because I couldn't do more. It gave me a bad feeling. I don't know how to get rid of rats, or get proper seats on a bus, or help you from busting your bladder because they won't let you use a "white" restroom.[22]

In Europe, the Second World War began in 1939, but Hitler only declared war on the previously neutral United States after the Japanese attacked Pearl Harbor in December 1941. As the nation finally entered the global conflict and mobilization began, Louis wanted to do his part. Cynics might suggest that Louis could not afford to remain aloof in the way Jack Dempsey, another heavyweight champion, had during World War I—Dempsey had paid a price for this decision, included being labeled a draft dodger by the *New York Times*, but he had been quickly forgiven after the war.[23] A black champion might not have been treated as generously. But strategic considerations aside, there is no reason to doubt that Louis sincerely wanted to serve the country. When one journalist asked him why he was risking his million-dollar championship title for nothing, he shot back: "I ain't fighting for nothing, I am fighting for my country." When a black journalist quizzed him about his support for a country riven by racist injustices, his laconically brilliant answer was: "Hitler won't fix them."[24]

The war against the Nazis created a new political environment in the United States. The enemy was not just openly racist and anti-Semitic; Germany was explicitly staking its quest for dominance on spurious theories of Aryan superiority. It became increasingly difficult to deny the ideological kinship between Nazism and U.S.-style white supremacy—a kinship that may well have delayed the U.S. entry into the war in the first place. If America wanted to fight Hitler effectively, the country would be forced to face up to the obvious contradictions at a time when black political movements were beginning to gain strength, creating considerable anxiety in the process. Detroit, in the meantime, was re-tooling for war, re-fashioning itself from Motor City to Arsenal of Democracy—a process that drew more and more workers to the city, creating ever-worsening conditions for them, particularly with regard to housing.

The complexities of the shifting ideological landscape posed a conundrum for black community leaders: Should they act as good Americans, suspend the internal fight and support the war wholeheartedly, in the hope of being rewarded later—driven by a trust and optimism for which U.S. history had given no cause? Should they demand the end of segregation and Jim Crow in exchange for support? Or should they refuse to take part in the war altogether, as at least one activist, Lewis Jones, decided to do (refusing to be conscripted into a segregated military unit, Jones was sentenced to three years in prison).[25]

During the summer of 1941, when Roosevelt was increasing arms expenditure in the expectation that the United States would join the war, A. Philip Randolph, America's most powerful black trade unionist as the leader of the Brotherhood of Sleeping Car Porters and one of the first leaders of the civil rights movement, created the March on Washington Movement, demanding that black workers be hired in the expanding defense industries, which were burgeoning in Detroit more than anywhere else. Unemployment was still sky-high after the Great Depression, and black workers were the last to find jobs. But Randolph's threat to bring one hundred thousand demonstrators to the capital delivered significant results: in June 1941, Roosevelt signed Executive Order 8802, creating a Committee of Fair Employment Practices, charged to ensure that all federal agencies involved in defense procurement should operate without discrimination as to "race, creed, color or national origin."[26] Private defense contractors in the sector were obliged to comply with the order as well. This was the first time that the U.S. government had created a policy explicitly designed to promote equal economic opportunity. The idea of the march laid the foundation for subsequent campaigns that would culminate in the Civil Rights Act of 1964. Randolph, fittingly, was one of the organizers of the March on Washington in 1963, where Martin Luther King Jr. would deliver the "I Have A Dream" speech to an audience of a quarter million—the same speech he had first given in Detroit, during the Walk to Freedom.[27]

As the United States entered the war, most of the black leadership settled on a policy known as "the double V"—victory abroad and at home. By committing fully to the war effort, so the idea went, African Americans would earn the country's respect as equal fellow citizens, leaving them well placed to obtain concessions on civil rights after the war.[28] To people such as Lewis Jones, the very fact that the U.S. armed forces remained segregated made this collaboration an outrage. And in fact, the U.S. secretary of war openly argued that integration would be destabilizing, since blacks allegedly did not show the military initiative of whites and segregation was "an established American custom."[29]

African American ambivalence with regard to the war effort was not just about Jim Crow, segregation, or other racist injustice. In 1941, the main theater of the war was Europe, and African Americans had fewer cultural ties to Europe than white Americans who would frequently identify with their ancestors' country of origin. More importantly, black Americans remembered their hopes of more equal treatment after loyal service during World War I, hopes quickly dashed when the war was over.[30] In sum, the U.S. government had a dire need for a man with the profile and charisma of Joe Louis to bring black citizens on board.

He was never sent to the front lines—he was too valuable an asset for that. Instead, Joe Louis agreed to a charity fight, a rematch against Buddy Baer, with whom he had a bit of unfinished business—half a year earlier, the six-feet-seven-tall Baer had knocked Louis out of the ring, even though Louis beat the count and Baer was disqualified later in the match. The rematch was scheduled for January 9, 1942, with all the proceeds to go to the Navy Relief Society. This was particularly notable as the navy was known to be extremely reluctant to recruit African Americans, and Louis took his share of criticism from a number of civil rights activists—why work to the navy's benefit, of all outfits?[31] In the end, however, it was probably a smart shaming strategy: Louis knocked out Baer in the first round and presented the Society with a check for $89,092.01—almost $1.5 million in today's money. Three days later, he joined the armed forces and became a national hero.

Thus began Joe Louis's tour as a goodwill ambassador and propaganda tool. His message was crafted to African American sensibilities. Posters portrayed "Pvt Joe Louis" in army uniform wielding a bayonet. The tagline read: "We're going to do our part . . . and we'll win because we're on God's side."[32] The language of faith played well to deeply religious black communities, and the noble private appealed to all demographics in a way a black officer might not have. As Randy Roberts writes: "The poster itself suggested Louis' iconic status. At a time when the government censored, and mainstream newspapers commonly refused to print pictures of black soldiers in uniform, let alone shots of them holding up rifles, Louis' image—in uniform, armed and aggressive—was slapped up on the walls of recruiting stations and government buildings in every section of the country. The tag line as well as his accepted persona had deracialized his image, transforming him into a symbol of patriotism. And not just black patriotism—American patriotism."[33] More boxing matches organized to support the war effort followed. By his own account, Louis lived at the barracks the way other black soldiers did, and while earning the rank of corporal, he refused to accept a higher rank offered to him.[34]

Joe Louis's deep ties to Detroit, now the industrial center of the war effort, probably made him an even more effective spokesman for the war. But in some ways, the most significant contribution that Joe Louis made to the war was financial, promoting government bonds that were funding the military. To that end, he gave speeches, made radio appearances, and starred in government-sponsored films about his life, produced in Hollywood and designed to persuade black America that this war was their war as well, never mind racial segregation in the country or its armed forces. *The Negro Soldier* (1944), produced by Frank Capra, is one of the most notable of these films—it was shown to almost every single African American soldier, and to significant numbers of white soldiers as well, to good reviews. Following race-based conflagrations in several major cities, not least the Detroit riot of 1943 (see chapter 19), the documentary took pains to replace the established Hollywood "Sambo" stereotypes of African Americans as lazy, foolish, and comical with an image of African Americans as thoughtful, patriotic, and brave. Langston Hughes declared it the "most remarkable Negro film ever flashed on the American screen."[35]

The army organized national tours for him where he would display his boxing skills to army base audiences—tours that also, however, gave him the opportunity to express his own views on segregation, which he did frequently. At one such gathering in Detroit, he caustically proclaimed that if blacks were given "an even break in the army we would show the world how to win this war."[36] He openly criticized the policy of not admitting well-educated blacks into the officer class, most notably in the case of Jackie Robinson, the baseball player, whom he spent time with at one army base.[37] And on one famous occasion, at Camp Sibert in Alabama, decades before Rosa Parks's famous protest, he joined the bus queue labeled "White Only" and refused to move to the black line—which promptly had him facing arrest.[38] Did he allow himself to be co-opted by a war machine that could not have cared less for the civil rights of African Americans? Perhaps, but he said his piece, he quietly and not so quietly held to his convictions, and he became a hero to much of America in the process—the first black man to do so in the history of the country, it has been asserted over and over again.

There is, however, a danger of overstating the degree to which white America accepted and respected Joe Louis. It is not surprising that the individual who was permitted to become America's first black hero was an athlete, because, much as it had done with music, the country had begun to carve out sports as one of the few niches where African Americans were allowed to excel. Neither is it a coincidence that it was a boxer: Major League Baseball would not be integrated for several years to come. As Howard Bryant observes:

Integrating team sports was a much greater threat to segregation than the rise of a fighter. . . . Team sports foreshadowed an
integrated society, for if blacks and whites could live together
during six weeks of spring training and six months of the baseball season, why not side by side in the classroom, the foxhole,
or on Main Street? "We sent the Harlem Hellfighters to France
to fight with General Pershing," Russel Honoré said. "And when
they got there, the Congress of the United States said, 'Don't let
them fight,' because if you do, they knew they'd want to come
back and have social justice."[39]

World War II did mark a turning point in American race relations, and
the seeds of the later civil rights movement were planted in the 1940s—some
of them by men like Joe Louis who had to walk the tightrope of respectability. But that did not mean that a man like Louis would be allowed to excel
beyond the confines of boxing. In 1948, Louis, $500,000 in debt to the
IRS (including taxes he owed on sizable sums he had donated to the Navy
Relief Society), wanted to acquire a Ford dealership in Chicago—selling
the same cars he had helped build in the 1930s when he worked at the
River Rouge factory. Henry Ford II asked for feedback from his dealers
and regional managers, and thirty-five pages of the correspondence are preserved among the papers of Walker A. Williams, Ford's sales manager in the
1940s.[40] The letters are a shocking read. District manager Johnston reports
that "we feel certain that we would lose all of the State of South Carolina's business which would involve over 400 units a year in normal times
and where we now enjoy a very favorable relationship," and that "many
present good Ford owners would never buy another Ford product." Houston weighs in: "Believes Ford Motor Company would be boycotted in the
South." Indianapolis worries that "whispering campaign might be started
by competition." Pennsylvania is "bluntly told that this would be construed
as supporting Harry Truman and the other left-wing groups, in an election
year, and that it would definitely give us bad public re-action, as they don't
given a 'damn' for Harry Truman. For your information a recent Gallup Poll
shows the South to be the most conservative of all sections of the country so
far as communists and left wings are concerned."

Some of the letters seem touched by a smidgen of bad conscience. Thus, Dearborn's district manager writes: "If we do not have anything to gain from a business standpoint, then in our opinion we should not make such an appointment. If, on the other hand, other factors should be given consideration such as human relations, constitutional rights or some such factors, then we would probably have to change our decision." Others don't even try. Alabama's "Mr. Lloyd strongly recommended that regardless of any circumstances, that we do not appoint Joe Louis, or any other negro, as a Ford dealer anywhere in the United States and that we keep the Ford business a white man's business." New Orleans: "Ford business is a white man's business and we do not want any negroes in it. Frankly, if we had a negro in the organization and it so happened that the writer was thrown into contact with the individual at a conference, meeting or presentation of Ford products, he would not attend."

Whether it was because Ford would lose business in the South, or because appointing a single black dealership would signal Ford's alliance with "communists of leftwings," or because respectable white dealers from the South would refuse to attend conferences, or because the competition would exploit it, or because Ford would be seen to side with Harry Truman and the civil rights legislation that was beginning its long march through Congress, one thing was clear: Ford could employ African Americans, but it certainly could not allow them to become employers in turn. If the "first black American hero" was going to find the money to pay his taxes, he had to return to the ring.

The "Freeman Field Mutiny" of 1945 is another case study both in how much and how little things were changing. Rather than a single protest, the "Mutiny" comprised a series of protests that would eventually see black officers arrested 162 times, some of them more than once—all in response to their determined opposition to Colonel Robert Selway, who insisted on segregating officer clubs in clear violation of a War Department's ban on discrimination. The black officers of the 477th Bombardment Group, which moved from Selfridge Field near Detroit to Kentucky and eventually to Freeman Field, Indiana, refused to bow to escalating threats, including a court-martial for "disobeying a direct order by a superior officer in time of war," punishable by death. More than a hundred of them were flown to

Kentucky, detained behind barbed wire for ninety-four days. Black newspapers soon got wind of the story, the NAACP got involved, and in the end, 104 officers received letters of reprimand, three were court-martialed, and one was convicted—it was not until the 1990s that the air force set aside the conviction and rescinded the reprimands.[41] As Daniel Haulman points out, this story, which is often hailed "as a forerunner of the modern Civil Rights Movement, in which peaceful nonviolent resistance resulted in the desegregation of facilities," is a more ambivalent tale: the immediate result was the removal of every white officer from the 477th—the air force would rather see an all-black unit than an integrated one.[42] And yet, the Freeman Field Mutiny was almost certainly crucial to the eventual integration of the air force in 1949, four years after the Tuskegee Airmen risked their careers and their lives.

One of the ringleaders of the uprising was Coleman Young, an experienced labor organizer and the future mayor of Detroit.[43] And on December 12, 1979, it was Coleman Young who opened the Joe Louis Arena, where the Red Wings played for forty years. Joe Louis died before the city could organize an event honoring him in the place named after him, and it is now demolished. But not far from where it stood for forty years, Joe Louis's giant clenched fist, suspended by steel cables from its pyramid frame, continues to sway in the wind.

SEVENTEEN

APRIL 28, 1949

Fred Matthaei leads the Detroit bid to host the 1956 Summer Olympic Games. The successful industrialist had been promoting Detroit as an Olympic city since 1938, and he will continue to do so for another two decades. Detroit had every reason to believe that its turn had come, but its bid flounders in part because of internal disagreements about the location of an Olympic stadium—a planning failure that would haunt future attempts.

When Detroit asked to host "the glorious pageantry" of the Olympics, it made an audacious argument. "The very pulsation of the Twentieth Century can be reckoned in the heart of Detroit where the crucial economic and social problems are focused as at no other place," a 1947 bid document argued on behalf of the city. And for that reason, the fate of Detroit was the fate of the nation—if the city could not solve the social ills that rapid industrialization had produced, they would spread far and wide: "Whatever presages ill for Detroit is ominous, for the evil can extend rapidly from it throughout the land and beyond." Among those evils were "cynicism" and a lack of "civic spirit and pride"—and those, at least, the Olympic Games could address: "It is neither wishful thinking nor imagining when Detroit's leaders say that a sublimation and unification of civic spirit and pride, that would eradicate the evils we fear, would result from the tremendous joint effort made necessary to conduct an Olympiad in all its glorious pageantry at Detroit."[1]

Fred Matthaei, the chair of Detroit Olympic Committee, fully expected the city to be nominated by the U.S. Olympic Association (USOA) in 1948 as the official U.S. candidate—he believed that Detroit had the inside track for the 1956 Olympic Games. Chicago, Minneapolis, Philadelphia, and San Francisco were the competition for the nomination, and a small USOA committee would visit each of the cities before making its recommendation.[2] Detroit confidently made its case in a brochure that laid out the city's commitment along with the reasons its bid should take precedence. After all, Detroit had been bidding to host the Olympic Games since 1938, longer than any other U.S. city. It had offered to host the 1940 Games, after Tokyo withdrew at short notice; it had offered to host the 1944 Games, which were later canceled because of World War II; it had offered to host the first postwar games in 1948, and it had bid for the 1952 Games.[3]

On each occasion, the bid was led by Fred Matthaei, a man who had made his fortune in the early part of the century. In 1917, Matthaei founded American Metal Products, a company that made steel tubes and other steel products for Detroit's booming automobile industry. By that time, Ford's River Rouge plant was already assembling three-quarters of a million cars per year, and there was plenty of business for enterprising young men like Matthaei. By 1939, the business was generating over $1 million per year in sales; during World War II, the plant converted to military production and increased its output tenfold within five years. By the end of the war, Matthaei was spending less time running the company than pursuing his dream project: to bring the Olympic Games to Detroit.[4]

Even when the 1952 bid failed, Matthaei did not despair: Avery Brundage, the preeminent U.S. representative on the International Olympic Committee, promised him that Detroit's time would come. Brundage had always argued on the basis of precedence: Helsinki was offered the 1940 Games because it had already bid, the story went, and London was awarded the 1944 Games because it was next in line, and nabbed the 1948 Games because Helsinki was not yet in a position to stage the event, so 1952 was Helsinki's turn. By that logic, Matthaei concluded, 1956 was in the bag for Detroit.[5]

By the spring of 1948, the USOA had conducted its visits and had agreed to declare its choice by June 15, when suddenly the process was put on hold.[6] Los Angeles had decided to enter a bid and, allegedly, the Olympic Association of Southern California was threatening to withhold funding for the U.S. team for the upcoming London Games if it didn't get its way. Matthaei, disturbed and outraged, wrote to Brundage: "If so, it can be classed with the all-time unethical, inconsiderate actions of a selfish and ungrateful member allegedly in the Olympic movement."[7] After all, Matthaei pointed out, Detroit was doing its part for the U.S. team, spending $100,000 to host the national swim trials in newly refurbished Rouge Park.

The inspection committee produced its report at the beginning of June, outlining Detroit's plans alongside those of Minneapolis, Philadelphia, Chicago, and Los Angeles. Detroit, the committee reported, would build an Olympic stadium and an Olympic village on the Detroit River waterfront, as part of a project to redevelop blighted land.[8] The swimming competitions would be held in Rouge Park, and the city had numerous existing facilities suitable for staging the other sports. On July 11, 1948, the USOA announced that Detroit was its preferred bidder, and soon after, everybody departed for the London Games, which took place between July 29 and August 14.[9]

On September 21, the mayor addressed the newly constituted Detroit Olympic Organizing Committee at its initial meeting, and the members elected an executive committee with Matthaei as chairman. The first and most pressing order of business concerned the construction of the Olympic Stadium. Unbeknownst to the inspection committee, nothing had actually been settled in this regard, and more than twenty-six sites were under consideration. In his opening statement, Mayor Eugene Van Antwerp, who had taken office in January of 1948, expressed his support for the Michigan Fairgrounds.[10] At its second meeting on October 11, the Organizing Committee learned that, with the assistance of the City Plan Commission, the options had been reduced to two: an open stadium in Rouge Park, which would cost around $6 million to build, or a covered stadium close to Wayne State University in midtown, with a price tag of $13 million.[11]

An open stadium would save money, the committee reasoned, but it would not get much use after the games, at best about a dozen football games (mainly for the Detroit Lions and Wayne State) that would produce a meager annual income of about $200,000. It might be possible to start out with an open stadium, with seats for one hundred thousand, and to add a roof later. This would make it a more attractive venue for hosting events such as circuses, trade shows, and pageants along with sports events, thus increasing the forecast revenues to $750,000 per year. Moreover, the city could build it in stages: a $6 million open stadium seating sixty thousand could even be ready by 1952, in case Helsinki failed to get its act together in time.[12]

The committee preferred this option and started discussing financing methods, including apparent commitments from the city, which had already budgeted $1 million, and from the State. Considering revenue bonds, they analyzed the experience of other cities and found that "in every instance the income from the stadium or convention hall in itself has not been adequate to service the indebtedness, except in the case of the Olympic Games Committee in Los Angeles." The Organizing Committee expected the Games as a whole to gross $12 million, not enough to pay for the costs of building the needed facilities, including an Olympic village. A construction company submitted a quote to build the village, on the basis of a "standard cabin" costing $700 each. Assuming two athletes per cabin and four thousand participating athletes, this added another $1.4 million to the bill—about $14 million in today's money.[13]

A 1948 report by the Detroit City Plan Commission had found that "the operating income from the Games cannot be expected to pay the capital costs of the physical facilities needed," and that hence "it is desirable and possible to so plan all new capital facilities built for the Olympiad that they can be used as permanent parts of the city's public plant."[14] While the plans appeared to be progressing along these lines, the Organizing Committee, which officially reported to the mayor, learned that there was resistance from various city departments. At a public hearing, attendees raised several objections with regard to the practicality and the cost estimates of the Wayne State option; the city treasurer, future mayor Albert Cobo, backed up the Organizing Committee estimates, but the city engineer suggested that a tab of $24 million (about $240 million in today's money) was more likely. Others argued that the facilities should be financed privately, and to cap it all, Van Antwerp still hankered after the State Fairgrounds site. In a letter to the mayor on December 28, 1948, Matthaei laid out the state of negotiations and put his conclusions starkly: "Unless you are willing to accept the recommendations of your Detroit Organizing Committee, there is nothing further for us to do."[15]

The stadium problem would dog the Detroit Olympic Committee in all subsequent bids for the Games of 1960, 1964, 1968, and 1972. This seems all the more baffling seeing that by the 1940s, the city government had wholeheartedly subscribed to the need for large-scale urban planning. By the end of the Great Depression, the city's infrastructure was in a poor state, and housing shortages were particularly dire—a problem further exacerbated by wartime immigration, which added a quarter of a million to the city's population. By 1950, more than 1.8 million people lived in Detroit, a number that had roughly doubled in thirty years, and was four times as high as forty years before. During this rapid growth, the city had barely invested in its infrastructure, and it was time. In 1942, the mayor established the Regional Defense Planning Committee to work on housing and other issues related to the influx of defense workers, and in 1944, the mayor's postwar improvement committee issued a plan sunnily entitled "Post-War Improvements to Make Your Detroit a Finer City in Which to Live and Work." The Planning Committee's staff was significantly enlarged, and by 1949, the city was well on the way to developing a master plan for the city, which would eventually be published in 1951.

In December of 1948, the Detroit Olympic Committee was well aware of this work and incorporated concepts of urban redevelopment into its pitch. With four months to go until the IOC would meet in Rome to make its final decision, Detroit's bid, which had looked so very promising, was teetering. That month, Brundage wrote to Matthaei, quoting a letter from IOC president Sigfrid Edström that invited Detroit to present its case in Rome—a presentation that needed to include details about facilities and organization along with the possibility of assisting with travel expenses for athletes and officials.[16] What Matthaei did not know was that Edström had already put his thumb on the scale. He had circulated to the IOC members the applications of, in this order, Melbourne, Buenos Aires, Mexico City, Detroit, and Los Angeles—describing Melbourne's bid as "wonderful." Detroit, by contrast, got a few noncommittal lines, and the question of precedence, which previously had been presented as oh-so-decisive, wasn't mentioned at all.[17]

There was clearly confusion about the American participation in the process. In August 1948, Gustavus Kirby, the grand old man of American amateur athletics, had written to Brundage suggesting he should meet with the Detroit bid organizers to discuss their plans.[18] In December 1948, a full six months after it had decided who to support, the USOA had written to the IOC stressing that "our organization wants it to be understood by the members of the International Olympic committee that Detroit has received this unqualified endorsement, and that such endorsement has been granted to no other American city."[19] In February 1949, however, Edström wrote to Douglas Roby, the U.S. member of the IOC (whom we encountered in chapter 13), to complain that he had not received a formal bid from Detroit.[20]

In the meantime, Matthaei continued to lobby for Detroit's bid, winning first the endorsement of the Michigan Senate and then a joint resolution of the U.S. Congress in March 1949. In 1949, Detroit could reasonably claim, as the bid brochure stated, to be the "industrial capital of the world" and Detroit's business leaders also lined up in support (though it is unclear with how much enthusiasm). Officially, the Fairgrounds had been chosen as the site for the Olympic Stadium, but ominously, the city had still not committed any financial support.

Disaster struck on April 28, 1949. The bid team arrived in Rome for the IOC's 43rd session expecting to represent the United States—only to find that Minneapolis and Los Angeles had also arrived to make their case. Los Angeles was represented by Jack Garland, who had just inherited his father's seat on the IOC. In January, Roby had written to Garland politely asking him to respect Detroit's prior claim, but Garland would have none of it.[21] Brundage tried to mediate, and Minneapolis agreed to withdraw as long as LA did as well. Garland refused, pretending the Los Angeles bid was just a formality, to place a marker for future bids. Then Brundage intervened in a somewhat bizarre manner. If those two cities insisted on bidding, he claimed, he "would be duty bound to enter the invitations of Philadelphia, San Francisco and Chicago." After all, those three cities, unlike LA and Minneapolis, had respected the USOA choice as binding—as it now turned out, to their disadvantage. And since those three were not actually present in Rome, he himself would present their cases. Confusion spread—the Americans agreed to ask the IOC to select one of what was now six America cities competing on behalf of the United States—but Brundage, it seems, never passed that message on to the IOC.[22]

Other deals fell through as well. Detroit, worried about a coalition of

British Commonwealth interests favoring Melbourne, had made a pact with Montreal, which was bidding for the 1956 Winter Olympics. If the British bloc were to recognize Detroit's precedence and shift Melbourne forward to 1960, Detroit, in exchange, would support Montreal. It is unclear whether Montreal reneged on the deal or never quite agreed to it.

In the end, Detroit's biggest failing might have been its naiveté with regard to financial matters. According to a report in the Dutch newspaper *De Rotterdammer*, "the manner in which the Olympics were assigned could be compared with an international auction, whereby the highest bidder was 'Number One.'" Juan Perón, the Argentine president, stated his willingness to commit $30 million to hosting the games. Melbourne didn't put a number to it, but offered to pay the expenses of all the athletes and all the IOC members. And Los Angeles, with its "token" bid, promised not only to cover IOC "member and lady" expenses, but to give the IOC half of the profits from staging the Games. "Detroit could not bid against this," the *De Rotterdammer* article stated.[23]

Having offered nothing in terms of financial inducements, Detroit won only two out of forty-one votes in the first round of bidding. Chicago, Minneapolis, Philadelphia, San Francisco, and Montreal were eliminated right away; Mexico City went out in the second round. That left Los Angeles, Buenos Aires, Melbourne, and Detroit. In the third round, Detroit came in last, but LA didn't do much better, and that was the end of the U.S. cities. In the final round, Melbourne defeated Buenos Aires, 21 to 20.

Could Detroit have afforded it? Take the city engineer's $24 million estimate of the stadium cost at face value, add $2 million for the Olympic Village and $4 million for other costs—that would match Juan Perón's $30 million bid. Allow $10 million of revenue from the event (below the Detroit Olympic Committee estimate) and then estimate the future value of stadium revenue from hosting the Lions and other events at $6 million (eight times expected annual revenues, not an atypical multiple). That would leave a deficit of $14 million to be subsidized by the city, an amount that could have been spread over the seven years between winning the Games in 1949 to hosting them in 1956—that comes to about $2 million a year. In 1954 the annual retail sales of Detroit equaled over $2.5 billion, generating sales tax for the state of $77 million.[24] In other words, the subsidy would have cost about 2.6 percent of the total sales tax revenue of the city: not nothing, but also not an immense financial burden. In 1950, Detroit was one the richest cities in the United States. The median income of the almost half million families in the city was $3,955—higher than New York City and the highest in the country, tied with Chicago.[25] The total income of Detroiters, therefore, was in the region of $2 billion per year—an income tax of one-tenth of 1 percent, spread over ten years, would have done the trick and covered the subsidy. Again, that's not nothing, but it is hardly an immense burden, either.

Oddly, the *Detroit Free Press* blamed Detroit's failure on the slovenliness of Mayor Van Antwerp. The man had not dressed property, the paper claimed, and he had turned up in an old suit, "a sports shirt, and a necktie with Detroit gravy stains."[26] Matthaei had quite a different explanation for the city's defeat. In a heated correspondence with Brundage, he laid the blame firmly at the feet of the president of the USOA and the chaotic presentation of multiple U.S. bids. Brundage demurred, claiming he could do nothing to stop the other cities from bidding, that LA would not withdraw despite the USOA's decision, that "the treachery of the Minneapolis representative was unexpected," and so on. "I did everything within my power to aid your campaign," he protested.[27]

In November, Matthaei replied: "Dear Avery, 'We cannot prevent Los Angeles or any other city from submitting invitations to the IOC.' Your persistent attitude in this regard has been largely responsible for the debacle that occurred in Rome. Unless there is a change in thinking on your part, it will be useless for a United States city—other than LA—to consider preparations for holding a future Olympiad."[28] The USOA, Matthaei continued, "is in ill repute with IOC membership," and "the President of the USOA necessarily must bear a part of this stigma." From Matthaei's perspective, the United States was a laughing stock for allowing so many rival cities to bid; in addition, the USOA had helped corrupt the process by conniving to allow financial considerations to affect decision making at the IOC. Brundage, Matthaei finally concluded, was jeopardizing his chances as the "heir apparent" to assume the IOC presidency. The British bloc, he predicted, was conspiring to pass him over and select Lord David Burghley instead.[29]

Matthaei's rage was understandable, but it was probably unwise to articulate his criticism in quite so much detail and with quite such intensity. Brundage was not a good man to cross. He was not known as a man who took to any critique kindly, and when he actually did become president of the IOC in 1952, his power grew exponentially. A *Sports Illustrated* profile from 1956 describes him as "the black villain who, in his twenty-four-year reign as president of the U.S. Olympic Association, threw Swimmer Eleanor Holm off the 1936 U.S. Olympic team in midocean for sipping champagne, who cold-heartedly took a new automobile away from the pretty Canadian figure skater, Barbara Ann Scott, who ruthlessly declared Jesse Owens a professional, who peremptorily suspended Babe Didrikson, who publicly chastised Charley Paddock, who refused to allow European countries to reimburse their athletes for the regular salaries they lost when they were away from their jobs competing at the Olympic Games. You may have heard him described as Slavery Avery."[30]

And any further Detroit bid would fall under his watch.

EIGHTEEN

OCTOBER 10, 1945

The Tigers win their second World Series, led by a returning war hero, the veteran Hank Greenberg, and an emerging young pitcher, Hal Newhouser. During the war, the All-American Girls Profession-al Baseball League offers an alternative to the major leagues, and in Detroit, Rosie the Riveter symbolizes the crucial role that women played in stocking the "Arsenal of Democracy." While the postwar years failed to deliver on the country's wartime promises to women and Americans of color, the Tigers' World Series trophy symbolizes Detroit's crucial contribution to the Allied powers' victory.

Skeeter Webb, the leadoff batter for the Tigers, takes Hank Borowy to a full count and then singles to right field. Next up, Eddie Mayo gets a base hit off the first pitch, and Webb hustles to third base. Doc Cramer takes a strike, but then manages to hook a ball over third base for the third hit of the inning, and Webb scores. After just nine pitches, manager Charlie Grimm takes the Cubs' ace pitcher out of the game.[1]

Hank Greenberg, the legendary Detroit slugger, steps up to the plate, and the field retreats. What the Cubs do not know is that Greenberg is injured. To everyone's surprise, he makes a sacrifice bunt, so now there are runners on second and third with one out and one run. Paul Derringer, the relief pitcher, intentionally walks Roy Cullenbine, creating the opportunity for a double play with the bases loaded. Rudy York, the Tigers' other slug-ger, is now up. A long fly ball to right field, which would have scored two or three runs, lands just foul, and York pops up the next pitch to third. Bases loaded and two out. The next batter, Jimmy Outlaw, plays a waiting game. He watches one, two, three and then, unbelievably, four pitches sail all around the plate. Another walk—but this time not intentional. It's a gift, 2–0 Tigers. Paul Richards steps up, and after getting behind on the count smashes the ball down the left field line, and this time the ball stays fair . . . just. All three men on base score. In the first inning of game 7 of the World Series, the Tigers lead 5–0 at Wrigley Field. A few hours later, it's 9–3, and the Tigers take home their second World Series title.

It was a peculiar World Series in many ways. Because of wartime restrictions, the teams changed venues only once, with the first three games played at Briggs Field and the last four in Chicago (normally, the sequence would be 2-3-2). And because a large segment of major league players had been called up for military service, most teams were made up of veterans, youngsters, or "4-F's"—men found to be ineligible for failing to meet "physical, mental or moral standards." In the previous season, the St. Louis Browns, who had been the worst drawing team in the American League since 1902, finally managed to win their first pennant largely because most of their players were 4-Fs. Detroit had some luck in this regard as well: Newhouser was not called up because of a heart murmur, Rudy York for having a loose knee. In 1944, Newhouser emerged as the leading pitcher in baseball, and he would dominate for a decade. He remains the only Detroit-born baseball player to enter the Hall of Fame as a Tigers player.

Rudy York had been with the Tigers since 1937, and he really came into his own during wartime. Between 1940 and 1945, he barely missed a game, and he led the league in home runs and RBIs in 1943. Oddly though, from about 1942 onward, the Detroit crowd started to jeer at him when he came to the plate. Sometimes referred to as Chief York or simply "the Indian," York had one Cherokee great-grandparent, which during that time was all it took for crowds to erupt in war whoops and other mockeries of Native American life (or rather its caricature). He was, however, much loved by his fellow players, who paid tribute to his generosity and cheerfulness.[2] After the Tigers won the pennant on the last day of the season in a rain-sodden game in St. Louis, thanks to a Hank Greenberg home run, York insisted on spending every last penny he had on paying for the party on the train home. Like many ballplayers, he struggled with alcohol, but his Native American ancestry made that a stigma none of the other players had to bear. The press often criticized his fielding—one journalist called him "part Indian and part first baseman"—but baseball experts today are of the view that it was perfectly fine.[3] In 1943, H.G. Salsinger, the respected baseball writer for the *Detroit News*, took the fans to task for the way they treated York, but it didn't stop them.[4]

Hank Greenberg was, without a doubt, the hero of the team. One of the "three G's" or "G-Men" from the team that won the 1935 World Series—the other two being Charlie Gehringer and Goose Goslin—Greenberg had been called up in 1940. Initially classified 4-F for flat feet, he demanded to be re-examined, and was admitted in April 1941.[5] Like most major league players, he was not exposed to combat, but as captain in the Army Air Corps (the predecessor of the U.S. Air Force), he ran reconnaissance missions in Burma. The longest serving baseball player in the military, he was finally discharged in the middle of June 1945, about a month after the war in Europe had ended. He played his first game for the Tigers on July 1, his return giving Detroit the edge in the second half of the season.

For some purists, the World Series of 1945 is not on a par with the peacetime editions, if only because many of the best players were not available. The government had in fact considered canceling the major league seasons altogether, but decided that it would be better for morale to keep it going, and President Roosevelt insisted the game go on in his famous "green light" letter to then MLB commissioner Kenesaw Mountain Landis. When the Tigers won the 1945 series, the V-J victory in Japan had just brought World War II to an end, and Detroit's triumph packed a symbolic punch: it was Detroit, after all, that had enabled the United States to outgun the Axis powers and to supply not just its own armies but those of the allies with seemingly endless amounts of equipment.

After Hitler's invasion of Poland on September 1, 1939, Britain and France had declared war on Germany. The Nazis attacked Denmark and Norway in April 1940 and France the next month, securing easy victories and bringing most of Europe under their control. Hitler had already signed a non-aggression pact with Stalin's Soviet Union, and in early June 1940, Britain stood alone and it looked grim. But in 1941, fortunes began to turn: first, Hitler made the disastrous decision to invade the Soviet Union in late June, and second, Japan attacked Pearl Harbor in December. As Hitler simultaneously declared war on the United States, the nation saw itself

under threat for the first time during the war. Until then, isolationist sentiment had run strong in America. Henry Ford went as far as turning down
a British order for aircraft engines in 1940, on the grounds that he would
help defend America, but not a foreign power.[6] While Ford's virulent and
well-known anti-Semitism might well have led him to secretly sympathize
with the Nazis, many business leaders in Detroit were not enthusiastic about
being drawn into war for other reasons.

Roosevelt and the government, however, had other ideas. The president
became convinced that U.S. involvement was inevitable, and from the middle of 1940, he formed a close bond with the British prime minister Winston
Churchill. From that year on, the government placed ever larger numbers
of defense orders in Detroit, and the process of adapting to war production began. Perhaps the most famous example was the Willow Run factory
that built the B-24 Liberator bomber aircraft. Ford agreed to take on the
production contract, and under the direction of his son Edsel and his chief
engineer Charles Sorensen, he built a plant that would produce aircraft on
a production line, just like cars. The plant, one mile long, was located near
Ypsilanti, west of Detroit, just inside Republican-voting Washtenaw County
rather than Democrat-controlled Wayne County, suiting Henry Ford's politics. While the plant initially struggled to meet its targets, by the end of the
war, it was turning out one bomber every hour.[7]

The government also received strong support in the war effort from
Walter Reuther and the UAW. Politically, the union's leaders were strongly
opposed to fascism (Father Coughlin and other homegrown fascists were
fanatically anti-union), and they found it easy to align with Roosevelt's outlook. In addition, the war posed an opportunity to collaborate more closely
with the employers, in pursuit of a shared goal. It might seem ironic that in
the middle of a war against Hitler, Reuther pushed for a model resembling
the German policy of co-determination ("work councils"), in which union
representatives serve on the supervisory board of directors in significant
numbers. But that model was hardly a fascist one: co-determination was
established in Germany in 1920, thanks to socialist and social-democratic
forces, and the Nazis had promptly suspended the work councils. That said,
Reuther's ideas were (and still are) too radical for American business leaders, who were interested in coordinating efforts, but were certainly not eager
to share power with the workers.

The union's focus on promoting the war effort—and the many well-paying jobs it created—came at a price. Issues such as race or gender equity took a back seat as union leaders did not want to be perceived to be rocking the boat during a national emergency.[8] The dislocation caused by the shift to wartime production was immense. In order to ensure that military production targets could be met, the government had obliged the auto companies to cease production of passenger cars by February 10, 1942.[9] Every factory in the city was retooled to produce planes, tanks, munitions, and every kind of military hardware, right down to pots and pans. The industrial workforce increased from just under four hundred thousand in 1940 to almost nine hundred thousand by 1943. By the end of the war, Detroit had supplied something like 10 percent of all wartime contracts, a figure only matched by New York, whose population was more than four times larger.[10] Soon after the war started, Detroit became known as the "Arsenal of Democracy,"[11] a title earned at considerable cost. One of the most dire consequences of the rapidly expanding military-industrial complex was the acute housing shortage as new workers flooded the city, a source of conflict in the city for decades to come.

One of the most devastating descriptions of the hardships that awaited migrants from the South comes in the form of a novel, Harriet Arnow's *The Dollmaker*.[12] Arnow herself had moved to Detroit in 1944, and her account, while fictionalized, is informed by her own experience living in the war industry's crowded projects. The novel relates the grim story of Gertie Nevels, a white farmer from the Kentucky hills who, with her five children, follows her husband to Detroit. For her, the city is not a site of prosperity but rather one of never-ending and deeply disorienting conflict between new and old residents, Catholics and Protestants, "the reds" and the anti-communists, union members and scabs, rich and poor—a cauldron of strife and resentment where the Appalachian "hillbillies" are as deeply loathed as the black workers from the South, and where the rhythms, sounds, crafts, and communities of the countryside disappear in a generation while Father Coughlin's fascist, anti-Semitic tirades on the radio function as a dystopian soundtrack to the struggle of the new urban proletariat.[13] Arnow and her husband had lived in a development that must have been quite similar to the sarcastically named "Merry Hill" of the novel. Joyce Carol Oates, viewing *The Dollmaker* as an "American Tragedy," writes: "In Kentucky, the Nevels are themselves a kind of domestic factory, producing their own food; in Detroit they are the exploited base of a vast capitalistic pyramid, utterly helpless, anonymous cogs in a factory that extends beyond the brutal city of Detroit to take in the entire nation."[14]

The wartime labor shortage and the depletion of the major leagues also led to one of sports history's most intriguing episodes, the creation of a female professional league for the national pastime—the All-American Girls Professional Baseball League (AAGPBL). Women had played baseball since at least the 1860s, but their participation in the sport had been both heavily constricted and controversial. Before World War II, "Bloomer girls" teams, named for the pants that had been developed for American women in the nineteenth century, were a bit of a novelty act; they were quite popular, but also greeted with a good amount of suspicion and disapproval—their misogynist critics habitually accused the women of being prostitutes. Still, the *Detroit Free Press* extended a warm welcome to the Star Bloomer Girls when they arrived in Detroit in August 1916, noting that "the team boasts several . . . performers who could draw salaries as semi-pros." Somewhat astonishingly, the Star Bloomers had come to play against Pfeiffer's Famous, a leading Detroit amateur men's club, "and the Famous boys seem due for a busy afternoon."[15] Sadly, we do not know how the game went, but the same paper had assured its readers a day earlier that "the Star Bloomer Girls' baseball team . . . is a real ball club," and that "Miss Cunningham is a real pitcher, who can field her position as well as any man in the game, and is known among her teammates as the second Eddie Plank [the Philadelphia Athletics' star pitcher]."[16]

Educationists had promoted baseball in high schools as an appropriate activity for girls, if suitably adapted. The development of softball, as a version of baseball for amateurs, had started in the 1890s, and the game became formalized in the 1930s. Both men and women's teams played across the country, and in 1935 *Time* estimated that there were as many as two million amateur players nationwide.[17] Softball was also a big game in Canada, and just as Detroit was a natural destination for migrating Canadian hockey players, Canadian women softball players were drawn into the city's orbit.[18] The national fastpitch championship for women started in 1933, and Detroit became a well-known center of softball (the University of Michigan in Ann Arbor still fields one of the winningest teams ever). The University of Detroit stadium played host to the national championship, for both men and women, between 1940 and 1943.[19]

As we mentioned above, there had been talk about closing down the major leagues during the war, for loss of manpower. And even though play continued, the war's effect on the quality of the game was noticeable. The minor leagues were even more badly affected. Before the advent of TV, minor league baseball was popular across the United States, particularly in smaller towns where folks had few or no opportunities to see a major league game. The idea of a women's league to fill the gap was the brainchild of Philip Wrigley, owner of the Chicago Cubs.[20]

The league launched in 1943 with four teams: Racine, Rockford, South Bend, and Kenosha—smaller cities located around Chicago in Illinois, Wisconsin, and Indiana. Detroit, alas, never fielded a team of its own, even though the city had plenty of amateur clubs. Perhaps most of the Detroit women didn't think it was worth their time, seeing that they were busy building bombers. Still, when the *Detroit Free Press* that year asked random citizens whether they favored "women participating in professional sports," the replies—at least the published ones—were unanimously positive. Mrs. Lauretta Reed, of 5607 Talbot, pointed out that "women are doing a man's job in plants throughout the country and I can't see why they couldn't do a man's job in athletic competition." Ralph Shanks, of 13200 La Salle, didn't "know whether or not they could play baseball, but one thing is certain and that is that they go all out to win—more so than men." Mrs. Margaret Reed, of 5532 Webb, acerbically pointed out that "they couldn't be any worse than were the Tigers last season."[21]

The time was clearly ripe—women had already proved themselves. Still, the league was organized as a trust rather than a for-profit business, in line with Wrigley's view that the league's primary purpose was to support the war effort. The players were not meant to take the place of the pros for long, and there were concerns that women performing to mixed audiences would be seen as not quite respectable. To counteract such misgivings, the players were expected to meet strict expectations—they had to wear make-up and conduct themselves at all times in a lady-like fashion, in notable distinction from the boisterous, foul-mouthed, chewing and spitting men of professional baseball. Absurdly, they were also expected to play in short skirts, outfits that made sliding painful and generated a good deal of skin abrasions. Each team had a male manager and a female chaperone, the latter expected to dispense discipline and act as both confidante and medical adviser. The pay was not generous, certainly far behind the major leaguers—but it was certainly comparable to if not better than that of the minor leaguers, who were notoriously underpaid and grossly exploited.

While Detroit did not have its own team, its amateur players, some quite well known, certainly attracted their number of recruiters, leading to grumbles. As one scout made an offer, the manager of the Hudson Girls' softball team, Harry Kaczynski, complained "there must be a law that will stop him from raiding the ball teams, those girls all hold defense jobs and are frozen."[22] In the end, few of the Detroit women ended up in the AAGPBL, but there were some: Eulah Elizabeth "Betty" Tucker, who got her start in the sandlots of Detroit and ended up playing for five different teams in the league. Arlene Buszka, of the South Bend Blue Sox, who died in Rochester Hills in 2006. Pitcher Mary Rini, of the Kenosha Comets and the Muskegon Lassies, of whom nothing more is known. And shortstop and second baseman Margaret "Marge" Stefani of the Blue Sox and the Rockford Peaches, much beloved for her gruff sisterly ways—in 2002, former Blue Sox comrade Betty Trezza said that her "fondest memory was the big sister treatment I received from Bonnie Baker and Marge Stefani. They took me under their wing and gave me the confidence I needed to continue to play."[23] Dolly Brumfield White, who used her AAGPBL earnings to finance her college education, remembered Marge as "the old warhorse" who "sounded like a circus barker," always yelling. "You gotta have pepper over there!"[24] Stefani went on to coach and to chaperone, but she died early, at age forty-six.

If Detroit's women left only a small mark on the enterprise most famously celebrated by the sweetly nostalgic film *A League of Their Own*, they certainly stamped their imprint onto the Detroit wartime industry. In the 1940s, Detroit needed a bigger labor force. There were only so many retirees, people with disabilities, and recent school and college graduates to draft, so most of the new workers were migrants, mainly from the South, and women, both black and white. In 1943, the *Pittsburgh Courier*, an African American newspaper, reported under the headline "Women Find Many Opportunities at Ford Co." that Ford appeared to be hiring women "at the approximate rate of 50 per day" and praised Ford's treatment of black workers:

> Prior to the outbreak of World War No. 2 women were not employed at all by the Ford Motor Company, but when Ford employees began to enter the armed services in large numbers, leaving more or less dependent women behind to bear the economic burdens, the policy at Ford changed almost overnight. Today women are employed in practically every department of the Ford Motor company and no distinction is made between white and colored. . . . Irrespective of race, women are now playing a great part in building airplane motors and tanks for the Allied Nations of the world under Henry Ford, and as William H. Woodstock, superintendent of the new aluminum plant puts it, "Women are as capable of making cylinder heads for planes as man, and that is true of our women generally, whether they be white or colored."[25]

One white woman became one of the most powerful images of wartime production: "Rosie the Riveter." Rosie made her first appearance in a song by that name, which celebrated the women who were contributing to the war effort in factories and shipyards. It quickly became a hit, and when the government sought to produce a promotional film about the home front, it searched for a woman to fit the already iconic name. They found her in Rose Will Monroe, an actual riveter who worked in the Willow Run factory, building B-24s.[26] To be sure, Rosie the Riveter was a figure open to interpretation; not everybody was unequivocally happy to see women enter what had been a male world. Norman Rockwell's 1943 cover for the *Saturday Evening Post* shows an unapologetically muscular woman, safety googles pushed up on her forehead, a sandwich in her left, a rivet gun on her lap, Hitler's *Mein Kampf* crushed under her right foot. Other Rosies are decidedly more feminine, often absurdly so, their lips glistening with lipstick, a flirtatious smile on their face, daintily holding a tool as if it were a hairstyling accessory. The most famous one is J. Howard Miller's Rosie, created as a poster for Westinghouse Company's War Production Coordinating Committee. Wearing a kerchief to cover her hair, Rosie is rolling up her sleeve, flexing her biceps, and definitely not smiling: "We Can Do It!" read the iconic slogan accompanying her image. One Michigan woman proved the slogan true: figure skating champion Esther Wrona, a war plant inspector in Saginaw, took a closer look at a machine gun and figured out a way to save "470 man hours and $500 worth of materials a month." She was the second woman to get hired at that General Motors plant and the first to receive a $1,000 war bond as a reward.[27]

Women were badly needed, highly motivated, and—as they quickly proved themselves—fully qualified, but recruiting them to the production lines created some challenges. Before the war, female workers and employees had mostly worked clerical jobs that usually paid badly. Given the much higher pay rates on the production lines, many were exceptionally keen on making the transition, but neither male employers nor male co-workers were equally, well, riveted by the idea. Many men refused to work alongside women just as they refused to work alongside African Americans, leading to the kind of hate strikes that racial integration in the workplace had generated.[28] Employers were often reluctant because, out of habit, they considered women less able—an assumption the women quickly set right once they arrived, and with lower rates of absenteeism to boot. One thing made them particularly attractive to employers: you could pay them less, eighty or ninety cents on the male dollar.[29] Unsurprisingly, women found it hard to get promoted, and if they had small children, they had trouble finding daycare.[30] While facilities were much expanded, the government underfunded them so significantly that many mothers could simply not afford to take up such offers as they were. Still, women's employment in Michigan rose from 392,000 in 1940 to almost 800,000 at the peak.[31] More than a quarter of the workforce at Willow Run was female.

The wartime labor shortage not only undermined the idea of "women's work," giving American women confidence and new aspirations beyond the workplace.[32] It was a momentous shift in gender roles, and one that could only be reversed for so long. When the war ended, most women in industrial jobs were simply expected to return either to the home or to the kind of jobs they had held before. Layoffs started in 1945, and women were the most likely to be dismissed, regardless of their record and certainly regardless of their wishes. The Women's League lasted a bit longer: Wrigley wanted to keep it going, and for a few years, he succeeded. Some teams folded, others emerged, and at its peak in 1948, the league numbered ten teams. After 1948, the league went into decline, and it collapsed in 1954, partially for the same reason that independent minor league baseball died out: TV had brought the major league into everybody's home, why bother with anything else?

The league had never come closer to Detroit than Muskegon and Grand Rapids, but in 2010, more than 50 of the 259 surviving members of the All-American Girls Professional Baseball League gathered in Detroit. They called their four-day reunion "Motown in Motion," and on August 5, you could see white-haired ladies in their seventies, eighties, and nineties pitch and catch in Comerica Park.[33]

NINETEEN

FEBRUARY 5, 1943

At the Olympia stadium, Sugar Ray Robinson loses to Jake LaMotta, and Jesse Owens comes to work at the Ford Motor Company—the most famous of a vast cast of athletes that the company employed. Tensions are rising as workers from the South, both black and white, pour into the city to fill the jobs the war effort creates. White neighborhoods threaten violence at the prospect of integrated housing projects, and in June 1943, the tensions erupt into a full-scale race riot, starting on Belle Isle and spreading to Black Bottom. The riot kills thirty-four people, twenty-four of whom are African Americans. City officials insist that the black community is to blame, in the face of ample evidence to the contrary.

Sugar Ray Robinson had been the favorite, at more than three to one as the match drew near. Betting was heavy. Olympia was sold out: 18,916 fans had shown up, the largest crowd for a boxing match at that venue ever. Gross receipts came in at $47,280.[1] In the end, he was saved by the bell from a knockout in the eighth round: "With Robinson sitting outside the ring, his legs across the bottom strand of ropes, Referee Sam Hennessy was about to raise his right hand for the count of 10 when the bell ended the round." He held on for all ten rounds, but the decision was unanimous: LaMotta on points. Thus, the "Raging Bull" of later Robert De Niro fame handed Sugar Ray his first defeat after 129 victories. The *Detroit Free Press* does not bother to mention that Sugar Ray grew up in Detroit—defeated, he becomes the "wraith-like Negro from New York's Harlem."[2]

The crowd, the paper reported, was in a mad uproar from beginning to end. Joyce Carol Oates says that "each boxing match is a story—a unique and highly condensed drama without words."[3] What was the story of this particular fight? Upsets, in a way, are always more satisfying than the outcomes we expect. They make for better stories. A few years earlier, the fight might have been framed as yet another black versus white confrontation, but mainstream newspapers were not selling that narrative anymore, though no doubt there were many who still saw it that way. The *Detroit Free Press* points out, in passing, that "LaMotta has made a specialty of beating [black fighters]" and that "Friday night's fight was the forty-eighth of Jake's career and Robinson was his fortieth negro opponent."[4]

It is important to keep in mind, though, that in the 1940s someone like LaMotta wasn't exactly "white"—"LaMotta knew there were those who called him a wop, though never to his face," Wil Haygood writes. Conversely, Robinson was not the "savage," as they had called Joe Louis—slim, elegant, cool, and hitherto undefeated, he was "the artist," with LaMotta "the proletarian." On that backdrop, Haygood casts the match as one framed by "fierce ethnic pride"—and part of a rivalry that would span a decade, "an opera in six brutal acts" that would end in Chicago with the Valentine's Day Massacre of February 14, 1951.[5] On that day, Sugar Ray's victory was so complete that LaMotta would joke later that "if the referee had held up another 30 more seconds, Sugar Ray would have collapsed from hitting me."[6]

Back in 1943, only a few weeks after Robinson loses to LaMotta, he is given another crack. In front of an Olympia crowd of 15,149, Robinson, who badly wanted the rematch a few days before he is due to join the army, wins on points and goes off to war. LaMotta's fans—he had gathered quite the following in Detroit—thought the verdict was a farce.[7] But while LaMotta's aggressive style may have pleased the audiences, history would judge Sugar Ray Robinson to be the classier boxer of the two, and many think of him as one of the finest boxers of all times on a pound for pound basis: in 2002, he was ranked number one on *The Ring* magazine's list of "80 Best Fighters of the Last 80 Years."[8]

The Detroit fights were marketed vigorously: LaMotta, born in New York, got into shape at a gym off Gratiot Avenue, a little northeast of Black Bottom, in the area where most of the Italian community lived at the time.[9] For Robinson (born Walker Smith Jr. in 1921), it was a homecoming. In the 1920s, his parents, Walker and Leila Smith, had moved from Georgia to Detroit, where his father found work in the construction industry.[10] The family first lived on Macomb Street in Black Bottom, but for a while, they did well enough to be able to move a few blocks north to Canfield Street, always a sign of economic success in black Detroit. Things didn't end well, though—Walker Sr. was a philanderer, and Leila took the children back to Georgia for a while, returned to Detroit for a bit, and finally ended the marriage and moved to Harlem in 1932.[11]

Junior had fond memories of growing up in Detroit, especially of spending time at the legendary Brewster Recreation Center. The rec center, a converted library, had opened in 1929 to serve the migrant community around Black Bottom. It had basketball courts, a swimming pool, and a boxing ring. Charged membership dues of one quarter a week, Sugar Ray spent his time watching the boxers, including the one everybody was watching then: a promising young fighter named Joe Barrow, who would rename himself Joe Louis. Junior would become Sugar Ray Robinson when, at the age of fifteen, he borrowed his friend Ray Robinson's birth certificate so he could get his first Amateur Athletic Union membership card—he needed one to enter his first boxing tournament, and, being younger than the required age of eighteen, could not qualify using his own birthdate.[12] As Louis and Robinson became friends in later life, both liked to remember that Junior had carried Joe's bags when he trained at the Brewster. But since Joe didn't start boxing seriously until sometime in 1932, and Junior left Detroit in the fall of that year, they couldn't have known each other that well. And although Sugar Ray always stressed that he was born in Detroit (contradicting those who claimed he was born in Georgia), he never had as close a connection to the city as Joe Louis did, though the two ended up spending a good deal of their wartime service together.[13]

Boxing was still big back then, and Detroit was one of its centers. That probably explains one of the most hilarious interludes in the annals of boxing, Francesco "Frank" Barbaro's "White Hope" tournament of 1941. By the end of the 1930s, not least because of Joe Louis and Sugar Ray Robinson, African Americans were dominating the fight game. Since the days of Jack Johnson, the business would trot out one "great white hope" after the other, but black boxers, especially in the heavyweight class, continued to rule, much to the displeasure of some. Barbaro was an Italian immigrant who had started out in the coal mines of Illinois. He then made some money in the meats business before losing it all in the Great Depression, after which he came to Detroit to work in the factories, eventually saving enough to open the Bowery, a nightclub in Hamtramck, in 1934. A vigorous self-promoter, he decided to move into the fight business, and his bright idea was to post an open call to white boxing talent: the winner, he promised, would get to challenge and defeat Joe Louis.

Hilarity ensued. "What Makes White Hope Necessary?" the *Detroit Free Press* caustically asked in September 1941:

> What I would like to ask and I hereby do ask is what is the matter with the man who is champion now? There never was a cleaner fighter than Joe Louis. . . . He minds his own business, he fights anybody and everybody who has the slightest pretense of being a heavyweight challenger. On nights when he looks like the great fighter that he is and scores a quick knockout he is modest and unassuming. When somebody makes him look bad, he admits it. He is generous with praise for others and stingy with praise for himself. He can be champion, for my dough, as long as can keep belting out the boys and if Mr. Barbaro would like some free advice, here it is: Forget those white hopes and confine the search to chorus girls for the night club.[14]

A few weeks later, the same paper reported that "White Hopes Fail to Stir Excitement."[15] The national press had a field day: "Oct. 17, the first night," *Newsweek* wrote, "brought forth the funniest fighting ever seen outside a Keystone Comedy as 38 fighters, most of them wretchedly inept, traded awkward roundhouse swings in nineteen bouts. They ranged in size from Albert Nassaney, 300 pounds of blubber from Hoboken, N.J., to a tall skinny youth named Eddie Organic, weighing in at a willowy 175. And most of Detroit stayed far away, for the shambles drew a mere 4,336 persons." It was 2,796 on the second night, "practically private," *Newsweek* scoffed, when "the short and baldish Sgt. Frank Zamaris of Fort Dix . . . descended so furiously on his opponent, Sgt. Johnny Pivovar of Fort Sheridan, that

Pivovar lost three teeth and was clubbed to sleep simultaneously." The whole thing just fizzles out eventually, but not before Barbaro sinks at least $50,000 into his pathetic dream while "the behemoths, of whom there were some 50 to start, clutter up the Hotel Detroiter and gulp thick steaks in Barbaro's night club."[16] The *Free Press*, which had described the hapless challengers as "a breed long since thought to be extinct," sums up that "from a fighting standpoint, the tournament was a flop, but it was a champion mirth provoker."[17] The tournament did not uncover a single remarkable talent, though one Lee Savold, a journeyman boxer, was eventually declared the champion, and he would get to fight Joe Louis a full ten years later—only to be knocked out in the sixth round.[18]

Barbaro's ill-fated tournament may well be symptomatic of a larger historical development in the United States, the invention of whiteness as a category that would supersede ethnic differentiation along lines of national origin. For a long time, Italian Americans, particularly those from the south of Italy, were considered to be "racially suspect," as historian Jennifer Guglielmo writes.[19] In the 1940s, whiteness had become a highly desirable commodity to which Italian Americans were not fully entitled—what better way to establish your racial credentials than a "white hope" tournament?

All over the city, white immigrants were jockeying for position along with the migrants from the South—their status in the city was as low as it can get. Even in the early 1950s, a survey conducted by researcher Arthur Kornhauser found that "poor Southern whites, hill-billies, etc." were seen as the second-most undesirable group in Detroit, just after "criminals, gangsters, etc.," and two slots ahead of "Negroes."[20] As war workers flooded into Detroit, the pressures on the housing stock had helped fuel ethnic, geographical, and racial tensions. Most of the 150,000 or so migrants arriving in the city came from the South, and about three-quarters of them were white.[21] In the cauldron that was Detroit, Southern whites looked down on African Americans, but as Arnow describes so vividly in *The Dollmaker*, to most of the natives, they were "hillbillies" and a "disgrace to the race."[22] The crisis that unfolded in 1942 had little to do with them, a despised and discriminated group in their own right—it was white-established Detroit that was flexing its muscle against newcomers and working-class African Americans—and even middle-class black Detroiters joined in.

In June of 1941, the Detroit Housing Commission and the Federal Housing Administration (FHA) announced plans to build a government-funded housing project named after Sojourner Truth, the legendary abolitionist and women's rights activist. Truth had been born enslaved in 1797, managed to escape in 1826, and devoted her life to the cause. Around 1856 she moved to Michigan, where she would spend the rest of her life. While not directly involved in the Underground Railroad, she did help former slaves find homes, and during the Civil War, she helped recruit African American regiments to the Northern army. After the war, she campaigned for land grants for emancipated slaves. She died in Battle Creek, Michigan, in 1883.

By the end of 1941, the construction of the Sojourner Truth housing project was almost complete, and African Americans lucky enough to be allocated a home were scheduled to start rental payments on January 1, 1942. The Detroit Housing Commission had already established that government-funded projects would be segregated. When the NAACP argued for integrated housing, the commission presented the organization with a stark choice: you can either accept segregation, or there will be no housing for African Americans. But once it became known that the Sojourner Truth housing project was intended for African Americans, the ethnically Polish residents of Hamtramck mounted their own campaign to convert it into housing for white Detroiters instead. The push was led by three men: Father Constantine Dziuk, a local Catholic priest; Rudolph Tenerowicz, a former mayor of Hamtramck who had been convicted on vice conspiracy charges in 1931 and was later pardoned by the Governor; and a local realtor by the name of Joseph Bulla.[23] Blacks moving into the area, they argued, would bring down the value of white residents' property, which was largely funded by FHA loans. That line of argument was well established, and segregationists trotted it out whenever they felt threatened by even a modicum of integration—in this case, it was actually a fully segregated project, but still too close to white neighborhoods for their liking. The Polish American community lent substantial support to the campaign, which would mark the beginning of a new pattern. A report by a government investigator, dated 1942, states:

> The conflict over the Sojourner Truth Project illustrates the changing attitudes of Poles towards the Negroes. Until the

time when the Project was occupied by Negroes, the Poles and
Negroes lived amicably in Hamtramck on the same street and
in the same house. The Poles expressed no anxiety over depreci-
ated property values in a mixed neighborhood until real estate
agents and the subversive groups involved in the Sojourner Truth
fight gave it to them when the projects were opened. The second
generation Poles were the first to take up the battle cry for segregation and discrimination. Like others of foreign descent in
Detroit, they were beginning to fear the competition of young
and status-conscious Negroes in jobs. The younger Poles are
now inducing anti-Negro attitudes among the older generation
and the Negroes are being forced out of Hamtramck.[24]

The older generation of Poles, no doubt, remembered well what it was
like to be despised, excluded, and mocked. Immigrants from predominantly
Catholic countries in particular had been subject to vicious discrimination
in the United States for a long time, and lines such as "No polish or colored"
or "No Catholic" or "No Irish" had been common in job advertisements.[25]
Some restaurants featured signs reading "No Jews or dogs allowed," and
the open and rampant discrimination generated a considerable sense of
solidarity between disfavored groups, which also, of course, included Jewish Americans.[26] But the country was moving toward a racial classification
where the category of "white" subsumed demographic groups formerly seen
as distinct, with Anglo-Saxon Protestants at the top. Younger Polish immigrants or Americans of Polish descent no longer shared the same experiences
with African Americans, and solidarity largely crumbled, though in one sad
regard, it held: the residents of Conant Gardens, a black middle-class neighborhood nearby, joined the white opposition to the Sojourner Truth project,
likely in an effort to protect their investments.[27]

Shamefully, the FHA reversed itself in the face of this pressure and
announced in January 1942 that the project would now be for whites only.
But the African American community was not without its own allies—liberal
factions within the UAW and other progressive organizations reacted with
intense counter-protests, both at the mayor's office and in Washington. The
FHA completed its pirouette and returned to its original position; the black

tenants were scheduled to move in on February 28. Once again, the white opposition organized itself, erecting billboards with slogans such as "We want white tenants in our white community."[28] On the 27th, the night before move-in day, the KKK flexed its muscle and burned a cross, and by morning, around twelve hundred white protesters harassed and intimidated the few blacks courageous enough to attempt to make their new homes in the project. Black protesters arrived to oppose the racists, and despite heavy police presence, street fights broke out. In the ensuing battle, the police arrested 220 people—217 of them black. The *New York Times* noted the startling disparity in how police responded toward black and white combatants.[29]

It was time for the government to take over, and after some delay, it did, with a massive show of force: in April, 1,100 police and 1,600 members of the National Guard were sent to guard the first six African American families to finally move in. In the face of clear evidence that the government was committed to backing the project this time, white opposition dissolved, and in the end, 168 black families moved into the Sojourner Truth project.

The intense hostility that the white population showed to the black residents in this case is mirrored in countless other stories of the period. Up until a Supreme Court ruling in 1948, it remained legal to make a covenant in the title deed of a house stating that it could not be sold to particular buyers, such as African Americans or Jewish Americans.[30] Faced with an intense housing shortage, black families who could afford to do so tried desperately to move into marginal white neighborhoods, and never without opposition. In 1941, about six miles west of Sojourner Truth, on Pembroke Avenue between Van Antwerp Park and Eight Mile Road, white residents built a wall six feet tall and half a mile long to separate themselves from black residents.[31] To this day, petty techniques of segregation can appear around the city. In 2015, the well-to-do, predominantly white city of Grosse Pointe erected huge planters on Kercheval at the border with the city of Detroit. The arrangement resembled a checkpoint in a country at war, although Grosse Pointe claimed it was decorative. Following a negotiation between the two cities, in 2019 Grosse Pointe took steps to restore both the appearance and the reality of traffic access.[32]

Such was the state of race relations when Jake LaMotta fought Sugar Ray Robinson, a match fraught with symbolic tension. By the beginning of 1943, so-called hate strikes had become common: white workers would simply refuse to work alongside black workers, and as many as twenty thousand white workers walked off the job in response to the promotion of a few black colleagues. Such strikes were particularly frequent in the Packard plant on the southeastern corner of Hamtramck.[33] The Packard Local 190 was widely believed to have been infiltrated by the KKK, whose members had pushed the confrontation over the Sojourner Truth housing. Black union members grew increasingly frustrated at the UAW's lukewarm measures to defend them. Although the senior leadership was sympathetic, local white organizers often were not. In April of 1943, in response to the mounting criticism, the NAACP and UAW jointly organized a march down Woodward Avenue. Five thousand joined, protesting discrimination and demanding jobs for black women in particular. Walter Reuther and other members of the union leadership addressed the marchers and pledged to fight discrimination.[34]

On June 20, tensions erupted once again, with disastrous consequences. It was a Sunday, a hot summer day, and families gathered on Belle Isle, relaxing, barbecuing, and, no doubt, drinking. Unlike most of the city, Belle Isle, one and a half square miles of parkland, was not segregated. The island is connected to the city by a bridge almost half a mile long. As black and white families made their way back in the late afternoon, a fight broke out— nobody has ever been able to establish why, but a horrendous rumor spread: a group of men had taken a baby from its mother and thrown it over the railing into the Detroit River. In some tellings, the child is black and the men are white, in others the child is white and the men are black.[35] By 9 p.m., pitched battles between white and black Detroiters had broken out around the bridge, and the unrest started to spread along Jefferson Avenue. Whites hurled bricks at cars driven by blacks, and vice versa. There were beatings and stabbings. By 11 p.m., the unrest had reached Black Bottom, and the local population had come out in force. There were some assaults on random whites trapped in the neighborhood, and in the disorder, the looting began. By 4 a.m., gangs of white youths on Woodward Avenue were assaulting black patrons leaving nightclubs and theaters.[36]

The next day, the entire city was in the grip of chaos, violence, and disorder. In 1943, about 10 percent of the city's population was black, and given the segregated structure of the city, white antagonists knew where to attack. The mayor witnessed five hundred white men pursue one black man, presumably intent on lynching him, only for the man to be saved by a police officer. There were stories of ten thousand white men hunting down "black meat" in Cadillac Square.[37] As the day wore on, there were running battles between the police and black rioters, and community leaders begged the governor to send the National Guard. African Americans had good reason to distrust the overwhelmingly white Detroit police force, which became plain for all to see when photos of the rioting were published in the newspapers. One picture in the *Detroit Free Press* showed two black men lying on the ground surrounded by a crowd of white rioters; another in the *New York Times* showed two policemen holding up a black man while a white man assaults him.[38] On Monday evening, six thousand federal troops arrived, and by the following morning, peace had been restored. When it was over, thirty-four people had been killed, twenty-five of whom were African American. Of these twenty-five, seventeen had been killed by the police, whereas none of the nine white victims were. Around six hundred people were injured, three-quarters of whom were black. Over one thousand had been arrested—predominantly black. Property destruction ran into the millions, most of it in the Paradise Valley neighborhood.[39]

The governor of Michigan commissioned an inquiry into the causes of the riot. The committee decided that "irresponsible" black community leaders were to blame for stirring up resentments against the white majority and encouraging lawless behavior.[40] The committee members identified most of the rioters as young hoodlums, and while black community leaders and those on the left reported that the KKK had been involved in organizing the white violence, nobody seemed eager to follow up on this line of inquiry. The United States was at war with the fascists, and it wouldn't do to look too closely into the homegrown variety. For the most part, the committee based its report on police reports and neglected to interview any of the rioters involved directly.[41] One man did conduct such interviews: Dr. Lowell Selling, a court psychiatrist, who sat with convicted offenders. He concluded that, while largely employed and educated, they were also mostly migrants from the South and therefore, clearly, somewhat simpleminded and prone to violence because of their Southern heritage—"incapable of thinking straight."[42] The white establishment, be it government officials or professionals, closed ranks and attributed the riot to African Americans, whom they deemed socially and mentally inferior.

In vain, representatives of black communities sought to draw attention to the long list of legitimate grievances that underpinned black anger, and to the racially biased conduct of the police that managed to arrest black rioters almost exclusively despite clear evidence that they had been vastly outnumbered by the white rioters.

Years later, research into the profiles of those arrested showed that they weren't young hoodlums but predominantly mature, working-class black Detroiters. By contrast, however, the few whites that had been arrested tended to fit the profile falsely attributed to the African Americans: young, unattached, roaming the streets intent on inflicting violence. Blacks were arrested close to their homes, whites more often at some distance from their residence. Blacks were more likely to be arrested for looting and destroying white-owned businesses, whites for rioting—and the latter were also more likely to be armed, suggesting they were there for one reason only: to attack and fight blacks.[43]

Unlike most disturbances that get called by that name, the riot of 1943 was an actual race riot. There is evidence, in other words, that many of the aggressors were motivated predominantly by racial animus. There may indeed have been some black rioters who were seeking retribution, following hate strikes in wartime production plants. There may also have been some black rioters who wanted to vent their hatred against racist policemen. But it seems that a majority of the white rioters were rioting against African Americans in general. What we do know is that white rioters outnumbered black ones, and that hardly any of them were arrested. Once again, the Detroit police force acted as an arm of white supremacy, aided and abetted by government and other establishment figures. The 1943 riot, then, differed decisively from the uprising of 1967. Many of the problems, of course, would have remained the same—poor housing, unequal employment opportunities, police brutality—but the 1967 protests were not a fight between black and white Detroit, but a reaction to the police force's conduct.

In the wake of the riot the city authorities, concerned that the war effort would be disrupted, tried to quickly engineer a return to normalcy rather than institute actual change. Tuesday's game against the Cleveland Indians at Briggs Stadium was canceled, but the Wednesday game was allowed to proceed, albeit with three hundred soldiers posted inside the stadium.[44] But in papering over the cracks, the city missed possibly the biggest opportunity in its history. In general, the North had long refused to acknowledge that its own version of Jim Crow was just as unjust as the Southern variety, and the country was committed to a wartime myth of national unity. Detroit embraced that myth even as Gerald L.K. Smith, the infamous leader of the "America First" party, was publishing his fascist rag, *The Flag and the Cross*, from a building in downtown Detroit. In fact, labor activists and other socialists were convinced that Smith had had his hand in the riot, either as an organizer or at least someone who fueled the flames. In 1945, Hal Draper, a leading American Trotskyist, published a pamphlet under the imprint of the Workers Party entitled *The Truth About Gerald Smith: America's No. 1 Fascist*. By then, they had driven Smith out of Detroit and he had moved on to Los Angeles, but the left remembered his collaboration with the car industry and particularly Ford's anti-labor force. Their ire went deeper, and Draper's account is an important contemporary corrective to the official narratives hastily assembled by local and state government and law enforcement:

> If the strike-breaking record of Gerald Smith was not fresh in [labor's] minds, the infamous Detroit race riots of June 1943 were. This was a deliberately organized pogrom upon the Negro people, one of the most shameful of recent years. Bands of white youths roamed through the main streets and invaded the Negro neighborhoods of Detroit, looking for colored victims—beating, clubbing, maiming and killing. Thirty-four were slain, of whom twenty-five were Negroes. Policemen stood around grinning or turned their backs. Hundreds were injured. Negro housing projects like Sojourner Truth were attacked. The stench of race hatred hung over the city. Cries were heard from some of the fascist scum: "The Jews are next!" Everybody knew that this was a deliberately organized bloodbath. Who were the Hitlerite fiends who were behind it? Fourteen labor, liberal and progressive

national organizations publicly accused Gerald L.K. Smith of instigating the pogrom.[45]

Smith denied the charges, and the city's leaders refused to listen to black leaders and left-wing activists alike. UAW president R.J. Thomas declared that there was "a substantial nucleus of KKK and Black Legion elements here and nobody in political life has the intestinal fortitude to move in and prosecute."[46]

Had the city authorities been willing to at least engage with the black community representatives and address their many valid grievances, integration could have made a giant leap forward. It must remain a speculation, but it is quite possible that the country would have taken a different turn if it hadn't waited to eradicate legalized racism until decades later. In a memorable formulation, Thomas Sugrue describes Detroit's continuing segregationist policies and practices of the time as "the coffin of peace." It is the same coffin in which Joe Louis's aspirations to a Ford dealership would be buried.

The UAW, coordinating with black leaders, did attempt to chart a way forward "to forestall future riots." This involved an eight-point plan, which included the provision of adequate park and recreational facilities, provision of adequate housing for African Americans, and a commitment to addressing racial intolerance and ensuring impartial justice.[47] Instead of systemic change, Detroit's power brokers opted for public relations stunts—the Ford Motor Company, in particular, turned to athletes, exploiting their popularity to polish its image without working towards actual change. In July 1943, a widely syndicated puff piece by Watson Spoelstra, a Detroit-based sportswriter who would later end up at the *Detroit News*, pays homage to the "autograph seeker's paradise [that] is the vast Ford industrial empire," sprawling with "yesterday's and today's heroes of diamond and gridiron, ring and rink." Spoelstra credits the infamous Harry Bennett (more about him in chapter 22), head of the "Services Department," known for his brutal union-busting, for keeping lions at his Ann Arbor estate, and for shooting guns in his office. At the Ford Hunger March of 1932, Bennett had his people open fire on the unemployed marchers, leading to the death of four of them—a fifth died months later from his injuries. In Spoelstra's column, however, Bennett is just "a wiry little man with a big bow tie," partial to hiring athletes, particularly boxers.[48] War hides all sorts of sins.

Bennett's most notable employee during the wartime years, however, must have been Jesse Owens, "the world's fastest man" who, after humiliating Hitler in 1936 by becoming the first athlete to win four gold medals in the Olympic Games, was quickly betrayed and dismissed by the country for which he had run. In 1935, Jesse Owens had stunned the athletic world at a Big Ten track meet in Ann Arbor by setting three world records (and equaling a fourth) in 45 minutes, remembered as "the greatest 45 minutes ever in sport." His greatest triumph, of course, was at the 1936 Berlin Olympics when "he grabbed Adolf Hitler's toxic theories of racial supremacy and stuffed them in the Fuhrer's face by winning gold medals in the 100 and 200 meters, the long jump and the 4x100 relay."[49] You would think that feat would have won him the nation's and the American sports world's everlasting gratitude—instead, they stripped him of his amateur status, effectively ending his athletic career, when he opted to return home rather than tour with the Olympic team. An athlete of his stature might have expected to be recruited by a college athletic department as a coach, but instead Owens was forced to take on menial jobs to support his family. One of the most humiliating moments came when two businessmen approached him, representing the Negro Baseball League. Owens, still in peak form, was "more excited than I'd been in months. Here it was—right at the last minute when I need it most—another opportunity of a lifetime! I hadn't played much baseball, I'd been too busy with track. But I was fast, and strong, and I'd learn. I'd learn."[50] What he did learn was that they didn't want him to play ball—they wanted him to run 100-yard races against horses. In other words, they wanted him as a circus act. Owens could not afford to say no, and for a while, that is how he made his money.

When the government came calling in 1942, it must have been an enormous relief. How could a segregated military of a nation that had broken every promise to African Americans convince them to buy war bonds and to send their sons into war? Its answer was to turn to black superstars like Joe Louis and Jesse Owens, who suddenly became immensely valuable to the nation. After a stint as National Director of the Physical Fitness Program for Colored People in Civilian Defense, Owens took a position under Harry Bennett at Ford, where he quickly rose to the position of Director of Negro Personnel at the River Rouge plant. The exact dates are unclear: the Ford archives will only confirm that Owens's employment started in 1942 and ended in 1945, declining to share any further details of his contract. What is notable is that the white press of the time refers to him simply as "a Ford worker," hiding the fact that he held an executive position.[51] The same is even true for Ford's internal newspaper, the *Ford Times*, where he is simply "of the Personnel department at the Rouge plant" or "working at a desk in the Employment division." The coverage is in marked contrast to that of the African American press: the *People's Voice*, for instance, reports that Jesse Owens is "slated to take over the [Negro Employment] office" as a "labor relations expert."[52]

Not much is known about Owens's time at Ford—possibly because Ford downplayed his role, but his own accounts are vague as well. In *Jesse: The Man Who Outran Hitler*, he writes that Roosevelt himself summoned him:

> "Jesse Owens," he said, "we're in a terrible war, one that will not be easy to win. I think you can help us to move toward victory." . . . What they wanted me to do was to supervise the hiring of Negroes for the wartime effort in the Ford Motor Plant in Detroit. . . . Not many Negroes had been hired for jobs in the auto plants before that, and it was up to me to pick the right ones, not only so they'd get along with the whites, but so that we'd all get the job done and win the war."[53]

In fact, Ford had always had a sizable African American workforce, and "getting the job done" meant that Owens, as William J. Baker writes, "constantly found himself caught in the squeeze between Harry Bennett's authoritarian policies and the UAW's determination to protect workers' rights. The quick-triggered Bennett fired him four times for failing to protect company interests, only to rehire him immediately." But Owens, it appears, was no working-class hero: "Jesse's allegiance was clear. 'I was working for the company, for the interest of the company,' he told an interviewer later. He toed the Ford line, he insisted, because 'we had a war going on' and the building of Pratt-Whitney motors, tanks, and B-24 bombers 'was a mighty important job.'"[54]

After the riot, with the city on edge and race relations as bad as they'd ever been, Jesse Owens was switched from HR to PR: "He worked closely with the Urban League to improve housing for Ford workers, with the local YMCA to provide wholesome recreation, and with the NAACP to air the problems facing black families who had recently moved to Detroit to work for Ford. In all those measures, Jesse projected a benign corporate image that had been sadly lacking under the domineering rule of Harry Bennett."[55] After Edsel Ford's death in 1943, a struggle for control of the company ensued. Henry was ailing, both physically and mentally, and Bennett fancied his chances of seizing control while Edsel's sons were still on active war duty. But Henry Ford II returned to the company in 1943, and though the power struggle lasted for two more years, Bennett was finally ousted, along with a thousand of his closest thugs. The new regime offered Owens a different job, with lower status. Owens declined and moved on. Unlike Joe Louis, he did not leave his mark on Detroit, and few have even heard of his brief interlude at Ford.

To be sure, Detroit was not the only city to be affected by race riots and both ethnic and racial conflict during the war. Serious unrest also broke out in Harlem, Mobile, and Brownsville, Texas. The opening paragraph of James Baldwin's soaring essay "Notes of a Native Son" mentions that "there had been, in Detroit, one of the bloodiest race riots of the century."[56] The great American writer tells his own story as a war worker in New Jersey to illustrate the roots of the rebellions. After being turned away from every lunch counter and every restaurant he enters because they "don't serve Negroes here," the growing bitterness turns into blind fury:

> That year in New Jersey lives in my mind as though it were the year during which, having an unsuspected predilection for it, I first contracted some dread, chronic disease, the unfailing symptom of which is a kind of blind fever, a pounding in the skull and fire in the bowels. Once this disease is contracted, one can never be really carefree again, for the fever, without an instant's warning, can recur at any moment. It can wreck more important things than race relations. There is not a Negro alive who does not have this rage in his blood—one has the choice, merely, of living with it consciously or surrendering to it. As for me, this fever has recurred in me, and does, and will until the day I die.[57]

The violence erupted all over the country. During those years, there were racially motivated attacks by whites on Mexicans and African Americans in Chicago and Los Angeles. There were hate strikes in Chicago, Baltimore, and Philadelphia. Racism was not a Detroit problem, it was an American problem—but in the long run, Detroit may have paid a heavier price than most other cities. The factory jobs began leaving the city in the 1940s, and when plant after plant moved to the suburbs, even those who wanted to stay had little choice other than to follow the work. Thus began the long exodus to the suburbs.

TWENTY

JUNE 22, 1938

It takes Joe Louis two minutes and four seconds to beat Max Schmeling, boxing representative of the Third Reich. Louis, already world champion, has now avenged his unexpected defeat in 1936. When much of America rejoices at the triumph, white supremacists have to eat their disappointment. Louis, who had grown up in Detroit, learned his trade in the publicly funded Brewster Recreation Center, during the time when the Black Legion, a splinter group of the Ku Klux Klan, terrorized the city.

At 10:08 p.m. the bell rings in Yankee Stadium.[1] What the audience sees is a white man who walks slowly toward his opponent, a black man. Race is everything this evening. This fight is fought over white supremacy, and for once, America is siding with the black man. Joe Louis is usually slow to advance in the first round, but this time, he bounds from his corner, eager to throw the first punch. For maybe seven seconds, the two boxers feint jabs at each other, and then Louis hits Max Schmeling, Hitler's boxer, with a strong left jab. Two more blows snap back Schmeling's head, followed by a left hook to his body. They clinch. As they break free, they face each other, Schmeling crouching now, extending his left arm as if this will keep Louis away; Louis leans forward and peers between his raised gloves, looking for an opening. He leaps at his opponent, who tries to hold him, but Louis manages two more hits to the head and drives Schmeling onto the ropes. Schmeling pushes forward and stems the tide for a moment, but as he steps back, Louis delivers a fierce left jab straight to the face. Barely thirty seconds have passed.

There's a lull, as the two men weigh where they stand. Schmeling thinks he may have weathered the storm and tentatively advances again, but as Louis continues to crouch forward, threatening to strike, the German slowly retreats to the ropes. He manages to duck under a huge left-handed swing, but as he tries to raise himself, an upper cut hits him full in the face, followed by another right. He is now defenseless. A huge swinging blow misses completely, and Louis steadies Schmeling's head with his right glove as if he were to deliver the full force of his left arm into Schmeling's face. Instead, he chooses to deliver a blow to stomach, one to the kidneys, then one to the head again. Left, right, left, right, left, right—Schmeling is now leaning on the ropes, looking out to the audience, and the referee pushes Louis away so Schmeling can catch his breath. Just over one minute of the fight has gone by.

Schmeling turns back into the ring, trying to steady himself with the rope as he leaves the security it offers. Louis walks straight at him and delivers a left and then a right to the head; Schmeling falls forward onto his knees, then onto his back, and rolls again so he is back on his knees. He stands up and faces Louis, his arms lolling by his side, now looking more like a drunk than anything else. He can barely raise his arms as Louis immediately hits him again on the side of the head with his right fist. He leans away, crouching now, trying to hold off his attacker, but the black man just uses his left arm to stand him up straight and throw another left jab. Schmeling is now leaning forward and so Louis withdraws his supporting arms and Schmeling stumbles to the floor. He gets up and the referee checks to see if he can continue; he can, so Louis advances again.

One more big punch to the kidneys and one more big right hand to the side of the head and Schmeling goes down for the third time. Louis briefly crouches over him, as if to check that he is really hurt and then retreats to his corner. Schmeling is lying on the canvas resting on one elbow, his legs seemingly gone. He manages to raise himself to his knees to start the impossible process of getting to his feet, but his first foot slips and he is back on his knees. The referee will let this continue if he can get to his feet. His cornerman runs into the ring to put a stop to it. Two minutes and four seconds have elapsed since the start of the fight. It is over. The black man won.

Why stress race to this extent? Because Schmeling's publicist had claimed that "no black man" could defeat him. Because the Nazis had used Schmeling to prove that whites, or "Aryans," were the superior race. Because after their first fight, which Schmeling had won, a Rome paper opined that Schmeling had "confirmed the supremacy of a race that could not be undone by brute force."[2] Because the Nazi rag *Der Weltkampf* declared that "the Negro is of a slave nature, but woe unto us if this slave nature is unbridled, for then arrogance and cruelty show themselves in the most bestial way."[3] Because the fight's winnings would go toward building German tanks, Schmeling's publicist announced. Because this was a fight framed as a fight between white and black, between Nazi Germany and pluralist America, however egregiously the United States fell short of its ideals. Germany had just annexed Austria. The entire world was watching, and they were watching not just an American fight a German, they were watching a black man fight a white man, with the stakes impossibly high. And for the first time, most of America was rooting for the black man: "The whole damned country was depending on me," Louis is quoted in a biography.[4]

They had fought once before, on June 19, 1936, but Schmeling had needed twelve rounds to knock Louis out back then. This time Louis needed exactly one to take Schmeling down. The fight would be spun as a victory for America and a defeat for fascism, but those two minutes are also shorthand for the entire history of Detroit. Joe Louis, world heavyweight champion from Detroit, crushes Max Schmeling, representative of the Nazi regime, whose dogma is founded on the concept of racial superiority. In two minutes, Joe Louis proved something that generations of biologists and social theorists could not: that theories of racial supremacy can be made risible by two minutes in a boxing ring. Jesse Owens had managed something similar during a few seconds at the Berlin Olympics in 1936. But a fight is a better symbol than a race, particularly at a time when boxing was huge and track was not.

In 1938, theories of white racial superiority were broadly accepted in America, of course, and Detroit was no exception. On the contrary: Father Coughlin's increasingly unhinged sermons were still on the air, broadcast from Detroit. Henry Ford thought of African Americans as inferior citizens in need of paternalistic care, and his policies were actually on the benign side—measured by the standards of the time, a man who paid black workers the same as white ones was a near miracle. To African Americans who had fled the South's Jim Crow and Ku Klux Klan, the lynchings, beatings, arson, and daily humiliations, industrial cities such as Detroit held a promise they rarely kept—James Baldwin's essays reflecting on those years lay waste to the notion of a more tolerant North. The color bar applied to professional athletes in the major leagues in the North as much as it did in the South. And in any case, the Klan had followed the migrants north—during the 1920s, the state with the largest Klan membership was Indiana, with Michigan not far behind.

It is impossible to understand how much Joe Louis meant to black Americans in Detroit in the 1930s without understanding the history of race relations in the city in the preceding decades. In 1910, about six thousand African Americans had lived in Detroit, but the black population started to grow in the following decade as the rapidly expanding auto industry attracted migrants from the South along with immigrants from Poland, Germany, Russia, Britain, Ireland, Hungary, Italy, and elsewhere. For most migrant communities, the pattern of settlement was common—at first they would crowd together into slums close to the central business district. As they adapted and learned to blend into their new country, ethnic organization gave way to social stratification. The consolidation of whiteness was far from complete in the 1930s, but for African Americans in Detroit, there was no blending, and unless you were a member of the small black upper-middle class, there was rarely a way out of the neighborhood. All migrants had to deal with the housing shortages plaguing Detroit, and life was immensely difficult for migrant workers of all races and ethnicities—but for African Americans, the problems would stay long after other detested groups such as Appalachians or Italians or Poles had become just white Detroiters.

Before the Civil Rights Act passed, racial segregation was largely legal, and not, as many Northerners liked to believe, just in the South—even if tactics varied. A common method for keeping African Americans literally in their place was to use restrictive covenants, which frequently excluded Jewish Americans as well—home buyers had to enter a contractual obligation never to sell to black or Jewish residents; in addition, banks did their part by making it exceedingly difficult for black residents to get mortgages on halfway decent terms. White supremacist organizations such as the KKK stood by in the rare cases where segregation by paperwork failed, quickly resorting to more overt tactics of intimidation and terror. (We described the lingering effects for black urban communities earlier in chapter 7.)

The most famous of such cases is the story of Ossian Sweet, which begins in 1925, thirteen years before Louis knocks out Schmeling. The black physician was one of the few who had managed to move out of Black Bottom after persuading a homeowner to sell him a modest house on Garland Street, in a white neighborhood on the East Side. He paid $6,000 over market value—a kind of racism fee that was the norm in Detroit. The "Waterworks Park Improvement Association," an organization whose sole mission was to dissuade black Detroiters from moving into white neighborhoods, thought they would make quick work of the transgressor, but Sweet was prepared. He knew that other houses belonging to black middle-class families in white neighborhoods had been attacked, and he gathered a group of friends and relatives to defend his home.

Representatives of the "Improvement Association," along with Sweet's new neighbors, all of whom he easily outranked in education and accomplishment, angrily confronted him on his very first day on Garland, September 8. As the angry white crowd swelled—estimates of the size vary widely, but it could have been up to two thousand—policemen were assigned to the area to keep the peace the next day. They couldn't have been too committed to their task: stones began to fly, an upstairs window shattered, and one of the men inside fired into the crowd from within the house. One white man was wounded, another one killed. The police arrested everybody in the house for murder, including Sweet's wife, Gladys. The press whipped the city into a frenzy.

It could have been the same old story, but this time, it came with a twist: the NAACP decided to put resources into the case, and they hired Clarence Darrow, one of the most famous defense lawyers in American history. The presiding judge, Frank Murphy, was young and considered a liberal. Before an all-white jury, the first trial ended in a mistrial. For the second one, Darrow managed to sever the cases of the eight defendants, and Henry Sweet, Ossian's brother, who was tried first, again by an all-white jury, was acquitted. As a consequence, the prosecution dropped the remaining cases, and Sweet and his friends went free—an outcome astonishing enough to have generated a play (Arthur Beer's *Malice Aforethought*, published in 1987), a celebrated book (Kevin Boyle's *Arc of Justice: A Saga of Race, Civil Rights, and Murder in the Jazz Age*, 2004),[5] another play based on Boyle's book, and a docudrama (Gordon C. Bennett's *My Name is Ossian Sweet*, 2011). The house at 2905 Garland Street was designated a Michigan Historic Site in 1975, and listed on the National Register of Historic Places in 1985.

A triumph in some ways, the story doesn't end happily: Gladys Sweet died of tuberculosis at the age of twenty-seven, as did Henry Sweet, in 1938—the year of Joe Louis's victory against Schmeling. Owing to financial difficulties, Ossian Sweet could not hold on to the house; his life steadily deteriorated, and he shot himself in the head in 1960.

Sweet's acquittal seemed to suggest that things were, indeed, better up North, but his story is an anomaly. In the 1920s, the Klan, now in its second incarnation, was no longer a Southern organization, and it had several strongholds in the Midwest, particularly in areas that were destinations of the Great Migration. In Detroit, the KKK quickly became powerful, and in 1924, the year of the Ossian Sweet incident, one Charles Bowles ran for mayor with the open support of the Klan. As the *Free Press* notes in a rundown of the worst mayors in Detroit history, "as more African Americans came to the city to work in factories, the Republican Bowles rode into office thanks in part to wide support from the Ku Klux Klan. It didn't help that a majority of the new recruits to the Detroit police force in the early 1920s were Southern whites—some of whom were Klansmen themselves."[6]

Eliminated in the primaries, Bowles had tried his luck as a write-in candidate instead, and would have won had it not been for fifteen thousand disqualified ballots. After running for office unsuccessfully several times, he finally succeeded in 1929—only to be recalled for "tolerating lawlessness" six months later in the biggest turnout special election in the city's history.[7]

By the start of the Great Depression, a new organization was emerging in the city: the Black Legion, a white supremacist group that served as the model for the 1937 film by the same title, starring Humphrey Bogart. An offshoot of the KKK, the Black Legion counted up to 135,000 members, including a significant number of public officials—possibly including, historian Rick Perlstein suggests, Detroit's police chief.[8] Harry Bennett was almost certainly a leading member. They were predominantly nativists, but their enemy list included not just all immigrants but also Catholics, Jews, and labor unionists—and, of course, African Americans. During their initiation ceremony, new members were asked what they surely took to be a rhetorical question: "Do you believe in white supremacy, and that no negro should have authority over a white man?"[9]

While immigration laws passed in 1921 and 1924 severely restricted the flow of migrants from Europe and imposed ethnic quotas, large numbers of Detroiters who had arrived earlier were either immigrants or the children of immigrants. Midwesterners whose families had been there for longer than one or two generations resented the competition for jobs, housing and, during the Depression, welfare support. The Black Legion, founded in Ohio, was active across the Midwest, but Detroit and Highland Park were among the principal recruitment centers. Organized on a paramilitary basis, the Black Legion claimed at one point to have one million members in Michigan—which was without a doubt self-aggrandizing bunk, as independent estimates put the figure closer to twenty-five thousand. Nonetheless, they inflicted severe terror on their victims. By one account, they would wait in a car at night on a quiet street until a black man passed and then simply shoot him, not only committing murder with impunity but instilling a growing sense of fear in black communities.

Shockingly, they flew under the radar for years—and not only because they largely targeted residents nobody in power cared much about. As historian Tom Stanton suggests in his wonderful book on "murder, baseball and the secret society that shocked Depression-era Detroit," on which much of our account here is based, they almost certainly enjoyed police protection, and law enforcement turned a blind eye.[10] The *Detroit Free Press* had made a few vague references to the organization in 1935, describing them as formed "to battle communism."[11] They would not be exposed until they killed a white man in 1936, Charles Poole—ostensibly for beating his wife, but more likely for being a Catholic married to a Protestant woman. Then, coverage exploded.

A year earlier, however, in May 1935, two Black Legion members, Dayton Dean and Charles Rouse, conspired in the senseless killing of a black man. They suggested to Silas Coleman that the three of them go for a ride to Rush Lake, fifty miles west of Detroit. This was the same day when, twenty miles away, Jesse Owens had set the world record in the long jump, the

220-yard dash, and the 220 low hurdles. Rouse owed Coleman money, and he told him that a fishing buddy at the lake would settle the debt. Around 11 p.m., they arrived at a cottage where Harvey Davis, a "colonel" in the Black Legion, was waiting for them, together with several other Legionnaires and their wives. Dean and Rouse told Coleman to wait in the car, while Davis instructed them to drive their victim to the Old Mill Pond in Pinckney. Davis and his men would follow, armed. Once they got to the lake, Coleman got out of the car, and Davis shot him point-blank in the stomach. Coleman turned and ran, and the rest followed him, firing. Desperate, he waded into the pond, but the bullets kept coming. After a while, the white terrorists were confident that their job was done and returned to Rush Lake to carry on drinking. Silas Coleman was found dead the next morning, leaning on a post six feet from the shore. He had gunshot wounds in the head, neck, and chest.

Davis had no motive, unless you want to call "wanting to know what it feels like to kill a black man" a motive. The police weren't keen on solving the murder. It was not until the Black Legion killed white Charles Poole in 1936 that the press and the police cracked down on them. Dayton Dean's testimony secured the conviction, and he confessed to several other criminal conspiracies. Among them was the murder of Silas Coleman. A subsequent trial eventually yielded several convictions—but if the Black Legion had kept to killing African Americans, they might have been left to do so in peace for years and years to come.[12]

Roughly ten years earlier, around the time Ossian Sweet stood trial for murder, the Barrow family from Alabama had joined the great migration to Detroit. In 1926, the family, including fourteen children, moved from rural subsistence farming to a crowded house on Macomb Street in Black Bottom. Joe, the youngest member of the family, was making little progress at school, and so his mother sent him to take violin lessons in the hope of uncovering a talent. On the way, he was persuaded by a school friend to use the fifty cents allotted to him for the lesson to enroll in a boxing gym instead. Thus began the career of perhaps the greatest heavyweight boxer in history—who might have become a great violinist instead, we will never know.

The need to outwit his mother was a bit of a theme—before one of his early fights, Joe Barrow changed his name because he didn't want his mother to see it in the newspapers—and thus it was that "Joe Louis" entered the boxing scene. He had fond memories of his Detroit childhood—paying five cents to spend all day at the movies, enjoying picnics on Belle Isle, hanging around the Eastern Market, where he did odd jobs at the produce stalls. In fact, he didn't recall anything too bad about Alabama either and remembered, instead, that "nobody white ever called me a 'nigger' until I got to Detroit."[13]

Initially the family thrived. His stepfather worked as a street cleaner, and one of his brothers got a job at Ford. But then came the 1929 Wall Street Crash and the start of the Great Depression. In 1929, the Detroit motor industry produced 5.3 million vehicles; by 1931, as demand collapsed, the number fell to 1.3 million. By 1932, the jobless population of Detroit was around one quarter of a million, or roughly one-third of the working population. As Louis said, "I'll bet you can predict a depression just by seeing how many black people are starting to lose their jobs."[14] Louis remembered standing in line at the soup kitchen to get food, and his mother receiving some relief money.

This was around the time that Louis took up boxing. He was bored at school, and he had transferred to a vocational college, where he was learning to build cabinets. But at the boxing gym they realized they had a talent on their hands, and Louis had found his vocation. There was one time he almost gave up: when Johnny Miler defeated him in 1932, in an amateur fight. Miler had represented the United States at the LA Olympics that summer, and thus was certainly a worthy opponent, but Louis was so demoralized that he decided to give up boxing and take a job at Ford, pushing truck bodies onto a conveyor belt. "Sometimes after work my back would hurt me so much I couldn't straighten up," he recalled—working the assembly line was tougher than fighting in the ring, in some ways.[15] By January 1933 he was back in training.

That year John Roxborough took him under his wing. Roxborough had become wealthy through the illegal numbers game (a kind of lottery that flourished in this era), but he was also a man with a sense of social responsibility and a commitment to supporting the African American community, where he was widely admired. He insisted, along with all the other trainers and managers that came to surround Joe Louis, that as a black professional boxer, Louis needed to set an example of respectability. Roxborough sent Louis to Chicago to train with Jack Blackburn, a fellow African American, who explained to him right at the start: "You know, boy, the heavyweight division for a Negro is hardly likely. The white man ain't too keen on it. You have to be something to get anywhere. If you really ain't gonna be another Jack Johnson you got some hope. White man hasn't forgotten that fool nigger with his white women acting like he owned the world."[16]

Louis turned professional in 1934, and he quickly rose to national prominence with nineteen fights and nineteen victories in under a year, including seven knockouts and only four fights going the distance. In July 1935, his stellar record won him a fight against former champion Primo Carnera at Yankee Stadium. Carnera was associated with Benito Mussolini, the Italian fascist dictator, and like the Schmeling fights to come, this one was framed in racial terms. At the time, Mussolini was threatening to invade Abyssinia, whose king, Haile Selassie, was a hero to much of America's black population. Louis gave Carnera a lesson in boxing, turning his face into a bloody mess and punching the strength out of him. In the sixth round, he knocked Carnera down three times, and the fight was over. Celebrations erupted in Harlem, and nationwide, African Americans had a new hero—nobody describes this scene in more moving terms than the celebrated poet Maya Angelou. In "Champion of the World," chapter 19 of *I Know Why the Caged Bird Sings*, she describes the despair that for a moment overtakes a crowd gathering in a store to listen to the fight on the radio:

> "He's got Louis against the ropes and now it's a left to the body and a right to the ribs. Another right to the body, it looks like it was low . . . Yes, ladies and gentlemen, the referee is signaling but the contender keeps raining the blows on Louis. It's another to the body, and it looks like Louis is going down."
>
> My race groaned. It was our people falling. It was another lynching, yet another Black man hanging on a tree. One more woman ambushed and raped. A Black boy whipped and maimed. It was hounds on the trail of a man running through slimy swamps. It was a white woman slapping her maid for being forgetful. The men in the Store stood away from the walls

and at attention. Women greedily clutched the babes on their laps while on the porch the shufflings and smiles, flirtings and pinchings of a few minutes before were gone.

This might be the end of the world. If Joe lost we were back in slavery and beyond help. It would all be true; the accusations that we were lower types of human beings. Only a little higher than apes. True that we were stupid and ugly and lazy and dirty and unlucky and worst of all, that God himself hated us and ordained us to be hewers of wood and drawers of water, forever and ever, world without end. We didn't breathe. We didn't hope. We waited.

Such were the stakes—in no small part because white America had made them the stakes. Max Schmeling, for instance, was not much of a Nazi—he had turned down an award from Hitler, he sheltered two young Jews during Kristallnacht, and he would later become friends of a sort with Joe Louis. But when Hitler's regime declared him the embodiment of Aryan strength and superiority, beating him meant beating the ideology that promoted him. And any time an American boxer became "a great white hope," his race erased his individuality and the individuality of his opponent. Angelou describes how this works, how sports and race become entangled, how entire worldviews enter the ring along with the fighters. After describing the moment Louis beats Carnera and remains the champion, she writes:

> Champion of the world. A Black boy. Some Black mother's son. He was the strongest man in the world. . . . It would take an hour or more before the people would leave the Store and head for home. Those who lived too far had made arrangements to stay in town. It wouldn't be fit for a Black man and his family to be caught on a lonely country road on a night when Joe Louis had proved that we were the strongest people in the world.

The Carnera match took place ten days after Max Baer, a Nebraskan of German origin, unexpectedly lost the heavyweight title to James Braddock—portrayed by Russell Crowe in the film *Cinderella Man*. Three months later, Louis took down Baer in four rounds, clearly making him a contender for the world title. He had disposed of recent champions so convincingly that to deny him the chance would have seemed ludicrous. But while negotiations for the title fight continued, his team arranged for him to fight another former champion, Schmeling, who had lost the title to Baer. Schmeling was the first and still the only German to win the heavyweight title—not in the most glamorous manner, however. In 1930, his opponent was simply disqualified for a low blow to the groin, and then Schmeling quickly lost the title again—to the same man, this time on a controversial decision on points. Schmeling had a bit of a following in the United States, but when the Nazis rose to power, they fully claimed him as their own, as an archetype of the Aryan superman and an ambassador for Nazi masculinity. In June of 1933, he was fighting Baer again, and the fight was promoted as "Aryan vs. Jew." Baer's shorts were embroidered with the Star of David— one of his paternal grandparents had been Jewish. Schmeling played along, and he became an ambivalent figure in the United States. At the time, most Americans were fearful about being drawn into another European war, and while most Americans disapproved of Hitler's militarism, a significant number openly admired his anti-Semitism. This was particularly true in Detroit, which in the 1930s was, according to documentary filmmaker Aviva Kempner, "the hotbed of domestic anti-Semitism."[17] At the time, the city had the sixth-highest Jewish population in the United States, but while there had been tensions between the Jewish and the black population in Detroit, both groups would have been united in rooting for Louis.[18]

When Louis first fought Schmeling in June 1936, the fight would turn into the ultimate propaganda spectacle for the Nazi regime. Louis was the heavy favorite, but allegedly, he became overconfident, played golf instead of preparing, and went down to an unexpected defeat. The Nazis were jubilant, and African Americans were in despair. Louis himself said he had "let a whole race of people down," and Angelou's poetic account cited above lends credence to that sentiment. While today the embarrassment that Jesse Owens inflicted on the master race at the Olympic Games in Berlin one month later seems to carry more historical significance, Louis was by far the more prominent African American athlete at the time.[19]

So now it was Schmeling who saw himself as first in line to challenge the world champion, James Walter Braddock. The political situation, however, worked against him. The ferociousness with which Nazis were persecuting German Jews had become harder and harder to deny, and while the United States would not lift a finger to help them for many years to come, distaste for Hitler was growing. Mike Jacobs, the Jewish boxing promoter who had Joe Louis under contract, was keen to get his man in first, and knocking Schmeling and his Nazi promoters out of the way was an added bonus. In addition, a Braddock-Louis fight was a bigger publicity draw than a Braddock-Schmeling fight—and so Louis got the nod in 1937. Although Braddock floored Louis in the first round, Louis quickly established how much of an aberration his loss to Schmeling had been, and he knocked Braddock out in the eighth round, in a match of fearsome brutality even for a sport not known for restraint. An African American was world heavyweight champion again.

This left one bit of unfinished business—Louis felt that in order to truly earn the title, he had to take Schmeling out as well. An agreement was reached in 1938, a year before war broke out in Europe. At the time the rematch was billed as "the fight of the century," and it's hard to argue with that even now, in light of the political significance it acquired.

After the fight, Schmeling was rushed to the hospital. His doctor reported "fractures of the transverse processes of the third and fourth lumbar vertebra with a hemorrhage of the lumbar muscles."[20] African Americans across the country partied through the night. In Harlem, it was said, half a million people crowded into the streets, and ecstatic crowds were celebrating in Washington, DC, and Philadelphia, in Chicago and Chattanooga, in Milwaukee and Memphis, in Cleveland and St. Louis.[21] The *Detroit Free Press* reported that ten thousand people danced in the streets of Black Bottom while Cecil Lee's band played "Flat Foot Floogie (with the Floy Floy)".[22] Similar scenes played out across America. As David Margolick reports:

> In the stands there was bedlam. Tallulah Bankhead sprang to her feet and turned to the Schmeling fans behind her. "I told you so, you sons of bitches!" she screamed. Whites were hugging blacks. "The happiest people I saw at this fight were not the Negroes but the Jews," a black writer observed. "In the row in front of me

there was a great line of Jews—and they had the best time of all their Jewish lives." . . . "Beat the hell out of the damn German bastard!" W. E. B. Du Bois, a lifelong Germanophile who rarely swore, shouted gleefully in Atlanta. In Hollywood, Bette Davis jumped up and down; she had won $66 in the Warner Brothers fight pool. . . ."Everybody danced and sang," Woody Guthrie wrote from Santa Fe. "I watched the people laugh, walk, sing, do all sorts of dances. I heard 'Hooray for Joe Louis!' 'To hell with Max Schmeling' in Indian, Mexican, Spanish, all kinds of white tongues."[23]

Joe Louis was now a national treasure—and he would remain one as long as he did not try to leverage his fame on behalf of racial justice with too much vigor. Perhaps his respectful demeanor in front of the press reassured anxious white Americans that he was not a threat anywhere outside the ring; the Jewish population, who often saw themselves as natural allies of African Americans anyway, were utterly delighted to see him crush the symbol of the Nazis.

As the world slid toward war, many Americans realized that they would have to take sides. And even those who didn't care about politics recognized the greatest heavyweight boxer the world had ever produced for what he was. His nicknames, "the Brown Bomber" and "the Dark Destroyer," were respectful, an homage. But even as he became the nation's champion, nobody should be under any delusions—Joe Louis's victory barely made a dent when it came to the racist discourse of the day. The *Washington Post* had this to say: "Joe Louis, the lethargic, chicken-eating young colored boy, reverted to his dreaded role of the 'brown bomber' tonight." UPI, the news agency, called him "a jungle man, completely primitive as any savage, out to destroy the thing he hates." Joe Louis was good enough to beat a Nazi to a pulp; he was good enough to recruit black soldiers to the war; he was good enough to make people buy war bonds. He was not good enough to eat with white officers or to sell cars.

How does it end? While Joe Louis may not sell Fords anywhere in the United States, Max Schmeling, the Nazis' icon, gets rich off selling soda—Coca-Cola, no less, that most quintessential American concoction. In the

1950s, he gains the exclusive rights to bottle and distribute Coke in Hamburg, a very lucrative career move. Until very recently, Coca Cola's website lovingly embraced him:

> The onslaught of employees was huge, as Max Schmeling visited the Hamburg-Wandsbek branch of Coca-Cola in the summer of 1957. Many employees could hardly believe that the legendary sportsman was suddenly standing there in front of them. Unlike any other German boxer before him, Schmeling had triumphed time and again in the ring. He was the world heavyweight champion. He had written boxing history with his 1936 knockout victory over the then-undefeated Joe Louis.[24]

His "reputation," Coke told you, is "unparalleled"; he is "the exceptional athlete," and if Joe Louis ever beat *him*, Coca-Cola certainly didn't want to tell you about it. In the meantime, Louis tours with the Daily Bros. Circus as one of its attractions. In the 1960s, he is mocked as an "Uncle Tom" by some members of an African American community increasingly less impressed by the respectability politics that had allowed Louis to become a hero. His health deteriorates, he takes drugs, he has paranoid episodes, his money evaporates, he eventually rides a scooter to get around. He works as a greeter in Las Vegas, at Caesar's Palace. He dies in April of 1981. Max Schmeling is one of his pallbearers, and pays for some of the funeral expenses. He will outlive Joe Louis by twenty-four years.

TWENTY-ONE

APRIL 18, 1936

While the sky darkens over Europe, Detroit, hosting a banquet to celebrate the success of its sporting stars, christens itself the "City of Champions." In 1935, the same year the UAW was founded, the Tigers had won their first World Series, to be followed by championships for the Red Wings and the Lions. The governor of Michigan proudly declares April 18th "the Day of the Champions." In the midst of the Great Depression, the celebration lifts the mood. At the same time, the economic suffering increasingly moves people to embrace progressive policies aimed at creating a social safety net— but some of those individuals, such as the infamous anti-Semitic Detroit priest Father Coughlin, merge these demands with rabid anti-Semitism and sympathy for Adolf Hitler. Coughlin's radio shows command an enthusiastic following, but he is eventually sidelined when the United States enter World War II.

When the Detroit Red Wings defeated the Toronto Maple Leafs to win their first Stanley Cup on April 11, 1936, Detroit became the City of Champions. On December 15, 1935, the Detroit Lions had defeated the New York Giants, 26–7, winning their first NFL championship. On October 7, 1935, the Detroit Tigers had defeated the Chicago Cubs in game 7, winning their first World Series. Thus Detroit held the three major league championships of the time simultaneously, a feat not achieved by any American city before or since.

It is hardly surprising that politicians rushed to make hay of it. The City Council declared April 18th to be "Championship Day." Governor Frank Fitzgerald issued a proclamation: "I am glad to designate Saturday,

April 18th as the 'Day of the Champions.' It is my earnest wish that citizens of the state will observe the day by a display of flags, banners and pictures of our champions where possible." In 1936, the State of Michigan couldn't do enough to associate itself with Detroit's success.[1]

On that Saturday evening, the Chamber of Commerce staged a testimonial banquet at the Masonic Temple, just two blocks from where the Little Caesars Arena is now located. Tickets cost $3. The temple is a remarkable neo-gothic structure completed in 1926, with its own athletic complex, including an elegant but sadly unfinished swimming pool. Today, it remains the largest Masonic building in the world. On Champions Day, six hundred guests attended, including the players from the three teams, along with Joe Louis. Louis wasn't world heavyweight champion yet, but he was widely considered the champion-in-waiting, and the city revered him for his string of twenty-four wins since 1934.[2] There are many photos from this era in which players from all teams pose with each other and with Joe Louis, who was a keen fan of all sports and especially baseball. As a black man in 1936, he would not have been allowed to play for any one of these teams.

Champions Day expanded to include a number of other sporting heroes from Detroit. Other champion teams included were the Dixie Oils, a fast-pitch professional softball team that had won the George H. Sisler Trophy in 1935, the Stroh's bowling team that had won the American Bowling Congress championship in 1934, and the Detroit Olympics, a minor league hockey team that won the International Hockey League title in 1935 and 1936. Individual achievement was recognized as well. In attendance were, among others, Gar Wood, who had held the Harmsworth Trophy for the world speed record since 1920; Walter Hagen, who had captained the U.S. golf team to victory in the Ryder Cup in 1935; Dick Degener, a champion diver who would win a gold medal at the Berlin Olympics later that year; Eddie Tolan, who had won gold medals in the 1932 Olympics in the 100 and 200 meters. The governor sent his apologies—he was unable to attend due to illness.

While the celebrations involved all kinds of sports, there is no doubt that the World Series victory was the centerpiece. Detroit had been a major league town since 1901, and before 1935, had appeared in and been defeated in four World Series. The most recent loss had come in 1934, when, after leading three games to two against the St Louis Cardinals in the best-of-seven series, the Tigers blew the last two games on their home field. The final game of that series had been particularly brutal, with a score of 11–0. When the Cardinals' players started showboating, a near riot erupted. The crowd only calmed down when Commissioner Kenesaw Mountain Landis demanded that St. Louis remove from the game the player who was irritating the Detroit fans the most.[3]

Frank Navin, who had been involved with the team since 1902 and been its principal owner since 1908, had despaired of achieving his dream of winning a World Series. Detroit was one of the most committed cities in baseball, but when it came to winning the big prize, it seemed cursed.

The 1935 team changed all that. It was blessed with the fearsome 3G's in the batting lineup: Charlie Gehringer—known as "the Mechanical Man" for his reliability—had been the star second baseman since 1924, and he is widely considered one of the greatest second basemen in history.[4] Goose Goslin had been in the majors since 1921 and had appeared in three World Series before joining the Tigers in 1924; he had a reputation for clutch hitting. Hank Greenberg was the handsome young star of the lineup, always dressed well and noted for his charm.

The team was led by Mickey Cochrane, known as "Black Mike," either for his swarthy skin or his dark moods. He was one of the best catchers in the league, and the Philadelphia A's had only traded him because they were in financial trouble in 1934.[5] At the time, Navin was working on a plan to hire Babe Ruth, and when this fell through, the opportunity to obtain the services of Cochrane was a stroke of good fortune. Navin made him player-manager.

Like all great baseball teams, Detroit in 1935 had dominant pitching. "General" Crowder, also acquired in 1934, was a reliable veteran. Tommy Bridges had debuted with the Tigers in 1930 and had come within one out of pitching a perfect game in 1932 (only 29 perfect games have been pitched in major league history). "Schoolboy" Rowe was twenty-three years old when he made his first appearance with the Tigers in 1933, and he had become an immediate sensation. When asked in 1934 to reveal the secret of his success, he confided, "Just eat a lot of vittles, climb on that mound, wrap my fingers around the ball and say to it, 'Edna, honey, let's go.'" Edna was the name of his childhood sweetheart whom he married that year.[6] The other starter on the team was Elden "Submarine" Auker, so named for his low-arm pitching style. The first batter he ever faced in the majors was Babe Ruth, whom he struck out. That was in 1933. Auker would be the single remaining member of the 1935 team who attended the last game in Tiger Stadium on September 27, 1999.

The Tigers had started the season badly and struggled to get into contention, but by the all-star break, they were only one game behind the Yankees. Then, at the end of July, they took the series in New York two games to one, and with it the top spot in the American League, and they never looked back. Due to a scheduling quirk, the Tigers played at home for a majority of the month of August, and by September, they were nine games ahead and knew they would clinch the pennant and with it, a return trip to the World Series. Their opponents in the Fall Classic were the Chicago Cubs. The first two games of the series were at home, and after they lost the first, fans feared a repeat of 1934. The Tigers won the second game, but they lost Hank Greenberg, the 1935 MVP who had led the league in RBIs and home runs. He broke his wrist sliding into home plate and was out for the series. Anxiety levels grew. Some say that winning the next game, the first to be played at Wrigley Field, was the key to the series. If the Tigers could prove they did not depend solely on Greenberg, the team's biggest star, hope was not lost. They did it. Having won Game Four, they had three chances left. Defeat in Game Five brought them back to Navin Field: surely they would not blow it again?[7]

In Game Six, it began to look like they might. In a tight game, the Tigers scored in the first, and the Cubs evened the score in the third; the Tigers led again in the fourth, but then conceded two in the fifth to give the Cubs a 3–2 lead. The Tigers leveled the score in the sixth, and the teams stayed even until the ninth. In the top of the ninth, Chicago's leadoff hitter tripled, leaving the winning run ninety feet from home. The crowd went silent, but Bridges demonstrated his control in a tight situation: he sent down the next three batters, stranding the runner on third. In the bottom of the ninth, Flea Clifton, Greenberg's replacement, who had not got a hit in the series to that point, struck out. Then Mickey Cochrane singled, and Gehringer hit a ground ball that moved the runner to second. Two out and a man on second, and Goose Goslin strode to the plate; known as a pull hitter, the second baseman stood back, almost a second rightfielder. Goslin hit the first pitch along right-field foul line but it landed foul. He connected with the second which looped into the outfield, just over the head of the despairing second baseman. As the Cubs fielders converged upon the ball Cochrane scurried home for the win. Detroit went crazy. The celebrations went on all night, and people who remembered said the city made more noise that day than on Armistice Day, which had ended the World War in 1918.[8]

Business was booming at the ballpark. Despite the 1934 World Series defeat, Detroit led the league in attendance that year with 919,000 seats sold, more than double the league average for the season. In 1935, the club beat its own attendance record with a figure of over 1 million—tops in the league again. By 1935 Frank Navin, who retained the majority of shares, had acquired a partner: the baseball fanatic Walter Briggs. After building two double-decker stands, between home plate and first and home plate and third, in 1912, Navin had renamed the field after himself—increasing capacity to thirty thousand seats had apparently obviated any need for modesty. The two owners now planned to extend the ballpark and enclose it completely. However, as work got under way, Navin suffered a heart attack while out on horseback, just six weeks after achieving his life's dream. Briggs immediately swooped in to acquire Navin's shares, allegedly sending a check to the very hospital where Navin lay dying. As sole owner, he not only continued the construction, but also followed Navin's example by naming the modernized stadium after himself—what good is being rich if you can't slap your name on big buildings? By 1938, the capacity had grown to 53,000, and Briggs Stadium was widely praised as the best stadium in baseball. It was in that year that the Detroit Lions started playing there, as they would continue to do until 1974, when they moved to Pontiac.[9]

In 1936, at least some Detroiters had grounds for economic optimism. After the horrors of the collapse in the early 1930s, car production was back up to over 3 million, and employment was rising. The city's finances were in better shape as well, not least due to mayor Frank Couzens, a man with political pedigree: his father had been Henry Ford's accountant before pursuing a career in politics and had been mayor of Detroit himself before becoming a U.S. senator.

Frank Couzens had overseen a restructuring of Detroit's $400 million debt, after the closure of several of the major banks in 1933.[10] That year, the city had defaulted on its debts. After borrowing heavily in the 1920s to meet the needs of the dramatic explosion in population, the city was completely unprepared for the collapse of tax revenues caused by the Depression. With higher interest rates on the city debt, the annual payments had forced major cutbacks in services. The younger Couzens had focused on extending the maturity of debt, and by 1936, much of it would not be due for repayment until 1945. This gave the city breathing space along with the capacity to spend money on basic services, such as streetlights and schools.

But below the sporting glory and a brightening economic outlook, dark forces were forming—in Detroit, in the nation, and globally. Political divisions were widening. As workers started returning to the factories, union organizers started to made inroads, especially among Polish Americans from Hamtramck. Detroit employers such as Henry Ford and Walter Briggs had always zealously opposed unionization, and had successfully obstructed previous attempts to organize, but the Great Depression changed the landscape in two major ways: already-appalling conditions for both employed and unemployed workers in the 1930s got even worse, and Franklin Roosevelt shepherded the National Labor Relations Act (NLRA) through Congress in 1935, preventing employers from invoking antitrust law to thwart unionization. Owners had claimed that they were buffeted by the forces of competition, and that an entire labor force organizing to represent their collective interest represented extortion. However, in a world where jobs were scarce and the alternative was abject poverty, it was clear that employers held all the cards. The credibility of the bosses was further undermined by the fact that they paid detective agencies to spy on their workers, hired goons to terrorize those who attempted to join a union, and used non-union labor to drive out unionized labor with the blessing and assistance of the police.[11] When the NLRA finally passed, the law compelled employers to recognize the union as the sole bargainer on behalf of the workforce, provided that a majority of workers chose to join it.

The United Automobile Workers (UAW) was founded in 1935 and immediately began recruiting members. There was no shortage of issues causing owner-worker disputes on the production lines: arbitrary hiring and firing decisions, pay cuts, dangerous pressure on workers to speed up the production line, and so on. Union organizers such as Walter Reuther quickly increased membership by demonstrating how effectively workers could focus their demands. But the main challenge was always to gain the owners' recognition so that bargaining could be institutionalized. And for that, you needed the support of the majority of the workforce, and to take on the industry as a whole, or at least one of the Big Three.

The key event actually took place in Flint, one of the main production centers of GM, seventy miles northwest of the city. Flint was dangerous territory for the unions. Wyndham Mortimer, the UAW's lead organizer there, would later recall that he had just checked into "the Dresden," his cheap Flint hotel, when the phone rang: "A voice said: 'You had better get the hell back where you came from if you don't want to be carried out in a wooden box!'" Mortimer was unimpressed: "I was fifty-two years old and nobody had taken me out in a box yet. I'd be damned if this was going to be the first time! I ignored the phone call, which I attributed to the Black Legion, and proceeded to plan my work."[12]

The work of Mortimer and his allies would culminate in what is known as the Great GM Sit-Down Strike, possibly the most important strike in the twentieth century, and it would kick off the golden era of unionization in Detroit. But when Mortimer arrived, a mere 122 of the 45,000 autoworkers in Flint were union members, and Mortimer "soon learned that the vast majority of the GM workers regarded these 122 men as paid agents of General Motors." All legitimate organizers had been "fingered as a Red and fired."[13] Mortimer and his team organized on the down low for a while, keeping the names of new members a secret. But then the UAW found its opening when the workers at a Cleveland plant went on strike. The union announced it would not settle the Cleveland matter unless GM entered into a national agreement, and got ready to shut down the Fisher No. 1 plant in Flint. Because Cleveland and Flint were the only two factories making the dies for car body components, GM was vulnerable. When the company's plans to move the dies out of the Flint factory became known, union members moved in and occupied the plant—in a reversal of the usual strike strategy of keeping workers from entering, a sit-down strike keeps management out, bars strikebreakers, and physically takes over the means of production. Howard Zinn describes the event here:

Committees organized recreation, information, classes, a postal service, sanitation. Courts were set up to deal with those who didn't take their turn washing dishes or who threw rubbish or smoked where it was prohibited or brought in liquor. The "punishment" consisted of extra duties; the ultimate punishment was expulsion from the plant. A restaurant owner across the street prepared three meals a day for two thousand strikers. There were classes in parliamentary procedure, public speaking, history of the labor movement. Graduate students at the University of Michigan gave courses in journalism and creative writing. There were injunctions, but a procession of five thousand armed workers encircled the plant and there was no attempt to enforce the injunction. Police attacked with tear gas and the workers fought back with firehoses. Thirteen strikers were wounded by gunfire, but the police were driven back. The governor called out the National Guard. By this time the strike had spread to other General Motors plants. Finally there was a settlement, a six-month contract, leaving many questions unsettled but recognizing that from now on, the company would have to deal not with individuals but with a union.[14]

A key figure in settling the dispute was Frank Murphy, the governor of Michigan, who encouraged the car companies to recognize the UAW. The companies pressured Murphy to call in the troops to evict the strikers, arguing they were guilty of trespass. Murphy did—but he sent the National Guard to *protect* the strikers, not to take them down.[15]

Although the GM strike turned into a triumph for the unions, Henry Ford, alone among the major owners, continued to hold out and would not sign the first contract with the UAW until 1941—shortly before the AFL agreed to a no-strike pledge for the duration of the war. Ford loathed unions with a passion, and the company's notorious "Service Department," under the leadership of Ford's enforcer Harry Bennett, intimidated everybody who sought to organize the company's workforce. His tactics were ugly: firings, spying, threats, beatings. The Service Department had up to eight thousand people at his disposal, and unionization was a blood sport.[16] Just a few months after the sit-down strike ended, in May 1937, the Detroit

"Battle of the Overpass" made nationwide news. The UAW had stepped up its efforts to conquer Ford, and billboards sprouted proclaiming that "Fordism is Fascism" and "Unionism is Americanism"—slogans that may sound a bit ham-fisted now, but the Nazis had taken over Germany, Ford had made his sympathies with Hitler fully known, and Father Coughlin, the still popular pro-fascist radio host, was railing against unions every day. On May 26, Walter Reuther scheduled a massive leaflet campaign at the Rouge Plant in Dearborn, specifically at Miller Road Overpass at Gate 4. He had recruited one hundred women to hand out the leaflets, and he had invited clergy and the press. Here is how the *Detroit News* describes the scene:

> Two hours before the scheduled time, newspapermen arrived at the site and saw 25 cars filled with men in sunglasses who warned them to get out of the area, and threatened photographers. An hour before shift change, just before 2 p.m., Walter Reuther, Richard T. Frankensteen, in charge of the overall Ford drive, Robert Kanter, and J.J. Kennedy, the UAW's East Side regional director arrived. The Detroit News photographer, James E. (Scotty) Kilpatrick, thought the backdrop of the Ford sign would make a great picture, and obligingly, the union men walked up the two flights of iron stairs to the overpass. Facing the photographers, Reuther and his partners had their backs to the thugs that were approaching them. The newsmen's warnings were too late. They were attacked brutally: punched and kicked repeatedly. Frankensteen recounted how two men held his legs apart while another kicked him repeatedly in the groin. One man placed his heel in his abdomen, grinding it, then put his full weight on it. Reuther was punched in the face, abdomen and back and kicked down the stairs. Kanter was pushed off the bridge and fell 30 feet. The women who were to hand out the leaflets were arriving on trolley cars and were brutally shoved back into the cars, or pulled out and beaten. A lone police officer, appalled at the scene, pleaded with the "service" men to stop beating one woman: "You'll kill her . . ." The Dearborn

police did nothing else. They stood by and said the Ford men were protecting their private property.[17]

Ford's goons went around confiscating photographic plates and ripping pages out of their notepapers, but the *Detroit News* photographer tricked them—he hid his plates in his trunk and handed over useless blanks. The next day, the photographs of the brutal assault were plastered all over the front page, and the wire services distributed them all over the world. As the paper writes in a retrospective published in 1997: "Ford won the battle but lost the war for public opinion. The NLRB castigated Ford and Bennett for their actions. In the next election the Labor candidates in Detroit won more than twice as many votes as they had ever gotten. Three years later Ford signed a contract with the UAW." As mentioned earlier, Bennett was fired in 1945, after a power struggle with the family.

The story of Ford and the UAW is central not just to labor relations, but also to the racial politics of Detroit. From 1917 on, Henry Ford had started hiring African American workers in large numbers. This was the beginning of the Great Migration, which, over the course of half a century, saw millions of black Americans leave the Jim Crow South in the hope to find better conditions in the rapidly industrializing North. In the 1920s and 1930s, Ford was by far the largest employer of black labor in the city. Notably and unusually, he paid them the same wages he paid white workers, and he developed links with Detroit's black community leaders, who in turn helped him recruit workers. Popular African American songs of the period talked about moving north to go work for "Mr. Ford."[18]

Ford, however, was also a virulent anti-Semite, convinced that there was a Jewish conspiracy to take over the world. In 1918, he had acquired the *Dearborn Independent*, a newspaper, and fashioned it into a bullhorn to rail against the "Jewish threat." In consequence, Henry Ford was the only American mentioned in Hitler's book, *Mein Kampf* (My Struggle): "Jews are the regents of the stock exchange power of the American Union. Every year they manage to become increasingly the controlling masters of the labor power of a people of 120,000,000 souls; one great man, Ford, to their exasperation still holds out independently there even now."[19]

Racism and anti-Semitism are closely allied ideological systems, so at first glance, it may seem surprising that the same man who rated a cameo in *Mein Kampf* treated African Americans as fairly as any employer at the time. Ford certainly did not think of black Americans as his equals—but he did see them as American citizens, whereas Jews, to his mind, would always be foreign interlopers intent on destroying what he thought of as the dominant "Anglo-Celtic" culture of America. Today, we would probably call him an "ethno-nationalist."[20] Blacks were racially inferior, as far as he was concerned, and they generally got the least pleasant jobs in his factories—but as Americans, they deserved to be protected. Paternalist Ford supported segregation, but he also felt that black families should enjoy the same amenities in their communities as white families. He did set up training programs for black workers, and in several cases, black foremen rose to positions of authority over white workers—an unthinkable event in most factories in Detroit at the time.

There is no direct evidence that Ford decided to hire large numbers of black workers in order to prevent unionization. However, for several years, that was the precise effect of his hiring practices. During that era, many white workers resented working alongside black workers, and well into the 1950s, they would engage in frequent "hate strikes" during which white workers chose to lay down their tools rather than work alongside black co-workers, as instructed. As a result, large segments of the African American community were suspicious of unions, a suspicion often borne out by the limited union support they encountered when demanding equal treatment.[21] As late as 1966, James Baldwin would write in *The Nation* that "the Negro in America can scarcely yet be considered—for example—as a part of the labor unions—and he is certainly not so considered by the majority of these unions."[22]

If Ford and Bennett had thought to exploit that tension to their benefit, they miscalculated. When they tried to bus in black strikebreakers in full view of white-staffed picket lines, African American leaders realized that management was exploiting racial animosity to defeat an organization fighting for better working conditions, and they wanted no part of it. The prominent black journalist George Schuyler scathingly described the Rouge factory as a "modern plantation," and he compared black leaders who supported Henry Ford to the conciliatory protagonist of Harriet

Beecher Stowe's 1852 novel *Uncle Tom's Cabin*: "Since every Uncle Tom's Cabin must of course have an Uncle Tom," he wrote, "it need occasion no surprise that there are any number of Uncle Toms in the Ford setup," willing to betray "their people for filthy lucre."[23] Guardedly, African Americans decided that they were better off joining organized labor—even if the unions harbored racists, they calculated, they at least stood some chance of finding support against the white employers who had power over their livelihoods. And while we cannot know for certain that Ford's early policies had been stratagems to divide and thus conquer his workforce, we do know this: once black workers joined the unions and Ford was forced to accept the UAW, his support for black citizens appears to have dwindled quickly, though he continued to employ large numbers of African American workers.

Thus began an uneasy alliance between the UAW, its white members, and black communities of Detroit. On the one hand, the white workers welcomed the solidarity and the improved work conditions of broad unionization; on the other hand, they clamored for segregation. And segregation they got—as mentioned in previous chapters, Detroit remained one of the most segregated cities in the North for decades to come.

Black workers, in turn, demanded equal rights as a condition for lending their strength to the cause. Union leadership expressed sympathy for them and their plight, but asked for patience—a refrain that echoes through the Reconstruction era, Jim Crow, the civil rights era, and beyond. Yet the union did deliver on some promises. In 1944, the UAW set up a Fair Employment Practices Committee that investigated cases of discrimination.[24] In 1952, it issued a four-point plan to eliminate hiring discrimination in Detroit, including the adoption of fair employment legislation that would outlaw discrimination in hiring; in 1955, the state adopted a fairly toothless Fair Employment Practices Code.[25] Finally, the Civil Rights Act of 1964 superseded this law, making discrimination both illegal and punishable. The alliance between black and white workers in Detroit remained an uneasy one. If the Walk to Freedom in 1963 was a high point, the accelerating white flight of the 1960s signaled that white Detroiters would rather self-segregate in the suburbs than share the city—though it is important to keep in mind that many of those who left had no choice but to follow the work as the main employers moved Detroit's jobs out of the city.

The NLRA was a part of the New Deal, on which President Roosevelt had campaigned to win the 1932 election. President Hoover's response to the Great Depression had been to cut spending and to balance the budget, regardless of unemployment and the state of the economy—the basic austerity strategy. Roosevelt, by contrast, used the power of the government budget to get people back to work. In 1933, as starvation became a real prospect in America, feeding the hungry was the first priority, though, and the federal government instituted food aid to supplement the relief programs that cities had undertaken. Detroit was a significant beneficiary. The establishment of the Works Progress Administration (WPA) in May 1935 added large federal programs including road construction and other public works in order to create employment. Unsurprisingly, many conservative auto manufacturers decried the profligacy, though quite a few of these same people had been lobbying for new roads over the previous quarter-century. In the long term, they would benefit—more roads meant more driving, which meant more cars. FDR's program turned out to be good for business, just as would be the government-funded Interstate Highway System, built under Dwight D. Eisenhower in the 1950s.

The mid-1930s were a watershed in Detroit politics. Since the 1910s, when the auto industry transformed Detroit, city government had been largely run along non-partisan, pro-business lines. Nominally Republican for the most part, the people running the city had devoted most of their energy to nuts-and-bolts issues: the most efficient way to organize the construction of sewers or the appropriate price of street car services. Radical politics played a limited role, and, amid and despite all the poverty and inequality, Detroit saw itself at the forefront of creating a new world order, solidly capitalist in outlook. The Depression changed all that. On one side, socialist and communist organizers won converts—they argued that the capitalist economies were at a standstill while the Soviet Union was enjoying rapid economic growth and sharing the fruits of that growth more equally. By contrast, in the United States the workers most heavily bore the brunt of market fluctuations, such as the drop in car production between 1929 and 1932 that had led to massive layoffs. A rational, planned system of production, the socialist argued, could prevent such hardship in the future. While not socialists, the New Dealers echoed many of these ideas, and a sense that the old methods were not working had brought Roosevelt to power. In the election year of 1936, the scale of Roosevelt's landslide victory made clear how popular the New Deal had become. He took 60.8 percent of the popular vote, won 523 out of 531 electoral votes, and took all but two states. No president since has won with a larger margin of victory.

Detroit reflected the national mood. The city had elected left-leaning figures such as Frank Murphy, mayor from 1930 to 1933 and governor of Michigan from 1937 to 1939. Murphy played a crucial role in the strikes of 1937. While freely acknowledging that such occupations were technically illegal, he refused to accede to the employers' demand that he send in the National Guard to end the occupations, effectively forcing the employers to the negotiating table where they would have to recognize the unions.

While the left argued for a fairer distribution of wealth and equality before the law, other forms of populism also prospered. Detroit was the poster child for the melting pot, with its diverse population of ethnicities whose origins lay in Europe (France, Britain, Ireland, Germany, Poland, Russia, Hungary, Italy, Scandinavia, Malta, and other countries), Africa, and, to a lesser extent, Latin America and Asia. As the economy turned sour, some politicians seized the opportunity to exploit ethnic tensions. Segregation of African Americans was already well established, and more or less the official policy of the city—no matter how liberal the mayors professed to be. Anti-Polish sentiment was also strong, particularly among immigrants who had arrived earlier, notably those of Anglo-Saxon origin who, as Protestants, feared that Catholicism might one day dominate. Ethnic slurs of all sorts were common, and anti-Semitism was on the rise.

The embodiment of these tensions was Father Coughlin, a Catholic priest from Canada who was sent to Detroit in 1923. In 1926, he founded the Shrine of the Little Flower, a church on Woodward and Twelve Mile Road, just north of the city. Before Coughlin arrived, the vehemently anti-Catholic Ku Klux Klan had burnt a cross outside the church. Protestant animosity to Catholicism had a long history in the United States, and it remained a force at least until the election of John F. Kennedy as president in 1960—Kennedy repeatedly had to assure the electorate that he would not take his orders from Rome. In the beginning, Coughlin preached a gospel of friendship and reconciliation, and he was one of the first leaders to realize the potential of the new mass communication medium: radio. He spoke on the city's radio station, WJR, in 1926, and quickly acquired his own weekly slot. His radio sermons became so popular that CBS offered him a contract in 1930, giving him national exposure.

After the Wall Street Crash of 1929 and the onset of the Great Depression in 1930, Coughlin's talks became more and more political. He views were homespun and his solutions simple. He viewed the banks of Wall Street as the great evil that had brought the country down, and he supported Roosevelt in 1932 because of his promise to get people back to work. In his view, the bankers of Wall Street had caused the Depression by the uncontrolled expansion of credit, and the federal government needed to take proper control over the supply of money. His support, which was embodied in his slogan "Roosevelt or Ruin," played a significant role in the election. Once Roosevelt was in power, however, Coughlin's views began to change. He now feared that the Depression would drive working people to godless communism, and therefore destroy religious life in the United States, especially Catholicism. He supported some form of capitalism, as long as it was nationalist first, but he also called for full employment, something like a minimum wage, and a social safety net including pensions.[26]

As politicians and union organizers on the left grew stronger from 1933 onward, Coughlin blamed Roosevelt for their success, and he started to campaign against him—he was now convinced that FDR was a Wall Street pawn. His own program would strike any contemporary American as rather left-leaning: in 1934, he established a political organization called the National Union for Social Justice (NUSJ), which called for higher taxes on the wealthy, monetary reforms, nationalization of railways and major industries, and the federal protection of labor rights. At the time, "social justice" was a central term in the Catholic social theory, often marshaled to lure the working class away from unions and into the bosom of the church. The NUSJ's membership ran into the millions. In 1935, Coughlin proclaimed that "I have dedicated my life to fight against the heinous rottenness of modern capitalism because it robs the laborer of this world's goods. But blow for blow I shall strike against Communism, because it robs us of the next world's happiness."[27]

A populist with a muddled economic message, he was also a raving anti-Semite, and in the late 1930s, he would support both Hitler and Mussolini—when the war broke out in Europe in 1939, the Roosevelt administration forced him off the air. In the mid-1930s, however, he was influential enough to form a political party, together with pension advocate Francis Townsend and Gerald L. K. Smith, who had taken over Huey Long's followers after the U.S. senator's assassination in 1935. In 1936, the newly formed Union Party nominated Republican William Lemke and labor lawyer Thomas O'Brien for the presidency. Their platform was incoherent, representing a mixture of the founders' views, and in the end, they won less than 2 percent of the vote. When the party dissolved, Coughlin focused all his energy on his NUSJ.

As the vicious nature of Hitler's regime emerged ever more clearly, Coughlin's anti-Semitism finally came into sharper focus as well. Coughlin supported the Nazis because he continued to see Communism as the biggest threat, and he became an apologist for Nazi atrocities. The Jews, he argued, had brought their fate upon themselves. Naturally, he was a fan of the fictional *Protocols of the Elders of Zion*, a notorious document used by anti-Semites to drum up hatred. Coughlin printed extracts from the tract in 1938—after all, so had Henry Ford in the 1920s. All the while, Coughlin's vast radio audiences absorbed these messages of hate.

By the early 1940s, Charles Coughlin was largely a spent force. He had been forced off the air, and the postal service refused him second-class mailing rights for his magazine, effectively pricing him out of circulation. In 1942, his bishop instructed him to cease all activities outside his parish, where he remained until his death in 1966. But even though Father Coughlin could eventually be neutralized, anti-Semitic slurs were an everyday occurrence in 1930s Detroit, as were ethnic insults of all sorts. Hank Greenberg suffered endless taunts while playing at Briggs Stadium, and he would remember later that at "every ballpark I went to, there'd be somebody in the stands who spent the whole afternoon just calling me names."[28]

In 1934, Greenberg had taken a career risk when he refused to play on Yom Kippur—a decision that some feared would add fuel to the anti-Semitic hate machine. In the end, though, his courage, along with his towering athletic talent and his clean-cut image, did much to counter the hatred of people like Coughlin, and for many Jews, Greenberg in the 1930s became a symbol of hope and pride. In 1938, Greenberg almost matched Babe Ruth's home run record for the season, and he later said: "I came to feel that if I, as a Jew, hit a home run, I was hitting one against Hitler."

Like Joe Louis and Jesse Owens, Greenberg knew well that sports and politics are not distinct spheres of endeavor, and that any triumph by those deemed inferior by the Nazis was a symbolic victory over them. Like Louis, Greenberg knew what he meant to other Jewish Americans. One morning, he was having breakfast with Manila "Bud" Shaver, the Detroit Times sports editor, while opening his mail. He showed Shaver a handwritten letter. It was from a thirteen-year-old Jewish girl who told him how much Max Baer had disappointed her when he lost to Jimmy Braddock. She had now transferred her loyalty to Hank, and, as Shaver remembered, "begged him not to fail her or his people."[29]

There is no doubt that during the 1930s, the City of Champions had a long way to go. If it pulled together, it was unbeatable, but its factionalism spelled calamity.

TWENTY-TWO

SEPTEMBER 2, 1933

After a twenty-year break, the racetracks in Detroit open again as a way of generating revenues and boosting the local economy that has collapsed. The car industry is the epicenter of the Great Depression, and Detroit struggles to support its homeless and hungry. In the city's hospitals, people die of starvation. In a rare bright spot, 1933 sees the Eighteenth Amendment repealed and Prohibition end. Detroit, with its roaring economy in the 1920s and its strategic position on the border, had never been dry, but the thriving bootleg business exacted a heavy cost in terms of gang violence and corruption.

Twenty thousand people attended the opening day of the Michigan Farm and Industrial Fair on the State Fairgrounds. The people crowding the grandstand—including Governor William Comstock and a number of other state officials—were not there to look at machinery or cattle. They had come to enjoy the first day of legalized horse racing in Michigan, with eight races on the program. It got exciting right away: in the first race, Mayco, a 10-to-1 longshot, won by a head's length. In the sixth race, the thoroughbred Gallant Sir, winner of eleven straight races, took the inaugural $2,500 handicap.

Gambling at the Fairgrounds was licensed under the pari-mutuel system: gamblers paid into a pot, and the winners were paid in proportion to their stake, with the operator taking a healthy slice. Licensees bid for the right to operate race days at the Fairgrounds, and the winning bidder guaranteed the state about half a million dollars.[1]

While horseracing had become popular across the United States by the 1890s, by 1910, a series of Michigan laws prohibiting lotteries, which covered gambling on horses, had effectively killed off the sport in Detroit.[2] The city had put its stake in a different kind of horsepower—the State Fairgrounds hosted motor racing instead, promoted by the car manufacturers. In June 1933, the state legislature, with the governor's support, passed a law that re-introduced horseracing to Michigan.[3] The law would have passed months earlier had it not been for a battle between those who favored just the ponies and those who wanted to see dog racing as well. In the end, the dog racers lost out—an odd result, since the dogs would have raised a good chunk of revenue for the state, and revenue was the sole reason for the law to begin with.

In the midst of the Depression, the state needed any dollar it could get its hand on, and the races were an excellent opportunity to raise much-needed cash. The sport would prove extremely popular both in Detroit and in Michigan more generally. In that first year, there were thirty-one race days, yielding a total attendance of 101,000, with $4 million staked. The State Fairgrounds was the only licensed racetrack during the 1930s, and seeing its success, the number of race days was raised to around sixty-five.[4] On Labor Day in 1936, Seabiscuit, possibly the most celebrated horse in history, won the Governor's Handicap in front of a crowd of 28,000. The champion thoroughbred became a symbol of resilience during the Great Depression, and he stars in numerous books and movies.[5] When he retired in 1940, he had brought in more money than any horse to date, and more than fifty thousand people came to visit him during his retirement years at Ridgewood Ranch.

By 1945, more racetracks had been licensed, and there were 142 race days each year, drawing 1.2 million spectators and $44 million in stakes. Between 1942 and 1995, Detroit racetrack crowds exceeded attendance at Tigers games every year, with the single exception of 1948. At their peak in 1971, almost 4 million people attended the races, four times as many as went to see the Tigers. Racing at the State Fairgrounds ended in 1950, when the Detroit Race Course in Livonia became the main venue, just beyond the western edge of the city. Other licensed racecourses included Hazel Park and Northville Downs. In the end, it was the state lottery that killed horse gambling: after the first state lottery was licensed in 1971, racetrack attendance declined.[6] In April 2018, Hazel Park Raceway closed, effectively ending the era of thoroughbred horseracing in Detroit.[7]

1933 was a year in which the state decided to relax its control of human vice. Betting on the ponies became legal at the same time the state repealed restrictions on the sale of beer, as long as the brews contained less than 3.2 percent alcohol. The end of Prohibition was here. Roosevelt, newly elected, issued a call for the repeal of the Eighteenth Constitutional Amendment—"the manufacture, sale, or transportation of intoxicating liquors within, the importation thereof into, or the exportation thereof from the United States and all the territory subject to the jurisdiction thereof for beverage purposes is hereby prohibited." Repeal required the passage of another amendment: the Twenty-First. Roosevelt had remained on the fence about repeal right up until his election in 1932; it had become increasingly popular in the country, but it could have cost him electoral votes in the more "virtuous" states. The fact that Eleanor Roosevelt supported Prohibition might have made it a tricky proposition as well.[8]

Prohibition had been a predictable failure. Colonel Ira Reeves, who led the New Jersey district federal Prohibition agency, was at first zealous in pursuing his enforcement duties, but later lamented the efficacy of his efforts. Instead of doing little to reduce supply, he explained, "I had raised the price of alcoholic beverages and reduced the quality."[9] While alcohol consumption fell dramatically at first, it quickly stabilized at around two-thirds of the pre-Prohibition level. The wording of the amendment did not help. The law made *selling* illegal, but not buying or possessing it. In 1919, wealthy Americans drinkers stocked up, and in some instances, their stocks lasted until repeal. The rest of the country had three main sources: kitchen-sink operations in the home, large-scale moonshine production and distribution, and cross-border smuggling.[10] Detroit, a narrow river's breadth away from Canada, was in an ideal location for the last of these.

According to a study by the Detroit Board of Commerce, in 1928, the city's trade in alcohol employed fifty thousand people and generated $215 million in annual sales, making it the second largest business in the city after the auto trade.[11] By 1925, the Hiram Walker Distillery in Canada was shipping one hundred thousand cases of Canadian whiskey from Windsor to Detroit, allegedly for transshipment to Cuba. The Canadian government made no bones about its disinterest in enforcing U.S. laws on the other side of the border. Seagram's whiskey made it all the way from Montreal across the river, and Detroit acquired another one of its many nicknames: "the City on a Still."[12]

While much of the alcohol was supposed to be shipped to a second destination, Detroit kept a goodly amount for itself: the city had one of the highest consumption levels during Prohibition. By 1923, Detroit boasted an estimated 7,000 speakeasies or blind pigs; by 1925, there were 25,000.[13] Nobody tried very hard to hide it, either. One wag wrote, "It was absolutely impossible to get a drink in Detroit unless you walked at least ten feet and told the busy bartender what you wanted in a voice loud enough for him to hear you above the uproar."[14] During the Ossian Sweet trial in 1925, lawyer Clarence Darrow was easily able to obtain a bottle of whiskey to consume in the courthouse office while he waited for the jury to return its verdict.[15]

Darrow was a fervent opponent of Prohibition, and he saw a clear link between the Anti-Saloon League, which pursued vigorous enforcement of the law, and the rise of white supremacism in the North during the 1920s. "The father and mother of the Ku Klux is the Anti-Saloon League."[16] Supporters of Prohibition, predominantly Protestant, welcomed the vigilante enforcement that the Klan could provide, while the Klan was delighted to position itself as proudly upholding the law of the land.

It is certainly a fact that during Prohibition, Detroit saw a serious breakdown of law and order. Even before Prohibition, a gangland culture had been developing in the city, and mob murders had become a problem.[17] In the Roaring Twenties, the enormous profits that could be reaped by bootlegging made Detroit one of the centers of American gangsterism. The Detroit River was the smugglers' focus of operation, and the gangs soon established protection rackets.

Daniel Okrent recounts that "gun violence turned the Detroit River into a combat zone. 'Indiscriminate shooting on the river' caused a group of local yachtsmen to make a formal protest to Congress. At any given hour, as many as fifteen hundred boats were dashing one way or another along its eighteen miles, either laden with illegal cargo or returning to the Canadian side for more."[18]

The River Gang, led by the Licavoli brothers from St. Louis, dominated much of the trade. They operated speedboats that would cross the river at night and offload cases of whiskey into cars waiting on the waterfront. They charged 25 percent of the retail price for the service; if you would rather run your own boats, they would let you do that—for a fee. Refusing to work with the River Gang was enough to get you murdered. While the border traffic was their main focus of operation, they also became involved in the operation of speakeasies.[19]

One way for the River Gang to avoid the city police was to operate along the river just to the west and to the east of the city limits. They might also have been keen to avoid the Purple Gang, a rival operation.[20] The Purple Gang was the most violent of the Detroit gangs during Prohibition. Unlike many of the mobs that were dominated by Italians, the Purple Gang was Jewish—members hailed from the Black Bottom area of the city, which had not yet been become a predominantly black neighborhood.[21] Their brutality was legendary. They would hijack shipments of liquor crossing the river and simply kill everyone on board. As a result, most of the traffic crossing the river within the city limits came under their control, and their speedboats became known as the "Little Jewish Navy." After their consignments landed, they'd usually take them to warehouses to "cut"—that is, dilute—the merchandise, handsomely increasing profits. Like the River Gang, the Purple Gang gained control of a number of speakeasies.

The Purple Gang earned much of its reputation during what was called the "Cleaners and Dyers War."[22] In the early 1920s, the laundry business in the city was highly competitive. The president of the Detroit Federation of Labor, Francis Martel, saw the Purple Gang as a welcome means to limit competition and raise prices, and he encouraged them to set about extorting all the cleaners in the city. Rumor has it that they gained their name because of the purple dye they'd toss into a load of laundry as a first warning if a business refused to co-operate. The second refusal would get the business bombed. By 1928, they had established firm control, and the entire city's laundry businesses were paying them protection money. And yes, prices rose, but any extra profit is more likely to have ended up in the Purple Gang's coffers than in the businesses' tills.

Other, more conventional mob business activities included brothels and gambling. Prostitution thrived in Detroit during Prohibition. African American sex workers tended to search for clients in Black Bottom, while their white colleagues worked just west of the downtown, out toward Navin Field and Corktown.[23] Soliciting on the streets was generally accepted, and in 1964, one woman recalled the era wistfully: "A very popular girl then could earn with tips over two hundred dollars in a twelve hour period. . . . The prostitute now makes far less than her older sister of the roaring twenties."[24]

Gambling by and large took the form of lotteries, banned in Michigan by a law passed in 1835, the same law that prevented gambling on horses. The illegal numbers games were called "policies," and runners would distribute tickets around the neighborhood, advertising odds of 300 to 1 or 500 to 1 (though the real ratio was more like 6,000 to 1). The operator would take up to 80 percent of the revenues generated, and with daily betting turnover estimated in the region of $50,000, this was a very profitable business.[25] As the gangs generated revenue, hired muscle, and paid off law enforcement while running the bootlegging business, they were able to extend their empires into these other illegal businesses.

Most of the murders those days involved either criminals killing each other, police shooting criminals, or criminals shooting police, although all these murders made the city an extremely dangerous place, and innocent bystanders could easily get shot by accident. The city government and police were either unwilling or powerless to do anything about it. In July 1926, the Rockefeller Foundation issued a 150-page report describing Detroit as "the vilest city on the continent."[26] The report claimed that law enforcement had being corrupted by the bootleggers, an accusation that was widely seen as plausible. In addition, Prohibition simply wasn't popular in Detroit, and so the effort to stamp out illegal drinking was half-hearted. "Local judges yawned at the liquor laws," writes Okrent.[27] More sinister were the bribes that the Purple Gang and others paid the police and city officials, payoffs that enabled the gangs to conduct their business with impunity, and more or less in the open.

Even before Prohibition ended, however, the era of the Purple Gang was drawing to a close. Charles Bowles, who in 1924 had almost won the mayor's office with the support of the Ku Klux Klan, actually succeeded in getting himself elected in 1929. He had distanced himself from the KKK, not because of its violent racism, but because the city's large Polish community did not countenance its faith in the superiority of Anglo-Saxon Protestants— and they voted accordingly. When Bowles took office at the beginning of

1930, he immediately began handing out jobs to friends and associates. He instigated a reform of the police department, which was clearly overdue, but crime rates immediately increased.[28] Rumors circulated that he had funded his campaign with contributions from gangsters and that, in return, he was letting them run the city without interference.

That May, while Bowles was away attending the Kentucky Derby, Police Commissioner Harold Emmons arranged a series of raids and arrested a number of well-known criminals. When Bowles returned, he demanded that Emmons resign—he refused, and Bowles fired him. That move turned out to be ill-advised—in the first successful recall campaign in a major U.S. city, Bowles was kicked out of City Hall, even after his supporters spent $100,000 opposing the recall campaign. The vote took place on July 12, 1930—Bowles had been in office for little more than six months. A key figure in the recall's success was Gerald Buckley, a journalist and radio broadcaster who had denounced corruption in general and Bowles in particular for some time. The day after Buckley announced the result on the radio—with considerable satisfaction, one imagines—he was gunned down in the LaSalle Hotel on the corner of Adelaide and Woodward. Growing disgust at bootleg-related murders was an important factor in bringing an end to Prohibition.

Indirectly, Prohibition had led to some beneficial infrastructure investment. In 1929, the Ambassador Bridge had opened, which was followed, in 1930, of the opening of the Detroit-Windsor road tunnel—also known as "the funnel," since it enabled Prohibition-era Americans to cross into Canada where they could drink legally.[29] The demand for crossings was so large that both projects could be privately funded. One reason was the passage of the new immigration laws in 1921 and 1924: passengers were now required to produce some kind of proof of identity, and ferry businesses were struggling with long lines. But then the Great Depression hit.

The scale of the economic collapse in Detroit was staggering. At the peak of 1929, Ford employed 128,000 workers; by 1931, the number had fallen to 37,000. By October 1930, 123,000 of the city's workforce were unemployed (18 percent), and by January 1931, unemployment stood at 32 percent. By the end of 1932, it was estimated that half of the city's working population was without steady employment.[30] In a city so dominated by a single industry, the collapse in demand for its product was catastrophic. The human misery was numbing. As during all major recessions, people did not simply lose their jobs, they frequently lost their homes as well. Owners defaulted on loans, renters were evicted for non-payment. It was not just men walking the streets looking for jobs; during the Depression, an estimated two hundred thousand children across the country were homeless, and many of them lived in Detroit. Workers who remained employed saw their wages cut. While the prices of goods fell about 20 percent, the average wage for autoworkers fell by 50 percent. In Inkster, a small city fifteen miles west of Detroit settled by African Americans trying to get out of Black Bottom, the city government ran out of money, closed the schools, and laid off the entire police force, while the power company disconnected all electricity.[31] It was a deadly time. According to Dr. John Ryan of the National Catholic Welfare Council, quoted in the *Detroit Free Press*, "a physician in one of the hospitals in Detroit reported not long ago that, on the average, four persons a day are brought to that particular hospital too far gone from starvation to be saved."[32]

We have already mentioned the many forms of ethnic and racial prejudices that thrived in the era—against African Americans, Jews, Poles, Italians, and so on. But one of the groups hardest hit was the Mexican community. As employment in Detroit and Michigan started to collapse in 1930, Hoover decided to mass deport not just Mexican immigrants but Americans of Mexican descent. Journalist Diane Bernhard writes: "The program, implemented by Hoover's secretary of labor, William Doak, included passing local laws forbidding government employment of anyone of Mexican descent, even legal permanent residents and U.S. citizens. Major companies, including Ford, U.S. Steel and the Southern Pacific Railroad, colluded with the government by telling Mexicans they would be better off with their own people, laying off thousands."[33] Detroit's community was hit hard, particularly migrant workers in the rural areas surrounding the city.

Organizations such as the Communist Party played a significant role in providing relief and bringing attention to the plight of the unemployed and marginalized. The magnitude of the crisis certainly appeared to support their anti-capitalist theories, which called for a system of worker control and a planned production process that would avoid the wild gyrations of the market system. They organized protest marches demanding that the factory owners and other capitalists contribute their conspicuous wealth to relieve the misery of the hungry and the homeless. On March 7, 1932, around four thousand demonstrators assembled in west Detroit at Fort Street and Oakwood with the intention of marching on Ford's River Rouge plant in Dearborn. Ford had long organized his own paramilitary security under Harry Bennett. They recruited from both the police force and from released criminals, whom Ford claimed he could rehabilitate. Members of Ford's "Service Department" were difficult to distinguish from the Dearborn police force. On that day, both stood together waiting for the protesters to arrive. As the marchers approached, police and Ford's thugs alike drew their guns and opened fire. Four demonstrators were killed, and sixty were injured. No one was ever brought to trial for these crimes. Instead, Dearborn and Detroit police raided Communist Party offices and arrested sixty "suspects"—including two who had been shot and wounded and were chained to their hospital beds.[34]

The events of that day reverberated around the country, and it was catastrophes such as these that set the stage for Roosevelt's election and the New Deal. To be sure, some thought that the Communist threat was real and had to be suppressed by all means necessary. More, however, concluded that shooting hungry unemployed workers was unjustifiable, and that radical change was required. The mayor of Detroit, Frank Murphy, faced significant criticism from the Communists, who accused him of complicity with the owners. Murphy threaded the needle—he acknowledged that the march, being unsanctioned, was illegal, but he also claimed that he was not opposed to the march. Most Detroiters were sure where his sympathies lay.[35]

Frank Murphy had been elected mayor after the recall of Charles Bowles, and then re-elected in 1931. He campaigned as a friend of the working class and called for radical change to provide a safety net for the poor. A devout Catholic, he was not opposed to capitalism, but he did think a significant safety net was necessary. Unlike Father Coughlin, he was not an anti-Semite, and unlike Bowles, he was not a segregationist. As a result, he won overwhelming support in the city. One of his first acts as mayor was to create the Mayor's Unemployment Committee, which distributed relief funds as long as the city had money.[36] His advice also helped Roosevelt to craft the New Deal and programs such as the WPA, which provided federal relief to Detroit. In 1933, Roosevelt appointed him governor-general of the Philippines, and in 1937 he was elected governor of Michigan. The president appointed him as attorney general in 1939 and to the Supreme Court in 1940, where he remained until he died in 1948.

When Hank Greenberg was a nineteen-year-old rookie with the Detroit Tigers, the Purple Gang, then in their pomp as rulers of Detroit, sought to befriend him. They were regular and visible patrons of Navin Field, and they must have been particularly pleased to see a Jewish kid playing for their team. By 1935, most of the gang were dead or behind bars. Then again, the gangsters of the area pretty much ran the prisons, so it was not unusual to find convicted criminals at the ball games in Detroit—incarcerated Purple Gang members were seen at both the 1935 and 1945 World Series games. In 1941, Abe Bernstein, one of the gang's leaders, personally arranged for Greenberg to play an exhibition game at Jackson State Prison. Greenberg played for the prison squad, and his two home runs led them to victory.[37]

TWENTY-THREE

MAY 11, 1930

Opening pitch at Hamtramck Stadium, the new Negro League ball-park. The stadium is located in the heart of Detroit's Polish com-munity, illustrating still positive relations between black and white immigrant communities—relations that were soon to shift. In 1930, the Polish mayor of Hamtramck is there to catch the opening pitch; a decade later he seeks political capital by opposing housing projects for black Detroiters. The Stars' star is Turkey Stearnes, one of the great baseball players of the time, denied the opportunity to prove himself on the national stage by the major leagues' strict if unofficial segregation policy.

On Sunday, a record throng attended the dedication ceremonies at the new Hamtramck Stadium and saw the Detroit Stars win both ends of a double-header. The Stars blanked the Hamtramck Municipal Nine, 11–0, in the ini-tial contest and trimmed the Cubans, 7–4, in the nightcap. Ty Cobb threw out the ceremonial first pitch in the Cuban game, with Dr. Rudolph Tenero-wicz, mayor of Hamtramck, on the receiving end. The teams were presented a floral offering by the fans.[1]

That day, ten thousand people watched the Detroit Stars of the Negro National League (NNL), whose home was now be in Hamtramck—a city that had incorporated eight years earlier to avoid being swallowed up by Detroit, which now surrounds it on all sides. Although the Sunday after-noon games were officially the opening games at the stadium, the chance to generate revenue on a Saturday had been too good to pass up, so the Stars and the Cubans had played the previous afternoon as well—the Cubans took the first game, 6–4, while the Detroit Stars took the second, 7–4.[2]

It was the Detroit Stars' eleventh season in the NNL. It had gotten off to a bad start when their star player of the previous seven years, Norman "Turkey" Stearnes, jumped to the Lincoln Giants of New York. The Giants had played in the rival Eastern Colored League, which had folded in 1928, then joined the American Negro League, which was born and died in 1929, and they were still looking for competition at the start of 1930.[3] In a segregated sport, hardly anybody in the mainstream sports press bothered to celebrate the achievements of black players; nonetheless, "Turkey" Stearnes, who owed his nickname to his unusual running style, was, without a doubt, one of baseball's greats. While only pieces of the statistical records of the Negro League players have survived, Stearnes stands out with a career 176 home runs and 585 RBIs for a batting average of .344 in over 3,000 plate appearances.[4]

John Roesink had bought the Detroit Stars franchise in 1925, and like owners Frank Navin and Walter Briggs, named the facility after himself (although it was renamed Hamtramck Stadium in 1935). The stadium reportedly cost around $30,000 to build, a bold investment in the wake of the Wall Street Crash of 1929.[5] It was a significant commitment by Roesink, a successful Detroit tailor who also owned a chain of haberdashery stores in the downtown.[6] The new build was required after Mack Stadium had burned down the year before. The stands could accommodate around six thousand people, and the whole arena ten thousand. Charmingly, fans could also sit on the other side of the stadium fence in the Grand Trunk Western Railroad, finding seats in the parked boxcars waiting to be loaded up at the Dodge Main plant next door.[7]

The eight teams of the NNL played a split season, with the pennant decided in a playoff between the winner of the first half and the winner of the second. Without Stearnes in the first half, Detroit finished in fourth place, behind the first-place St. Louis Stars. By midseason, however, the Lincoln Giants had folded, and Stearnes returned to Detroit for the second half.[8] A week after his return, on June 27, the stadium staged a first for Detroit baseball: a night game. Lighting equipment had been acquired by the Kansas City Monarchs, who loaded it on trucks and took it with them on the road, no doubt in exchange for a share of the gate. The system was basic, with a noisy generator placed in midfield; wires everywhere threatened to trip up the fielders.[9] But the evening was a success, and the *Detroit Free Press* reported that 6,432 packed into the stadium to witness the innovation.[10]

Detroit won the second half of the split season, tied on win percentage with St. Louis. For the first time in their history, the Stars had a shot at the pennant. By contrast, the Tigers were coming to the end of a dismal season, and by mid-September were twenty-five games behind the leaders, with only two weeks left to play. The seven-game NNL title series started on September 13. The first four games were in St. Louis, and the teams returned to Detroit with the series tied a week later. The home team won game 5 and needed just one more victory on home soil to take the championship. Game 6 ended in a 4–3 loss, even though Stearnes hit a huge home run. His batting in the series was remarkable. In twenty-two at bats, he had thirteen hits, including four doubles, one triple, and three home runs, for a slugging percentage of 1.273. But game 7 was a huge disappointment: Stearnes went without a hit in five appearances at the plate, and St. Louis overwhelmed Detroit 13–7 to take the pennant.[11]

Even when they were playing for the championship, the Detroit Stars were already on the skids. One reason Stearnes had left at the beginning of the season was the grim outlook for baseball in Detroit at that time. The Wall Street Crash of October 1929 was already weighing down on planned automobile production for 1930, and it didn't look good for leisure spending. Everyone in Detroit was dependent on the economic health of the car industry, but the businesses that served the 8 percent of the population who were black were especially at risk. While the motor industry had welcomed black workers, few others did, and they were always the first to be laid off. Apart from the car industry, the African American economy in Detroit in that era depended largely on bootlegging and gambling.[12]

The Detroit Stars played baseball at a very high level, but the sport's segregation meant that they could never hope to prove themselves superior by beating a white team. The major leagues' ban of African Americans was strictly enforced in the absence of any written policy—in theory, any owner could have hired a black player at any time. In 1942, Commissioner Landis actually stressed there was no rule preventing them from doing so: "If [anybody] wants to sign one or 25 Negro players, it is all right with me." One of the leading owners, Larry MacPhail of the Brooklyn Dodgers, replied: "Judge Landis was not speaking for baseball when he said there was no barrier; there has been an unwritten law tantamount to an agreement between major league clubs on the subject of the racial issue."[13]

Of course, much of the blatant racism in baseball can be characterized as "unwritten law." The status of Cuban players illustrated the hypocrisy: Afro-Cubans would have been labeled "colored" in the America of the 1920s, but because they were foreigners, the major league clubs were willing to hire them—everyone simply pretended not to notice the hue of their skin.[14] And black players did get to play against their white counterparts in exhibition games, which the black teams frequently won.[15] Everybody was aware of the hypocrisy—Charlie Gehringer, the Tigers Hall of Famer, reportedly told Willie Foster, who played for the Chicago American Giants, "If I could paint you white, I could get $150,000 for you right now." Landis opposed exhibition games by the major league teams, although white players could still join "all-star" teams, which in those days meant invitation teams that would undertake barnstorming tours.[16] Gehringer also remembered playing a number of games against black nines, and he found them highly competitive.[17]

Some white players would come and watch Negro League teams. Several New York Giants players, in St. Louis for a game against the Cardinals, attended game 2 of the 1930 pennant series and saw the Detroit Stars' third baseman, Bobbie Robinson, complete a remarkable triple play to win the game. Afterward, they asked to be introduced to him so they could shake his hand.[18] The composition of the crowd at Detroit Stars games is unknown, but it was said that when the Tigers were out of town many white fans went to watch the Negro League team. For owners, however, this was probably a limited source of income at best. The reality was that the team was highly dependent on the economic well-being of Detroit's minority population.

The location of the stadium was a drawback for the Detroit Stars. Most black people had no choice but to live in Black Bottom, and the four-mile trek to Hamtramck Stadium was inconvenient at best. Streetcars could get you there for five or six cents—the price was a major political issue in Detroit—and cost was a consideration. Hamtramck was almost entirely Polish, but, around this time, there appears to have been little hostility between

African Americans and Poles. Some African Americans lived in Hamtramck and, as we saw, Mayor Tenerowicz was happy to officiate at the opening of the stadium.

In fact, ties between the African American and Polish communities went back some time. According to his obituary in the *Detroit Free Press* in 1908, Charles Roxborough, a black lawyer, had built his practice representing Poles.[19] One of his sons, John, would go on to manage Joe Louis, and the other, Charles Jr., would follow his father's career in the law. In 1930, Charles Jr. became the first black representative in the Michigan State Senate. But there was always competition for jobs. Hamtramck Stadium was convenient for those African Americans who worked next door at Dodge Main, but Poles wanted the jobs there, too, and might well refuse to work alongside black workers. African Americans were slow to support unionization precisely because the white workers did not see them as equals, and white employers were willing to pay black workers to break strikes.

Roxborough lost his seat to a Polish American from Hamtramck, and was then defeated three times, standing against Polish Americans, including Tenerowicz, in elections for Michigan's First U.S. Congressional District. Whatever the state of African American–Polish relations in 1930, they would certainly change over the next decade. Tenerowicz was immensely popular in the Polish community and, after a spell in jail in 1931, would go on to win a second term as mayor in 1936, and in 1938 was elected unopposed as representative for Michigan's First District in Congress, where he served until 1943.[20] From this position he would lead the opposition against allocating housing to African Americans at the Sojourner Truth project.

Roesink sold his interest in the Detroit Stars at the end of the 1930 season to Everett Watson, a man well known in the black community from the numbers racket. He had an extravagant reputation, handing out money freely when he had it, but in 1931 the Detroit Stars were not bringing in crowds and the players were struggling to get paid; by the end of the season the team had folded.[21] The NNL would struggle on for another couple of years, and there was an attempt to build a new team in Detroit to play at Hamtramck, but it all fizzled out in the Depression. Between 1929 and 1933, attendance at Navin Field had fallen from 869,318 to 320,972. Attendance at the Detroit Stars games was a small fraction of that at Tiger games, and the collapse in attendance was even more devastating.

In 1933 the NNL was re-founded, and after a few precarious years established itself again. By the late 1930s, it incorporated East Coast teams from New York, Philadelphia, Baltimore, and Washington, DC. In 1937, the Negro American League was founded. This league would end up with teams in Chicago, Kansas City, Cleveland, Indianapolis, Memphis, and Birmingham. Another attempt was made to start a Detroit team, and once again it would fail. The following ten years were the heyday of Negro League baseball, and between 1942 and 1948 the pennant winners of the two leagues played in the Negro World Series.[22] Ironically, it was integration of the major leagues, starting with Jackie Robinson in 1947, that sounded the death knell for the Negro Leagues. Detroit would not integrate until 1957, though plenty of amateur black nines played baseball in the city. Joe Louis started up his own team in the 1930s—the Brown Bombers softball team—and often made cameo appearances. A keen baseball fan, he was regularly seen at Tigers games. In 1936, Louis was approached as a possible owner of a new Detroit team in the resurgent NNL. He liked the idea of owning his own professional team, and had the money to finance it. But his management talked him out of making the purchase, because many of the new teams were associated with money from the rackets, which didn't sit well with Louis's clean-cut image.[23] While Detroit no longer had a black professional team, Walter Briggs was willing to rent out his stadium in the late 1930s to touring Negro League teams putting on exhibition games, and black Detroiters flocked to watch them.[24]

The heyday of black baseball in Detroit was the 1920s, when the Detroit Stars played at Mack Park. This stadium, about four miles east of Black Bottom, was also located in a white residential area. Today the site borders the vast Conner Creek industrial plant of Chrysler, the last car plant entirely located in the city of Detroit. Mack Stadium had been built by John Roesink in 1914. His approach to the sports business was entrepreneurial— he brought a number a Major League Baseball teams to the stadium to play games against his own team, and in 1920 he also founded one of the first pro football teams in Detroit. He was friendly with Frank Navin and several Tigers players, including Cobb, who threw the first pitch at Hamtramck as a favor. Since his main business was on Hastings Street, in the heart of Black Bottom, Roesink was also well connected to many influential black Detroiters.[25]

Because segregation in baseball was always a "gentleman's agreement," never written into the rules, deciding if a particular individual was "colored" could pose a problem—and the decision did frequently hang on a player's ability. There were clearly instances of African American players appearing in the minor leagues in the nineteenth century. But by the 1890s the policy of segregation was more actively pursued as the Jim Crow "separate but equal" philosophy took hold.[26] As a result, all-colored teams started to appear and play games against each other. One of the most successful of these in the first two decades of the twentieth century was the Chicago American Giants run by Rube Foster, which barnstormed the country. In 1920, Foster created more stable competition by founding the NNL. Foster knew Detroit well, and arranged for John "Tenny" Blount to run the Detroit franchise, which he arranged to play at Mack Park.[27]

The league was a success, and the rival Eastern Colored League was founded in 1923. The Negro World Series was inaugurated the year after, played between the champions of each league. In January 1927 the two leagues held a meeting at the Detroit YMCA to discuss policy issues, and Mayor John Smith addressed the delegations, saying how proud he had been in earlier years to throw the inaugural pitch for the Detroit Stars at the beginning of the NNL season. He also said rather pointedly that "there is no scandal in colored baseball, the record is clean." No doubt he had in mind the "Black Sox" gambling scandal that had almost brought down the whites-only major leagues in 1919.[28]

In purely baseball terms, the Detroit Stars were never dominant in the league, but neither were they doormats. As a business, the franchise was successful during the Roaring Twenties. Coleman Young, the future mayor, came to Detroit as a five-year-old in 1923, and remembered growing up in Black Bottom in this era: "We did particularly well during Prohibition, which can be said for all of Black Bottom and Paradise Valley. I never saw such prosperity in the black community—hell, in the city—as there was then. The money was practically jumping from pocket to pocket in those days. If you weren't making any, you either weren't trying or were inhibited by an unusual code of lawfulness."[29] Bootlegging, gambling and vice recycled the money coming out of the car factories. Almost anyone could get work, and as people flooded into the city willy-nilly, the patterns of segregation that later became established had not yet been laid down. Young could remember growing up surrounded by families with ethnic roots in Italy, Germany, and Syria, and the smell of rye bread emanating from the Jewish bakery.

More important than baseball in the 1920s was the emerging black music scene. Blues, boogie-woogie, and jazz were all to be found in Paradise Valley during this era, and although less well known today, famous artists such as Bessie Smith, Ma Rainey, Rufus Perryman, and Maceo Merriweather all played in Detroit. They laid the foundations for artists who would become Detroit regulars in the 1940s such as Billie Holiday, Cab Calloway, Nat King Cole, and John Lee Hooker. These artists served the growing black population, while white audiences proved less fastidious about black entertainers in the music industry than in the sports industry.

Black political opposition to discrimination and segregation was also starting to emerge in Detroit in 1930. In that year, a little known preacher called Wallace Fard Muhammad turned up in Detroit and on July 4 founded the Nation of Islam. Its purpose, he said, was to "teach the downtrodden and defenseless Black people a thorough Knowledge of God and of themselves, and to put them on the road to Self-Independence with a superior culture and higher civilization than they had previously experienced." Where Fard was from or where he went is shrouded in mystery. He used many aliases, including "Ford."[30] Under his disciple, Elijah Muhammad, the Nation of Islam would go on to be a major political force in 1960s America.[31] At the same time, about ninety miles west a young boy called Malcolm Little was growing up in Lansing, the state capital of Michigan. The following year his father would die in a streetcar accident, which the family believed was the work of the Black Legion. Malcolm and his family would move east, and when he joined the gangs in New York in the 1940s he was nicknamed "Detroit Red." In later years he took the name Malcolm X.

The end of Mack Park came on Sunday July 7, 1929. The previous day's game had been canceled and the ground was still waterlogged. The ground staff followed the usual practice of covering the field in gasoline, which they would set alight in order to clear the water. However, a fire suddenly burst out in the stand where fans were waiting. No one was killed, but about 220 people were treated for burns, many of them serious. While a subsequent investigation did not find evidence of negligence, quite a few people believed that Roesink had stored tanks of gasoline under the stand, and that it was these that had caused the fire. While Roesink compensated the players, he did nothing for the injured and his reputation among his patrons was severely tarnished. Despite building a new park and having a winning team, attendance stagnated in the following season. Some journalists claimed that this was attributable as much to boycotts as it was to the incipient economic crisis.[32]

After the Detroit Stars folded, Turkey Stearnes went on to play for the Chicago American Giants and then the Kansas City Monarchs, finally retiring from baseball in 1940. He did work for Walter Briggs, which involved not playing ball in his stadium but spraying cars in his car body works, jokingly referred to as the "Briggs slaughterhouse."[33] Stearnes was a quiet man. He didn't drink, womanize, or gamble. He was intense, with a habit of talking to himself in angry tones when he struck out or misfielded, an idiosyncrasy that many found disconcerting. Yet the great players of the Negro Leagues remembered him as one of the very best.

After integration, the Hall of Fame in Cooperstown started to admit Negro League players, not an easy task given the incomplete statistical record. Ted "Double Duty" Radcliffe, so called because he played both pitcher and catcher, played with and against Stearnes. Himself one of the great players and ambassadors for Negro League achievements in later years, he said of Stearnes: "There were a lot of great players came through Detroit with the Stars. I guess the names don't mean much now. Seems to me, a man can play ball that good, he ought to be remembered."[34] Thanks mainly to efforts of his widow, Nettie Mae, Norman "Turkey Stearnes" was inducted in the Baseball Hall of Fame in 2000, more than two decades after he passed away.

Miraculously the Hamtramck Stadium has survived. For years it stood unused, the iron frame of the grandstand slowly rusting away. The site is next to Keyworth Stadium, the WPA edifice opened by President Roosevelt in 1936 and now renovated as the home of Detroit City FC. The team owners have worked with the Friends of Historic Hamtramck Stadium and city authorities to develop a plan for the old ballpark, and money has been raised to bring this special location back to life.

TWENTY-FOUR

MAY 10, 1927

Ty Cobb returns in triumph to Detroit, where he had played for the Tigers for two decades. Even though he has recently moved to the Philadelphia Athletics in the twilight of his career, the city rolls out the red carpet. Ty Cobb, surely the greatest Tigers player ever and arguably the greatest player of all time, is a deeply controversial figure, although biographies differ as to the extent of his bad temper, his racism, and the degree to which he was hated.

Thirty thousand people had crowded into Navin Field when Mayor Smith stepped up to the microphone: "Cobb this day has the key to the city and to our hearts." Ty Cobb had arrived that morning on the *City of Cleveland* luxury steamer, which had made its way across the Lakes to Detroit. At a luncheon in the Masonic Temple, the mayor and other local dignitaries paid tribute to the great man. "It is hard," he responded, "to come back to the city, of which one for so long has been a part, in the role of an enemy, and I cannot work up a competitive spirit to play against my old team. But even though I must try to beat the Tigers, I have nothing but best wishes for the club." In the game, Cobb appeared at the plate four times, getting a double and a walk. His new team, the Philadelphia Athletics, comfortably beat the team he had played on for twenty-two years, 6–3.[1] Even if he played against them now, Detroit still loved Ty Cobb. Thanks to that new invention, the radio, not only the fans in the stadium could witness events, but so could all Detroiters and Michiganders with a wireless receiver. Baseball radio broadcasts in Detroit had started three weeks earlier on opening day with the very first game of the post-Cobb era.

The technology was as revolutionary in its day as television or the internet later, and commercial radio stations started to appear around 1920. In that year, WWJ in Detroit became one of the first stations in the United States to send out regular programming. The first baseball game broadcast via radio took place in Pittsburgh in 1921, and by the time regular broadcasts of Tiger games started, the New York Giants, the Chicago Cubs, the White Sox, the Cleveland Indians, the Boston Braves, and the Red Sox had already aired games.

The announcer for the first Tigers game was Ty Tyson, whose career would continue into the 1950s. He was known for his rather laconic style, and for developing his own nicknames for the players: "Mr. Tiger" for Charlie Gehringer, "Hancus Pancus" for Hank Greenberg. Some found him a little too cynical for their liking, even "bitter."[2] In 1934, Tyson acquired a rival in the form of Harry Heilmann; Heilmann had not only played seventeen seasons for the Tigers at first base and right field, he had been American League batting champion four times. He had only retired a couple of years earlier, and he was not a wordsmith like Tyson. His down-home style appealed to many fans, though, and he was known for recounting lengthy anecdotes about his time with baseball's greats while paying only cursory attention to the game being played in front of him. Heilmann worked for the WXYZ station, which broadcast largely to rural Michigan, while Tyson's WWJ audience sat in metro Detroit. Their rivalry continued for the next two decades, with most fans declaring staunch allegiance to either Tyson or Heilmann.[3]

By 1930, more than 50 percent of Michigan households had a radio, and just as Father Coughlin owed much of his popularity to the medium that he used to spew his venom, professional baseball reached a greater following thanks to broadcasting. During the 1930s, following America's game on the radio became a national pastime, and people said that you'd always be within earshot of a radio playing if you walked the streets of Detroit. A journalist visiting the city in 1934 claimed he was able to drive from Dearborn to Detroit and listen to the game uninterrupted, thanks to countless radios blaring through the air.[4]

Ty Cobb largely missed out on radio's golden age of baseball, but he was without doubt the sport's first great star. To some, his achievements on the field made him the greatest player of all time, and few would fail to include him in their all-time nine. His major league career started in 1905 with the

Tigers, where he stayed until those two final seasons with the Athletics. During his twenty-four-year career, he won the American League batting title eleven times, and his lifetime average of .366 is the highest in the history of baseball for players with over 3,000 plate appearances. He ranks fourth in all-time career stolen bases. He set ninety major league records during his career.[5] When the Baseball Hall of Fame was established in 1936, he received over 98 percent of votes cast, still one of the highest percentages ever recorded.

Cobb was also one of the first sporting superstars to generate significant income from endorsements. Thanks to the Reserve Clause, under which players were effectively contracted to a team in perpetuity unless the owner chose to sell them, salaries were not very high. In 1919, the Black Sox scandal, in which players were bribed to throw the World Series, had rocked the game. Shoeless Joe Jackson was alleged to have received a bribe of $5,000—equivalent to about $75,000 in today's money. It's hard to imagine a would-be fixer today approaching a major league star and offering such a paltry sum to fix any game, let alone the World Series, but those were different times. As the biggest star in the game, Cobb's salary was well above the norm and peaked at $85,000 in 1927, but it was still a fraction of what players now earn.[6]

He had other sources of income, however. Cobb was closely associated with Coca-Cola, a product that had been concocted in the same year that Cobb was born, and, like him, hailed from Georgia. He did not just advertise the soda, he ended up owning a lot of Coca-Cola stock, as well.[7] But it wasn't only Coke: his name was slapped on sporting goods, tobacco, candy, whiskey, and health supplements such as "nuxated iron." Between his endorsements and investments in the stock market, journalists noted, Cobb was the only millionaire baseball player to that point in history.[8]

For all his genius on the field, Cobb was a controversial figure in his own time, and just as controversial later. Here is a particularly scathing description of him in a 2017 article published in the *Metro Times*:

> He was known as a bigot with a short temper and a penchant
> for sadism. One local sportswriter described his style of play as
> "daring to the point of dementia." A later Tiger player said Cobb

regarded the game as "something like a war," recalling that "every time at bat for him was like a crusade." Cobb inspired fear in his opponents and hatred in his teammates. His reputation as a dirty player was well known—his contemporaries described how he'd sharpen his cleats in the dugout, then slide feet-first into a bag with those razor-sharp spikes aimed high. Given his thirst for blood and spurred soles, it's hardly surprising his career record for stealing home (54 times) still stands. It's also not a shocker he retains the dubious honor of committing more errors (271) than any American League outfielder.[9]

All sides acknowledge that he was an intense man who played to win, and many found him aloof, a bookish guy who preferred reading and taking baseball notes to carousing with his teammates. He often got into fights. One of the most infamous incidents came in 1912 during a game in New York, when a heckler named Claude Lucker yelled that Cobb was a "half-nigger," and that his mother had slept with a black man. Cobb was a product of Georgia and of his time, and he rushed into the stands, climbed up twelve rows of seats, and beat the guy senseless. Few at the time would have blamed him had Lucker not been missing a hand and a half. Even though his team threatened to strike if Cobb received punishment for his actions, the American League suspended him for ten days.[10]

Cobb's terrifying habit of sliding spikes-first into infielders did not help. Charlie Gehringer called him "a real hateful guy," and said he never knew anyone so hated by so many players as "Butcher" Cobb.[11] The numerous bust-ups with other players started at the very beginning of his career when, as a rookie, he appears to have been the victim of particularly vicious hazing.[12] Cobb may have cemented his terrible reputation when, near the end of his life, he hired the journalist Al Stump to ghostwrite his autobiography. Cobb died just before it was published, and it's difficult to imagine that he would have approved of the final copy. Freed of constraints, Stump painted a picture of an aggressive, difficult, money-grubbing misanthrope. He did, however, also point out that Cobb gave much of his fortune to an educational fund to help needy kids through college, and that he would often break down in tears when students came to thank him.[13] Stump's book started one of the most malicious urban legends: comparing Cobb with his biggest rival during his playing days, Babe Ruth, the author wrote that in 1948, a quarter of a million fans filled Yankee Stadium to pay their respects at the coffin of the Sultan of Swat, but "Ty Cobb drew just three men from big-league ball to his funeral."[14] Cobb-critics have maintained for a long time that only three people altogether showed up at his funeral, even though that is clearly not how Stump describes it.

A 2015 biography of Cobb challenges not just the funeral story but a number of other established narratives.[15] With the help of Cobb's descendants, Charles Leerhsen shows that actually Cobb's funeral was a very big affair. While *Ty Cobb: A Terrible Beauty* does not deny that Cobb could be aggressive or irascible, the book argues that baseball was a rough game, especially in those times, and that Cobb was no different from many of his contemporaries, except for being exceptionally talented. And much of the evidence does not suggest that he was especially unpopular, as his reception in Detroit in 1927 attests.

Perhaps the thorniest issue is the question of Cobb's racism—taken as a fact by many of his critics. As a white southerner, "Georgia Peach" Cobb is an easy target—Northerners like to think that racism is a Southern problem, after all. And since Cobb had migrated to Detroit a mere forty years after the Civil War ended, it seemed plausible to suspect him of harboring views on race that would stand out in Yankee Michigan. But Cobb's grandfather was a Methodist abolitionist who had been run out of North Carolina's Haywood County for his unpopular opinions, and while that hardly clears Cobb, we shouldn't jump to conclusions. We've already seen that he was happy to throw the opening pitch at a Negro League ballpark, and, after baseball integrated, Cobb made relatively supportive comments at a time when other Southern baseball players were openly hostile to black players' advancement. In 1952, he told a reporter: "I see no reason in the world why we shouldn't compete with colored athletes as long as they conduct themselves with politeness and gentility. Let me say that no white man has the right to be less of a gentleman than a colored man. In my book that goes not just for baseball but for all walks of life."[16]

The conviction that Cobb mistreated or lacked respect for African Americans rests upon more than speculation and conjecture, however. In 1910,

Cobb was playing in an exhibition game in Cuba against Double Duty Radcliffe, who was playing catcher that day. Always an extravagant character, Radcliffe's chest protector had "Thou shalt not steal" written on it. Radcliffe later told this story: "We barnstormed against all of 'em, Ty Cobb and them. Ty Cobb comes up to bat and says to me, 'No nigger's gonna catch me stealing.' He gets to first, tries to steal. I get him. As he's coming off the field, I yell at him, 'No nigger's gonna catch you stealing? Well this nigger just done did it.'" After this incident, Cobb is said to have vowed never to play against black nines again.[17] While his alleged vow is not well attested, it is an established fact that Cobb never played exhibition games against Negro League teams after 1910, even though numerous white players did.

And then, there is the story of Henry Cummings, a well-liked black groundkeeper at the Tigers' spring training camp in Augusta, Georgia. It's reported that in 1907, Cobb got into a dispute with Cummings—allegedly, the groundskeeper approached the baseball star in a manner that Cobb considered too friendly, and he pushed him away. An altercation ensued, and a teammate, Charlie Schmidt, ended up fighting Cobb. Schmidt later claimed that Cobb had assaulted Savannah Cummings, who was trying to defend her husband.[18]

A year later, Cobb assaulted Fred Collins, a black man who worked for the Detroit United Railway Company. Collins was working, laying asphalt, when Cobb emerged from the Pontchartrain Hotel on Cadillac Square, adjacent to Campus Martius. Because of the freshly laid asphalt, Collins said "you can't cross here"—Cobb took offense and attacked Collins. Cobb received a summons for the attack and appeared in court, finally settling with Collins privately.[19]

In 1909, Cobb was staying at the Euclid Hotel in Cleveland, where he returned late one night, apparently intoxicated, and asked the bellhop to take him on the elevator up to a room where some teammates were playing poker. Dissatisfied with the response he got, Cobb became involved in a brawl with the bellhop and the nightwatchman, George Stanfield. Stanfield filed suit, accusing Cobb of stabbing him with a knife; Cobb pleaded guilty to a charge of simple assault and paid a $100 fine. Depending on who tells the story, both Stanfield and the bellhop were black.[20]

In 1919, there was another incident at the Pontchartrain Hotel. Cobb assaulted Ada Morris, a black chambermaid. While she was trying to replace linen he pushed her out of his room, kicked her in the stomach, and pushed her down a flight of stairs. She was hospitalized for weeks. The story surfaced a month later when Morris filed suit against Cobb, and the *Chicago Defender*, an African American newspaper, reported it as a racially motivated attack. The case was dropped, and the paper alleged that Tigers owner Frank Navin and the American League were involved in a cover-up. Perhaps Morris was indeed paid off—there are no published records to shed more light on the incident.[21]

There are certainly quite a few of these types of stories. Bill Moore, a pitcher whose major league career consisted of exactly one game—played on April 15, 1925, for the Tigers—had this one to tell: "I can't remember exactly where it was—some small town in Georgia—but I remember the incident. We were in a restaurant after the game when Cobb asked this black waiter something. I don't know what was said, but the waiter said 'No.' God almighty, you would've thought a bomb had exploded in there! Cobb jumped out of his chair and grabbed that waiter by the lapels and told him 'You so-and-so nigger, it's "No, sir" and "Yes, sir" when you talk to a white man.' And then he went on a tirade about the blacks."[22]

Leerhsen's book takes pains to dismiss or minimize these accounts as evidence of Cobb's racism. The only eyewitness to Cobb assaulting Mrs. Cummings, he writes, was a disgruntled teammate; there is no record of Cobb using a racial epithet when addressing Collins; there is no proof that the bellhop was black, and Stanfield may have been white; Bill Moore got his story confused. Only the Morris story seems to leave Leerhsen struggling for an excuse. In general, Leerhsen appears to believe that Cobb has been unfairly singled out for behavior that was common at the time—but the fact that racism was commonplace hardly erases its import. It may indeed be correct to view Cobb's behavior as that of a typical white bigot of his era, and that his views may have evolved later in his life.

Double Duty Radcliffe doesn't appear to have much doubt about where Cobb stood, even though he links Cobb's conduct to that of the majors in general. Here is his take, from a biography published in 1994:

I played against Ty Cobb. I didn't pitch against him—they wouldn't let me pitch in the league then 'cause they couldn't touch me. Was Ty Cobb as good as they say? Oh yeah. He was dirty, though. He didn't play but two games against us because he was a racist. He beat up a colored woman in the stands one time when he was with the Detroit Tigers. He was nasty. See, we played the Detroit Tigers and beat 'em and that's when the major league commissioner, Judge Landis, stopped us from playing a team intact. We had to play all-star teams so they couldn't say we beat a major league team. We beat 'em seven out of nine so they took us away! We didn't get a chance to play 'em no more until Landis died in '41.[23]

Cobb rehabilitators such as Leerhsen are likely to dismiss this testimony because it contains several inaccuracies. Landis died in 1944, not 1941; the story of the "colored woman in the stands" seems to be confusing the Lucker incident with the Ada Morris assault; the claim of "seven out of nine" victories against the Tigers sounds suspiciously precise in the midst of a vague account. Yet, for all this, Radcliffe was better placed than most to assess the racial attitudes of Cobb. He did play against him, and he spent many seasons in Detroit where he had opportunities not only to meet Cobb but to meet dozens of players, both black and white, who had played with and against Cobb.

In the end, we see what we want to see. Since sport and race are so closely linked in the history of the United States, his conduct toward African Americans has come under especially harsh scrutiny, while his anti-social behavior with regard to others is simply subsumed as that of an anti-social athlete. But in the context of Detroit in the first few decades of the twentieth century, the categories of white and black had not yet congealed into the dominant racial paradigm—as we have seen in previous chapters, ethnicity, national origin, and religion played crucial roles as well. This was especially true in the early 1920s, at which point about one-quarter of the city's population had been born in another country.

During the Ty Cobb era, Americans' perceptions about their country underwent significant changes. Though the United States had always been a nation of immigrants, the country's involvement in the First World War had sparked a re-evaluation of its relationship to Europe, the continent of origin of most immigrants at the time. Not surprisingly, anti-German feeling had grown considerably once the United States entered the war in 1917, forcing most German Americans to play down the importance of their roots. It is possible that the general hostility toward all things German helped smooth the way for Prohibition, since many German brewers such as Busch and Stroh had fostered close relations with Germany and were now seen as unpatriotic.

Many Americans would have preferred to stay out of European entanglements, and others feared the consequences of the war, not least the Bolshevik revolution in Russia. Figures like Henry Ford associated both communism and banking with Judaism, and large swaths of Protestants objected to the large-scale migration of Catholics from Poland and Italy. Protestantism has always been the dominant form of Christianity in the United States, and hostility to "the Papists" went back to colonial days and the French and Indian War, which led to the long-standing accusation that Catholics were more loyal to the Pope than to the nation. As we mentioned earlier, the Klan, at its 1925 peak, was alleged to have up to 6 million members, of whom around one-third were to be found in the Midwest. Chicago, Indianapolis, and Detroit were particular strongholds. This surprised many observers given the traditional association of the KKK with the South. But the Great Migration from the South and the large inflow of Catholics and Jews from Europe fed the beast. The rise of the KKK in Detroit was extraordinary in its speed. The first KKK organizer set up in the city in 1921, and by 1923, they were able to burn crosses with up twenty-five thousand people in attendance.[24]

Anti-Catholicism, anti-Semitism, and white supremacy by and large came as a bundle—as with Italians, Jews were not perceived to be white, in any case, and the idea of a homogenous "white America" that would include older and newer immigrants, Catholics and Protestants, had not congealed yet. As Brent Staples writes in the *New York Times*, "Congress envisioned a white, Protestant and culturally homogeneous America when it declared in 1790 that only 'free white persons, who have, or shall migrate into the United States' were eligible to become naturalized citizens. The calculus of racism underwent swift revision when waves of culturally diverse immigrants from the far corners of Europe changed the face of the country."[25]

Unlike anti-black racism, however, the brutal discrimination against white European minority groups eventually ended. Consequently, events such as the lynching of eleven Italian immigrants in New Orleans in 1891—which gave rise to the proclamation of Columbus Day—have all but disappeared from the national discourse.[26] And while it is an unambivalently good thing that Americans of Polish, Italian, or Appalachian descent no longer have cause for fear, the consequent loss of solidarity between disfavored groups was a heavy price to pay, for the nation in general but for Detroit in particular.

TWENTY-FIVE

JULY 12, 1921

Alphonse Kronk, a twelve-year-old boy, is run over and killed by a motor truck, a terrifying new hazard of everyday life in the city. His father, John Kronk, an immigrant from Poland and local politician, is inspired to lobby for facilities that will keep youngsters occupied and off the newly dangerous streets. In 1922, he officiates at the opening of a city-funded gym at 5555 McGraw Avenue, which will be named after him a few years later. The Kronk Gym was part of the larger agenda of progressive mayor James Couzens, the business architect of the Ford Motor Company who had persuaded Henry Ford to pay his workers the unheard-of wage of $5 a day. Couzens sought to give Detroit capitalism a human face by supporting leisure facilities, parks, and other urban amenities. The Great Depression put an end to those programs, a loss that would significantly contribute to the neighborhood blight to come.

At 6 p.m., young Alphonse Kronk was hit by a motor truck on the corner of Junction and Kopernick, about two and half miles up Michigan Avenue from Navin Field, and about fifty yards away from his front door. The driver of the truck was Joseph Kraemer, who was delivering heavy equipment; he was driving alongside a streetcar at the time of the accident. Alphonse was playing in the street with one of his cousins. When the streetcar stopped, Alphonse ran into the road; he did not see the truck, which a witness said was traveling at around 20–25 miles an hour. The truck knocked Alphonse down, ran over his chest, and did not stop. Alphonse was still alive when the ambulance arrived, but he died on the way to hospital. An hour later Kraemer turned himself in to the police; he did not possess a driver's license.[1]

Cars were changing the city, and the price of the new prosperity could be heartbreakingly steep.

We tend to think of sports in terms of the big games, the fierce rivalries, the legendary teams and players—but sports is also about pick-up games in the park, swimming in the rivers, tossing balls with your friends, batting practice with the neighborhood kids. When the car arrived to change American cities forever, the streets were no longer the space for any of that, though it took municipalities some time to come to terms with the new reality and the challenges it posed.

The scale and speed of the changes had been impossibly rapid. In 1910, a Model T Ford cost $950. By the early 1920s, the price had dropped to around $300, while over the same period average incomes had doubled. In 1910, Detroit produced more 100,000 cars for the first time; by 1923, the number had reached 3 million. Today, it is hard to comprehend the sheer scale of the changes that the automobile brought to Americans' lifestyle. Previously, the road had been occupied by people going about their business, by kids playing, by horses, and by electric streetcars. Horses vanished from the streets almost immediately, and automobiles took up all the space on the roads. Pedestrians were relegated to the sidewalks, if there were any. Noise, traffic jams, and road accidents were not new, but they increased dramatically in the urban environment. By 1924, 23,600 people died in car accidents each year—more than half of today's number but in a population one-third the size.

The history of the mass-market motor car is inextricably linked to the name of Henry Ford. The motor car evolved in two key stages in the first two decades of the twentieth century. The first of these, between roughly 1900 and 1910, entailed a series of technological innovations in the design of the automobile, making it into a relatively safe and reliable means of rapid transport. Many of these innovations were developed in Detroit, where Ford was a major player, but far from the only one. The second, between 1910 and 1920, transformed the automobile from a luxury item of the rich into an object every American could aspire to own. This stage entailed the development of a process of mass production that exploited economies of scale and lowered unit costs, and thus made the product affordable. In this process, the Ford Motor Company led the way almost single-handedly. As every schoolchild still learns today, Ford developed the assembly line, which enabled workers to build cars in a steady flow, replacing with machines the physical human effort of lifting and moving the parts. Today we are nearing the logical end of this process, as humans almost entirely disappear from the assembly process in a wide range of manufacturing activities.

Henry Ford did not hit on this idea entirely on his own. The logic of the assembly line had been articulated by Frederick Winslow Taylor, a management consultant whose book *The Principles of Scientific Management* is considered one of the most influential texts on business management ever written—it gives "Taylorism" its name. In 1911, when it was published, Taylor was already well known for his analysis of production techniques through his work at Bethlehem Steel.[2] The design and implementation of the Ford factory in Highland Park where his ideas were put into practice was largely the work of lieutenants such as Ed Martin, Charles Sorensen, and William Knudsen (the latter two were Danish-born immigrants).[3] The building itself was designed by the doyen of industrial architects, Prussian-born Albert Kahn.

If Ford's vision was ultimately the driving force, it was a vision rooted in the homespun philosophy of self-reliance and autonomy that he had inherited from his father. In 1909, Ford articulated his ambition "to democratize the automobile. When I'm through, everybody will be able to afford one and about everyone will have one."[4] The Model T Ford was the car and the Highland Park assembly line was the place where this vision would become a reality. The first T was built in 1908, the Highland Park plant opened in 1910; between 1908 and 1913, production at Ford rose from just over 10,000 units to 168,000. By 1916, it was 735,000.[5]

Mass production both reduced the price of automobiles and restructured the auto industry. One critical factor that had enabled the car industry in Detroit to grow in the early years was the sheer number of small engineering companies that could make the necessary parts. The early car producers needed very little capital because they contracted out most of the production—all they really did in their workshops was assemble the pieces. It was the suppliers who bore the financial burden of investing capital to manufacture the parts. Ford brought all of these supply chains in-house. That move considerably sped up the production process—but it also required a lot more capital. Small-scale outfits could not match the mass producers on cost, and the number of producers required to supply the entire market fell. As this Ford-initiated process played out over the decades, Detroit would eventually see the number of major car producers cut to three or four.[6] The Highland Park plant was followed in 1920 by an even bigger one, the River Rouge in Dearborn, which became known as the engineering miracle of the century. People would visit from all over the world to see this monument to modern production, and Diego Rivera would immortalize it in his complex murals commissioned by Edsel Ford and exhibited to this day in the Detroit Institute of Arts.

These new plants became islands of self-sufficiency in the urban landscape. From these strongholds, industrialists were able to shape urban policy and influence the economic destiny of the city. In 1914, Ford adopted another revolutionary policy—the $5 daily wage. This move was actually the brainchild of James Couzens, future mayor and U.S. senator. Couzens had been the business manager of the Ford Motor Company since its foundation in 1902, and in the first decade of the company's existence, the two men formed a close bond. Couzens admired Ford's engineering skills and visionary ambitions, while Ford recognized the need to find an ally in a company that, despite it bearing his name, he did not control fully until 1907. As one writer put it, "It can be presumed that Ford, by himself, could not have managed a small grocery store, and Couzens could not have assembled a child's kiddie car."[7] Charles Sorensen, who worked for Ford for forty years and controlled the production for twenty years from the mid-1920s on, gave a good deal of credit for the early success of the company to Couzens:

> From 1903 to 1913 was the Couzens period. True, the company had Henry Ford's name, its product and production were his. There never would have been a Ford car without him. But the Ford Motor Company would not have made Ford cars long without James Couzens. He controlled expenditures, organized sales, and set the pattern for business operation. He drove Ford and the production side to produce cars to meet the public's demand. He yelled for plant expansion and drove us from

the Piquette Avenue Plant into Highland Park. Everyone in the company, including Henry Ford, acknowledged him as the driving force during this period.[8]

In those early years, Couzens and Ford shared a progressive vision that put industry at the service of the people and considered corporate ownership to be a responsibility held in trust, rather than a source of vast personal enrichment. As mass production of the Model T turned the two men into millionaires, Couzens became wracked with guilt at the visible hardships of the working families on which the company relied. Socialist ideas were gaining ground in the United States and the rest of the world, organized labor was beginning to flex its muscle, and Couzens persuaded Henry Ford that paying his workers $5 a day—twice the going rate at the time—would mark a new way forward for the capitalist enterprise.[9] Of course, it also helped that higher-paid workers were more likely to be loyal, absenteeism being a perennial problem of factory labor. In one year in the 1910s, the Ford Motor Company "somehow managed to hire more than 52,000 people, despite having less than 15,000 on payroll at any one time."[10]

A well-paid workforce had an additional benefit—they could buy Fords. But there was a catch: if you wanted to make five bucks a day, you had to live by Henry Ford's idea of moral conduct. In 1915, the company published a booklet titled *Helpful Hints and Advice to Employees to Help Them Grasp the Opportunities Which Are Presented to Them by the Ford Profit-Sharing Plan*. The company, we learn in its preface, "has organized a staff of men, whose business it is, to help and encourage every man that needs assistance to grasp the opportunities that are his." And indeed, these men were "trained to offer useful advice on hygiene and on how to manage household finances. Behind them stood the Ford legal department, whose lawyers would help, free, with everything from buying a house to becoming an American citizen. Should an employee get sick or be injured, the company maintained a full-time staff of ten doctors and a hundred nurses."[11]

But they were also there to inspect your life, and soon, they'd be a force of two hundred men who were keeping a close watch on Ford workers' lives. They were the "Sociological Department," which would morph into Harry Bennett's "Services Department" later on, and they were there to see if you were married, if your house was clean, if your kids seemed healthy, if your wife was around. The company would not tell its employees where to live, "but it does expect that they, to be profit-sharers, will choose wholesome and decent neighborhoods and buildings, and keep their homes and surroundings clean, sanitary and healthful."[12] The preface may have promised that "no rules or regulations, of a general nature, are employed" and that "each individual is given a chance to work out the very best condition for himself in a way that will give him the most pleasure and satisfaction and foundation for further growth," but in reality, rules and regulations poured forth in abundance. Anyone who wanted the daily wage of five bucks had to "qualify as to sobriety, industry and cleanliness." Women qualified only if they had "some relatives solely dependent upon them for support." You also had to have worked at Ford for six months—an elegant solution to the absentee problem.

By 1915, workers were already wise to their employers' regime—the booklet notes, with evident pique, "that some young men, in order to qualify as profit-sharers, have hastily married without giving serious thought to such an important step in their lives. Seldom does such a marriage prove a happy one." Of course, heavy-handed regimes invariably produce enterprising schemes to subvert them. Richard Snow relates the fine anecdote of eleven young Ford workers who lived in a boarding house: "Whenever an agent stopped by, the man he was visiting would borrow the generous-spirited landlady and present her as his wife. Fortunately . . . the social workers never called on all eleven at the same time."[13] And apparently, quite a few scammers saw an opportunity and posed as Ford investigators to sell their wares, prompting the booklet's authors to issue the following warning: *This Company has nothing to sell but Motor Cars, and is in no way connected with any company, firm or individual engaged in selling real estate or anything whatsoever. No one who tries to sell an employe [sic] anything is an agent of the Ford Motor Company. If he says he is, he lies. Do not buy anything from him.*

Such anecdotes aside, Ford was serious about controlling the moral life of his employees and put real resources behind the undertaking. "A staff of investigators has been chosen whose duties are to explain the profit-sharing plan, and collect information and data from every one of the employes," the book lays out. If the investigators found you unworthy of profit-sharing, your case would go before a committee of the Sociological Department, which would pass final judgment. Foreigners were under special notice: "The investigators have found, upon going into the homes of many employes, and particularly some of those of foreign birth, that in many cases they were living and sleeping in overcrowded rooms and tenements. Often these rooms and tenements were dark, ill-ventilated and foul smelling, with poor sanitary conditions as to toilet accommodations and the disposal of garbage and refuse. . . . Notice that the most advanced people are the cleanest."

Ford's Sociological Department is, without a doubt, the forerunner of the sort of "private government" corporations impose on their employees that Elizabeth Anderson analyzes in her 2017 book of the same title.[14] She notes that to this day, "if the government imposed such regulations on us, we would rightly protest that our constitutional rights were being violated. But American workers have no such rights against their bosses. Even speaking out . . . can get them fired." To be sure, Ford and Couzens were convinced that they were acting in their workers' best interests—a new age, they thought, needed new cultural norms, and an industry heavily reliant on an immigrant workforce had to forcefully acculturate them to run smoothly. In fact, when foreigners graduated from Ford's "English school," the Henry Ford Museum tells us, they went through a ritual ceremony in which they literally stepped into a giant cauldron labeled "'American Melting Pot.' After going through a virtual smelting process, the immigrant's identity was boiled away, leaving a new citizen to emerge from the pot wearing American clothes and waving American flags."[15]

These clean, thrifty, sober, married, moral, well-paid workers were meant to produce the next generation of well-bathed, thrifty, moral Americans. *Helpful Hints* warns in particular against the kids running wild: "Children who are compelled to resort to the streets and alleys of the city for playgrounds are not getting what they need. To insure good health, and enable them to enjoy in fullest measure the desires of happy childhood, they should have open ground and space for play. Choose a home in a locality where ample room, with good wholesome surroundings, will enable the children to get the greatest benefit possible from their play, under conditions that will tend to clean and healthful ideas, rather than those likely to be formed in the streets and alleys of the crowded section of the city." Of course, the city would not have been nearly as crowded, dirty, and dangerous were it not for the Ford Motor Company and its competitors. Little Alphonse Kronk was just one of scores of victims—there were tens of thousands of cars on the streets of Detroit when he was hit, and a feature in the *Detroit News* mentions that in "the 1920s, 60 percent of automobile fatalities nationwide were children under age 9. One gruesome Detroit article described an Italian family whose 18-month-old son was hit and wedged in the wheel well of a car. As the hysterical father and police pried out the child's dead body, the mother went into the house and committed suicide."[16]

Ford was right that the city's children needed room to play, but where would all these parks and playgrounds for wholesome frolic and exercise come from in this city? At least, citizens like John Kronk tried to step up. Today, the only reason anybody knows Kronk's name is the Kronk Recreation Center, a venue linked to the heyday of Detroit boxing in the 1980s. Back in the 1920s, however, he was instrumental in finding funding for recreational facilities, finally an integral part of city policy. John Kronk himself was born on Polish land in 1883, at a time when Poland had been divided for more than a hundred years by the encircling powers of Russia, Prussia, and the Austro-Hungarian empire.[17] The family had emigrated soon after he was born, and they eventually moved to the southwest corner of Detroit, near the railyards, an area that was one of the main industrial centers of the city at the time. Back then, it was considered a Polish neighborhood—nowadays it is known as Mexicantown. Young Kronk worked as machinist and for the Detroit Union Railway before opening a saloon in 1910, just off Michigan Avenue.

When it was time to enter politics, however, the saloon had to go—he sold it in the same year he became an alderman, for in order to succeed in city politics, he needed the favors of the Prohibitionists.[18] At that time, the City of Detroit was organized politically in a ward system—small sections that tended to reflect local ethnic interests. The city elected forty-two aldermen, and an arcane network of committees made the decisions—a system rife with influence trading and backroom deals. The rising stars of the auto industry, who were achieving national acclaim, felt unrecognized in their own backyard, and they had little influence on city policies, which tended to be live-and-let-live. Local politicians supported ethnic schools, customs, and habits, tolerated alcohol consumption, gambling, and, to some extent, prostitution and brothels—exactly the kind of life Ford's Sociological Department had made it its mission to stamp out. Led by Henry Leland, president of the Cadillac Motor Company, the industrialists formed the Detroit Citizens League (DCL) to lobby for electoral reform. In essence, they wanted the city to be run like a corporation—and with greater deference to their interests.[19] Their clean-living regimes made them natural allies to the Prohibition movement, and if John Kronk wanted them as allies, selling his saloon was probably essential.[20]

Detroit might not have been exactly a company town, but the car industry's muscle was massive by then, and the DCL got what it wanted. In June 1918, the city voted to accept a new charter drawn up by the League. It gave power to the mayor and an elected council of nine "at-large" representatives—a system that survives to the present day. In 1919, John Kronk was elected to the first City Council. In 1920, he opened a bank, no doubt helped by the influential business figures who were now his friends. Throughout the rest of his life, he would serve on the council on and off, winning some elections and losing others—he was still serving at his death in 1953.[21]

Perhaps his most interesting, if ill-fated proposal, advanced in 1939, was that Detroit and the surrounding region of Southeast Michigan should secede from the state of Michigan and form their own state. In general, however, his politics tended toward the mundanely pragmatic, including his celebrated victory over the Detroit Union Railway (DUR), which had sought to raise streetcar fares to six cents: the "Kronk Ordinance" fixed them at five.[22] In this endeavor, he allied with James Couzens, who had entered politics after leaving Ford and continued a bitter campaign to bring the streetcars under municipal ownership and eliminate the private monopoly of the DUR. When Couzens succeeded in 1922, having been attacked as a "socialist" by his opponent, he had finally brought to fruition an idea first proposed by Mayor Hazen Pingree, an earlier "Republican socialist."[23]

Kronk's most lasting imprint, however, may have been his role in the expansion of recreational facilities. The DCL saw overcrowding in the central city as the root of much evil in urban Detroit. It advocated expanding affordable housing along with the creation of municipal recreation facilities.

In 1919, Couzens's new city administration won voter approval to spend $10 million in bond revenue to construct new playgrounds and playing fields and to extend the city's park system. Wholesome recreation was meant to foster wholesome politics: according to the DCL, "one of the best weapons for fighting against radicalism and for completing the solution of the saloon problem lies in a generous supply of recreation facilities."[24] Such facilities, as Kronk understood only too well, would also help to keep children off streets made more dangerous by the explosion of motorized road traffic. New developments mushroomed, and the city expanded from 47 square miles in 1915 to 140 square miles by 1926.

One of the very first steps of the new council was to approve the construction of a "community house" at 5555 McGraw Avenue, just nine months after Alphonse's death and just a mile away from where he died. At a cost of $160,000, the house consisted of a gymnasium, a swimming pool, changing facilities, and an auditorium. Clarence Brewer, appointed commissioner of the Department of Recreation in 1921, claimed it was one of the finest in the country. Mayor Couzens and Councilman Kronk officiated at the opening in March 1922.[25] In 1926, the council passed a resolution naming the community house after Kronk, in recognition of the fact that he had been the leading advocate for its creation.[26] Brewer had even more ambitious plans. In December 1921, he proposed the construction of a fifty-thousand-seat municipal stadium with a view to hosting the 1928 Olympic Games. It was to be funded by municipal bonds and would cost $900,000—a modest price tag if you consider that that figure in 1921 dollars amounts to $12 million today.[27] Compare that with the cost of the $863 million Little Caesars Arena that opened in 2017! But the price was considered too steep, the stadium was never built, and Detroit would never see the Olympic Games.

That doesn't mean that the city didn't invest. In 1920, Detroit spent $350,420 to maintain 144 recreation centers under paid leadership.[28] By 1927, the budget had increased to over $1 million, serving over a million users; it reached $3.5 million by the beginning of 1930.[29] The Recreation Department was responsible for a dizzying array of activities: managing parks and gyms; maintaining facilities such as tennis courts, swimming pools, and baseball diamonds; running competitions for children and adults; and organizing camps, festivals, and outdoor entertainments. It was even responsible for licensing dance halls, a tricky issue in Prohibition Detroit—they were very popular, but dancers frequently felt quite a bit more nimble after a drink or five, and accommodations had to be made.

The extent to which these programs in the 1920s had the desired effects of reducing delinquency and vice is not clear, and because of the excesses of Prohibition, the outcomes remain cloudy. However, it is hard to believe that publicly funded recreation facilities did not do quite a bit of good. Parks do break up the oppressiveness of urban landscapes, and children do need to play outdoors—which had become much more dangerous in the automobile era, as John Kronk learned in the hardest possible way.

As is so often the case, these lovely developments had a dark underbelly—by and large they excluded Detroit's growing African American population, both with regard to housing and to the accompanying recreational facilities. This is where the roots of Detroit's extreme segregation lie, which would continue to define and haunt the city—first as a matter of official city policy and then as a matter of city practice. In the 1920s, as we noted earlier, the KKK was powerful in Detroit and the Midwest, and the Klan's growing influence cowed even the white politicians who claimed to be sympathetic to the black housing crisis. Redlining and other blatantly discriminatory practices were the order of the day.

The Recreation Department did take some steps to meet the needs of the African American community. Forrester Washington, a pioneer of African American social work, commented approvingly:

> Another encouraging feature of the development of recreation among Negroes is the active steps that certain cities are taking to provide recreational facilities in those sections where large numbers of colored people live. Detroit stands foremost in this particular. In this city in 1915 there was one paid colored play director; in 1927 there were five; in 1905 there were one hundred colored summer playground directors; in 1925 there were three hundred and twenty-five. On April 6, 1928, the City Council of Detroit, on the direction of Mayor Lodge, voted $268,000 for the erection of a recreational center at 637 Brewster Street, in the heart of a large Negro community. This new structure

will consist of six large club rooms, an auditorium with stage, a gymnasium with balcony, a swimming pool with balcony, and will altogether be one of the best recreational centers in the country.[30]

Kronk and other civic dignitaries were in attendance when the Brewster opened on October 25, 1929—the same gym where Joe Louis would enroll as a sixteen-year-old, one year later.[31] Unlike the Kronk, it has survived—after a long period of dereliction, the site is now under redevelopment.

TWENTY-SIX

OCTOBER 9, 1910

The Chalmers Batting Race ends in acrimony as Ty Cobb is declared the batting title winner, allegedly leading Nap Lajoie by a difference of .00086. Both sides fling allegations of cheating, made more plausible by the league's questionable record keeping. Seventy-one years later, statisticians conclude that Lajoie had been the rightful winner. Hugh Chalmers, an acclaimed marketing wizard, was thrilled by the controversy, but his sincerely held belief that marketing was more important than engineering would be his downfall.

On the final day of the season, Nap Lajoie produced eight hits in a double-header, thus finishing the season with the highest batting average—or so he thought. For the next six days, he thought he had won the title and a brand new Chalmers automobile—and for the rest of his life, he would think that he should have. But six days later, his fortunes were reversed, and both award and car went to Ty Cobb instead. Seventy-one years later, in one last twist, the *Sporting News* reported that there had been a mistake—record keepers had counted a Tigers box score twice.[1] Lajoie had been right—he was the rightful batting champion of the 1910 season.

Batting average in baseball is a relatively simple concept—you divide the number of batters' hits by the number of times they went up to bat. Of course, a "hit" is more than just making contact—you have to hit the ball well or far enough to enable you to get safely to first base or beyond, without an error by the opposing team, and without the fielders taking out another base runner. A hit, then, advances the team's chances to score a run. Batting average is the most venerable of baseball statistics, originally developed and promoted in the 1870s by Henry Chadwick, the "father of baseball."

Even though some of today's statistical purists are rather sniffy about it, it remains a good measure of batting effectiveness.[2]

Hugh Chalmers, president and proprietor of the Chalmers Automobile Company of Detroit, thought it a perfect measurement. As a man who had entered the auto industry just three years earlier, he did not know much about engineering, but he knew good publicity when he saw it. He came up with a scheme to promote his product that he took to be foolproof: early in 1910, he told the National Commission—representing the long-established National League and the newbie American League—that he was offering a Chalmers car, valued at $1,500, to the player with the highest batting average at the end of the season. In the previous season, the winner of the batting crown had received nothing more than a silver cup, and the commissioners[3] saw in Chalmers's offer a chance to promote their leagues along with his cars, and the deal was struck.[4]

Early on, Detroit's Ty Cobb was everyone's favorite to win the title. He had topped American League averages for the previous three seasons, and while Honus Wagner was thought a plausible contender, few others were considered credible competition. When, at the beginning of the season, Chalmers hosted a reception in Detroit to get the word out about his prize, most fans were not yet particularly focused on the batting contest—there were 155 games to come. By midseason, however, when the American League announced the official averages, fans started to take an interest.

Major League Baseball was still in its infancy in 1910, and it was much more challenging to collect data than it is today. The official scorer, appointed by each team, recorded the events of each game and mailed them to the league offices within five days, where they were, in turn, entered by hand into ledgers. Scorers were usually journalists, whose degree of familiarity with the game varied. There was no reason to think the official scorer's tally would match exactly with those of the other journalists producing the unofficial box scores that were published in the papers. The official scorer did not share his record, and the league secretary did not reveal the season averages until the season was over. Published scores could differ in various ways. Some were a matter of judgment—what appeared as an error to one baseball expert might not seem so to another. But simple errors of recording or transcription were possible as well. Decades later, a baseball commissioner would even set up a committee to correct discrepancies in the records.[5]

However (un)reliable the figures might have been, when the American League announced theirs in the middle of the season (the National League would wait until the end of it), they certainly came as a surprise. Instead of Ty Cobb, it was Napoleon Lajoie who topped the chart, one of the great players of the early twentieth century. "Nap," or "Larry," as he was affectionately known, had played in the National League since 1896 and had won the batting title three times. He was so popular with players and fans alike that they had decided to nickname the Cleveland team "the Naps" in his honor. But by 1910, he was aging, and being both his team's manager and a batter, he had struggled—not many fans expected him to return to form.

Ty and Nap were in a batting race now, and from the middle of the season onward, a baseball fever overtook the country as fans eagerly anticipated the outcome. After each game, newspapers issued updates on the state of the race, and each month, the fortunes of the players waxed and waned. As the climax of the season approached, the batting race appeared to generate a good deal more interest than the World Series. By early September, it looked as if Cobb had gained the lead, but when an eye infection forced him to take time off, the race tightened again.[6] By the last week of the season in early October, however, his lead appeared solid.

And then the shenanigans started. Detroit were due to play their last two games of the season in Chicago, but Cobb suddenly asked to be excused. Allegedly, he needed to remain fresh for an all-star game in Philadelphia. Most fans suspected that he was simply protecting his lead: if he didn't play, his batting average couldn't get any worse.[7]

On the last day of the season, Cleveland was due to play a doubleheader in St. Louis, against the always-awful Browns. By common consent, Lajoie now needed something of a miracle—and something of a miracle he got. In his first at-bat, he hit the ball to centerfield for a triple—though some claimed the fielder should have caught it. In his second, he noticed that Red Corriden, the rookie third baseman, was standing well back, so he bunted. Shortstop fielded the ball and lobbed it to first base, rather than throwing hard, and Lajoie was ruled safe. In Lajoie's third appearance, Corriden was still standing well back. Maybe it was out of respect for batter's hitting power but Lajoie decided once again that the bunt was his best option and, sure enough, he had another hit. In his last at-bat of the first game, once again Corriden stood well back and Lajoie bunted—Lajoie had four hits in four at-bats now.[8] According to the statisticians, another four-for-four showing in the nightcap would have him overtake Cobb. Surely that wasn't possible?

It had been made possible, it seems. Later, the manager would say that Lajoie had simply outfoxed them by bunting when they expected him to drive. Each bunt was pretty much a guaranteed hit, and Lajoie accumulated four more—miracle achieved![9] Of the eight hits Lajoie needed that day, seven had come from bunts. Corriden claimed that the manager had ordered him to stand back; unsurprisingly, the bizarre denouement gave rise to speculation that the outcome had been fixed. After all, Lajoie was popular, Cobb was not—not even with some of his teammates, who sent a congratulatory telegram to Lajoie. Quite a few newspapers, however, even those in St. Louis, proclaimed that the Browns had disgraced baseball.[10] The original agreement between Chalmers and the National Commission, which ran baseball at the time, stated that the final decision as to the winner would rest with the Commission. Chalmers, when asked, declared that "our company probably will not ask that the alleged quitting of the St. Louis club be investigated, relying on the commission to take any such action that it may deem necessary or expedient. I regret very much that any scandal should arise over the batting race. . . . We had no reason to anticipate anything of this sort and trust that the fans will reserve judgment until all the facts come out."[11]

The twists were not yet over. The National Commission was in charge of announcing the winner, once they had calculated the official record for the season. Before doing so, Ban Johnson, founder and president of the American League, promised an inquiry into what had happened in St. Louis. On October 15, he released a statement exonerating the Browns—Lajoie's hits, he had decided, were undisputed. He went as far as to argue that Lajoie should have been given a fifth hit in the last game instead of an error, based on the scoring of a St. Louis journalist. And then . . . he proclaimed Ty Cobb the winner of the batting title, with an average of .384944 over Lajoie's .384084.[12]

To add to the shock and dismay, Johnson's math, according to his own numbers, was wrong—Cobb had indeed won, but his 196 hits from 509 at-bats actually put the percentage at .385069. The margin between the two batters, however, was a single hit—and Johnson himself had just declared that Lajoie should have been awarded that fifth hit, which would have put him over the top.[13] Accordingly, Lajoie went to his grave believing he should have won that title and that car. And in 1981, twenty-two years after his death, an analysis of the American League records proved him right. He should have won—not because of the extra hit, but because they had mis-recorded Cobb's hits, who had two fewer than the official record showed. The injustice, however, could no longer be remedied—the commissioner declared that the statute of limitations had run out on the issue, and Ty Cobb would stand as the 1910 batting champion.[14]

Back in 1910, Ban Johnson promised that this race would never be run again, but Hugh Chalmers, of course, was delighted. The competition and the ensuing controversy had given him more publicity than he could have hoped for in his wildest dreams, and he was more than happy to smooth things over by agreeing to award both players a Chalmers. He even managed to persuade Johnson to run another competition the following year. This time, however, it would be for MVP of the American League, and the winner would be voted in by the leading journalists—averting another statistical headache.[15]

The 1910 batting race would turn out to be the high watermark of Chalmers's career. He had risen to prominence about a decade earlier as the star salesman of the National Cash Register (NCR) Company, one of the nation's fastest-growing businesses at the end of the nineteenth century. In 1900, at the age of twenty-seven, Chalmers had become NCR's vice president and general manager, second only to company founder John Patterson, who had taken him under his wing. Over the next seven years Chalmers continued to thrive, and by 1907 he was earning an annual salary of $84,000, equivalent to over $2 million in today's money—long before excessive corporate salaries made such sums seem normal. Patterson, however, was a difficult and aggressive man who frequently dismissed employees to whom he took a dislike. In 1907 it was Chalmers's turn, and he was fired.[16]

Chalmers would have his revenge. With a market share of around

90 percent, NCR attracted an antitrust investigation into some of its more aggressive marketing policies. During a trial in 1912, Chalmers gave evidence against his former employer. Another salesman described in court the kinds of practices that Patterson had sanctioned: he would "blackjack the salesmen of competitors" and "bribe freight agents to hold up shipments, or drop sand in competitors' machines to put them out of order, open offices next door to competitors and cut the prices to knock them out of business—these were all things that his knockout squad had been doing."[17] Patterson and several executives were convicted and handed down jail sentences, although these were eventually commuted.

Chalmers, by this point enjoying a national reputation, was persuaded by a group of automobile engineers to take over the Thomas-Detroit Motor Company. These engineers had previously worked for Ransom Olds, who had set up the first auto manufacturing plant in Detroit in 1899, and within two years they would leave to start up the Hudson Motor Car Company. By 1909, Chalmers was on his own, and he renamed the company for himself.[18] Still, he had a brand new factory to move into, designed by the great Albert Kahn, who had also built Chalmers a home. The factory was located far out on the city's East Side, and the house was a few blocks away in Indian Village, where a lot of the city's wealth congregated—to this day a lovely, leafy, highly prosperous neighborhood of vast mansions.[19]

Chalmers was convinced that he knew how to be successful in this business because he thought of it as simply one business among others. The key to all, in his view, was marketing, and he was the best marketer around. By then, Chalmers was a well-regarded public speaker, and he used his public platform to downplay the importance of manufacturing expertise in the production of automobiles. In a number of speeches, he claimed that it was much easier to build things than to sell them.[20] And in fact, Chalmers's print advertising campaigns in 1908 were quite successful. While drab by today's standards, the campaign entitled "This Astounding Car for $1500" prompted something of a revolution in car advertising and gave a significant boost to sales.[21] In another ploy, widely used in the industry, he also entered his cars into auto races, under the name of the Bluebird racing team.[22] There, too, he had some early success, but it was not enough to reach the well-to-do middle-class market for which he was aiming. Broad exposure came with his next idea, the baseball batting prize.

Some of his public lectures made more sense than others. On some issues, Chalmers seemed in tune with the industry that he had entered, for instance when he argued publicly for improving the roads at public expense. A self-serving proposal, needless to say, but the government would come to agree. On other topics, however, he was hopelessly at sea. When Ford raised the daily wage to $5, Chalmers pompously declared that Ford should have first consulted with the rest of the industry before doing so.[23] And in 1912 he delivered a diatribe in *Scientific American*, decrying large-scale production:

> Overproduction is the greatest danger to the automobile industry; or, at least, to those manufacturers who do not immediately realize that building and selling automobiles is a manufacturing proposition just like the building and selling of any other commodity. There is a great market, for instance, for adding machines. Yet it would be ridiculous to think that manufacturers could build two or three hundred thousand adding machines every year and not flood the market. I think some manufacturers of automobiles have not yet come to a full realization of the fact that they can build too many cars.[24]

This deep insight, which must have owed much to his time at a company building cash registers, of which there can, in fact, be too many, came during the time when Ford had raised annual production from 10,000 to 80,000 in the space of just four years and would further increase it to almost 750,000 in the next four years.

It seems likely that after 1910, Chalmers was simply losing interest in running his company, becoming more interested in participating in political life instead. He was involved in organizing the Employers' Association of Detroit, which pioneered the industry opposition to unionization. The organization was created in 1902 but had little influence until 1910, when Chalmers created the automobile division.[25] In 1912, Henry Leland, president of Cadillac, organized the Detroit Citizens League to lobby for municipal reform, culminating in the successful 1918 referendum to revise the city charter that we described in the previous chapter. Chalmers led the Citizens' Charter Committee on the referendum campaign.[26] He also became a leading light in the Detroit Athletic Club (DAC), which elected him president in 1913.

The DAC had formally come into existence in 1887, but it could trace its roots back to the Peninsula Cricket Club, founded in 1857. By 1910, it was largely moribund.[27] With a committee consisting of Detroit's elite, including the emerging aristocracy of the new motor industry, the club engaged Albert Kahn to build a grand new clubhouse. Modeled on a Renaissance Italian palace, the DAC was built on six floors with 108 bedrooms, fancy dining rooms, a Turkish bath, a gymnasium, and two squash courts. At the grand opening in 1915, Chalmers declared that "the DAC has become recognized all over the world as one of the greatest clubs. It will continue to impress our guests as the crystallized spirit of Detroit."[28] One of the best ways to admire the DAC nowadays is from behind home plate at Comerica Park. When the building was refurbished in 2011, one of the sixth-floor suites was transformed into the Hugh Chalmers Board Room in honor of the former president.

At around the same time the new DAC building was drawing acclaim, Chalmers's car company began to struggle. The cars were good-looking, and in 1908, they had been state of the art, but by 1915 they were out of date. As the industry advanced, Chalmers stood still, technically speaking. Moreover, he imagined that the car would remain the plaything of the well-to-do middle and upper classes rather than reaching a mass market, so he was quite content to sustain his high prices. Inevitably, sales started to shrink, and in 1917 Chalmers Motor Company entered into a business alliance with the Maxwell Motor Company in order to share costs.[29] By 1920, the shareholders had installed Walter Chrysler to bring the struggling Maxwell company back to life, and in 1922 a creditor forced Chalmers into receivership. Maxwell took over Chalmers entirely before eventually morphing into Chrysler.[30] The last Chalmers car was produced in 1923.[31]

Chalmers had enough money to remain on the fringe of the Detroit social elites, throwing garden parties on his swanky estate in Bloomfield Hills. His factory would remain operational as part of the Chrysler Corporation until 1990, when it was demolished.[32] The area today forms part of the much larger Chrysler complex—one of the last remaining car production sites located within the city of Detroit.

Chalmers passed away unexpectedly in 1932, already a largely forgotten figure. His obituary praised his marketing skills and his general contributions to the social life of Detroit, but there was no glossing over the fact that his car business had failed.[33] As it turned out, making cars was more difficult than marketing them. At mid-century, auto industry veteran Eugene Lewis had this to say about the man: "If Hugh had been as fine a manufacturer as he was a salesman, his car would probably be well known today."[34] In the end, his invention of the Chalmers Batting Race may have been his most interesting contribution to history.

TWENTY-SEVEN

OCTOBER 10, 1901

Henry Ford drives his own car to victory in a motor race that helps to establish his name as a particularly talented manufacturer of the horseless machine. In the early years, Ford is adventurous and open-minded, and in partnership with James Couzens, he builds a reliable, affordable, and mass-producible car. The more successful he becomes, the more arrogant, suspicious, and peculiar he grows. His dislike for bankers morphs into virulent anti-Semitism, which earns him an approving remark in Hitler's manifesto, Mein Kampf. *Couzens leaves to pursue his political ambitions.*

In the end, there were only two entries for the big race of the afternoon. One was Alexander Winton, a bicycler-turned-car mechanic who built his own cars, driving "Bullet." The other was Henry Ford, who was trying to raise funds to build more cars. He had named his machine "Sweepstakes." The race covered twenty-five miles, and Winton took a clear lead in the first few laps—Ford, who was not used to racing, took the corners far too sharply. Each driver had a mechanic on board, to assist and to act as ballast. After seven miles, Winton had opened a half-mile lead, which included one mile covered in one minute and twelve seconds, a world record. But then Winton's car started to slow down and to trail smoke; as his mechanic poured oil on the engine in hope of preventing a complete burnout, Ford passed Winton to cross the finish line victorious.[1] When he climbed out of Sweepstakes, Ford is said to have muttered, "Boy, I'll never do that again. I was scared to death."[2]

Around ten thousand people turned up at the Grosse Pointe racetrack that day to watch a series of motor car races, billed as the "First Big Auto

Race Meet of the West."[3] First raced the steam cars, next the electric cars, and finally, for the climax of the day, the gas cars, which were clearly the fastest. Ford's victory in this race is often described as the turning point in his career, the moment when he received recognition for his engineering skills and gave investors the confidence to back him. Perhaps so, but next day's report in the *Detroit Free Press* focused predominantly on Winton and his world record. The paper noted that the crowd was primarily interested in the obstacle race, where the cars had to manoeuver their way around tightly spaced barrels. The bookmaker apparently did a brisk business on the later races of the day. Street cars ran from the city every three-quarters of an hour to the racetrack, and one writer proved himself prescient by wondering if the event "denoted the approach of the horseless age."[4]

In later life, Ford would complain that he did not care for motor sport: "I never thought anything of racing, but the public refused to consider the automobile in any light other than as a fast toy."[5] In fact, there is no evidence that he was interested in sport of any kind. His real interest turned out to be the construction of a reliable car that could be sold in volume at a low cost. But he needed financing to start production, and winning races generated buzz, which in turn convinced investors that the product would sell. Ford had already seen one venture fail: the Detroit Automobile Company, founded in 1899, folded because the investors couldn't see sales materializing quickly enough.[6] It was in this period that he came to develop his hatred for finance and banking, which would later merge with his anti-Semitism. In 1901, the victory at Grosse Pointe garnered the needed publicity, and a group of backers provided $30,000 to start the Henry Ford Company. It may come as a surprise, considering the now-iconic status of that business name, but this venture quickly failed as well. The shareholders believed the race had sufficiently proven the technology, and they expected the rapid production and sale of a great many cars, generating quick and handsome returns. Ford, however, thought there was still work to be done, and he first wanted to develop another racing car. Following an acrimonious settlement, Ford kept his name, his patents, and a small payoff, while the investors put Henry Leland in charge of the renamed company—the first car the company produced was called the Cadillac.[7]

In 1902, Ford partnered with a cyclist to produce his second racer. Tom

Cooper, born just outside Detroit, was a champion cyclist of the 1890s. He knew how to take corners, and he taught Henry Ford—it appears that the pair became good friends.[8] Cooper, a celebrity in his own right, may even have advanced money to Ford, and he considered driving one of the two racing vehicles that Ford produced, the "999" and the "Red Devil." However, when Cooper and Ford realized how difficult and in fact frightening the vehicles were to drive, they decided to hire someone else to risk his life. That man, Barney Oldfield, another cyclist attracted to the new motor sport, would become one of the great names of early motor racing.[9]

Ford had built the 999 for himself and the Red Devil for Cooper. But, again, race cars really weren't his thing. A few weeks before the race, he sold the 999 to Cooper, and just before the race, he panicked and tried to dissuade Oldfield from driving it—he feared that a fatal accident was inevitable. That was exactly the kind of challenge that Oldfield relished, and he laughed off Ford's suggestion. He knew what he was doing—the newspaper reported that Oldfield "slid around turns, tore down stretches and ripped things loose generally. The drivers gave him a wide berth."[10] The Cooper-Ford vehicle won the five-mile manufacturer's race easily, achieving an average speed close to sixty miles per hour. Winton's car, once again the main rival, once again broke down.

If Oldfield was the hero of the race, Ford was recognized as the creative genius, and even though he no longer owned the 999, he was able to capitalize on its success. Oldfield and Cooper would carve out fine careers for themselves over the next few years, barnstorming around the country and racing the Ford cars against all comers—and when no one came, then against each other.[11] Henry Ford capitalized in a different way, catching the attention of financial backers for his third company, the Ford Motor Company. Now in collaboration with James Couzens, Ford introduced his Model A, producing 1,750 vehicles between 1903 and 1904.

As he began to build cars on a larger scale, Ford didn't forget how valuable racing was for generating publicity. In perhaps his boldest step yet, he announced at the beginning of 1904 that he would break the world record for the mile in a car. On January 12, on the frozen surface of Lake St. Clair, thirty-five miles north of Detroit, Henry Ford, driving his own car, completed a mile in thirty-nine seconds, a full seven seconds faster than the previous record. It was a remarkable achievement, one unmatched by any of his rivals in the design and manufacture of automobiles.[12] While Ford made one more attempt to break the land speed record, he never participated in races again. But with his encouragement, others did, and Ford cars became dominant on the racetracks between 1904 and 1907. The fact that these racers were propelled by engines very similar to those of the Model B Ford helped him sell the road cars. By 1907, Ford cars were established as the fastest and most reliable in the country. With Ford's reputation now shining in the eyes of the American public, he was able to more or less give up on racing—which must have come as a relief to him.[13] In 1908, the Model T Ford started production.

Ford was by no means the only manufacturer who discovered racing as a way to generate fame and capital. Chevrolet takes its name from Louis Chevrolet, a Swiss racer, who was racing Buick cars in Detroit by 1907. As a result, he got friendly with William Durant, who would go on to found General Motors. In 1911, the two men started Chevrolet together, but they later quarreled, and Louis gave up mass-market cars in 1918—he focused on racing until his death in 1941. Manufacturers also often hired driving aces, like Barney Oldfield, to drive for them. Another early racing champion was Eddie Rickenbacker, now best remembered as an ace fighter pilot in the First World War. Before that, he raced Maxwell cars during the Chalmers era.

Despite those forays, however, the American manufacturers lagged behind the Europeans, who had begun making cars not long after Gottlieb Daimler and Karl Benz invented the internal combustion engine in the 1870s. In the United States, by contrast, the honor of producing the first American automobile is usually accorded to the Duryea Motor Wagon Company of Springfield, Massachusetts, whose first vehicle did not go on sale until 1893. Another difference between Europe and the United States was the quality of the roads. Generally speaking, roads were better in Europe, which made it easier to concentrate on speed: in the thirty years between 1898 and 1927, a European held the land speed record for all but four years and three months. Americans, by contrast, had to ensure that their machine did not break apart on their rough roads, and the longer distances made endurance a main focus: the Glidden Tour, for example, established in 1904, took competitors on a two-hundred-mile course around the Midwest.

In Detroit, the first automobile appeared on the streets in March 1896—it had been built by Charles Brady King in his workshop on St. Antoine, just south of Jefferson and about three hundred yards west of the Renaissance Center, present-day home of General Motors. Within a decade, Detroit had established itself as the preeminent center of automobile production in North America. Detroit companies were pivotal to the invention and standardization of many of the design elements of what came to be the standard car. These included the steering wheel and gear shifts, pneumatic tires, improved suspension, canopy tops, headlamps, the throttle pedal, drum brakes, the electric starter, better spark plugs, and oil pumps. Superior materials also played a key role, especially when it came to steel. Most of these innovations were the result of individual efforts, usually patented—but during this period, Detroit manufacturers worked together on the standardization of parts in order to achieve maximum flexibility in production.[14]

Why did Detroit, rather than some other city, become the center of the U.S. motor industry? Given that this was a revolution that could happen only once, we will never know what exact weight we should give to each explanatory factor, but we can identify a number that were significant. By the 1890s, Detroit had developed as a medium-sized industrial center serving a hinterland consisting of Michigan and parts of Ohio and Indiana. It was a transport hub for the railroads, connecting to Chicago in the West, to the eastern seaboard via Cleveland to the southeast, and up to Toronto and Montreal in Canada to the northeast. The railroads north of Detroit connected to the mining towns of the Upper Peninsula and to the state's farming areas. As a major port on the Great Lakes, Detroit was also a key center for transshipment: bulk goods from the region were taken to the Mississippi by rail. Transport infrastructure created transport manufacturing, and together with the Pullman Car Company, the railroad companies trained large numbers of engineers in the maintenance of engines and the construction of carriages to be hauled by the engines. In addition, the city, which by the 1880s had become a center of stove manufacturing, was full of men skilled in metal working.

The geography of the city was conducive to networking and the exchange of ideas. The railroads had formed a circle around the city, with the main artery running southwest to northeast, connecting to the upper part of Ohio, while another branch followed the riverfront. The Belt Line completed the circuit. Unlike many cities, where manufacturing districts were separated from residential ones, the two lived side by side in Detroit at that time. The network of streetcars made for relatively easy movement around the city. People tended to live among their own ethnic group, but the distances were by no means as great as they would become later.

The geographical advantages are nicely illustrated by the evolution of Ford factories. The workshop where he produced his first vehicle in June 1896 was on Bagley Avenue, just behind Grand Circus Park in the heart of the downtown.[15] His first factory proper was on Mack Avenue, on Detroit's East Side, close to the railroad and about three blocks from the modern Heidelberg Project.[16] He then moved to 461 Piquette Avenue, where the factory still stands, located between Poletown, Woodward Avenue, and Wayne State. The move to Highland Park took him just a few miles up Woodward.

If any place denotes the dawn of the horseless age, it is Detroit. Perhaps oddly, then, the preeminent U.S. motor racing circuit is actually in Indianapolis. The Indianapolis Motor Speedway, constructed in 1909, is a purpose-built oval with banking on the turns, representing a conscious effort to meet the demand of a motor-racing audience. This was quite different from the Grosse Pointe racetrack, where Ford cars raced in 1901 and 1902, which was simply a repurposed horse racing track. As a journalist for the *Detroit Free Press* wrote, with what we must assume is some poetic license, "A mettlesome pacer, with sleek coat, high head, extended nostrils, stood uneasily in a stall at the Grosse Pointe race track yesterday. As he pawed the floor and jerked at his halter, it was easy to see that something was wrong with his equine majesty. For the first time in his career the horse was getting no attention, though a crowd stood about, and he resented it."[17]

That horse would not be the last to see his status shrink. A harness track for trotting races, called Grosse Pointe, opened in 1894.[18] The track was not actually in Grosse Pointe, the swish neighborhood on the northeastern limit of the city on the shores of Lake St. Clair, but on Detroit's East Side, very close to where the giant Chrysler plant is now. Trotting, which had grown out of county fair entertainment, was a popular form of horse racing in the United States from the early nineteenth century on, and Detroit became one of the centers of the sport. In harness racing, the horses pull riders seated in a lightweight cart known as a "sulky" around a track. Quainter in look, it seemed better suited to the region's rural history than the flat racing associated in those times with New York, Chicago, and New Orleans. Just like flat racing, however, it attracted gambling—technically illegal thanks to the Michigan law against lotteries.

The earliest written records of trotting races in Detroit go back to 1843, when there was a racecourse built in Hamtramck, but the practice was already in swing.[19] By 1850, as many as a thousand people would turn up to watch races—not half bad at a time when Detroit's population counted 20,000. In 1884, the Detroit Driving Club was formed to organize the sport in the city, joined in 1887 by the American Trotting Association, largely through the efforts of D.J. Campau, scion of one of the oldest families of the city.[20] When Recreation Park was built in 1879 as the home of Detroit's first professional baseball team, it included a trotting track encircling the park.

Because of its association with gambling, the favors of trotting and other forms of horseracing tended to rise and fall with the political tides. During the early 1900s, horse racing came under criticism nationally, and trotting declined as motor races increased. As at Grosse Pointe, popular trotting tracks such as the State Fairgrounds were converted into motor racing tracks in the early years of the new century.[21] In New York, thoroughbred racing weathered the storm of those years and made a strong comeback in the early nineteen teens. This was not the case in Detroit, where race cards seem to have become shorter and shorter; in 1918, the *Detroit Free Press* reported that the Detroit Driving Club would no longer be able to stage races.[22]

Key to these developments was the ascent of the motor industry moguls into the elite ranks of Detroit society. No doubt, the local motor manufacturers and their racing teams had a vested interest in seeing the ponies decline—they had cars to sell, but they were also committed to an ethos of disciplined austerity, which ran counter to the drinking and the gambling that were par for the horseracing course. Horseracing has always been a kind of accommodation between those in the working class who like to bet on the ponies and the super-rich who can afford to maintain a racing stable, each gambling in their own way. The publication that best represented the mindset of the new industrial elite was a magazine called *Horseless Age*— and at the dawn of that age, those who made it their business to render the horse obsolete as a beast of burden hardly had much interest in sponsoring horse races for fun.

The Ford race of 1901 thus stands on the precipice of a new era. Back in 1899, one of the backers of Ford's first business venture was Detroit's mayor, William Maybury. His statue still stands on Grand Circus in downtown Detroit, scowling across Woodward Avenue at his political opponent, Hazen Pingree. Maybury not only invested in Ford on his own account, he found other investors and even awarded Ford a driving license, which in those days was not a necessity but a mark of respect.

In 1901, Maybury asked prominent Detroiters to write letters to the Detroit citizens of 2001, "for those whose good fortune it will be to live in Detroit at the opening of the 21st century." He wrote one himself:

> We communicate by telegraph and telephone over distances that at the opening of the nineteenth century were insurmountable. We travel at a rate not dreamed of then . . . by railroad and steam power from Detroit to Chicago in less than eight hours, and to New York City by several routes in less than 20 hours. How much faster are you traveling? How much farther have you annihilated time and space and what agencies are you employing to which we are strangers?
>
> We talk by long distance telephone to the remotest cities in our own country, and with a fair degree of practical success. Are you talking with foreign lands and to the islands of the sea by the same method? . . . May we be permitted to express one supreme hope that whatever failures the coming century may have in the progress of things material, you may be conscious when the century is over that, as a nation, people and city, you have grown in righteousness, for it is this that exalts a nation.[23]

Perhaps the city's current mayor should ask Detroiters to write back and ask the powers of the fin de siècle what they would have done differently had they known the path on which they set the city more than a hundred years ago.

TWENTY-EIGHT

OCTOBER 24, 1887

The Detroit Wolverines win the thirteenth game of the World Series at Recreation Park. Baseball is developing into the people's sport. The Wolverines will be driven into bankruptcy by other members of the league, upset by the team's aggressive recruitment policy. The city is booming, serving as an industrial base for the westward expansion into Michigan and beyond. In a city of migrants, tensions are ever present between the new arrivals from countries such as Germany, Poland, and Italy, and those who had come earlier. City politics, which reflect the various struggles, produces Mayor Hazen Pingree, one of Detroit's most superb politicians, who will become known as the "Idol of the People." Pingree's finest hours come when he first fights the street car monopolies and public utilities and then insists, against rabid opposition, to parcel out public gardening land to immigrant families who are in danger of dying of starvation.

In the bottom of the fourth, in game 13 of the World Series, two Detroit players, to the jaunty tunes of a band, propel a wheelbarrow filled with 520 silver dollars toward home plate at Recreation Park. As the music fades, they call for Detroit catcher Charlie Bennett to come onto the field. Three burly policemen enter and inform Bennett that they will have to take him into custody unless he takes the wheelbarrow around the bases. With the crowd in jubilation, the whole troupe parades off the field to the tune of "Yankee Doodle Dandy."[1]

A crowd of around four thousand supporters had packed Recreation Park to watch this pageant featured during the game between the National League's Detroit Wolverines and the American Association's St. Louis

Browns. They were in high spirits, largely because the Detroits had already won the fifteen-game contest by winning eight games to the Browns' three. Detroit mayor Marvin Chamberlain addressed the new world champions: "Detroit is famed for beauty, culture, intelligence, energy and enterprise. But Detroit's base ball club has carried far and wide, even beyond the bounds of our nation, the renown of our fair city, and in honoring the club we simply honor the city."[2]

Even before the regular season had ended, the teams' business managers had agreed to play all fifteen games no matter what, so they could squeeze as much revenue from the event as possible. The Wolverines had secured their eighth win in Baltimore as the peripatetic competition meandered across the country, with games in New York, Pittsburgh, Philadelphia, and Boston, as well as in the two teams' hometowns. Now it was back in Recreation Park, constructed in 1879, one and a half blocks east of Woodward Avenue, between Fremont and Brady Street. Today, it is the location of the Detroit Medical Center, but back then it was part of the Brush Estate. Elijah Brush had bought the property in 1806 when it was still farmland, running two or three miles north from the river into open country. His son Edmund Brush developed the area in the 1850s into an upscale residential district. In the streets just south of Recreation Park, Detroit's elite built some of the grandest houses in the city toward the end of the century, houses that a hundred years later would become derelict, their images paraded across the world as emblematic of Detroit's decay—these days, however, Brush Park is making a comeback, and the neighborhood has once again become desirable real estate.

The Brush family had leased the area for the park, and they were financially involved in the venture, designed to host any number of recreational activities, including cricket, croquet, lawn tennis, lacrosse, and the newfangled foot-ball. It was surrounded by a half-mile trotting track where gentlemen could exercise their horses, and one corner was dedicated for use as an open-air skating rink in winter.[3]

The project's backers included many of the city's emerging industrial barons, men who had grown rich during the era of rapid growth brought by the railroads. Some were self-made, but many had inherited property that was becoming more and more valuable, providing collateral for new and profitable investments. One such man was James McMillan, whose Michigan Car Company, in partnership with John Newberry, had supplied railroad cars to the Union Army during the Civil War. They went on to invest in a wide range of new technologies, including street cars and the Detroit telephone system. McMillan and his contemporaries saw themselves as benefactors, serving the public interest by running profitable businesses. The new president of Recreation Park would now serve to bring commercial sport to the people of Detroit.[4]

Before 1880, cricket had been the more popular sport in Detroit, but base ball (not yet a single word) was on the ascent. Various ancestors of this game had been played in England and the colonies for centuries, but in the 1840s, the Knickerbocker Club of New York had formalized a set of rules that caught on across the country. At first, clubs were amateur organizations, serving mostly the players who enjoyed the game. By the 1860s, however, the sport had become popular enough to attract an audience, and there was money to be made from exhibition games. Many of the best amateurs decided to organize themselves into a professional association, and in 1871, the first baseball league, the National Association, was founded. Badly organized, it folded in 1875, and in 1876, the National League was established by William Hulbert, a Chicagoan involved in the retail grocery business.[5]

For all this time, Detroit had been a baseball backwater, but the worthy founders of Recreation Park decided they wanted a professional team at their facility, and so they worked with William Hollinger to create one dedicated to the park. Hollinger had gained experience in putting together a professional team in Cleveland, where he had been ousted by his business partner. With financial support from the Recreation Park Company, he organized the Hollinger Nine, Detroit's first professional baseball team, and set up a schedule of games against a number of strong teams across the country. The plan was to join a league the following year. Interest in Detroit, however, proved modest, and once it became clear that ticket sales would not support the player salaries, the team folded. Hollinger didn't suffer too much—a star performer at the billiard table, after 1879 he could usually be found competing at one or another of Detroit's numerous pool halls.[6]

The following year, another member of the Recreation Park Company, William G. Thompson, decided to have a go. Thompson had recently been elected mayor of Detroit, but the job wasn't so onerous as to prevent him from engaging in a little business on the side.[7] Thompson set about raising the funds. But which league should they join? The National League's William Hulbert sought to run his shop on good Republican principles, and he opposed drinking and gambling—two things the majority of players enjoyed a great deal. At the time, Hulbert was engineering the expulsion of the Cincinnati Red Stockings. Cincinnati, a charter member of the league, had been the first baseball team to turn professional in 1869, and its supporters, predominantly of German origin, were committed to having a few pints while watching Sunday baseball. Hulbert did not just object to the beer, he opposed playing baseball on the Lord's day altogether.[8] When Thompson inquired about a franchise for Detroit, organized on Hulbert's principles, Hulbert persuaded Cincinnati to resign from the National League and to found its own, the American Association, commonly referred to as the "Beer and Whisky League." In 1881, the newly formed Detroit Wolverines took Cincinnati's place in the National League.[9]

In anticipation of enthusiastic crowds, the club directors spent $400 on a new grandstand seating 1,200. On opening day in May, 1,265 people showed up, and Thompson reckoned that an average gate of 1,000 would be enough to turn a profit.[10] Professional baseball, however, failed to capture the city's imagination, and in the years to follow, attendance did not live up to expectations. No doubt, the team's mediocre performance in the league did not help. After finishing mid-table in its first season, the Wolverines' performance deteriorated, and in 1884, they finished at the bottom of the standings, with an embarrassing .250 win percentage. By the end of the year, Thompson had decided to stand down as director, though nobody would accuse him of doing so gracefully: he declared that the financial failings of the team were not the owners' fault but were instead to blame on "the dishonesty and ungratefulness of the players."[11]

Thompson's grievances reveal much about the labor relations of the day. In 1879, Hulbert had introduced the Reserve Clause, a mechanism that effectively tied a player to his club in perpetuity as long as the owner wanted to retain his services—the employer, by contrast, was free to release any player on short notice. Relationships could get testy. The *Detroit Free Press* reported on Thompson's gripes in 1884. Thompson recalled telling a player that "he was not batting as he ought." Apparently, the player, not unreasonably, responded that if Thompson was not happy he should release him from his contract so he could play for another club.[12] Thompson was scandalized: "Impudent as a bootblack," he grumbled, promising that he would "never again, directly or indirectly, employ a man I cannot discharge"—a familiar demand from American moguls then and now.

To be sure, Thompson might have had some cause for complaint. Young male athletes in that age liked to party, which meant drinking, womanizing, and gambling. The clubs, who now tended to see the players as assets they had invested in and hence were entitled to protect, tried to impose strict discipline and even went so far as hiring private detectives to monitor their activities.[13] But as the *Detroit Free Press* reported, they did not follow through on their threats of hefty fines, and the "result has been that players have gone upon the diamond so intoxicated that they could not stand still; with eyes so bleared from a night's carouse that if a ball came to them they could see three or four. . . . In this condition, they have muffed, fumbled, thrown wildly, and played like chumps generally; disgusted the patrons of the game, and reduced attendance nearly to the vanishing point."[14]

After Thompson resigned in a huff, another businessman, Frederick Stearns, stepped forward in 1885 to lead the Detroit club. He decided that the only way to make the club successful was to acquire the league's best players, and in September 1885, he bought the ailing Buffalo franchise in order to acquire its stars, known as the Big Four. The strategy paid off: after coming close in 1886, they won the league pennant and the World Series in 1887. Growing success brought a growing fan base, and the games now raised gates sufficient to fund the most expensive payroll in the league.[15] The *Detroit Free Press*, too, changed its tune, publishing this editorial:

> The success of the Detroits, in capturing all the base ball honors of the year is something in which the city and citizens may justly take a good deal of pride. It may not be the highest possible preeminence for a city to have a winning nine; but it is very pleasant and gratifying, and it has an actual mercantile value. The stalwart striking and rapid running, the precise pitching and careful catching that the "boys" have done in behalf of the city, have

advertised Detroit in a manner and to an extent which could not readily have been achieved in any other way.[16]

Stearns's ploy, however, had angered his fellow owners. While happy to engage in sporting competition, they were not interested in business competition. They preferred to control the league in the manner of the emerging business trusts that were dominating the American economy. Businesses like Standard Oil made money by amalgamating competing enterprises and coordinating on prices while resisting organized labor. Stearns was not playing this game, and as Detroit was one of the low-drawing teams in the league, he was vulnerable to retribution. His punishment arrived when the other teams replaced the 30 percent gate share for the visiting team with a guaranteed minimum payment. The Wolverines had relied on making large returns while on the road, and the new rule was the beginning of the end. That end came very quickly. Within a year of Charlie Bennett's triumphal procession, the directors closed down the team, citing large financial losses, and left Detroit without a professional baseball team.[17]

That era in American history is known as the Gilded Age for a reason. The great commercial enterprises of the times accumulated untold wealth for their owners; to this day, the names of Rockefeller, Vanderbilt, and Carnegie evoke visions of conspicuous opulence. But the rapid economic expansion and the vast profits it enabled also generated poverty and hardship, notably among the huge immigrant populations arriving from eastern and southern Europe. The worthies of Detroit, a large fraction of whom had inherited substantial wealth, sang the still-familiar tune: anyone can make it as long as he works hard and shows a spirit of enterprise. Financial failure is moral failure; there are no legitimate workers' grievances, just the complaints of the lazy, the ungrateful, and the dishonest. The catchphrase of the day, coined by the social Darwinian Herbert Spencer, predicted and condoned the "survival of the fittest." Meanwhile, the wealthy organized their trusts and combines to avoid competition, keep labor down, and further increase profits. The philosophy of the Republicans was popular with the white Anglo-Saxon and Irish-American men whose families were relatively established in the country. Already substantial landowners, they prospered as the economy grew, and they dominated Michigan politics—while Detroit was largely Democratic, the city did not yet have much influence in the then overwhelmingly rural state.[18]

After Thompson, who as a popular Republican had bucked Detroit's preference for Democrats, the position of mayor and many of the Common Council seats had fallen into the hands of the Democrats—better liked than their counterparts, not least because they opposed the temperance movement. That movement had become so unpopular that it began to affect Republicans' chances at the ballot box. By 1889, they were searching for a candidate who could generate broader appeal. The leading Republican figure in the state was James McMillan, who had been elected that year as U.S. senator of Michigan, a post he would hold for the rest of his life. He led a small cabal that identified Hazen Pingree as a suitable candidate for mayor—leading to one of the greatest bait-and-switch operations in the history of American municipal politics.

The statue of Hazen Pingree, as we mentioned, sits on the corner of Woodward and Adams; he leans forward as if ready to jump up and start an argument with William Maybury, whose statue he faces—a fitting posture since there were few things Pingree relished as much as arguments. He had fought in the Civil War in the First Massachusetts Heavy Artillery, and he heard from Union soldiers that there were good opportunities in the growing city of Detroit. He moved there in 1865 and found work cutting leather in a shoe factory. After some years, he used his savings to buy out the owner and rose to become one of Detroit's major manufacturers—his shop went from eight to seven hundred employees in a few years, and before you knew it, he was running one of the biggest shoe factories in the country. This was just the kind of rags-to-riches story Republicans liked. On October 31, 1889, they sent Pingree a letter, signed by nearly a hundred of the city's prominent Republicans, asking him to stand for mayor. The Detroit *Plain-dealer* published the letter, a remarkable document in itself:

> We, the undersigned, desiring to have at the head of our city government a man whose business career will be a guarantee that the same ability shown in his business will be brought to bear in the administration of city affairs, to the end that economy shall be affected and a policy pursued which shall have in view

the reduction of our present extravagant rate of taxation . . . , earnestly request you to allow the use of your name as a candidate for mayor, pledging to you in the event of your selection our hearty and active support to secure your election to that position.[19]

It soon transpired that Mayor Pingree, elected with the pledged "hearty and active support" of his fellow businessmen, had no interest in lowering anybody's taxes, and even less interest in furthering the causes of the men who had heaved him into office. When he was done four terms later, he had emerged as the Bernie Sanders of Detroit. A fine homage by Bill Loomis sums up the high points:

Pingree got private corporations to lower the price of natural gas, telephone service and street car rates. He reconstructed the sewer system and improved Detroit's horrible unpaved streets that were considered among the worst in the country for a big city. He constructed public schools, the first public parks, and free public baths. He exposed corruption in the school board and bribery at the private lighting company. He initiated the first publicly owned transit company and city-owned electric company after he found that Detroit was paying nearly double the rates charged in Toledo, Cleveland, Grand Rapids and Buffalo. He implemented equal tax policies for the city, and he forced down the rates for river ferries. He started competitive bidding for street car companies and he brought about electrified rapid transit. He did away with the old toll roads and began his nationally famous potato patch plan that helped feed thousands through a devastating economic depression.[20]

Pingree was particularly enthusiastic when it came to addressing corruption in the way city contracts were handled. When he took office, Detroit had a sum of four paved streets—the rest were made of wood, much of it rotting. Bribes to council members and city inspectors were common, whether in the construction of roads, sewers, or school buildings. Pingree started out in the most straightforward manner: by establishing the best method of construct-ing a street, by ordering contractors to adopt best practice, and by checking their bills against their actual expenses. The business community was not pleased, and his early backers began to suspect that they had made a fateful mistake. They were relieved of all doubt when in summer of 1894, Pingree, furious about the continuing grift, had the entire school board arrested after documenting their demand for bribes in a sting operation.

As Pingree's star fell with the monied elite, it rose with the citizens he served. His intense hatred for the railway and streetcar industry in par-ticular made him popular with the working-class residents that depended on public transportation. Detroit's first "urban railway" had begun operat-ing in 1863, with carriages drawn by horses along tracks. Those streetcars soon became an essential mode of transportation for Detroit's workers. When other cities started to electrify their streetcar systems in the 1880s, the Detroit City Railway Company, which held the monopoly franchise in the city, refused to invest—while charging the high fare of five cents a ride. In 1891, the company's employees went on strike, and three days of bloody rioting ensued, with angry citizens overturning street cars in protest of the owners' profiteering—among them a young James Couzens who would lat-er pioneer Ford's $5-per-day wage.[21] The owners, furious, asked for state troops, but Pingree refused. Siding with the workers, he campaigned to end the company's monopoly franchise and to force through lower prices. On May 12, 1891, the parties reached an agreement, and the streetcar compa-nies had to recognize a new union, an AFL-affiliated local.

Mayor Pingree became a passionate advocate for public ownership of pub-lic transportation. He conducted studies and personally paid to send City Council members on field trips to study how other cities operated munici-pally owned streetcar systems. He quickly became a hero to working-class Detroit while making implacable enemies of the Republican elite. James McMillan, whose business interests in the streetcar industry were under attack, became a lifelong foe. The men who had placed their hopes for lower taxes in Hazen Pingree now furiously sought to find anybody who could challenge him for his position—to no avail. McMillan even backed a Demo-crat to get rid of Pingree, but he won his re-election handily—his policies earned him the honorific of the "Idol of the People," written now into the stone of his monument.

Pingree was responding to the increasing monopolization of economic life in the United States. In 1890, the U.S. Congress had passed the Sherman Act, which prohibited collusion and the deliberate monopolization of industries. This was also a direct response to the growing threat that concerted business interests posed in American life, and Mayor Pingree would come to embody the new archetypal politician of the "Progressive Era." Pingree viewed the emergence of monopolization as a form of extortion practiced at the expense of the working class, and his campaigns were vocally indignant about the rampant exploitation. His political convictions and his policy prescriptions would now get this Republican businessman identified as a socialist: he saw municipal control of core services, provided at the city's expense, as the only way to forestall a revolution. He didn't stop with streetcars but also challenged local monopolies on telephony, another business in which McMillan was heavily invested, and on the ferries that crossed the river to Canada or to Belle Isle, the lovely island the city had acquired in 1879.[22] He led a successful campaign to eliminate the last of the toll roads in the city, which he saw as a regressive tax on the poor, and he took on widespread tax evasion, which was depleting the city's budget.[23] Many of the shipping lines on the riverfront, for instance, declared their head offices to be located in landlocked Hamtramck to avoid the higher Detroit taxes—the same strategy Henry Ford would employ twenty years later when he located his assembly line to Highland Park.[24]

Pingree's finest hour may have come in 1894, after Detroit was hit by the nationwide economic recession following the Panic of 1893. The banks were hit hard, and manufacturers laid off workers until the male unemployment rate rose to an estimated 33 percent, with immigrants hit even harder. Street riots broke out, violently suppressed by armed police. Loomis reports that "500 men armed with shovels attacked Sheriff C.P. Collins and two deputies who emptied their revolvers into the charging mob, but soon shovels came down on them and beat them into a 'senseless bloody mass,' according to the *Detroit Tribune*." Mainstream Republicans and Democrats alike counseled austerity—cutting public services just when they were needed the most. Pingree first responded by asking bakeries to lower the price of bread, and he created jobs by banning trucks, allowing at least some men to earn a living by hauling rock with wheelbarrows.[25] But none of that was enough, so Pingree turned to urban farming. Why not turn vacant city land over to anybody who wanted to feed themselves? The city's rich, the papers, and the churches scoffed, and his fund-raising efforts came to nothing. Undeterred, the mayor sold one of his dearest possessions, a prize-winning horse, and kicked off his potato patch program on 430 acres of Detroit land. In the end, over 1,500 families were able to sustain themselves on Pingree's Potato Patches, a program that became famous across the United States.[26]

Hazen Pingree's political career was forged in the upheavals of Detroit in the early 1890s, but his vision extended far beyond the city he led. He went on to campaign nationally for municipal control and social reform, first in his capacity as mayor, and then as state governor, a position he held from 1897 until his death in London in 1901. Although few people outside of Detroit know his name now, many of his ideas would emerge over the course of the twentieth century in the form of policies crucial to a humane industrial society. Echoes of his urban farming initiative live on in modern-day Detroit, where derelict land has been turned into beloved community gardens.

Hazen Pingree also presided over the end of Detroit's pro-baseball drought. In 1894, the Detroit Creams were launched. They played their first two seasons at League Park, a venue their owner George Vanderbeck had renovated on the East Side at Helen and Lafayette, not far from the bridge to Belle Isle. The Creams joined the Western League, organized by Ban Johnson. Even though they finished poorly in their first season, enough fans showed up to keep the business going. The opening of the 1895 season was a moving affair, in honor of Charlie Bennett—the same catcher of the old Wolverines who had played in the 1887 World Series but later had tragically lost both feet in a railroad accident. Still much beloved by Detroit baseball fans, he was enthroned behind home plate while the mayor of Detroit, Hazen Pingree, threw out the opening pitch—on May 1, the international day of labor, also known as "May Day."[27] Within a few short years, the Creams would move to a new stadium at the corner of Michigan and Trumbull, named Bennett Park in Charlie's honor; the Western League would become the American League, and the Creams, too, got a new name: the Detroit Tigers.

TWENTY-NINE

AUGUST 8, 1859

The Detroit Base Ball Club and the Early Risers Club meet for the first game of "base ball" recorded in the city. The final score is 59–21. City leaders, worried about the perils of a local culture dominated by young men living in boarding houses, promote baseball as healthy exercise and a fine alternative to the rampant drinking and gambling. Throughout the country, idyll turns into horror all too frequently, often with little warning. Baseball and violent riots go hand in hand, each as American as the proverbial apple pie. Detroit has known all about that over the course of its history. On the eve of the Civil War, the city is a dangerous place with a growing crime problem. Despite the fact that the African American population is tiny, white resentment bubbles under the surface, and in 1865, a white mob forms, resulting in the murder of two African Americans, injuries of twenty more, and the destruction of African American property.

On August 8, 1859, the city saw its first game of baseball—the experienced men of the Detroit Base Ball Club against the youngsters of the Early Risers Club, played at Cass Farm. The *Detroit Free Press* benevolently pointed out that "within a few years a good deal of attention has been turned among young men to field sports, such as cricket and base ball. The encouragement of these games will prove of incalculable benefit to young men in many ways; it will tend to occupy their leisure time in healthy exercise, counteracting the growing tendency to visit loons and other places of resort with which the city abounds, thus saving them from early immorality; it affords them with the sport, the most wholesome and effective exercise, bringing into violent use every muscle of the body, and creating of the puny, enervated boy, a robust, muscular, active, hearty man."[1]

The game, the paper speculated, would better the health of the city's young men, and curb their appetite for vice and sloth: "The more such games are patronized, the greater the zest and spirit with which they are entered into, the better it will be for the young men of the city. Those who hang around the billiard saloons and liquor shops, constantly complaining of a lack of exercise and consequent loss of appetite, would do well to join one of the base ball clubs, and take regular exercise with them." Of course, as we have seen in the previous chapter, the paper would soon have cause to speak quite differently about that wholesome exercise, but for now, it all was quite sweet and gentlemanly, and the young men in need of so much improvement acquitted themselves well, all things told:

> The Early Risers is a club organized this season, composed principally of younger persons. They number about twenty members. They take their name from their hour of practice, which is at 4 o'clock in the mornings of every Monday, Wednesday, and Friday. They play on Campus Martius in front of the Russell House. In the match that was played yesterday, this club was the challenging party. They were offered odds in the match by the other club on account of their inexperience and acknowledged inferiority, but with the true Young America spirit they declined accepting the offer, and went in on equal terms. They were of course beaten, but, as they expected this, they took it in good part, consoling themselves with the recollection that they had an even share of the sport, as well as the opportunity of practicing with superior players.

The score had been 59–21, reported in the *Detroit Free Press* along with a box score of sorts, indicating the hits and runs attributed to each player, plus the names of the umpire and scorers.[2] Baseball was noticeably different from the professional game played half a century later, let alone the game of today. Pitchers, for example, were obliged to pitch the ball in a manner that best suited the batter, while batters were out if the ball was caught on the bounce.

Scoring runs, evidently, was much easier. But the newspaper report is hardly interested in the nature of the game at all—what *does* capture its interest is the city's need to contain and channel the energy of idle young men.

Detroit in 1859 was still a small town, with a population of around forty thousand. The fact that the Early Risers played on Campus Martius, where they regularly broke windows of the Russell House Hotel, illustrates the small-town nature of Detroit at the time. Cass Farm, where the game had been played, was located somewhere around the Cass Tech High School playing fields, about a mile further north—at the time, it was still farmland. Four o'clock in the morning, in the days before daylight saving time, would have been about an hour before dawn in the middle of summer. It must have posed a challenge to see the ball in the early twilight; perhaps the Early Risers were aided by kerosene street lamps. Detroit had grown rapidly: ten years earlier, there had been ten thousand people; forty years ago, one thousand. There had not been a great deal of city planning to accommodate the growth, and the strains were beginning to show. Only a few years earlier angry residents had torn up a railroad track laid along Gratiot Street, simply because of the disturbance caused by the noise—it is important to keep in mind that nineteenth-century Americans rioted for any reason at all, or sometimes for no reason.[3]

Still, over the course of the 1850s, disorder became a matter of increasing concern in Detroit. As immigration swelled the population, and trade expanded, via the Great Lakes and the railroads, the once-quiet town became a bustling metropolis with a population in constant flux. The largest immigrant groups of this period were Irish and "German," a catchall term that no doubt included many Poles, whose kingdom had been partitioned by Prussia, Austria, and Russia at the end of the previous century. German immigrants in particular congregated on the city's East Side and maintained a distinctive cultural life. Those who came last tended to be poorly represented politically; power rested firmly in the hands of the Anglo-Saxon immigrants who had arrived earlier, claimed priority access to the region, and owned most of the land and businesses.

In these days, there was no concept of zoning, and factories grew up alongside residential districts, tenements were built alongside the docks, and mansions were built back-to-back with cheap boarding houses. This seems to have been especially true of nineteenth-century Detroit, which may serve as a model of the so-called melting pot (where no actual melting ever took place). As John Schneider writes: "The homes of some of Detroit's richest men along Congress Street West or Jefferson Avenue, for example, were but a long stone's throw from cheap bordellos and saloon flophouses. From the vantage point of today's sprawling metropolis, with its vast distances isolating various urban groups and activities, this was an extraordinary urban environment."[4]

For those who had at least a little money to spare, there were three main forms of entertainment. The first was drinking. By 1857, the city boasted over five hundred bars and saloons, serving a population of little more than 40,000—a ratio of 1 to 80.[5] For the sake of comparison, currently, about a thousand premises in Detroit have a liquor license, for about 675,000 inhabitants—a ratio of 1 to 675. German-style beer gardens proliferated, especially around the German East Side, and brewing became one of the city's most important industries.

The second kind of entertainment was billiards, a game that stretches back at least to Renaissance Europe and is still played today. It became popular in Britain, France, and Germany in the early nineteenth century and quickly reached the United States. As a competitive game, billiards evolved into a number of different varieties, which in the mid-nineteenth century would have involved three or four balls—you scored points by hitting the cue ball at a target ball, setting up ricochet effects with the remaining ones (similar to the present-day version).

A billiard craze swept the country in the 1850s, and Detroit was no exception. In April 12, 1859, a challenge match was staged at Firemen's Hall, on the corner of Jefferson and Randolph (opposite where the RenCen now stands). Michael Phelan of New York, champion of the east, played John Seereiter of Detroit, champion of the west. The prize money was substantial—$7,500, about $225,000 in today's money. The elegant building, which had hosted Detroit's first ever art exhibition in 1851, could seat up to a thousand people.[6] Seereiter was born in Alsace, then part of France, and his family had emigrated to the United States in 1830, when he was five years old. He moved to Detroit in 1849, and he would run billiard halls in the city until the 1890s, passing away in 1896.[7] Although Seereiter lost to

Phelan, the event established provincial Detroit as a recognized center of the sport.

Not everybody could have been happy with that: though it had originally been a gentleman's game, billiards was widely considered a disreputable activity, far too closely associated with drinking, gambling, and indolence. The name conjured up the same image as the "pool hall" did in the following century, and of course, modern pool is an adaptation of billiards. Like saloons, billiard halls were licensed, and in the second half of the nineteenth century, renting a table cost $5.[8]

Along with saloons and billiard halls, the "bachelor transient sub-culture," as historian John Schneider calls it, frequented brothels, which also proliferated in 1850s Detroit. Some observers claimed there were more than one hundred in 1850 already, and by the 1860s business appeared to be booming.[9] All these entertainments vied for the patronage of the many men who lived in the boarding houses dotted around the city. The problem, as many people saw it, was unattached young men with time on their hands: U.S. cities like Detroit were teeming with single men as the country industrialized and the population expanded westward—some were local, others came from back east, yet others had crossed the Atlantic. All of them were frequently at loose ends.[10]

In the 1850s, Detroiters in the German parts of the city started to demand that the city government close down the brothels in their districts. But since there was, as yet, no such thing as a city police force, the authorities declared themselves powerless to do anything. As a result, the citizenry took matters into their own hands and started systematically demolishing the houses where brothels stood, smashing windows and furniture, even setting fire to them. Between 1855 and 1859, there were twelve major incidents, and at least seventeen brothels were damaged or completely destroyed—to the abject terror, one must presume, of the sex workers inside them. All of this happened on the East Side, near Gratiot, along Hastings and the Detroit & Milwaukee train tracks. Typically there were over one hundred rioters operating at night, and their targets were the cheaper bordellos, especially those where black men sought out white women.[11]

Where the city government was unwilling to do anything about prostitution, the growing strength of the temperance movement posed a significant threat to the operation of the beer gardens, which was a serious assault on the culture of at least one immigrant group. Schneider writes: "Detroit's beer gardens were filled to capacity on Sunday afternoons with crowds of Germans enjoying their lager, singing and dancing to the music of the old country. Germans reacted sharply to the temperance movement, which was dominated by native-born Protestants, as an attack on legitimate immigrant customs."[12] In consequence, tensions were high as the temperance leaders tried to enforce the state's strict Sabbatarian drinking laws.

Until the 1850s, the city had enjoyed a reputation as being relatively free of crime, but that changed during this decade. Increasingly, Detroiters always had to fear being mugged and assaulted on the street, and burglaries, too, became a major problem. The wealthier citizens were particularly vulnerable, in person as they walked the streets, or as property owners whose domestic or commercial property could be looted at any moment. Murders became more frequent. While the general population called, with rising urgency, for a police force to be created, the rich preferred to hire their own private protection instead—after all, a public police force would have been obliged to protect the poorer as well as the richer districts of the city—at least in theory.[13]

In light of these circumstances, it is less surprising that the newspaper had high hopes for baseball—anything to keep the city's young men from committing more mayhem. And the sport did begin to emerge as a popular hobby, at least with the white Anglo-Saxon crowd—that much is suggested by the names on the rosters of that first game in the summer of 1859: Dumon, Peirce, Craig, Niles, McDonald, Newberry, Anderson, Folsam, Fellers, Fyfe, Field, Wright, Hawley, LeFavour, Gorton, Young, Pierce, and Winter.[14] To be sure, there is a smattering of French names—Dumon and LeFavour—representing property-owning families who had been residents since the age when Detroit was a French town.

By the 1850s, the social structure of baseball had already changed, compared with the early forms of the game played twenty or thirty years earlier. Judge Melvin McGee, who grew up in the village of Concord ninety miles west of Detroit, reminisced in the 1890s about the games of his childhood in the 1830s. In those days, he remembered, an entire neighborhood would come together to raise a house or a barn, and after the work was done, a communal meal had been consumed and the children and young men would play baseball. "It seems to me now," he wrote, "as I look back and recall those early days that the young people enjoyed their sports and games and entered into them with far more zest than young people do at the present day. There was no feeling of envy or superiority, or the feeling that you don't belong to my set. All were on a level, and everyone was just as good as any other."[15]

While the poor frequented saloons and billiard halls that anyone could enter, the elite formed clubs—and base ball clubs were just one activity among many suited to this form of organization. The very notion of a club— a form of exclusivity that enables insiders to "belong" precisely because it prevents outsiders from joining—was a vehicle for separating classes and ethnicities. The early baseball clubs tended to place great emphasis on the notion of gentlemanly conduct, which also implied a proper sense of social status. In this way, social elites could meet on an informal basis, which often promoted business contacts and opened up career opportunities—the equivalent of today's golf course. The roster's "Newberry," for instance, is the same John Newberry who, in partnership with James McMillan, went on to become one of the leading industrialists of the city, and for a while, he was in fact the president of the Detroit Club.[16] "Fyfe" was Richard Fyfe, who would end up a millionaire from shoe retailing, and crops up as a supporter of Hazen Pingree in later years.[17]

While these men, never having had a reason to think of themselves as anything other than worth emulating, wanted to set a good example to the city's less favored, they certainly did not want to mix with them socially. In the early years, a base ball club would seek to establish itself by issuing a challenge to an established club, which would be honor-bound to accept the challenge. But honor had its limits: when one or two African American baseball teams started to play and issue challenges, the established clubs breached etiquette by refusing outright to accept.[18] Playing against women was equally outré—actually, even women playing among themselves was enough to lead to social ostracism, which probably doomed the numerous attempts to form women's clubs between 1860 and 1880.[19] And finally, the clubs were firmly wedded to the notion of amateurism: they refused to play against any team suspected of remunerating its players.

The gentle, wholesome game, then, had a dark underbelly of racism, classism, and misogyny. In this regard, it's actually curious that the *Free Press* would clamor for young men to take up the game: teams such as the Detroit Club and the Early Risers would have been unlikely to welcome challenges from teams made up of German or Irish immigrants. Perhaps what the author of the article envisaged was a form of segregation, where members of each social class would compete with each other, but never mix with different strata. There is no doubt that such a mindset limited the spread of the game in its early days. Between 1850 and 1870, the term "base ball" appeared 718 times in the *Detroit Free Press*, with "billiard" or "billiards" appearing 1,643 times. Nonetheless, over the next thirty years, the outdoor sport triumphed in popular imagination, achieving 12,399 mentions, while "billiard" or "billiards" managed only 5,339. Despite its early elitism, baseball did become a democratic sport, at least as far as white men were concerned. It thrived, at least in part, as a solution to the problem of policing threatening young men, who were responsible, or at least perceived to be responsible, for an increasing level of disorder in the city.

This was the eve of the Civil War. Detroit was still a rowdy frontier town and Michigan had been a state for less than twenty-five years. Riotous behavior was commonplace in the saloons, brothels, and billiard halls, on occasion spreading to the streets. Tensions over race and ethnicity simmered. Late in 1862, the city started to muster troops to send off to war, and soon thereafter, what had been lingering tension exploded into the open. James Massie, an English traveler who visited Detroit in 1863, described the antipathy and hateful slurs that faced African Americans everywhere he went, demonstrating, in his words, "a strong prejudice against people of colour" in the Northern states.[20] Irish and German immigrants to the United States, in particular, feared African American competition in the labor market.[21]

When the hostility turned to violence, it was cataclysmic. In March of 1863, white Detroiters vented their fury on their black neighbors—one of the few events thus named that actually *deserve* the name "race riot." It started when a black man, William Faulkner, who owned a brothel, was accused of having molested two nine-year-old girls, one black and one white. Faulkner was arrested, tried, and sentenced to life imprisonment. A mob consisting mainly of Irish and German immigrants set out to lynch Faulkner while he was being escorted by soldiers from the courthouse to the jail. The soldiers fired into the crowd as it advanced, one person was killed, and Faulkner was delivered safely to jail. Being deprived of their particular target, the mob turned on the black population of Detroit, with cries of "Kill all the damned niggers."[22] It headed to Beaubien and Lafayette, where a number of African Americans lived. In the ensuing assault, two were killed, including a seventy-nine-year old man; at least twenty were seriously injured; and more than thirty homes were destroyed. Later, evidence established that Faulkner was innocent. He was released six years later.

Silas Farmer, whose monumental history of Detroit was published in 1884, documents the horrific event as follows:

> One of the darkest pages in the history of Detroit is the record of March 6, 1863. The events that led to the doings of that day are as follows: A mulatto named William Faulkner, had been arrested, tried, convicted, and sentenced to prison for life for an alleged outrage on a little girl. The war with the South was then in progress; a draft was feared, and the ignorant and vicious were glad of an opportunity to vent their ill-nature on a race which was claimed to be the cause of the war. Faulkner was arrested on February 26. His trial began on March 5, and on that day, while he was being conveyed back to jail, he was struck on the head with a paving-stone and knocked down. The mob which sur-rounded him then sought to seize him, but the officers succeeded in getting him inside the jail. The next day he was again taken to court. The trial was concluded and he was sentenced. While he was being conveyed back to jail, a squad of the provost-guard, who were aiding the sheriff, were attacked. They fired, and one man was killed. The mob now became infuriated, and an attack was begun on the colored people. Many of them were fearfully beaten; their buildings were set on fire for the purpose of burn-ing those who were inside; and paving-stones were torn up and thrown at those who tried to escape, thus driving them back into the flames. Many had always doubted Faulkner's guilt, and after

seven years had passed, the doubt becoming almost a certain-
ty, a pardon was procured, and on Friday, December 31, 1869,
greatly to his surprise, he was released.[23]

Murderous mobs always have a pretext—allegedly, the riot was caused by
the resentment white men felt over having to go to war to free the enslaved.
The history of similar assaults, including the shocking violence of the 1921
Tulsa riot, which cost between one hundred and three hundred black Americans their lives and destroyed thirty-five city blocks, suggests that it doesn't
take a draft to incite an anti-black pogrom. In any case, the political elite
was shaken by the riot and finally agreed that the city needed to act. Thus
the regime of "law and order," which would come to haunt the city over the
next hundred years, came to the city—in February 1865, the City Council
voted to create a Detroit Police Force.[24]

THIRTY

JUNE 2, 1763

At Michilimackinac, nearly three hundred miles north of Detroit, Ojibwa warriors and their wives fool the commander of the British garrison into letting them capture the fort by luring them to a game of baggattaway—now known as lacrosse. This event takes place during Pontiac's revolt, which culminates in the Native American leader laying siege to Detroit. While the siege fails, Pontiac is remembered for his resistance to the destruction of the indigenous population and its way of life. Historical accounts of Detroit have marginalized Native Americans, as have those of the country in general, but, in a small and belated sign of acknowledgment, the Haudenosaunee (Iroquois) nation is now represented in international lacrosse competition.

In 1851, roughly eighty years after Pontiac's revolt, historian Francis Parkman would picture that fateful morning as "warm and sultry." It had been the fourth of June, he claimed, King George's birthday (though he was actually mistaken about the date). The soldiers at Michilimackinac had some license to celebrate their monarch, and it seemed like a nice day for a game. "Encamped in the woods, not so far off," Parkman wrote, "were a large number of Ojibwas, lately arrived; while several bands of the Sac Indians, from the River Wisconsin, had also erected their lodges in the vicinity. Early in the morning, many Ojibwas came to the fort, inviting officers and soldiers to come out and see a grand game of ball, which was to be played between their nation and the Sacs."[1]

Nothing like a fun outing in early summer—half of the fort's population attended, leaving the place largely undefended. This is how Parkman wants us to imagine the scene:

> The houses and barracks were so ranged as to form a quadrangle, enclosing an extensive area, upon which the doors all opened, while behind rose the tall palisades, forming a large external square. The picturesque Canadian houses, with their rude porticoes, and projecting roofs of bark, sufficiently indicated the occupations of their inhabitants; for birch canoes were lying near many of them, and fishing-nets were stretched to dry in the sun. Women and children were moving about the doors; knots of Canadian voyageurs reclined on the ground, smoking and conversing; soldiers were lounging listlessly at the doors and windows of the barracks, or strolling in careless undress about the area.

Outside, everything was chill as well; the soldiers sat in the shade of the palisades, watching the Native Americans play. "Most of them were without arms, and mingled among them were a great number of Canadians, while a multitude of Indian squaws, wrapped in blankets, were conspicuous in the crowd. Captain Etherington and Lieutenant Leslie stood near the gate, the former indulging his inveterate English propensity; for, as Henry informs us, he had promised the Ojibwas that he would bet on their side against the Sacs."

Suddenly, the narrative turns ominous: "Indian chiefs and warriors were also among the spectators, intent, apparently, on watching the game, but with thoughts, in fact, far otherwise employed." But before we learn what was really going on, Parkman treats us to a description of the sport:

> The game in which they were engaged, called baggattaway by the Ojibwas, is still, as it has always been, a favorite with many Indian tribes. At either extremity of the ground, a tall post was planted, marking the stations of the rival parties. The object of each was defend his own post, and drive the ball to that of its adversary. Hundreds of lithe and agile figures were leaping and

bounding upon the plain. Each was nearly naked, his loose black hair flying in the wind, and each bore in his hand a bat of a form peculiar to this game. At one moment the whole were crowded together, a dense throng of combatants, all struggling for the ball; at the next, they were scattered again and running over the ground like hounds in full cry. Each, in his excitement, yelled and shouted at the height of his voice. Rushing and striking, tripping their adversaries, or hurling them to the ground, they pursued the animating contest amid the laughter and applause of the spectators.

Fate turns on a dime—when a ball soared out of the crowd and descended in a wide arc towards the pickets of the fort, it must have looked like a mistake, an accident, and when the ball players, all at once, "a maddened and tumultuous throng," rushed after it, the spectators may have wondered about the rules of the game. And then, the players were at the gate.

The amazed English had no time to think or act. The shrill cries of the ball players were changed to the ferocious war-whoop. The warriors snatched from the squaws the hatchets, which the latter, with this design, had concealed beneath their blankets. Some of the Indians assailed the spectators without, while others rushed into the fort, and all was carnage and confusion. At the outset, several strong hands had fastened their grip upon Etherington and Leslie, and led them away from the scene of the massacre towards the woods.

The account, first published in 1851, is part of Parkman's famous account of Pontiac's War, which focuses primarily on the siege of Detroit. This is, possibly, the earliest recorded instance of a sporting event in Michigan. While Michilimackinac is about three hundred miles from Detroit by canoe, skirting around Lake Huron, and roughly the same distance by car today, the event is closely connected to the city.

Parkman's classic history, which went through ten editions in his lifetime, has come under heavy criticism by modern scholarship. Like many historians of his time, he gave himself considerable license when it came to filling in the inevitable gaps in the sparse written record. The way he characterizes Pontiac and Native Americans in general, while sympathetic by the standards of his day, is riddled with prejudice and stereotypes. He relied almost entirely on the words of Europeans for his sources, never thinking to ask for Native American views or accounts. It appears that he got even simple details wrong. By Etherington's own eyewitness account, for instance, the events at Michilimackinac took place on June 2, not June 4.[2] That said, the roughly dozen extant accounts of the incident he describes, including some by Native Americans, at least appear to confirm the basic outline of his story. The subterfuge by ball game was a historical event.

Pontiac was a tribal leader of the Odawa (Ottawa), one of the Algonquin peoples, and, along with the Ojibwa (Chippewa) and the Potawatomi, a part of the Three Fires Alliance that had been formed one thousand years earlier at Michilimackinac.[3] These nations dominated the hunting grounds around Lakes Huron, Michigan, and Superior, which enclose the territory of what is now the state of Michigan. The first European settlers they encountered were the French, following the voyages of Jacques Cartier over two hundred years earlier. In 1608, Samuel de Champlain founded Quebec; in 1682, Sieur de La Salle reached the Mississippi from Lake Michigan, canoed the length of the river, and claimed Louisiana for France; and in 1701, Antoine de la Mothe Cadillac founded a settlement on the straits joining Lake Erie to Lake St. Clair and Lake Huron. He called it Detroit. In the French plan to build a colonial empire from Quebec to New Orleans, the fort at Detroit was a critical link at a time when the only viable means of long-distance trade was by water, and the route from north to south went through the Great Lakes.[4]

The French colonization of the region focused on two main interests: furs and Catholicism. While Jesuit priests sought to convert Native Americans, French traders lived in close contact with them and disturbed their way of life far less than the English, Scottish, Welsh, and Irish tribes who built farms, brought whole families, and claimed ownership of land. Both French and British settlers, however, did tremendous damage by introducing guns, whiskey, and disease.[5]

In the 1700s, Britain and France were the two great global powers struggling for mastery of the trade routes. Their conflict played out in the so-called French-Indian wars, which culminated in the capture of Quebec and the surrender of all French interests in Canada in 1760.[6] At first, the competition between Britain and France may have seemed to work to the benefit of the Native Americans, as the two competing European powers lavished gifts upon them in the hope of building alliances. The British had allied with the Haudenosaunee (Iroquois) nation, who were the dominant power before the European arrivals, while the Algonquins acknowledged the French King as their "Great Father." The victory of the British over the French was thus a double blow to the Algonquin peoples: not only had their ally lost, but the end of French competition meant that the British no longer needed to compete for favors. In the fall of 1760, British garrisons were dispatched to the frontier forts, carrying copies of the treaties signed by the French ceding their interest, meant to convince Native Americans that the regime change was permanent. At Detroit, the French commander Sieur de Belêtre reluctantly surrendered to Major Robert Rogers, and the French town formally came under British rule.[7]

The disadvantages of living with a British monopoly soon became apparent to the Native Americans, allies or not. The British became less generous in the provision of gifts, rationing alcohol and gunpowder, and generally treating the indigenous peoples as the inferiors they no doubt thought them to be. Worse, the tribal leaders soon realized that the defeat of the French would likely mean that a flood of settlers would move into the Ohio Valley and further west, steal their lands, and destroy their way of life.[8]

In 1761, the Lenni Lenape (Delaware) prophet Neolin, from the Ohio Valley, recounted visions in which he visited the Great Spirit, who instructed his people to return to the old ways of life and to give up the use of guns, alcohol, and other European goods. The Great Spirit also told him to drive the Europeans out of their country. Pontiac had some edits: he understood the message to dictate that only the British needed to be cleared out—so that the trading relationship with the French could resume.[9]

While he is often referred to as a general, Pontiac's exact role as a leader is contested—the nineteenth century portrayed him as a mastermind, but later scholars believe his importance might have been exaggerated. While he had a following in his own right, the success of his plan to attack the British and restore the French rested on his capacity to persuade other tribes to join his enterprise. By 1763, he had achieved that goal.[10] In addition, he had listened to the promises of French Canadians, who assured Pontiac that the king of

France would soon send troops to aid the displacement of the British—it is unclear whether this was a deliberate lie or a delusion on the part of the French. While we do not know how much of a role Pontiac played in coordinating the seizure of British forts such as Michilimackinac, he was the unquestioned leader of the siege of Detroit.[11] The plan to seize the fort was settled at a meeting on the Ecorse River about ten miles south of the fort, now known as Council Point Park.[12]

The siege began on May 7, 1763, when Pontiac planned to enter the fort under the guise of friendly negotiations with the commander, only to murder the entire garrison. This plan failed when Major Henry Gladwin, the commander, got wind of it.[13] A standoff followed—Pontiac did not have the means to take the fort by force, so he waited for the French to come to his aid, while the British did not have a large enough force to break out. Pontiac's allies foiled Detroit's first attempt to bring reinforcements, and on July 31, he and his men defeated a second British detachment during the Battle of Bloody Run, fought by a stream just east of the downtown that has now dried up, on the site of what is now Elmwood Cemetery, a hundred yards away from where the Detroit City FC Fieldhouse now stands.[14]

While Pontiac triumphed in that battle—twenty-seven British soldiers were killed and a further thirty wounded—the fort remained invincible, and the promised French soldiers did not arrive.[15] As winter approached, many of Pontiac's confederates started to drift away; the siege was finally raised at the end of October.[16] In the end, then, Pontiac's War was a failure, and he was assassinated two years later.[17] However, the conviction that had driven his attacks, the principle that the land belonged to the Native Americans and not the European invaders, made him a hero to generations of Native Americans and to some thoughtful descendants of the invaders.

The French may have given up possession of Detroit in 1760, but the French settlers did not leave, and many of the city's leading figures would be drawn from their ranks. The families of Joseph Campau, Francois Rivard, Charles Peltier, Peter Desnoyers, and Charles Girardin would wield considerable influence in nineteenth-century Detroit.[18] Even in the 1990 census, 6.8 percent of the residents of Grosse Pointe, the wealthy enclave north of the city, still claimed French ancestry, more than twice the national average.[19] In contrast to a city like New Orleans, little of French culture, language, or cuisine has survived in Detroit, but French origins still echo in the names of families, streets, or places—foremost among them, "Detroit," city of the straits. The streets running perpendicular to the Detroit River also still carry the names of families who owned the strip farms of the early settlement—Beaubien, St. Antoine, Rivard, Riopelle, DeQuindre, St. Aubin, Dubois, Chene, Beaufait, and Bellevue. The same is true for some of the grand avenues of the city: Gratiot, Kercheval, and Livernois. The name of Cadillac is to be found everywhere, not least in the name of the luxury cars. One-quarter of the city's flag carries the fleur-de-lis, the symbol of Royal France.

There is no such recognition of Native American origins in the flag, and none of the major streets is named after prominent Native families, while Woodward, Campau, and Macomb are the names of slaveholders. At least the name of Michigan itself derives from an Ojibwe word meaning "large lake." Additionally, the great arteries of Detroit—Michigan, Woodward, and Gratiot—are thought to be built following old Native American trails. Pontiac is remembered in the city bearing his name, twenty-five miles northwest of Detroit, for a few decades the home of the Detroit Lions, and there is the Pontiac division of General Motors, founded in 1926. You can learn Ojibwa at the University of Michigan, but not Kickapoo, Menominee, Miami, Ottawa, Potawatomi, Mesquakie-Sauk, or Huron. And nobody seems to remember that Detroit's history of slavery includes the owning of both Native and African Americans and that it was established under the French, tolerated by the British, and maintained by the U.S. government even when the Northwest Ordinance of 1787, establishing American rule, outlawed slavery.[20]

What survived, as the names were erased, was that ball game that drenched a sunny June day in 1763 in blood, "baggattaway" to its inventors, named "lacrosse" by French missionaries. European witnesses describe variants of it from the seventeenth century on.[21] It involved a crooked stick, attached with deerskin strips, that enabled the players to scoop up a small ball and propel it toward a goal. Those goals could be set at great distances apart, and a game could involve hundreds of players—not unlike the folk football played in early modern English towns. Many of the Europeans remarked upon the game's violence, but the British, whose own games of football often involved a good amount of bloodshed, would have taken that in stride.[22] Baggattaway had a spiritual as well as physical dimension, and there is a significant mythology surrounding the Native American tradition. In some cases, it appears to have been a preparation for battle, as indicated by its alternate name: "the little brother of war." In other versions, it simply seems to have been a joyous form of communal self-expression. Like Captain Etherington, the players liked to gamble on the outcome, and they often ruined themselves in the process—not unlike the English lords who played cricket around the same time.

Lacrosse was formalized as a game by William Beers, a Canadian dentist, at the end of the 1850s. He envisaged the sport as a manly form of physical exercise, along the lines of the many versions of football that were being codified around this time, but with truly Canadian roots.[23] It soon spread to the rest of the English-speaking world—the United States, Britain, Australia, and New Zealand, where it is played to this day.

Continuing their general pattern, the colonizers took over the game and proceeded to exclude the ones who had invented it. While Native Americans were "pure" and "natural" and "noble" when it served the invaders' purposes, they did not make for acceptable opponents at their own game. Since many of the Native American lacrosse teams could simply not afford to pursue their sport without some form of compensation, the ruling Anglo-Saxon elite insisted on rigid amateurism—at least when it suited them. And it certainly suited them to refuse to compete against professional or semi-professional Native players.

By the early twentieth century, North America had generally accepted professional lacrosse, but the Olympic Games still insisted that competitors be amateurs, which barred some of the greatest players from international competition, many of whom were Native Americans. From the mid-century onward, Haudenosaunee players began to campaign for the right to compete as a national team in international competition, stressing their independence from either Canada or the United States. In 1987, the men's national Haudenosaunee team was finally recognized by the Federation of International Lacrosse as the Iroquois Nationals. In the World Championships of 2014 and 2018, they took the bronze medal—an impossibly small token in recompense for centuries of erasure. As Tiya Miles writes in her formidable introduction to *The Dawn of Detroit*:

> For centuries the fire has raged, consuming lives, igniting passions, churning up the land and animals, swallowing humans whole. The burn that Detroiters feel—that the nation uncomfortably intuits as it looks upon the beleaguered city as a symbol of progress and defeat—traces back to distant times, to the global desire to make land into resources, the drive to turn people into things, the quest for imperial dominance, and the tolerance for ill-gotten gain. . . . Deep histories flow beneath present inequalities, silent as underground freshwater streams.[24]

The history of Detroit runs deep indeed, and we have sought to pay attention to its joy and its sorrow alike. In the end, all history ought to be in the service of imagining a different future—or multiple, intertwining futures. In closing, we want to pick up, in a light-hearted key, one strand of the possible futures of Detroit and return to the image of the City of Champions—but in this vision, the champions come to Detroit.

EPILOGUE: AUGUST 1, 2032

Start on the spot on the Detroit River where Antoine de la Mothe Cadillac made landfall in 1701. A short stroll takes you past the Hart Plaza where five thousand temporary seats have been erected to host the Beach Volleyball competition. On your left there is a bustle of tennis fans heading to the TCF Center—until 2019, it was known as the Cobo Center, but it was renamed when Detroit decided to no longer honor segregationists. Now it serves as the venue for gymnastics, badminton, judo, table tennis, taekwondo, trampolining, and fencing. High up on the Center's roof, which takes up half a million square feet, they are playing the Olympic Tennis Final. Millions of viewers across the world have grown used to the spectacular views across the Detroit River.

Head east along Jefferson and past the Renaissance Center, which has been converted to house the Olympic Village. You pass bustling neighborhoods, developments encouraged by the extension of the QLine—the trams now run from Woodward to Grosse Pointe. Today the trams are taking the crowds to Belle Isle to watch the rowers in the coxless fours and to admire the beautiful fin de siècle glass conservatory—designed by Albert Kahn, it is home to a jungle of exotic plants. Those who like horses can stroll a short distance to reach the fabulous cross-country course for the equestrian competition, next to the dressage arena and the show-jumping course; if they prefer the water, they can watch the sailboats heading out into Lake St. Clair. In the coming week, idyllic Belle Isle will welcome the canoers and the kayakers, the archers, and the shooters.

Heading back into town, a throng of visitors crowds into Campus Martius. It's just a ten-minute walk to the main events from there: the TCF Center, Ford Field (rugby sevens, field hockey, soccer, and flag football),

Comerica Park (baseball, softball), Little Caesars Arena (basketball, volley-ball, handball) are all a stroll away. The lush grandeur of the Fox Theatre is a novel backdrop for the boxing, wrestling, and weightlifting competitions. Never in the history of the Games has it been possible to stage all the main events in such close proximity in the center of a city.

There is one main excursion: the Canadian government, co-hosting, has funded the Aquatic Center and the Velodrome, and those who want to watch those competitions will have to hop over to Windsor. On the Detroit side, the only significant construction is the new Olympic Stadium. Recent developments in modular construction techniques have allowed the IOC to finance the building of a fifty-thousand-seat stadium, built to a Swiss design, which can be easily dismantled and shipped on to the next athletic event, anywhere in the world. For now, the stadium stands in Roosevelt Park, next to the old Michigan Central Train Depot, beautifully renovated by the Ford Motor Company. A few hundred yards back along Michigan Avenue, there is an arena where the softball teams practice—Detroiters still know the place as "The Corner," the site of old Tiger Stadium.

What has happened to make this possible? How did Detroit, after try-ing and failing nine times, finally get its chance to host the Olympics? Let's say that Los Angeles, which had been awarded the 2028 Games back in 2017, was forced to withdraw following a bribery scandal in 2023. Let's say that this latest ignominy finally forced the International Olympic Com-mittee to rethink its policies, its practices, and its priorities. Following a lengthy internal review, the IOC's leadership decided they could no longer lean on host cities to provide ever more lavish facilities with no practical use after the event. It was time to return to the Games' roots, the simple idea of athletes from around the world coming together to compete. Anyone who has been caught up in Olympics fever is inspired not only by the athletic performances but by the global community that springs up for two glorious weeks. After all, few among us will watch a runner do the 100 meter in nine seconds or a marathon in two hours and think, "One day, that could be me!" But coming together as a city to host the world's greatest athletes can build an unrivaled spirit of unity and pride—provided the city is not drained of its resources in the process and left with the future ruins of mammoth stadiums where no one wants to play.

So the IOC recognized that it had to change its ways—the power balance had flipped and it was now the Committee that had to make the offer, and it was the city that had to be persuaded. That would take a new ideal—too much of Olympic razzmatazz had come to focus on brand new extravagant showcases rather than on the humanity of the athletes. The stage had become more important than the play. But what the world wants to watch are the athletes, and if you brought them into the spaces you already had, the city could see itself in their performance. You would have to scale the Games down to human proportions. The IOC decided to stop ferreting out cities that were prepared to spend money on white elephants. Instead, they turned to a city that had a proven commitment to sport, at a scale that served the community.

All of a sudden, Detroit looked near perfect. As a world-class sports city, it was well endowed with facilities of all kinds, including venues to practice. Beyond downtown, there were the facilities of Wayne State, such as the Matthaei Center. There was Detroit University, the Brennan Pool, the reconstructed Brewster Recreation Center, Keyworth Stadium in Hamtramck, the Detroit City Fieldhouse, the New Kronk, and so many more. Of course, some say that Canada floated the idea first—Windsor, or "South Detroit," as it had been known for a while, had every reason to play up the attractiveness of cross-border Games. So in the end, the two countries created a fifty-mile Olympic zone around Detroit, taking down the border for the duration of the event.

At the time, many cities had bowed out of the Olympic bid business—too expensive, too inconvenient. But Detroit's citizens were behind it from the start: Motown is known for its sports, after all, with a long and proud history. A City of Champions would now bring the champions to the city. But the final nod also came as belated recognition of the many times Detroit had offered and had been turned down: a bit of restitution for the shenanigans of the past.

For a few summer weeks every four years, one city becomes the center of the world of sports—it is second only to the FIFA World Cup in global viewership. The State of Michigan, which had treated Detroit as a stepchild for so long, finally saw a city worth investing in: suddenly, there was money for public transportation systems that linked Detroit to its suburbs—and the suburbs, in turn, were happy to claim Detroit as their own for once. To be sure, there were critical voices as well. On the right, any investment in America's cities is wasteful by definition and must always be opposed. Elsewhere, skeptics were wondering if the money could not be spent on better things than a two-week jock party. But the Olympics were changing, and the new model prioritized the city over the glitz. The supporters won the debate handily.

Is it too fanciful to imagine Detroit as an Olympic city? Is it worthwhile to do so? Would the Games take care of any of Detroit's deeper troubles? Would they heal any of the wounds decades of neglect and disdain have inflicted? Of course not. But for two weeks, the nation's eyes would be on Detroit, with all the love and pride the city deserves. Sure, the literature has long shown that the economic impact of hosting the Games is, at best, minimal, and in the end, there is always something trivial about sports in a world where mayhem is the order of the day. Then again, a city that has saved its art from its creditors knows that price and value are different things: the same literature that shows us that the Olympics are a bad investment financially also shows that the Olympics make cities happy—and no city deserves an abundance of happiness more than Detroit, the City of Champions.

ACKNOWLEDGMENTS

We are, first of all, deeply indebted to all who have written about Detroit: the journalists, the historians, the novelists, and the poets. We have learned from everything we read, and we could not have begun thinking about this book without their work. And to the people who run the archives and keep memory alive: at the Detroit Public Library, the Ford Motor Company's archive, the Benson Henry Ford Research Center, the Detroit Historical Center, the Bentley Historical Library.

We owe friends and colleagues at the University of Michigan, who have been so supportive of this project, many of whom have spent hours upon hours listening to us, reading drafts, asking questions, giving feedback or just simple encouragement: Ketra Armstrong, John U. Bacon, Kerstin Barndt, Charlie Bright, James Cogswell, Walter Cohen, Rod Fort, Andreas Gailus, Daniel Herwitz, Fiona Lee, Marjorie Levinson, Allison McElroy, Karla Mallette, Johannes von Moltke, Benjamin Paloff, Yopie Prins, Helmut Puff, Patricia Reuter-Lorenz, Mark Rosentraub, Robert Sellers, Feodies Shipp III, Heather Thompson, Antoine Traisnel, Ron Wade, Liz Wingrove, and the College of LSA and the School of Kinesiology.

Our children, some of whom care about sports a lot, others who kindly tolerate their parents: Leon Sunstein, Stella Sunstein, Edward Szymanski, Kitty Szymanski, with a special shout-out to Will Szymanski.

Friends and scholars in Detroit and elsewhere who have helped in ways big and small, not least by not laughing out loud when Silke said she'd write about sports: Ian Balfour, Yago Colas, Keenan Covington, Ben Dettmar, Ismaila Verron Conteh, John Drabinski, Gidon Jakar, Stuart Kirschenbaum, Jason Krol, Todd Kropp, Dan Lijana, Lindy Lindell, Sean Mann, Daniel McLean, Imke Meyer, Jon Morosi, J.C. Reindl, Heidi Schlipphacke,

Bill Shea, Tom Stanton, Khali Sweeney, Gwendolyn Wells, the Detroit City Football Club along with the indefatigable Northern Guard, and Stefan's students in his classes on "Sports of Detroit" and "The Detroit Olympics."

Thank you to our wonderful editors, Carl Bromley and zakia henderson-brown, our equally wonderful agent, Gordon Wise, our meticulous copy-editor, Brian Baughan, our excellent production editor, Emily Albarillo, Todd Maslyk, who compiled the bibliography, and the entire team at The New Press.

Last, and also first, the City of Detroit and its people, the inspiration behind this book. In particular Mayor Hazen Pingree.

NOTES

Introduction

1. Christopher Morley, *Where the Blue Begins*, chapter 6 (public domain, available at https://www.gutenberg.org/ebooks/1402).

2. As quoted by John J. Macionis and Vincent N. Parillo, *Cities and Urban Life* (Bloomington: Indiana University Press, 2007), p. 218.

One: September 5, 2017

1. Kevin Shea, "One on One with Mike Ilitch," Hockey Hall of Fame, https://www.hhof.com/htmlSpotlight/spot_oneononeb200301.shtml.

2. "Tigers, Red Wings Owner Mike Ilitch, Founder of Little Caesars Pizza, Dies at Age 87," *Chicago Tribune*, February 10, 2017.

3. Elisha Anderson and Hasan *Dudar*, "LCA Opens to Fanfare, Excitement in Detroit," *Detroit Free Press*, September 5, 2017.

4. "World's Best Cities: 94. Detroit," Best Cities, www.bestcities.org/rankings/worlds-best-cities/detroit.

5. Allan Lengel, "The Making of the District Detroit," *Urban Land*, April 9, 2018, www.urbanland.uli.org/development-business/making-district-detroit.

6. "TERRIBLE ILITCHES," www.google.com/maps/d/u/0/viewer?mid=14j7a XjlU9GxOkzOAD2UWyos4EZA&shorturl=1&ll=42.33990916492976%2C-83 .05959105&z=14.

7. Tom Perkins, "Big Promises for a Thriving Urban Core in Detroit Vanish in a Swath of Parking Lots," *The Guardian*, October 8, 2018.

8. Louis Aguilar, "Cass Corridor Neighbors See Unfilled Promises in Little Caesars Arena District," *Detroit News*, November 5, 2018.

9. There is a now a large economics literature on this issue. See, for example, Dennis Coates and Brad R. Humphreys, "The Growth Effects of Sport Franchises, Stadia, and Arenas," *Journal of Policy Analysis and Management* 18, no. 4 (1999): 601–24, and also John Siegfried and Andrew Zimbalist, "The Economics of Sports Facilities and Their Communities," *Journal of Economic Perspectives* 14, no. 3 (2000): 95–114. These findings extend to hosting mega-events such as the Olympics Games: Robert A. Baade and Victor A. Matheson, "Going for the Gold: The

Economics of the Olympics," *Journal of Economic Perspectives* 30, no. 2 (2016): 201–18.

10. Tim Delaney and Tim Madigan, "The Sociology of Sport," in *The Sociology of Sports: An Introduction* (Jefferson, NC: McFarland, 2009), 3–25. There is growing evidence that major sports events can generate a significant "feel-good factor." See, for example, Georgios Kavetsos and Stefan Szymanski, "National Well-Being and International Sports Events," *Journal of Economic Psychology* 31, no. 2 (2010): 158–71 and Paul Dolan et al., "Quantifying the Intangible Impact of the Olympics Using Subjective Well-Being Data," *Journal of Public Economics* 177 (2019): 104043.

11. Bruce Katz and Jennifer Bradley, *The Metropolitan Revolution: How Cities and Metros Are Fixing Our Broken Politics and Fragile Economy* (Washington, DC: Brookings Institution Press, 2013).

12. If you want to learn more about the league, go to www.detroitrollerderby .com.

Two: October 24, 2012

1. See, for example, Thomas Boswell, "Justin Verlander Is Rocked by Pablo Sandoval in Shocking Start to 2012 World Series," *Washington Post*, October 25, 2012; Ian Casselberry, "One Bad Start or Did Justin Verlander Fold Under Pressure?," *Bleacher Report*, October 25, 2012.

2. See, for example, Charlie Scrabbles, "2012 World Series Odds: Tigers favored over Giants," *SB Nation*, October 24, 2012.

3. "Source: Tigers to Sign Prince Fielder," *ESPN*, January 24, 2012.

4. Michael Maidenberg, "Police Recruitment Doubles in 1970," *Detroit Free Press*, April 19, 1970.

5. U.S. Department of Justice, Crime in the United States 2012, Table 78, Michigan, ucr.fbi.gov/crime-in-the-u.s/2012/crime-in-the-u.s.-2012/tables/78tabledatadecpdf /table-78-state-cuts/table_78_full_time_law_enforcement_employees_michigan _by_city_2012.xls.

6. Nathan Bomey, *Detroit Resurrected: To Bankruptcy and Back* (New York: W.W. Norton, 2016), 51.

7. *Comprehensive Annual Financial Report, City of Detroit*, 2012, https:// detroitmi.gov/Portals/0/docs/finance/CAFR/Final%202012%20Detroit%20 Financial%20Statements.pdf and *City of Detroit Annual Report*, 1970.

8. Paige Williams, "Drop Dead Detroit," *New Yorker*, January 27, 2014.

9. Bomey, *Detroit Resurrected*, 43.

10. See Josh Hakala, "How Did We Get Here? A Look Back at Michigan's Emergency Manager Law," Michigan Radio, February 3, 2016, and Jonathan Oosting, "Snyder Signs Replacement Emergency Manager Law: We 'Heard, Recognized and Respected' Will of Voters," MLive, December 27, 2019.

11. Nick Brown, "Chapter 9 Bankruptcy Puts Detroit in Driver's Seat of Its Restructuring," Reuters, July 18, 2013.

12. David Ng, "Detroit Institute of Arts Collection Worth Billions, Report Says," *Los Angeles Times*, July 11, 2014.

13. Hamilton Nolan, "Sell Detroit's Art, Save Detroit's People," *Gawker*, July 10, 2014.

14. Bomey, *Detroit Resurrected*, 117, 122–23.

15. Mark Caro, "Will Detroit Have to Sell Its Art to Pay Its Bills?" *Chicago Tribune*, October 18, 2013.

16. For examples of the debate's coverage, see Philip Kennicott, "Detroit Institute of Arts Fire Sale: The Worst Idea Out of Motor City Since the Edsel," *Washington Post*, October 4, 2013, and Karen McVeigh, "Detroit Mired in Fresh Controversy over Sale of 60,000-Piece Art Collection," *The Guardian*, August 14, 2013.

17. See Maureen B. Collins, "Pensions or Paintings: The Detroit Institute of Arts from Bankruptcy to Grand Bargain," *U. Miami Bus. L. Rev.* 24, no. 1 (2015): 1–29.

18. Louis Aguilar, "Putting a Price Tag on Properties Linked to Gilbert," *Detroit News*, April 29, 2016.

19. At the time of writing, late 2019, this project is now uncertain.

20. Louis Aguilar, "Putting a Price Tag on Properties Linked to Gilbert," *Detroit News*, April 29, 2016.

21. For examples of such reactions, see Dana Afana, "'We Screwed Up Badly,' Says Dan Gilbert After Advertisement Sparks Outrage," MLive, July 24, 2019.

22. See "About DCFC," Detroit City FC, www.detcityfc.com/page/show/1570886-about-dcfc.

23. "Meet the Northern Guard," www.noonelikes.us/about-ngs.

24. This YouTube video shows Tetris being performed at the team's first home, Cass Tech. Do Haeng Michael Kitchen, "NGS Does the Tetris," Video, www.youtube.com/watch?v=VXAkavgsQSs.

25. Bill Shea, "Detroit City FC Raises $741,250 for Stadium Renovation Project," *Crain's Detroit Business*, February 16, 2016.

26. Larry O'Connor, "Detroit City FC, Manchester Club Share Common Bonds," *Detroit News*, July 29, 2016. and Sean Spence, "Detroit City FC Hosts FC St. Pauli in Front of 7,264," *Detroit City FC*, May 19, 2018. www.detcityfc.com/news_article/show/919588.

27. Larry O'Connor, "Club Necaxa visit to DCFC Taps into Latino Community's Soccer Passion," *Detroit News*, July 11, 2018.

28. The Fieldhouse is adjacent to the Mount Elliot Cemetery and the location of the Bloody Run, where a battle took place on July 31, 1763, between British troops and the Native Americans under Pontiac who were besieging Fort Detroit. Pontiac's forces were victorious, killing 20 British soldiers and wounding 32. The battle is described in detail in chapter 15 of Francis Parkman's *The Conspiracy of Pontiac and the Indian War After the Conquest of Canada* (London; New York: J.M. Dent; E.P. Dutton, 1851).

29. David Lengel, "World Series 2012: Tigers vs Giants—Everything You Need to Know," *The Guardian*, October 24, 2012.

Three: December 28, 2008

1. "Detroit Lions Lose to Finish 0-16," *Washington Post*, December 29, 2008.

2. In 2017 the Cleveland Browns emulated their neighbors to produce another 0-16 season. Comparisons of awfulness may seem odious, but arguably, Cleveland 2017 was not as bad as Detroit 2008—the Browns lost by smaller margins on average (11 points compared with 16) and even managed to take two games to overtime.

3. Tom Goldman, "Detroit Lions: Worst NFL Team Ever?," *NPR*, December 29, 2008; Seth Livingstone, "0-16 Lions Enter Hall of Shame," *USA Today*, December 29, 2008; "Zero-Sum Game for Lions, Who Finish 0 for 16," *Washington Post*, December 29, 2008; Karen Crouse, "0-16: Milestone the Lions Would Rather Forget," *New York Times*, December 29, 2008; John Niyo, "Perfectly Awful," *Detroit News*, December 29, 2008.

4. Niyo, "Perfectly Awful."

5. Joe Posnanski, "Darkness Falls Across the Land," *Kansas City Star*, December 31, 2008.

6. Bob Wojnowski, "Reviving the Lions Will Take Far More," *Detroit News*, December 30, 2008.

7. John U. Bacon, "An Appreciation of William Clay Ford, Sr.," March 14, 2014, www.johnubacon.com/2014/03/an-appreciation-of-william-clay-ford-sr.

8. Nick Kostora, "Detroit Lions: The 5 Best Quotes of the Matt Millen Era in Detroit," *Bleacher Report*, September 22, 2011.

9. Michael Rosenberg, "The Seven-Year Glitch," *Sports Illustrated*, December 2, 2013.

10. Peter Collier and David Horowitz, *The Fords: An American Epic* (New York: Encounter Books, 2002). On Bill's early years, see 188–89; on the Continental, 205–8 and 216–19; on alcoholism and the acquisition of the Lions, 256–57.

11. A good analysis of the relationship between the decline of Detroit and the motor industry can be found in George Galster's *Driving Detroit: The Quest for Respect in the Motor City* (Philadelphia: University of Pennsylvania Press, 2012).

12. As we were writing this book GM first announced the closure of the other remaining plant, Poletown, in the city's other enclave, Hamtramck, then announced a temporary reprieve, and then in early 2020 announced that the plant would be converted to the construction of electric cars. It overlooks Detroit City FC's Keyworth Stadium.

13. Mitt Romney, "Let Detroit Go Bankrupt," *New York Times*, November 18, 2008.

14. See Bill Vlasic, *Once upon a Car: The Fall and Resurrection of America's Big Three Automakers—GM, Ford, and Chrysler* (New York: HarperCollins, 2011), chaps. 27–31 for a good account of the bailout.

15. See Kimberly Amadeo, "Auto Industry Bailout," *The Balance*, June 25, 2019, for a detailed accounting of the bailout costs and returns, https://www.thebalance.com/auto-industry-bailout-gm-ford-chrysler-3305670. Her skepticism about the benefits of the bailout perhaps stems from the fact that she places little weight on the social costs that closing GM would have created for Detroit's population.

16. Mike Wilkinson, "Nearly Half of Detroit's Workers Are Unemployed: Analysis Shows Reported Jobless Rate Understates Extent of Problem," *Detroit News*, December 16, 2009.

17. Alexandra Marks, "'Hip Hop Mayor' Aims to Rev Motor City Engine," *Christian Science Monitor*, August 7, 2002.

18. "Kwame Kilpatrick," Wikipedia, en.wikipedia.org/wiki/Kwame_Kilpatrick.

19. Robert Snell and Mike Martindale, "New Witness Says There Was a Manoogian Party: Unsealed Filing Asserts Broad Cover-Up in Death of Stripper," *Detroit News*, November 22, 2010. For an example of dog-whistle news coverage, see Awr Hawkins, "Detroit: A Microcosm of Democrat Failure," *Breitbart*, July 22, 2013.

20. See, for instance, Robert Snell, "Consultant: Fouts Called Kwame Kilpatrick an 'N-word,'" *Detroit News*, January 21, 2019; Gus Burns, "Report: Relative Calls Kwame Kilpatrick Prosecution Racist, Detroit Brainwashed," MLive, February 21, 2013.

21. Mark Guarino, "Kwame Kilpatrick: Disgraced Detroit Mayor Gets 'Massive' 28-Year Sentence," *Christian Science Monitor*, October 10, 2013. For other analysis comparing Kilpatrick's sentences with others, see Breanna Edwards, "Was Kwame Kilpatrick's Sentence Too Harsh?," *The Root*, October 11, 2013, www.theroot.com/was-kwame-kilpatricks-sentence-too-harsh-1790898437.

22. Mike Riggs, "Why Kwame Kilpatrick Should Not Serve 28 Years in Prison," *CityLab*, October 11, 2013.

Four: November 19, 2004

1. Jonathan Abrams, "The Malice at the Palace: An Oral History of the Scariest Moment in NBA History," *Grantland*, March 20, 2012, grantland.com/features/an-oral-history-malice-palace. The words are from Mark Montieth, a journalist who covered the Pacers for the Indianapolis Star.

2. "NBA Commissioner David Stern Recalls 'Malice at the Palace' as Toughest Crisis He's Dealt With," *Indianapolis Star*, November 12, 2013.

3. Greg Sandoval, "Four NBA Players Suspended for Melee; Incidents Involving Athletes, Fans Are Increasing in U.S. Leagues," *Washington Post*, November 21, 2004.

4. The story of this series and the story of the Pistons' 2003–04 season is told in Detroit News, *Detroit Pistons: Champions at Work* (Detroit: Sports Publishing, 2004), which provides a collection of news stories published in the *Detroit News* about the team in that season. Much of what follows is drawn from this book.

5. Abrams, "The Malice at the Palace."

6. Abrams, "The Malice at the Palace."

7. Most of the whole sequence of events can be seen on YouTube here: "Pacers / Pistons Brawl (2004) Original," Video, www.youtube.com/watch?v=UdyqIh4nJ3Y. At the end of the video you can just make out Ron Artest lying on the bench and getting up to brawl with the fan who had thrown his drink at him.

8. Jeffrey Lane, *Under the Boards: The Cultural Revolution in Basketball* (Nebraska: Bison Books, 2007), 86.

9. You can watch the routine here: "Bill Burr | How You Know the N Word Is Coming | Shaq's Five Minute Funnies | Comedy Shaq," Video, www.youtube.com /watch?v=w8b81UM74Ow&feature=youtu.be&t=2m46s.

10. Rudy Martzke, "TV Sports," *USA Today*, November 23, 2004.

11. Abrams, "The Malice at the Palace."

12. Jeremy Peters and Liz Robbins, "5 Pacers and 5 Fans Are Charged in Fight," *New York Times*, December 9, 2004.

13. Matthew Kitchen, "How the 'Malice at the Palace' Changed Basketball Forever," *Men's Journal*, November 19, 2014.

14. For a detailed account of "the assault on blackness," including an analysis of the "Malice," see David Leonhardt, *After Artest: The NBA and the Assault on Blackness* (Albany: SUNY Press, 2012), as well as Boulou Ebanda de B'béri and Peter Hogarth, "White America's Construction of Black Bodies: The Case of Ron Artest as a Model of Covert Racial Ideology in the NBA's Discourse," *Journal of International and Intercultural Communication*, 2, no. 2 (2009): 89–106.

15. Zack Graham, "How David Stern's NBA Dress Code Changed Men's Fashion," *Rolling Stone*, November 4, 2016.

16. Candace Buckner, "As 'Malice at the Palace' Brawl Turns 10, Impact Lasts," *USA Today*, November 16, 2014.

17. Santiago Colás, *Ball Don't Lie! Myth, Genealogy, and Invention in the Cultures of Basketball* (Philadelphia: Temple University Press, 2016), 135.

18. Andrew Seifter, "Limbaugh on NBA fight: 'This Is the Hip-Hop Culture on Parade,'" *Media Matters*, November 23, 2004, www.mediamatters.org/rush -limbaugh/limbaugh-nba-fight-hip-hop-culture-parade.

19. Derek L. John, "New Fallujah, Michigan," *Recount*, December 15, 2004, www.nyujournalismprojects.org/recount/article/102.

20. Harvey Araton, "One Year After Pacers-Pistons Fight, Tough Questions of Race and Sports," *New York Times*, October 30, 2005.

21. In the 2000 census, the racial makeup of Auburn Hills was 75.9 percent white, 13.2 percent African American, 0.3 percent Native American, 6.3 percent Asian, 0.04 percent Pacific Islander, 1.6 percent from other races, and 2.6 percent from two or more races. Hispanic or Latino of any race made up 4.5 percent of the population.

22. Eminem and Sacha Jenkins, *The Way I Am* (New York: Plume, 2009), 115.

23. You can still find an ad for "The Fabulous Ruins of Detroit Tour" here: www.detroityes.com/fabulous-ruins-of-detroit.

24. The history of the theater is described here: Dan Austin, "Michigan Theatre," Historic Detroit, www.historicdetroit.org/building/michigan-theatre.

25. Thomas Morton, "Something, Something, Something, Detroit," *Vice*, July 31, 2009.

26. Tom Walsh, "Success Story Goes to Work at the Palace," *Detroit Free Press*, October 28, 2003.

27. Detroit News, *Detroit Pistons*, 79.

28. Chris McCosky, "Pistons Smother Bucks; Out-of-Sync Milwaukee Looks Out of Place in Rout," *Detroit News*, April 19, 2004.

29. For a detailed account of the line and all it implies, see Yago Colás, "'Ball Don't Lie!' Rasheed Wallace and the Politics of Protest in the National Basketball Association," *Communication & Sport*, 4, no. 2 (2016): 123–44.

30. Joanne C. Gerstner, "Pistons Say Rasheed Had a Huge Role," *Detroit News*, June 16, 2004.

31. Detroit News, *Detroit Pistons*, 114.

32. Detroit News, *Detroit Pistons*, 119.

33. William Rhoden, "Pistons' Championship Is What Detroit Needed," *New York Times*, June 17, 2004.

Five: September 27, 1999

1. The events of the final game and of the final season are lovingly chronicled in Tom Stanton's *The Final Season: Fathers, Sons, and One Last Season in a Classic American Ballpark* (New York: St. Martin's Press, 2001).

2. Lee Lamberts, "Robert Fick Reflects on Final Home Run at Tiger Stadium," *Holland Sentinel*, June 5, 2015.

3. Stanton, *The Final Season*, 238.

4. Richard Bak, *A Place for Summer: A Narrative History of Tiger Stadium* (Detroit: Wayne State University Press, 1998), 323ff.

5. Patrick J. Harrigan, *The Detroit Tigers: Club and Community, 1945–1995* (Toronto; Buffalo: University of Toronto Press, 1997), 258–59.

6. Harrigan, *The Detroit Tigers*, 351–53.

7. "The Way It Was—Briggs Stadium, 1958," *Hour Detroit*, https://www.hourdetroit.com/from-the-magazine/the-way-it-was-briggs-stadium-1958.

8. Harvey Briggs, "Great Grandson of Former Tigers Owner: Turning a Racist Legacy into One of Hope," *Detroit Free Press*, August 22, 2017.

9. Documentation related to the Cochrane Plan can be found on the website of the Detroit Chapter of the Society for American Baseball Research (SABR), sabr-detroit.org/wordpress/?p=70.

10. John Holusha, "Detroit Journal; Baseball Fans to Give an Aging Tiger Stadium a Great Big Hug," *New York Times*, April 20, 1988.

11. Citizens Research Council of Michigan, "Memorandum No. 1040," February 1996, crcmich.org/PUBLICAT/1990s/1996/memo1040.pdf.

12. Bak, *A Place for Summer*, 355–64. A hagiography commissioned by Monaghan that seeks to place his view of the world in its religious context can be found in Joseph Pearce's *Monaghan: A Life* (Charlotte, NC: Tan Books, 2016). Bak explains that he decided to sell the Tigers because Domino's Pizza was in financial difficulties and the banks gave him little choice (pp. 163–65). He also boasts of making a large profit from his ownership—he was paid $103 million in 1992, a much greater sum than the $53 million he paid in 1983, which doesn't include the $40 million taken out of the club in profits over his tenure. This amounts to a 14 percent annual rate of return, compared with average return on the stock market (S&P 500) of 11 percent over the same period. Fans might say that if Monaghan had taken a

smaller profit out of the ball club and used the money for a better team, or for investing in the stadium, then his stewardship might have been a bit more fruitful. However, he is unapologetic, pointing out the average win percentage under his tenure
(52 percent) was better than either the nine years before him (43.8 percent) and the
nine years after (41.8 percent). The problem with that argument is that Monaghan
inherited a good team, and winning a World Series in his first year of ownership is at
best a shared achievement with the prior ownership. The fact is that under his tenure
the team was on a downward trend, and the first few years of the Ilitch tenure must
to a large part be attributable to the signings of the Monaghan era. His description
of his tenure as "a golden era" is not only lacking in proper Christian modesty, it
would be unlikely to be endorsed by most fans.

13. Bak, *A Place for Summer*, 370.

14. Bak, *A Place for Summer*, 380–81.

15. Tina Lam, "Tigers, City Agree on Stadium," *Detroit News*, October 28, 1995.

16. Harrigan, *The Detroit Tigers*, 274.

17. Dennis Archer and Elizabeth Atkins, *Let the Future Begin* (Grosse Pointe
Farms, MI: Atkins & Greenspan Writing, 2017), 317.

18. The mayor's perspective on this deal is described in his autobiography, Archer
and Atkins, *Let the Future Begin*, 317–21. See also Bak, *A Place for Summer*,
385–89.

19. Tina Lam and Daniel Fricker, "Team Effort," *Detroit Free Press*, August 21,
1996. The Citizens Research Council Memorandum, written in advance of the referendum, sets out the background in some detail.

20. Much has been written about blackmail strategies employed by major
league teams in the United States. A good summary of the financial shenanigans and
the costs, to taxpayers and fans, can be found in Neil deMause and Joanna Cagan,
*Field of Schemes: How the Great Stadium Swindle Turns Public Money into Private
Profit* (Lincoln: University of Nebraska Press, 2008).

21. Payroll data for Major League Baseball can be downloaded from Profes-
sor Rodney Fort's "Rodney Fort's Sports Business Data," sites.google.com/site
/rodswebpages/codes.

22. See, e.g., Bak, *A Place for Summer*, 396.

23. The festival is a joint celebration between Detroit and Windsor, Ontario,
of Independence Day and Canada Day. See Ronnie Minor and Laurie Tamborino,
Detroit's Thanksgiving Day Parade (Chicago: Arcadia Publishing, 2003).

24. For a picture see Cheri Y. Gay, *Detroit: Then and Now* (London: Pavilion
Books, 2015), 40.

25. You can watch a video of the demolition here: "J.L. Hudsons Department
Store - GUINNESS WORLD RECORD!! - Controlled Demolition, Inc.," Video,
www.youtube.com/watch?v=JP1HJoG-1Pg.

26. Homrich Inc., "J.L. Hudson's—Detroit, MI," www.homrichinc.com/wp
-content/uploads/2012/09/J.L.-Hudsons-Detroit-MI1.pdf. A history of the Hudson's site that includes the current construction of an 800-foot skyscraper com-
bining retail, residential and office space by Dan Gilbert's Bedrock company, see
Paul Sewick, "The past, present, and future of the Hudson's site," *Curbed Detroit*,
November 21, 2017.

27. "Sorrow of Hudson's," *Michigan Now*, October 1, 2012, www.michigannow
.org/2012/10/01/sorrow-of-hudsons.

28. The final pitch can be viewed here: "The final out at Tiger Stadium," Video, www.youtube.com/watch?v=uljvXvdYHoE.

Six: October 27, 1995

1. Viv Bernstein, "Red Wings Draw on New Line," *Detroit Free Press*, October 25, 1995.

2. Keith Gave, *The Russian Five* (Ann Arbor, MI: Gold Star Publishing, 2018), 165. Our account of how the Russian Five came to play for Detroit is based on his book.

3. There is a lot of detailed historical work on the Detroit Tigers, as there is with baseball in general. But when it comes to Detroit's other major league teams, the record is patchy. There are many books written in praise of individual players, e.g., Stan Fischler, *Detroit Red Wings: Greatest Moments and Players* (New York: Skyhorse Publishing, 2012), or famous victories, e.g., the *Detroit News*–published *Stanley's Back! The Detroit Red Wings and the Capture of the Cup* (Detroit: Sports Publishing, 2002), or even arenas, e.g., Rich Kincaide, *The Gods of Olympia Stadium: Legends of the Detroit Red Wings* (Detroit: Sports Publishing, 2003). But a complete narrative history of the club remains to be written. This is problematic when looking at periods when the team was not successful, such as the Dead Wings era. What Stefan found the most instructive was talking to hockey fans in his class at the University of Michigan, who were able to ask their parents and grandparents about it—there was a lot of shared misery. Much of this can be picked up on Wikipedia and other websites. See, for example, "1967–82: The 'Dead Wings' Era," kaisercoolcat.weebly.com/dead-wings.html.

4. Before 1942 there were more teams in the NHL, but the Great Depression forced several of them to fold, and the Original Six were the last men standing.

5. On the cultural significance of hockey in Canada, see Richard Gruneau and David Whitson, *Hockey Night in Canada: Sports Identities and Cultural Politics* (Toronto: University of Toronto Press, 2012), and David Whitson and Richard Gruneau, eds., *Artificial Ice: Hockey, Culture, and Commerce* (Toronto: University of Toronto Press, 2012).

6. Estimates vary: one suggested figure of $107 billion per year comes from Kurt Nagl and Alexa St. John, "Bridge Promises New Trade Gateway for Automakers in U.S., Canada," *Automotive News*, July 17, 2018; another, of $120 billion, comes from "The New International Trade Crossing," July 2012, www.detroitchamber
.com/wp-content/uploads/2012/12/NITC-The-Facts.pdf.

7. "Million Dollar Arena Will House Detroit's High Priced National Hockey League Team," *Detroit Free Press*, May 3, 1926.

8. U.S. Census Bureau, "2009–2013 American Community Survey."

9. Reports of active discrimination in professional hockey most often concern French Canadian players, who are rarely drafted by Anglo-Canadian teams and are paid less when they are (a practice that is improving with the expansion of U.S. franchises).

10. Coleman Young and Lonnie Wheeler, *Hard Stuff: The Autobiography of Mayor Coleman Young* (New York: Viking, 1994), 232.

11. On the Underground Railroad, see, for example, Eric Foner, *Gateway to Freedom: The Hidden History of the Underground Railroad* (New York: W.W. Norton, 2015).

Seven: June 19, 1988

1. Mitch Albom, "Oh So Close!," *Detroit Free Press*, June 20, 1988.

2. Much of the information presented here is contained in the ESPN "30 for 30" documentary *Bad Boys*. The story of the Bad Boys is also told in Cameron Stauth, *The Franchise: Building a Winner with the World Champion Detroit Pistons, Basketball's Bad Boys* (New York: William Morrow, 1990), Isiah Thomas with Matt Dobek, *Bad Boys! An Inside Look at the Detroit Pistons' 1988–89 Championship Season* (Grand Rapids, MI: Masters Press, 1989), and Isiah Thomas, *The Fundamentals: 8 Plays for Winning the Games of Business and Life* (New York: HarperCollins, 2001). Sam Smith, *The Jordan Rules* (New York: Simon and Schuster, 1994), describes what it was like playing against the Pistons.

3. You be the judge: "Bill Laimbeer Phantom Foul," Video, www.youtube.com /watch?v=SSHGG0sGUOc.

4. Mitch Albom, "Bad Boys? These Pistons Are Pussycats," January 25, 1988.

5. "Raiders of the N.B.A.," *New York Times*, February 19, 1988.

6. Thomas, with Dobek, *Bad Boys!*, 24–25.

7. Thomas, *Bad Boys!*, 25.

8. Dan Holmes, "How the Detroit Pistons Came to Be Known as the Bad Boys," *Vintage Detroit*, April 27, 2016, www.vintagedetroit.com/blog/2016/04/27/how-the -detroit-pistons-came-to-be-known-as-the-bad-boys.

9. Holmes, "How the Detroit Pistons."

10. Thomas, *The Fundamentals*, 1.

11. Ira Berkow, "Thomas Keeps Promise to Mom," *New York Times*, May 11, 1987.

12. Thomas, *The Fundamentals*, 97.

13. Thomas, *The Fundamentals*, 31.

14. Santiago Colás, *Ball Don't Lie: Myth, Genealogy, and Invention in the Cultures of Basketball* (Philadelphia: Temple University Press, 2016), 129. The "myth of blackness," for Colás, is an operation that "groups together decontextualized descriptions of playing style, clothing, and on- and off-court behavior with stereotypes about urban black men and boys common in the 1980s and especially the 1990s" (123).

15. Albom, "Bad Boys?"

16. Ze'ev Chafets, "The Tragedy of Detroit," *New York Times*, July 29, 1990.

17. Jeffrey Lane, *Under the Boards: The Cultural Revolution in Basketball* (Nebraska: Bison Books, 2007), 150.

18. Scott Ostler, "Those Unfortunate Remarks about Larry Bird Just Don't Fly," *Los Angeles Times*, June 1, 1987.

19. Lane, *Under the Boards*, 142.

20. Lane, *Under the Boards*, 142.

21. Lane, *Under the Boards*, 150.

22. Mike Downey, "Isiah 'Hurt' by 'Joke' About Bird," *Los Angeles Times*, June 4, 1987.

23. Roy Johnson, "Thomas Explains Comments on Bird," *New York Times*, June 5, 1987.

24. Johnson, "Thomas Explains Comments."

25. Charles A. Murray and Richard J. Herrnstein, *The Bell Curve: Intelligence and Class Structure in American Life* (New York: The Free Press, 1994).

26. Johnson, "Thomas Explains Comments."

27. Downey, "Isiah 'Hurt.'"

28. See Smith, *The Jordan Rules*, 7–20.

29. Duane Noriyuki and Dan Gillmor, "Kings of Basketball Bring Crown Home," *Detroit Free Press*, June 15, 1989.

30. Dori Maynard and Jim Schaefer, "Fans Sweep Detroit Area with Championship Revelry: A Little Violence, Damage Reported," *Detroit Free Press*, June 15, 1989.

31. Paul Kersey, *Detroit: The Unauthorized Autopsy of America's Bankrupt Black Metropolis* (self-pub., SBPDL Publishing, 2014). SBPDL (Stuff Black People Don't Like) is the name of his blog. His name appears to be a pseudonym taken from the hero of the "Death Wish" movie franchise. Kersey's strategy is to list acknowledged crimes committed by black people, cite the decline of Detroit, and then wave his hands to say that the one was the cause of the other. Of course, there is no mention of the endless crimes perpetrated by white people on black people throughout the history of the city.

32. The National Center for Victims of Crime, "Urban and Rural Crime," ovc .ncjrs.gov/ncvrw2016/content/section-6/PDF/2016NCVRW_6_UrbanRural-508 .pdf. According to the statistics, in urban areas there are 3.8 aggravated assaults per 100,000 people, while the figure for rural areas is 4.9 per 100,000.

33. Firearm density was measured by a combination of the proportion of armed robberies in total robberies and the proportion of suicides using firearms. David McDowall, "Firearm Availability and Homicide Rates in Detroit, 1951–1986," *Social Forces* 69, no. 4 (1991): 1085–101.

34. Ching-Chi Hsieh and M. D. Pugh, "Poverty, Income Inequality, and Violent Crime: A Meta-Analysis of Recent Aggregate Data Studies," *Criminal Justice Review* 18, no. 2 (1993): 182–202.

35. Ta-Nehisi Coates, "The Case for Reparations," *The Atlantic*, June 2014.

36. Coates, "The Case for Reparations."

37. Samuel George, Amber Hendley, Jack Macnamara, Jasson Perez, and Alfonso Vaca-Loyola, "The Plunder of Black Wealth in Chicago: New Findings on the Lasting Toll of Predatory Housing Contracts," a study conducted at the Samuel DuBois Cook Center on Social Equity at Duke University in collaboration with the Nathalie P. Voorhees Center for Neighborhood and Community Improvement at

the University of Illinois in Chicago, the Policy Research Collaborative at Roosevelt University, and the Center for Urban Research and Learning at Loyola University Chicago, available at socialequity.duke.edu/wp-content/uploads/2019/10/Plunder -of-Black-Wealth-in-Chicago.pdf.

38. Lewis Wallace, "In Detroit, a Risky Alternative to Mortgages," *Marketplace*, October 6, 2016, www.marketplace.org/2016/10/06/inside-land-contracts.

39. Lindsay Gibbs, "The Story Behind The Biggest Brawl in WNBA History," *Deadspin*, September 12, 2019.

40. Carl Bialik, "WNBA Brawl Shows Toughness, Poor Judgment," *Wall Street Journal*, July 24, 2008.

Eight: April 15, 1985

1. George Puscas, "Marvin's Just Marvelous: TKO in 3," *Detroit Free Press*, April 16, 1985.

2. P. Coster, "Hagler Humbles the Great Pretender," *Courier-Mail*, April 17, 1985.

3. "Past Winner of The Ring's Year-End Awards," *The Ring*, February 24, 2012, www.webcitation.org/6E2HQNrhM?url=http://ringtv.craveonline.com/blog /171651-past-winners-of-the-rings-year-end-awards.

4. Brian Hughes and Damian Hughes, *Hit Man: The Thomas Hearns Story* (Lancashire, UK: Milo Books, 2009), 140.

5. The quote comes from Donald Curry, professional boxer, in "Marvin Hagler vs. Thomas Hearns," Wikipedia, https://en.wikipedia.org/wiki/Marvin_Hagler_vs ._Thomas_Hearns.

6. Hughes and Hughes, *Hit Man*, chapter 2.

7. Tommy George, "Hearns Won't Rest with Fewer than 4 Titles," *Detroit Free Press*, June 11, 1984.

8. George, "Hearns Won't Rest with Fewer than 4 Titles."

9. Associated Press, "Thomas Hearns Raises Money to Pay Tax Debt Through Auction," April 4, 2010.

10. Mark Kram, "The Heavyweight Who Created Kronk," *Detroit Free Press*, April 14, 1985.

11. Much of the following is drawn from the official Kronk website: Richard T. Slone, Sylvette Steward, Scott Eisner, and Janae Freeman Stacks, "History," kronksports.com/history. The website is run by his relatives.

12. Kram, "The Heavyweight Who Created Kronk."

13. See, for an example, Ivan Light, *Ethnic Entrepreneurship in America* (Berkeley: University of California Press, 1972).

14. Sterling Bone et al., "Shaping Small Business Lending Policy Through Matched-Paired Mystery Shopping," working paper, bit.ly/2UsKbTt.

15. Andy Lee with Niall Kelly, *Andy Lee: Fighter* (Dublin: Gill Books, 2019), 100–105.

16. Lee, *Andy Lee*, 218.

17. Personal interview, June 12, 2017.

18. Martin Mulcahey, "Boxing's a Driving Force in Detroit," *Dog House Boxing*, January 29, 2011, www.doghouseboxing.com/DHB/Mulcahey012911.htm; Jackie Kallen, "New Prospects in Detroit," *Boxing Insider*, January 9, 2012; Jackie Kallen, "Detroits Boxing Scene on the Upswing," *Boxing Insider*, December 12, 2013.

Nine: June 6, 1982

1. Shav Glick, "Detroit Passes Test, So Does Watson," *Los Angeles Times*, June 7, 1982.

2. Cooper Rollow, "Detroit Grand Prix Was Grand," *Chicago Tribune*, June 7, 1982.

3. American Motors Corporation was the smallest of the Big Four and would eventually be swallowed up by Chrysler in the 1980s, leaving just the Big Three.

4. An outline history of activities undertaken by Detroit Renaissance can be found at "History Archive: 1970–2000," Business Leaders for Michigan, businessleadersformichigan.com/history-archive-1970-2000.

5. The planning and construction of the Renaissance Center is described at length in Joe Darden, Richard Hill, June Thomas, and Richard Thomas, *Detroit: Race and Uneven Development* (Philadelphia: Temple University Press, 1987), 44–54.

6. "The Circuit," Racing Sports Cars, www.racingsportscars.com/covers/_Detroit-1984-06-24t.jpg.

7. Jackie Jones, Roger Martin, Mike Robinson, and Marcia Stepanek, "The Prix Was Grand for Some Merchants and Grim for Others," *Detroit Free Press*, June 20, 1982. Detroit Renaissance put estimated revenues at $4 million, and it was suggested that the Detroit economy could be boosted by as much as $12 million (Curt Sylvester, "Grand Prix Primer," *Detroit Free Press*, April 11, 1982). However, promoters can claim almost any number they like, since nothing is provable after the event.

8. Jones et al., "The Prix Was Grand for Some."

9. "Practice Delayed on Detroit Course," *Toronto Globe and Mail*, June 4, 1982.

10. United Press International, June 5, 1982, and *Toronto Globe and Mail*, June 5, 1982.

11. "The Cars Have Come and Gone, but Is Detroit Any Better?," *Detroit Free Press*, June 12, 1982.

12. Tim Sablik, "Recession of 1981–82," Federal Reserve History, www.federalreservehistory.org/essays/recession_of_1981_82. Since then only the Great Recession of 2008–9 has been worse.

13. "7 Michigan Cities Are in Top 10 For Worst Unemployment Rates," *New York Times*, January 20, 1981.

14. Sally Smith, "Minority Vendors Seek More Contracts," *Detroit Free Press*, December 7, 1982.

15. Of the seventeen teams entering cars in the 1982 Formula One World Championship, thirteen were powered by Ford engines: "1982 Formula One World Championship," Wikipedia, en.wikipedia.org/wiki/1982_Formula_One_World_Championship.

16. Production figures for the United States by make for every year from 1899 to 2000 can be found here: "U.S. Automobile Production Figures," Wikipedia, en.wikipedia.org/wiki/U.S._Automobile_Production_Figures.

17. Thomas Klier, "From Tail Fins to Hybrids: How Detroit Lost its Dominance of the U.S. Auto Market," *Economic Perspectives* 33, no. 2, (2009): 3.

18. Micheline Maynard, *The End of Detroit: How the Big Three Lost Their Grip on the American Car Market* (New York: Doubleday, 2003), 10.

19. Kent Trachte and Robert Ross, "The Crisis of Detroit and the Emergence of Global Capitalism," *International Journal of Urban and Regional Research* 9, no. 2 (1985): 186–217.

20. CARE (Cooperative for American Remittances to Europe) packages were sent to Europeans when Americans became aware of the terrible postwar conditions. Kat Eschner, "How WWII Created the Care Package," *Smithsonian Magazine*, November 27, 2017.

21. William J. Mitchell, "Care Packages for Detroit," *Detroit Free Press*, February 27, 1983. Schmidt said, "If soup kitchens have to be set up in Detroit, it amounts to a depression there. Such a state of affairs is unbelievable. It is grotesque to think of German automobile workers sending packages to Detroit." A spokesman for the German autoworkers at a GM-Opel plant, who contributed $20,000, said, "We criticize the social policy of the Reagan administration and we say his policy of armaments does no good for the social situation of all American workers."

22. Helen Fogel and Sandy McClure, "Devil's Night Hellish for City's Fire Fighters," *Detroit Free Press*, November 1, 1983.

23. Keeanga-Yamahtta Taylor, *Race for Profit: How Banks and the Real Estate Industry Undermined Black Homeownership* (Chapel Hill: University of North Carolina Press, 2019), 88–92 and 211–23.

24. Fogel and McClure, "Devil's Night Hellish."

25. Ze'ev Chafets, *Devil's Night: And Other True Tales of Detroit* (New York: Random House, 1990).

26. Ze'ev Chafets, "The Tragedy of Detroit," *New York Times*, July 29, 1990.

27. For more, see Khalil AlHajal, "Detroit Radio Station Calls Out Rush Limbaugh over False Statements on Motor City History," MLive, August 3, 2013.

28. Trachte and Ross, "The Crisis of Detroit and the Emergence of Global Capitalism," 186.

29. For a description of the history of Poletown, see John J. Bukowczyk, "The Decline and Fall of a Detroit Neighborhood: Poletown vs. G.M. and the City of Detroit," *Wash. & Lee L. Rev.* 41, no. 1 (1984): 49–76.

30. Bukowczyk, "The Decline and Fall of a Detroit Neighborhood," 58–59.

31. Bukowczyk, 60–64.

32. Bukowczyk, 64–71.

33. Bukowczyk, 66.

34. Barbara Ehrenreich, *Nickel and Dimed: On (Not) Getting By in America* (New York: Metropolitan Books, 2001).

35. John Maynard Keynes, *A Tract on Monetary Reform* (London: Macmillan, 1923), Ch. 3, p. 80. Keynes, a British economist, was responding in 1923 to the

argument that in the long run markets will adjust to full employment, during a UK recession in the aftermath of World War I.

36. Coleman Young and Lonnie Wheeler, *Hard Stuff: The Autobiography of Mayor Coleman Young* (New York: Viking, 1994), 246.

37. Janice Bockmeyer, "A Culture of Distrust: The Impact of Local Political Culture on Participation in the Detroit EZ," *Urban Studies* 37, no. 13 (2000): 2417–40.

38. See, e.g., David Fasenfest, "Community Politics and Urban Redevelopment: Poletown, Detroit, and General Motors," *Urban Affairs Quarterly* 22, no. 1 (1986): 101–23, and Lynn W. Bachelor, "Regime Maintenance, Solution Sets, and Urban Economic Development," *Urban Affairs Quarterly* 29, no. 4 (1994): 596–616.

39. Something similar exists in the world of sports. Research often suggests that goalkeepers facing penalty kicks in soccer would do better simply to stand still, since many kickers drive the ball at the center of the goal; goalkeepers tend to dive, either left or right, often vacating precisely the space where the ball will go. However, a goalkeeper who simply stands still will often be accused of doing nothing. Thus, it might seem better to be busy and wrong, even if you might be right more often by being idle. This issue is discussed in Simon Kuper and Stefan Szymanski, *Soccernomics* (New York: Nation Books, 2018), chapter 10.

40. Bachelor (1994) calls this tendency "policy replication."

41. Neil DeMause and Joanna Cagan, *Field of Schemes: How the Great Stadium Swindle Turns Public Money into Private Profit* (Lincoln: University of Nebraska Press, 2008).

Ten: April 1, 1977

1. The coining of the phrase "Pathetic Pistons" seems to have happened during the 1966 season, when the team lost 58 games in an 80-game season. Joe Falls, "Pathetic Pistons Need Leadership," *Detroit Free Press*, March 22, 1966. The title "Dead Wings" came much later, and appears to have emerged in the late 1970s. The first mention in the *Detroit Free Press* is on January 29, 1979: Tom Henderson, "OK, Here's What's Wrong with the 'Dead Wings' . . ."

2. Robert Ostmann Jr., "Red Wings Going to Pontiac," *Detroit Free Press*, April 2, 1977.

3. Curt Sylvester, "Pistons Won't Rule Out Move to Pontiac," *Detroit Free Press*, April 2, 1977.

4. Tom Henderson, "Our Pro Teams: Do They Make Money?," *Detroit Free Press*, July 3, 1977.

5. Records of purchase and sale prices of professional sports franchises in the United States can be found at Rodney Fort's "Rodney Fort's Sports Business Data," sites.google.com/site/rodswebpages/codes. Some caution must be exercised, since the only numbers available are based on press reports. However, the general picture of large capital appreciation is very clear.

6. Strictly, Grand River Avenue intersects Woodward five hundred yards north of Campus Martius, although in the original Woodward Plan developed after the fire of 1805, the street plan was to be formed on a pattern of intersecting hexagons with streets running along the edges and from the center of each hexagon to

its vertices. June Manning Thomas and Henco Bekkering, eds., *Mapping Detroit: Land, Community, and Shaping a City* (Detroit: Wayne State University Press, 2015), 36–39.

7. "Olympia Stadium," The Concert Database, theconcertdatabase.com/venues /olympia-stadium. The website is a project aimed at documenting as much of Michigan's blues, jazz, and rock history as possible.

8. Joe Falls, "Red Wings in Pontiac, Too," *Detroit Free Press*, May 24, 1976.

9. Jim Neubacher, "Oakland Arena Still a Big Maybe," *Detroit Free Press*, October 8, 1976.

10. Joe Falls, "Pistons Will Have to Follow," *Detroit Free Press*, April 3, 1977.

11. Jim Schutze, "Executive Is Slain Near Olympia," *Detroit Free Press*, November 8, 1976.

12. Curt Sylvester, "Pistons Sold for $8.1 Million," *Detroit Free Press*, July 30, 1974. Accounting for inflation, this would have been worth about $42 million in 2019.

13. Curt Sylvester, "He Considered Only 2 Sports," *Detroit Free Press*, August 15, 1974.

14. Johnette Howard, "Pistons Owner Knows What He Wants," *Detroit Free Press*, November 12, 1986. The rest of the paragraph comes from this source.

15. Howard, "Pistons Owner Knows What He Wants."

16. STRESS stands for "Stop The Robberies, Enjoy Safe Streets." Coleman Young and Lonnie Wheeler, *Hard Stuff: The Autobiography of Mayor Coleman Young* (New York: Viking, 1994), 192–93, 205.

17. Young and Wheeler, *Hard Stuff*, 212–13.

18. Heather Ann Thompson, new prologue to *Whose Detroit? Politics, Labor, and Race in a Modern American City* (2004; repr., Ithaca: Cornell University Press, 2017), xiii.

19. "Memorial Ceremony for Ernest C. Browne, Jr.," Detroit Historical Society, November 11, 2015, detroithistorical.org/things-do/events-calendar/events-listing /memorial-ceremony-ernest-c-browne-jr.

20. Jim Crutchfield, "Browne Wooing White Vote, Too," *Detroit Free Press*, June 26, 1977; Wilbur C. Rich, *Coleman Young and Detroit Politics: From Social Activist to Power Broker* (Detroit: Wayne State University Press, 1999), 110–12; Herb Boyd, *Black Detroit: A People's History of Self-Determination* (New York: HarperCollins, 2017), 247.

21. Kirk Cheyfitz, "Detroit White Voters Shift, Support a Black Candidate," *Washington Post*, September 15, 1977.

22. Young and Wheeler, *Hard Stuff*, 230–32. On his redevelopment strategy for Detroit, see June Manning Thomas, *Redevelopment and Race: Planning a Finer City in Postwar Detroit* (Detroit: Wayne State University Press, 2013), chapter 7: "Coleman Young and Redevelopment."

23. Manning Thomas, *Redevelopment and Race*, 35–45.

24. Browne took advertising space to publish a letter in the *Detroit Free Press* on April 20, 1977. Under the heading "The Riverfront Arena: Let the People

Decide," he expressed his opposition to the proposed arena, describing it as "an economically unsound project."

25. Robert Ostmann Jr., "City Pushes Arena but Key Queries Are Unanswered," *Detroit Free Press*, February 14, 1977.

26. Rich, *Coleman Young and Detroit Politics*, 172–76.

27. Young and Wheeler, *Hard Stuff*, 222–23, 229–31.

28. M.L. Elrick, "How Coleman Young Got Joe Louis Arena Built, and Kept the Red Wings in Detroit," Fox 2 Detroit, April 6, 2017.

29. Jim Crutchfield, "Riverfront Arena Given Court OK," *Detroit Free Press*, May 20, 1977.

30. Jim Crutchfield and William J. Mitchell, "Quiet Beginning for New Arena," *Detroit Free Press*, May 21, 1977.

31. Jim Crutchfield, "Mayor Young Pulls Off Coup: Red Wings Will Play Downtown," *Detroit Free Press*, August 4, 1977.

32. Jim Crutchfield and Allan Sloan, "Garage Is Key to Arena Deal for Wings," *Detroit Free Press*, August 5, 1977.

33. Curt Sylvester, "It's Official: Pistons Sign Pontiac Deal," *Detroit Free Press*, September 27, 1977.

34. Drew Sharp, *Dave Bing: A Life of Challenge* (Champaign, IL: Human Kinetics, 2013), 197–98.

35. See Sharp, *Dave Bing*, chapter 13, "The (Almost) Deal" for an account of the failed attempt to bring NBA basketball back to the city.

Eleven: December 26, 1970

1. "Super Bowl–Starved Lions Roar Today," *Detroit Free Press*, December 26, 1970.

2. George Puscas, "Why the Lions Lost: They Wouldn't Pass," *Detroit Free Press*, December 27, 1970.

3. Between 1966 and 1985 the Cowboys reached the playoffs in every season except two.

4. "Propose $900,000 Stadium for Athletics in Detroit," *Detroit Free Press*, December 22, 1921. According to the article, three possible locations were proposed: Memorial Park, on East Jefferson Avenue (downtown), Pingree Park (the northwest side), and Northwestern Field (the east side).

5. Jeffrey R. Wing, "Olympic Bids, Professional Sports, and Urban Politics: Four Decades of Stadium Planning in Detroit, 1936–1975" (PhD diss., Loyola University Chicago, 2016), 74.

6. Wing, "Olympic Bids," 94.

7. Wing, 47–48, 56.

8. Wing, 74.

9. Peter Benjaminson, "Lions Never Liked Idea of a Riverfront Stadium," *Detroit Free Press*, February 3, 1971.

10. Wing, "Olympic Bids," 139.

11. Wing, 146.

12. Planners in Pontiac started working on the idea at the end of 1967 (Larry Adcock, "Stadium Proposal Shocked Pontiac Officials in 1967," *Detroit Free Press*, February 3, 1971), but the plans did not become public until mid-1969 (George Puscas, "Pontiac Enters a Bid for Pair of Stadiums," *Detroit Free Press*, July 1, 1969).

13. Larry Adcock, "Lions OK a Pontiac Site, If . . . ," *Detroit Free Press*, October 28, 1970.

14. June Manning Thomas, *Redevelopment and Race: Planning a Finer City in Postwar Detroit* (Detroit: Wayne State University Press, 2013), 154.

15. Dave Smith, "Downtown Stadium Is the Core of Plan to Revitalize the City," *Detroit Free Press*, January 21, 1970. The article stated, "A new plan for the 'economic revitalization of Detroit' with a domed downtown stadium at its focal point has been formulated by the Greater Detroit Chamber of Commerce, it was learned Tuesday. Called 'Detroit Renaissance for the 1970s,' the plan calls for the formation of a 'blue ribbon leadership group.'"

16. Joe Darden, Richard Hill, June Thomas, and Richard Thomas, *Detroit: Race and Uneven Development* (Philadelphia: Temple University Press, 1987), 48.

17. Manning Thomas, *Redevelopment and Race*, 144–46.

18. Eric J. Hill and John Gallagher, *AIA Detroit: The American Institute of Architects Guide to Detroit Architecture* (Detroit, Wayne State University Press, 2003), 26.

19. Darden et al., *Detroit*, 49–51.

20. Darden et al., 51–54.

21. On the process of acquisition, see Dennis Archer and Elizabeth Atkins, *Let the Future Begin* (Grosse Pointe Farms, MI: Atkins & Greenspan Writing, 2017), 308–11.

22. Philip Power, "Racial Shadow over the Stadium," *Detroit Free Press*, March 28, 1969.

23. Coleman Young and Lonnie Wheeler, *The Hard Stuff: The Autobiography of Mayor Coleman Young* (New York: Viking, 1994), chapter 2.

24. Young and Wheeler, chapter 3.

25. Young and Wheeler, chapter 5.

26. Gordon Skene, "1952—HUAC Hearings Come to Detroit—Coleman Young Testifies—Past Daily Reference Room," *Past Daily*, October 24, 2017, past-daily.com/2017/10/24/coleman-young-past-daily-reference-room.

27. Her many achievements are set out in her obituary: Ika Koznarska Casanova, "Mary V. Beck, Trailblazer for Women on American Political Scene, Ukrainian Activist," *Ukrainian Weekly*, February 20, 2005, www.ukrweekly.com/old/archive/2005/080509.shtml.

28. Michael Maidenberg, "Mary Works On in Defeat," *Detroit Free Press*, September 11, 1969.

29. David Cooper, "Austin Hurt by Racial Split," *Detroit Free Press*, September 11, 1969.

30. Michael Maidenberg, "The Mayor's Race: Survey Shows Voters Are Divided," *Detroit Free Press*, August 3, 1969.

31. Heather Ann Thompson, *Whose Detroit? Politics, Labor, and Race in a Modern American City* (2004; repr., Ithaca: Cornell University Press, 2017), 80–81.

32. Thompson, 82–90.

33. Thompson, 82–83.

34. Herb Boyd, *Black Detroit: A People's History of Self-Determination* (New York: HarperCollins, 2017), 225–34.

35. Thompson, *Whose Detroit?*, 99–100.

36. Sidney Fine, *Violence in the Model City: The Cavanagh Administration, Race Relations, and the Detroit Riot of 1967* (East Lansing: Michigan State University Press, 2007), 457.

37. Heather Ann Thompson, "Rethinking the Politics of White Flight in the Postwar City: Detroit, 1945–1980," *Journal of Urban History*, 25, no. 2 (1999): 163–98.

Twelve: October 10, 1968

1. "It Was a Mad, Mad Scene When Downtown Erupted," *Detroit Free Press*, October 11, 1968.

2. "Tigers Avoid Welcoming Mob," *Detroit Free Press*, October 11, 1968.

3. "Tigers Avoid Welcoming Mob." Oddly, with rose-tinted hindsight some writers have tended to see the celebrations as entirely peaceful. For example: "Detroit Mayor Jerome Cavanaugh [*sic*] ordered fire and civil defense to be on alert, they weren't needed as more than 150,000 peacefully crowded the downtown sector." Tim Wendel, *Summer of '68* (Boston: Da Capo Press, 2012), 197. A more wary description is given in George Cantor, *The Tigers of '68: Baseball's Last Real Champions* (Lanham, MD: Rowman and Littlefield, 1997), 210: "There were a few scattered reports of violence during the night. But almost no looting or gunplay."

4. "Tigers Avoid Welcoming Mob."

5. "It Was a Mad, Mad Scene When Downtown Erupted."

6. Bill McGraw, "How 1968 Detroit Tigers Soothed a Rebellious City's Racial Tension," *Detroit Free Press*, September 7, 2018.

7. Patrick J. Harrigan, *The Detroit Tigers: Club and Community, 1945–1995* (Toronto; Buffalo: University of Toronto Press, 1997), 123.

8. William Serrin, "In the Wake of a Pennant, Color Blindness Prevails," *Detroit Free Press*, September 19, 1968.

9. "Looting Reported as Fans Celebrate," *Detroit Free Press*, October 11, 1968.

10. George Cantor, "Tigers Split . . . in Hole Now: Must Win Last 2 for Tie," *Detroit Free Press*, October 1, 1967.

11. George Cantor, "It's All Over: Tigers Lose Finale, Finish 2nd," *Detroit Free Press*, October 2, 1967.

12. The Saturday games' attendance had been a mere 20,421, in a stadium with a capacity of 54,000. Richard Bak, *A Place for Summer: A Narrative History of Tiger Stadium* (Detroit: Wayne State University Press, 1998), 305.

13. Bak, *A Place for Summer*, 307. See also Joe Dowdall, "Fans Rip Apart Tiger Stadium," *Detroit Free Press*, October 3, 1967.

14. Jack Saylor, "Horns Blow, Sirens Sound—Bosox Did It," *Detroit Free Press*, October 2, 1967.

15. U.S. Department of Justice, "Crime and Justice Atlas 2000," www.jrsa.org /projects/Crime_Atlas_2000.pdf.

16. Graham C. Ousey, "Explaining Regional and Urban Variation in Crime: A Review of Research," *Criminal Justice*, 1 (2000): 261–308. See exhibit 4, p. 274, and exhibit 6, p. 276.

17. Ousey, "Explaining Regional and Urban Variation in Crime," 280–95.

18. Kelley L. Carter, "Motown Mastermind Behind 'Dancing in the Street' Recalls the 1967 Detroit Riots—When Black Folks Took to the Streets," *The Undefeated*, https://theundefeated.com/features/motown-1967-detroit-riots/, no date.

19. David E. Nantais, "That Motown Sound: Berry Gordy, Jr. and the African-American Experience," *America*, February 16, 2009.

20. Mark Clague, "What Went On? The (Pre-)History of Motown's Politics at 45 RPM," *Michigan Quarterly Review*, 49, no. 4, Fall 2010.

21. "Motown Mastermind."

22. For a fuller account, see Suzanne Smith, *Dancing in the Street: Motown and the Cultural Politics of Detroit* (Cambridge, MA: Harvard University Press, 1999).

23. James Baldwin, "A Report from Occupied Territory," *The Nation*, July 11, 1966.

24. Chris Hayes, *A Colony in a Nation* (New York: W.W. Norton, 2017), 33.

25. Hubert G. Locke, *The Detroit Riot of 1967* (Detroit: Wayne State University Press, 2017), 110.

26. Steve Light, "Why 'Race Riot'? On the Need to Change a Misleading Term," *Los Angeles Review of Books*, November 12, 2016. See also: Ken Coleman, "Rebellion, Revolution or Riot: the Debate Continues," in *Detroit 1967: Origins, Impacts, Legacies*, ed. Joel Stone (Detroit: Wayne State University Press, 2017).

27. Fine, *Violence in the Model City*, 135–36, and Locke, *The Detroit Riot of 1967*, 65–66.

28. "Urban Renewal . . . Means Negro Removal. ~ James Baldwin (1963)," Video, www.youtube.com/watch?v=T8Abhj17kYU.

29. For a detailed chronology of events, see Stone, ed., *Detroit 1967*, 119–36.

30. National Advisory Committee on Civil Disorders, *Report of the National Advisory Committee on Civil Disorders* (Washington, DC: Government Printing Office, 1968), 60–61. (This is generally known as the Kerner Report.) Even in 2019 terms, the value of the property damage, less than $400 million, sounds small. Initially the newspapers were citing figures ten times higher than this.

31. Quoted after Stephen C. Finley, "'We Needed Both of Them': The Continuing Relevance of Rev. Albert B. Cleage Jr.'s (Jaramogi Abebe Agyeman's) Radical Interpretations of Martin Luther King Jr. and Malcolm X in Scholarship and Black

Protest Thought," in *Albert Cleage Jr. and the Black Madonna and Child*, ed. Jawanza Eric Clark (New York: Palgrave Macmillan, 2016), 66.

32. "Cities: The Fire This Time," *Time*, August 4, 1967.

33. Thomas J. Sugrue, *The Origins of the Urban Crisis: Race and Inequality in Postwar Detroit* (Princeton, NJ: Princeton University Press, 2014), 273.

34. For a history of those policies, see Richard Rothstein, *The Color of Law: A Forgotten History of How Our Government Segregated America* (New York: Liveright, 2017).

35. Richard Bak, "Fifty Years Later: A Look Back at the Tigers' 1968 World Series Win," *Hour Detroit*, June 21, 2018.

36. Denny McLain, *I Told You I Wasn't Perfect* (Chicago: Triumph Books, 2007), 111–13.

37. Wendel, *Summer of '68*, part VI; and Cantor, *The Tigers of '68*. In Cantor, chapters 28–32 provide blow-by-blow accounts of the World Series.

38. Horton's life story up until 2000 is told in Grant Eldridge and Karen Elizabeth Bush, *Willie Horton: Detroit's Own Willie the Wonder* (Detroit, Wayne State University Press, 2001).

39. Jim Bouton, *Ball Four* (New York: Wiley, 1970), 302.

40. Lynn Henning, "Rage Too Much for a Tiger to Tame," *Detroit News*, July 20, 2017.

Thirteen: October 18, 1963

1. The film was subsequently repurposed by Mayor Cavanagh as a promotional film entitled "Detroit, City on the Move," which is still widely available on YouTube, see, e.g., William Hynde, "You Have to See Detroit's 1968 Olympic Bid Video," *Detroit Metro Times*, June 1, 2016. The President's involvement in the bid is also recorded in the John F. Kennedy Presidential Library archives, and can be found online here: "United States Olympic Committee," *John F. Kennedy Presidential Library and Museum*, www.jfklibrary.org/asset-viewer/archives/JFKPOF/110/JFKPOF-110-007.

2. Lyall Smith, "Olympic Loss Laid to Anti-US Bias: Detroit 2nd as Mexico Gets Games," *Detroit Free Press*, October 19, 1963.

3. Lyall Smith, "Anti-US Feeling Hurt City," *Detroit Free Press*, October 19, 1963.

4. David Maraniss, *Once in a Great City: A Detroit Story* (New York: Simon & Schuster, 2015), 257.

5. In 1959, an editorial in the *Detroit Times* had accused him of attempting to sabotage earlier bids: "Why Detroit Lost," *Detroit Times*, May 27, 1959.

6. This article, though somewhat starry-eyed, gives a good sense of the relationship between Garland and Brundage: John A. Lucas, "'Almost the Last American Disciple of Pure Olympic Games Amateurism': John J. Garland's Tenure on the International Olympic Committee, 1948–1968," *Olympika: The International Journal of Olympic Studies* 15 (2006): 113–26.

7. Lyall Smith, "How Cold War Perils Detroit Olympic Bid," *Detroit Free Press*, October 14, 1963.

8. Daniel Lawrence, "Dashed Dreams: Detroit and the 1968 Summer Olympics," *Michigan History* 96, no. 4 (July–August 2012).

9. Fred Matthaei bequeathed all of his files relating to Detroit Olympic bids to the Detroit Public Library, where they are archived in the Main Branch on Woodward Avenue. The archive runs to some twenty boxes of material, and has yet to be fully catalogued.

10. The list of committees is contained in a document headed "Detroit Olympic Committee," February 25, 1963, Detroit Public Library, Detroit Olympics Archive.

11. All of this was illustrated in the official bid document, "XIX Olympiad 1968: An Invitation to the US Olympic Committee," Detroit Public Library, Detroit Olympics Archive.

12. The interaction between politics, local teams, and the Olympic stadium site debate is set out in Jeffrey R. Wing, "Olympic Bids, Professional Sports, and Urban Politics: Four Decades of Stadium Planning in Detroit, 1936–1975" (PhD diss., Loyola University Chicago, 2016). On the Fairgrounds consensus, see page 58ff.

13. See David Wiggins and Patrick Miller, *The Unlevel Playing Field: A Documentary History of the African American Experience in Sport* (Chicago: University of Illinois Press, 2003), 347–54, on Johnson's community work. Competing in the Decathlon, he won a silver medal in the 1956 Olympics and gold in the 1960 games. He was a civil rights activist and was also among the group that apprehended Sirhan Sirhan after he assassinated Robert Kennedy. Johnson was selected to light the Olympic flame at the 1984 Olympics in Los Angeles.

14. Maraniss, *Once in a Great City*, 253–255.

15. Frank Beckman, "Mayor Blasts Booing Pickets," *Detroit Free Press*, October 12, 1963.

16. Hal Cohen, "Law to Ban Housing Bias Rejected by Council, 7–2," *Detroit Free Press*, October 9, 1963.

17. Lloyd D. Buss, "The Church and the City: Detroit's Open Housing Movement" (PhD diss., University of Michigan, 2008), 140.

18. Sidney Fine, *Violence in the Model City: The Cavanagh Administration, Race Relations, and the Detroit Riot of 1967* (East Lansing: Michigan State University Press, 2007), 18–19.

19. Maraniss, *Once in a Great City*, chapters 11 and 12.

20. The experience of the Model Cities program is evaluated in Bernard J. Frieden and Marshall Kaplan, *The Politics of Neglect: Urban Aid from Model Cities to Revenue Sharing* (Cambridge, MA: MIT Press, 1977).

21. See for example, Angela Dillard, *Faith in the City: Preaching Radical Social Change in Detroit* (Ann Arbor: University of Michigan Press, 2007), 269–73.

22. He was the father of Aretha Franklin, Queen of Soul.

23. Dillard, *Faith in the City*, 273–74, and Fine, *Violence in the Model City*, 25–30.

24. Romney's commitment to government intervention and spending to address problems of social inequality, as well as his intense interest in promoting civil rights and affirmative action made him in many ways indistinguishable from Democrats, and out of place in the Republican Party of his time and ours.

Fourteen: December 29, 1957

1. "Can These Be OUR Lions?," *Detroit Free Press*, December 30, 1957.

2. The details are described here: "Play-by-Play of Victory," *Detroit Free Press*, December 30, 1957.

3. Baseball was still the national pastime, but thanks to TV, the NFL was flexing its muscle. The year before, eleven of the twelve teams in the league landed a deal to broadcast regular season games. While court challenges, based on antitrust law, delayed collective deal-making until 1961, forcing teams to make individual deals, the co-ordination itself differed sharply from the baseball model, where each club focused on the local broadcasting market.

4. The blackout rule survived, in different form, until 2014, and it has been suspended on a year-to-year basis since. From 1973 to 2014, games would be blacked out only if ticket sales did not reach a set percentage, a rule designed to increase ticket sales and ensure robust attendance in the stadiums.

5. "What Blackout? Have a Beer," *Detroit Free Press*, December 30, 1957.

6. Bob St. John, *Heart of a Lion: The Wild and Woolly Life of Bobby Lane* (Dallas, TX: Taylor Publishing, 1991), 71–72.

7. Taylor T. Room, "The Incomparable Bobby Layne," *SB Nation Barking Carnival*, September 11, 2008. Layne's influence on the culture of the team persisted for many years. In 1963 the journalist George Plimpton joined the Lions training camp as a third-string quarterback on the unlikely proposition that a thirty-something non-athlete could just pick it up. He recounted his experiences in the book George Plimpton, *Paper Lion: Confessions of a Last-String Quarterback* (New York: Harper & Row, 1965). In one scene he describes being forced to stand on a chair and sing a song, a form of hazing imposed on rookies. "Friday explained that the hazing—the singing of school songs mostly—was a tradition fomented originally by Bobby Layne," p. 26.

8. The history of the Edsel car is told in Peter Collier and David Horowitz, *The Fords: An American Epic* (New York: Encounter Books, 2002), 211–25.

9. U.S. Department of Commerce, Bureau of Census, "Current Population Reports," November 1956, Series P-60, No. 23, Washington, DC.

10. Collier and Horowitz, *The Fords*, 214–15.

11. Jamie Page Deaton, "Why the Ford Edsel Failed," How Stuff Works, auto.howstuffworks.com/why-the-ford-edsel-failed.htm.

12. For a history of the car's failure, see Kathleen Ervin, "Edsel: An Auto Biography," *Failure Magazine*, March 7, 2002, failuremag.com/article/edsel-an-auto-biography.

13. Edward S. Hanawalt and William B. Rouse, "Car Wars: Factors Underlying the Success or Failure of New Car Programs," *Systems Engineering* 13, no. 4

(2010): 389–404. McNamara went on the in the 1960s to oversee the escalation of U.S. involvement in Vietnam as secretary of defense.

14. James J. Flink, "Three Stages of American Automobile Consciousness," *American Quarterly* 24, no. 4 (1972): 451–73.

15. June Manning Thomas, *Redevelopment and Race: Planning a Finer City in Postwar Detroit* (Detroit: Wayne State University Press, 2013), 51–52.

16. Thomas J. Sugrue, *The Origins of the Urban Crisis: Race and Inequality in Postwar Detroit* (Princeton, NJ: Princeton University Press, 2014), 58.

17. Ken Coleman, "Black Bottom & Paradise Valley, What Happened?," *Detroit Is It*, October 5, 2017, detroitisit.com/history-black-bottom.

18. Sugrue, *Origins of the Urban Crisis*, 81–88.

19. Manning Thomas, *Redevelopment and Race*, 55–65.

20. Ryan Patrick Hooper, "Detroit's Black Bottom Neighborhood Resurrected in Photo Exhibit," *Detroit Free Press*, January 24, 2019.

21. Michael Ranville and Gregory Eaton, "Bob Mann Arrives in Detroit After Stellar Career at U of M," *Michigan Chronicle*, October 26–November 1, 2005.

22. Taken from Scott Ferkovich, "The First Black Player to Play for the Detroit Lions," *Vintage Detroit*, October 9, 2016. Mann went on to become a noted defense lawyer in Detroit.

23. See Richard Bak, *A Place for Summer: A Narrative History of Tiger Stadium* (Detroit: Wayne State University Press, 1998), 238 and 242.

24. Although Willie Horton, recalling growing up in Detroit, commented, "No one thought Virgil was black. Larry Doby was the first black." Richard Bak, *Turkey Stearnes and the Detroit Stars: The Negro Leagues in Detroit, 1919–1933* (Detroit: Wayne State University Press, 1995), 212.

25. Klier, "From Tail Fins to Hybrids," 5–6.

26. Bobby Layne with Bob Drum, *Always on Sunday* (Englewood Cliffs, NJ: Prentice Hall, 1962), 47.

27. Peter King, "Searching For Bobby Layne," *Sports Illustrated*, March 2, 2009.

Fifteen: April 15, 1952

1. This was the era of the Big Six, referring to the small group of six teams in the league (alongside the Red Wings were the Boston Bruins, New York Rangers, Chicago Black Hawks, Montreal Canadiens, and Toronto Maple Leafs), which meant there were only two playoff rounds. In today's NHL, with thirty teams and four playoff rounds, the chances of another postseason sweep are slim.

2. Roy MacSkimming, *Gordie: A Hockey Legend* (Vancouver: Greystone Books, 2003). See chapter 5, "Working on the Production Line." Gordie Howe's own account is contained in his autobiography, *Mr. Hockey: My Story* (New York: Berkley Books, 2014): "The newspapers ended up calling us 'The Production Line.' I didn't know if it was because of the goals we scored or if it was a nod to Detroit's auto industry. Maybe it was both," p. 73.

3. MacSkimming, *Gordie*, chapter 1.

4. MacSkimming, 49

5. Kevin Shea and Jason Wilson, *The Toronto Maple Leaf Hockey Club: Official Centennial Publication* (Toronto: McClelland & Stewart, 2016).

6. MacSkimming, *Gordie*, chapter 6.

7. MacSkimming, 82–85.

8. Marshall Dann, "Wings Nip Rangers, 3–2, in NHL Opener," *Detroit Free Press*, October 12, 1950. Howe is mentioned only once in the match report, with no reference to his miraculous recovery.

9. In the decade 1950–59, Howe led the league in scoring four times, was second four times, and ranked fifth in 1955 and sixth in 1959.

10. MacSkimming, *Gordie*, 65–66.

11. MacSkimming, 91.

12. Lindsay's efforts are recounted in J. Andrew Ross, "Trust and Antitrust: The Failure of the First National Hockey League Players' Association, 1957–1958," *Business & Economic History On-Line: Papers Presented at the BHC Annual Meeting* 8 (2010).

13. Ross, "Trust and Antitrust," 5.

14. Data from "Rodney Fort's Sports Business Data," https://sites.google.com/site /rodswebpages/codes.

15. Thompson, *Whose Detroit?*, 11–12.

16. Arthur Kornhauser, *Detroit as the People See It: A Survey of Attitudes in an Industrial City* (Detroit MI: Wayne University Press, 1952), 91.

17. Quoted in Thompson, *Whose Detroit?*, 21.

18. This brief outline is based on David M. Lewis Colman, *Race Against Liberalism: Black Workers and the UAW in Detroit* (Urbana: University of Illinois Press, 2008), 55–57.

Sixteen: October 26, 1951

1. "Marciano Gets 8th-Round TKO over Bomber," *Detroit Free Press*, October 27, 1951.

2. Tim Belknap, Billy Bowles, Mary Trueman, and Marianne Rzepka, "Ex-Athletes, Others Recall Boxing Great," *Detroit Free Press*, April 13, 1981.

3. "Marciano Gets 8th-Round TKO over Bomber," *Detroit Free Press*, October 27, 1951.

4. William C. Rhoden, "Joe Louis Moment," *New York Times*, November 5, 2008. In 2017 the Ukrainian boxer Wladimir Klitschko exceeded Louis's tenure by 113 days but, unlike Louis, he did not hold the title continuously.

5. Howard Bryant, *The Heritage: Black Athletes, a Divided America, and the Politics of Patriotism* (Boston, Beacon Press, 2018), 33.

6. Bryant, *The Heritage*, x.

7. Thom Greer, "America Loses Its Greatest Hero," *Daily News*, April 14, 1981.

8. Thomas E. Wagner and Philipp J. Obermiller, *African-American Miners and*

Migrants: The Eastern Kentucky Social Club (Urbana/Chicago: University of Illinois Press, 2004), 129.

9. Frank Sinatra, foreword to Neil Scott, *Joe Louis: A Picture Story of His Life* (New York: Greenberg, 1947).

10. On Jack Johnson see Theresa Runstedtler, *Jack Johnson, Rebel Sojourner: Boxing in the Shadow of the Global Color Line* (Berkeley: University of California Press, 2013). On Tommy Burns see Dan McCaffery, *Tommy Burns: Canada's Unknown World Heavyweight Champion* (Toronto: Miles Kelly Publishing, 2000).

11. Paul Beston, *The Boxing Kings: When American Heavyweights Ruled the Ring* (Lanham: Rowman & Littlefield, 2017), 100.

12. David Margolick, "Only One Athlete Has Ever Inspired This Many Songs," *New York Times*, February 25, 2001.

13. The story is often repeated but may be apocryphal: see David Margolick, "Save Me, Joe Louis!," *Los Angeles Times*, November 7, 2005.

14. Beston, *The Boxing Kings*, 104.

15. "Black Moses," *Time*, September 29, 1941.

16. Randy Roberts, "Jack Dempsey: An American Hero in the 1920's," *Journal of Popular Culture*, 8, no. 2 (1974), 411–26.

17. Randy Roberts, *Joe Louis: Hard Times Man* (New Haven, CT: Yale University Press, 2010), 201.

18. See William H. Wiggins, "Boxing's Sambo Twins: Racial Stereotypes in Jack Johnson and Joe Louis Newspaper Cartoons, 1908 to 1938," *Journal of Sport History* 15, no. 3 (1988): 242–54, for a comparison of the treatment of the two champions in the media.

19. Margolick, "Only One Athlete Has Ever Inspired This Many Songs," 171–72.

20. Dominic J. Capeci Jr. and Martha Wilkerson, "Multifarious Hero: Joe Louis, American Society and Race Relations During World Crisis, 1935–1945," *Journal of Sport History* 10, no. 3 (1983): 5–25.

21. Joe Louis, Edna Rust, and Art Rust, *Joe Louis: My Life* (New York: Harcourt, 1978), 246–47.

22. Louis, Rust, and Rust, 245–46.

23. Roberts, "Jack Dempsey: An American Hero in the 1920's."

24. Capeci and Wilkerson, "Multifarious Hero."

25. Lee Finkle, "The Conservative Aims of Militant Rhetoric: Black Protest During World War II," *Journal of American History*, 60, no. 3 (1973), 692–713.

26. Finkle, "The Conservative Aims of Militant Rhetoric."

27. Charles C. Euchner, *Nobody Turn Me Around: A People's History of the 1963 March on Washington* (Boston, Beacon Press, 2010).

28. Finkle, "The Conservative Aims of Militant Rhetoric," 692–96.

29. Lauren Rebecca Sklaroff, "Constructing G.I. Joe Louis: Cultural Solutions to the 'Negro Problem' During World War II," *Journal of American History* 89, no. 3 (2002): 958–83.

30. Neil A. Wynn, *The Afro-American and the Second World War* (New York; London: Holmes & Meier, 1993), 6–11.

31. Roberts, *Joe Louis*, 207–11.

32. Beston, *The Boxing Kings*, 121.

33. Quoted in Bryant, *The Heritage*, 33.

34. Louis, Rust, and Rust, *Joe Louis*, 172.

35. Roberts, *Joe Louis*, 228–29.

36. Capeci and Wilkerson, "Multifarious Hero," 21.

37. Louis, Rust, and Rust, *Joe Louis*, 179.

38. Louis was putting on exhibition matches with another boxing great, Sugar Ray Robinson, and the two spent much of the war together. The incident is detailed in Wil Haygood, *Sweet Thunder: The Life and Times of Sugar Ray Robinson* (Chicago: Chicago Review Press, 2011), 79–82.

39. Bryant, *The Heritage*, 31.

40. Box 33, Accession 998, Walker A. Williams records subseries, 1934–1961, Benson Ford Research Center, The Henry Ford. We want to thank Sam Rood at the Benson, who drew our attention to this particular folder.

41. "NAACP Asks Action Against Col. Selway, Old 477th Commander," *New York Age*, July 21, 1945.

42. Daniel Haulman, "Freeman Field Mutiny: Victory for Integration or Segregation?," *Air Power History* 63, no. 3 (2016): 41–45.

43. Coleman Young and Lonnie Wheeler, *Hard Stuff: The Autobiography of Mayor Coleman Young* (New York: Viking, 1994), 67–73.

Seventeen: April 28, 1949

1. The passage is well worth reading as a whole: "During the sixty years that have elapsed since 1887, when Detroit became one of the fourteen charter members of the Amateur Athletic Union, there have been many changes. During this period Detroit has made tremendous mechanical contributions improving the living standards of the entire world. Mass production has indeed proceeded at a furious pace, but incident thereto, Detroit has agglomerated a vast population from world sources; and the great plants building automobiles, trucks, accessories, machines, chemicals and drugs have sprawled out along the river and the lakes with the people dispersed among them. Difficult social problems have always accompanied industrial progress, and there are admittedly factions and classes in Detroit, and there is some cynicism; and there are many who are now concerned that we might irretrievably lose the best attributes of Detroit's civic character. . . . The very pulsation of the Twentieth Century can be reckoned in the heart of Detroit where the crucial economic and social problems are focused as at no other place . . . . Whatever presages ill for Detroit is ominous, for the evil can extend rapidly from it throughout the land and beyond. But it is neither wishful thinking nor imagining when Detroit's leaders say that a sublimation and unification of civic spirit and pride, that would eradicate the evils we fear, would result from the tremendous joint effort made necessary to conduct an Olympiad in all its glorious pageantry at Detroit." "Brief on Behalf of the City of Detroit Urging Acceptance of Detroit's Invitation to Act as Host of the Olympic Games, to Be Filed with the United States Olympic Association, Pursuant to Its Resolutions Adopted Monday,

July 28, 1947," Detroit Olympic Committee archive, Burton Collection, Detroit Public Library.

2. The findings about Detroit, Minneapolis, and Philadelphia are contained in the seventeen-page *Report of the Inspection Committee of the United States Olympic Association*. There is also a five-page supplementary report on Chicago. Detroit Olympic Committee archive, Burton Collection, Detroit Public Library.

3. The 1940 and 1944 offers are supported by a letter from Mayor Richard Reading, dated July 26, 1938, in the record of the Common Council, p. 1745. The process for deciding the host of the 1948 Games was hastily organized by postal ballot in March 1946, and there is some confusion over the identity of the bidding cities, but an article from the *Detroit News* on February 23, 1946, "Detroit's Olympic Committee Has Stadium Plan," cites a report from Matthaei to Mayor Reading claiming that "to date it is a 50-50 proposition" whether Detroit will get the 1948 Games. The 1952 bid was submitted to the IOC at its 40th Session in Lausanne, Switzerland, in September 1946, and then again at its 41st Session in Stockholm in June 1947, when the Games were awarded to Helsinki. Copies of all documentation are found in the Detroit Olympic Committee archive, Burton Collection.

4. In 1966 Matthaei sold American Metal Products to inventor William Lear, and the business survives to the present day as part of the Lear Corporation. Matthaei's life story is recited in his obituary: Larry Bush, "Regent-Emeritus Fred Matthaei Dies," *Ann Arbor News*, March 26, 1973, available at https://aadl.org/node /83737.

5. Brundage's theory of precedence was explained in a series of letters from the Detroit Olympic Committee archives: "A strong battle for the Games of the XIII Olympiad 1944 will place you in a better tactical position for 1948," Brundage to Matthaei, January 23, 1939; "Detroit, with its invitation lodged with the Committee in 1939, has priority so far as American cities are concerned," Brundage to Matthaei, April 12, 1946, Detroit Olympic Committee archive.

6. Brundage to Matthaei, April 28, 1948, Detroit Olympic Committee archive.

7. Matthaei to Brundage, May 25, 1948, Box 20, Avery Brundage Collection, University of Illinois at Urbana-Champaign.

8. *Report of the Inspection Committee*, Detroit Olympic Committee archive.

9. A formal letter confirming the decision was sent by Asa Bushnell, secretary of the USOA, to Otto Mayer, secretary of the IOC, on December 22, 1948. Detroit Olympic Committee archive.

10. "Initial Meeting of the Detroit Olympic Organizing Committee, Hotel Statler, September 21, 1948," Detroit Olympic Committee archive.

11. "Meeting of the Detroit Olympic Organizing Committee, Michigan Room, Hotel Statler, October 11, 1948," Detroit Olympic Committee archive; Chairman, Sub-committee on Finance, to Matthaei, November 11, 1948, and Matthaei to Van Antwerp, December 28, 1948, Detroit Olympic Committee archive.

12. Minutes of Executive Committee Meeting, Detroit Olympic Organizing Committee, October 8, 1948; Edward Jeffries, Chairman of Finance Sub-committee, to Mayor Van Antwerp, November 16, 1948, and Matthaei to Mayor Van Antwerp, December 28, 1948, Detroit Olympic Committee archive.

13. The Paul Bunyan Company, April 20, 1948, Detroit Olympic Committee archive.

14. Detroit City Plan Commission, *Report on Study of City Planning Aspects of the Olympic Games*, Detroit City Plan Commission, December 1948, Detroit Olympic Committee archive, December 1948.

15. Matthaei to Van Antwerp, December 28, 1948, Detroit Olympic Committee archive.

16. Brundage to Matthaei, December 18, 1948, Detroit Olympic Committee archive.

17. Edstrom to IOC, December 17, 1948, IOC archives, copy provided by Dr. Benjamin Dettmar.

18. Kirby to Brundage, August 13, 1948, Detroit Olympic Committee archive.

19. Asa Bushnell to Otto Mayer, Detroit Olympic Committee archive.

20. Roby to Edstrom, February 22, 1949, in reply to Edstrom's letter of February 28, Detroit Olympic Committee archive.

21. Roby to Jack Garland, January 17, 1949, Detroit Olympic Committee archive.

22. "Duplicity Balks Matthaei's Valiant Effort," *Michigan Manufacturer and Financial Record*, May 1949, p. 60, Detroit Olympic Committee archive.

23. Article translated from *De Rotterdammer*, Netherlands, Detroit Olympic Committee archive.

24. Sales tax revenues from the United States: Bureau of the Census, "The County and City Data Book, 1956, Supplement to Statistical Abstract of United States," p. 389. The Michigan sales tax rate in 1950 was 3 percent (Michigan Sales and Use Taxes, Tax Analysis Division, Bureau of Tax and Economic Policy, Michigan Department of Treasury, "Michigan Sales and Use Taxes," August 2004).

25. "The County and City Data Book, 1956," 364–420. Strictly, this relates only to cities with populations in excess of two hundred thousand. Also, Chicago actually beat Detroit by $1 in terms of median income—a statistical tie.

26. "As We See It . . . ," *Detroit Free Press*, May 10, 1949.

27. Brundage to Matthaei, n.d., Detroit Olympic Committee archive.

28. Matthaei to Brundage, November 29, 1949, Detroit Olympic Committee archive.

29. Matthaei to Brundage, n.d., Detroit Olympic Committee archive.

30. "The Embattled World of Avery Brundage," *Sports Illustrated*, January 30, 1956.

Eighteen: October 10, 1945

1. This account of Game 7 of the 1945 World Series is based on Burge Smith, *The 1945 Detroit Tigers: Nine Old Men and One Young Left Arm Win It All* (Jefferson, NC: McFarland, 2010), 244–62.

2. A fine biography is Terry Sloope, "Preston Rudolph 'Rudy' York," Etowah Valley Historical Society, https://evhsonline.org/archives/45477.

3. "Super Slugger: Georgia Hall-Bound Rudy York Had a Shrewd Eye for Pitchers," *Atlanta Journal-Constitution*, February 26, 1977.

4. H.G. Salsinger, "One for Psychologists: Why Do Fans Ride York?," *Sporting News*, September 2, 1943. p. 5.

5. Hank Greenberg (with Ira Berkow), *The Story of My Life* (Chicago: Ivan R. Dee, 1989). His wartime service is recounted in chapter 9.

6. A.J. Baime, *The Arsenal of Democracy: FDR, Detroit, and an Epic Quest to Arm an America at War* (Boston: Houghton Mifflin, 2014), p81.

7. Baime, *The Arsenal of Democracy*, chapters 11 and 12.

8. Nelson Lichtenstein, *Walter Reuther: The Most Dangerous Man in Detroit* (Urbana: University of Illinois Press, 1997), chapter 10.

9. Richard J. Overy, *Why the Allies Won* (New York: Norton, 2014), 194–98.

10. Alan Clive, *State of War: Michigan in World War II* (Ann Arbor: University of Michigan Press, 1979), 34.

11. The phrase "Arsenal of Democracy" was coined by President Roosevelt in a radio speech to the American people on December 29, 1940, at the time referring to the entire nation.

12. Harriet Arnow, *The Dollmaker* (1954; repr., New York: Simon and Schuster, 2012).

13. It is worth noting that Arnow takes creative license here since Coughlin himself had been forced off the air by the mid-1940s; his numerous fans, however, were still around.

14. Joyce Carol Oates, "An American Tragedy," *New York Times*, January 24, 1971.

15. "She's the Eddie Plank of Bloomer Girl Team," *Detroit Free Press*, August 13, 1916, p. 22.

16. "Girls Put Up Regular Game," *Detroit Free Press*, August 12, 1916, p. 12.

17. Lois Browne, *Girls of Summer: The Real Story of the All-American Girls Professional Baseball League* (Toronto: HarperCollins, 1992), 16.

18. Carly Adams, "Softball and the Female Community: Pauline Perron, Pro Ball Player, Outsider, 1926–1951," *Journal of Sport History*, 33, no. 3(2006), 323–43.

19. "Detroit Still Softball Hub in War Setting," *Detroit Free Press*, December 26, 1943.

20. The story is recounted in Browne, *Girls of Summer*, and was made into the 1992 film *A League of Their Own*.

21. "Inquiring Reporter Asks: Do You Favor Women Participating in Professional Sports?," *Detroit Free Press*, February 28, 1943.

22. Bob Latshaw, "Mixed Emotions Greet Attempt to Sign Detroit Girls for Pro Softball League," *Detroit Free Press*, May 4, 1943.

23. "A Thrilling Time: Women Baseball Players Recollect Years on the Diamond That Sparkled," *South Bend Tribune*, September 22, 2002, p. 64.

24. Merrie A. Fidler, *The Origins and History of the All-American Girls Professional Baseball League* (Jefferson, NC: McFarland, 2015), 192.

25. John E. Williams, "Women Find Many Opportunities at Ford Co.," *Pittsburgh Courier*, April 24, 1943.

26. Though oddly, the film *Rosie the Riveter* was set in California. Once again, LA was undermining Detroit.

27. Alfred J. Hudson, "Her Tip on Gun Wins $1,000 Bond," *Detroit Free Press*, November 11, 1942.

28. On hate strikes directed against African Americans, see Clive, *State of War*, 141–42; James Sparrow, *Warfare State: World War II Americans and the Age of Big Government* (New York: Oxford University Press, 2011); 184–88, and Thomas J. Sugrue, *The Origins of the Urban Crisis: Race and Inequality in Postwar Detroit* (Princeton, NJ: Princeton University Press, 2014), chapter 4. On a hate strike directed at women, see Lichtenstein, *Walter Reuther*, 200.

29. Clive, *State of War*, 189–90.

30. Clive, 193–98.

31. Clive, 186.

32. Ruth Milkman, "Redefining 'Women's Work': The Sexual Division of Labor in the Auto Industry During World War II," *Feminist Studies* 8, no. 2 (1982): 336–72.

33. Mac Slavin, "All-American Girls Baseball League Visited Comerica Park," *Medium*, August 5, 2010, https://tigers.mlblogs.com/all-american-girls-professional-baseball-league-48b69afbd33d.

Nineteen: February 5, 1943

1. Dale Stafford, "To Whom It May Concern," *Detroit Free Press*, February 5, 1943.

2. Charles P. Ward, "18,930 See LaMotta Floor Robinson in Scoring Upset Victory," *Detroit Free Press*, Feb 6, 1943.

3. Joyce Carol Oates, *On Boxing* (New York: Doubleday, 1987), 8.

4. Charles P. Ward, "Ward to the Wise," *Detroit Free Press*, February 28, 1943.

5. Wil Haygood, *Sweet Thunder: The Life and Times of Sugar Ray Robinson* (Chicago: Chicago Review Press, 2011).

6. Haygood, Sweet Thunder.

7. "Harlem Hurricane Drubs Bronx Rival," *News Journal* (Wilmington, DE), February 27, 1943.

8. Andrew Eisele, "Ring Magazine's 80 Best Fighters of the Last 80 Years," 2002, https://www.liveabout.com/ring-magazine-fighter-rankings-4153939.

9. Haygood, *Sweet Thunder*, 197–200.

10. Haygood, 14–16.

11. Haygood, 18–20.

12. Haygood, 19.

13. Sugar Ray Robinson would go on fighting for more than twenty years. He fought his last fight in November 1965. After his defeat to LaMotta, he would not lose another fight until 1951, and thirteen of the nineteen losses of his career, which spanned more than 200 professional fights, occurred in the 1960s. Sugar Ray would step into the ring in Detroit eight more times, seven times at Olympia, and once, in 1961, at the Cobo Arena. But his ongoing rivalry with LaMotta would go

down in boxing history as an epic series: they went at it six times, LaMotta winning exactly once. The final fight, in 1951, is known as the St. Valentine's Day Massacre. LaMotta took a horrendous beating, and by round 13, he had lost the ability to punch at all. In the end, the referee simply stopped the fight.

14. Harry Ferguson, "What Makes White Hope Necessary?," *Detroit Free Press*, September 7, 1941.

15. Charles P. Ward, "White Hopes Fail to Stir Excitement," *Detroit Free Press*, October 25, 1941.

16. "Sponsor of White Hope Tourney Pays and Pays as Hungry Heavyweights Haunt the Motor City," *Newsweek*, November 3, 1941.

17. Charles P. Ward, "Ward to the Wise," *Detroit Free Press*, August 28, 1941; "Boxing Promoters Rise, Only to Fall with a Thud," *Detroit Free Press*, December 28, 1941.

18. Savold fought once more, in 1952, going down to Rocky Marciano; Louis would fight only three more bouts.

19. Jennifer Guglielmo, "White Lies, Dark Truths," in *Are Italians White? How Race is Made in America*, eds. Jennifer Guglielmo and Salvatore Salerno (New York: Routledge, 2003), 8.

20. Arthur W. Kornhauser, *Detroit as the People See It* (Detroit: Wayne State University Press, 1953), 45.

21. John Hartigan, *Racial Situations: Class Predicaments of Whiteness in Detroit* (Princeton, NJ: Princeton University Press, 1999), 32.

22. Hartigan, *Racial Situations*, chapter 1.

23. Joe Darden, Richard Hill, June Thomas, and Richard Thomas, *Detroit: Race and Uneven Development* (Philadelphia: Temple University Press, 1987: 114–19.

24. Darden et al., *Detroit*, 115.

25. See Larry Kress, "1917: A Discrimination Tale," *Tales from a Schmo*, January 11, 2017, https://middleageschmo.wordpress.com/2017/01/11/1917-a-discrimination-tale.

26. Noam Hassenfeld, "Hank Greenberg: Caught Between Baseball and His Religion," WBUR, September 22, 2017, www.wbur.org/onlyagame/2017/09/22/hank-greenberg-rosh-hashana-tigers.

27. Sugrue, *The Origins of the Urban Crisis*, 41.

28. Sugrue, 74.

29. See "Sojourner Truth Housing Project," Detroit 1701, http://www.detroit1701.org/Sojourner%20Truth%20Housing%20Project.html.

30. Wendy Plotkin, "'Hemmed in': The Struggle Against Racial Restrictive Covenants and Deed Restrictions in Post-WWII Chicago," *Journal of the Illinois State Historical Society* 94, no. 1 (2001), 39–69.

31. Sugrue, *The Origins of the Urban Crisis*, 63–64. A photograph of the wall is shown on 65.

32. Ian Thibodeau, "Big, Heavy Planters Placed at Grosse Pointe Park-Detroit Border," *Mlive*, posted Jul 14, 2015, updated Apr 03, 2019, https://www.mlive.com/news/detroit/2015/07/big_heavy_planters_placed_at_g.html.

33. August Meier and Elliott M. Rudwick, *Black Detroit and the Rise of the UAW* (Ann Arbor: University of Michigan Press, 2007), 109–10, and 125–26.

34. "5,000 at Rally Ask Jobs for City's Negro Women," *Detroit Free Press*, April 12, 1943.

35. Janet L. Langlois, "The Belle Isle Bridge Incident: Legend Dialectic and Semiotic System in the 1943 Detroit Race Riots," *Journal of American Folklore* 96, no 380 (1983): 183–99.

36. Dominic J. Capeci and Martha Wilkerson, *Layered Violence: The Detroit Rioters of 1943* (Jackson: University Press of Mississippi, 1991), chapter 1.

37. Capeci and Wilkerson, *Layered Violence*, 13.

38. "Cars Overturned and Burned, Negroes Beaten by Rioting Crowd on Woodward," *Detroit Free Press*, June 22, 1943, p. 13, and "Mob Rule: Twenty-Three Persons are Killed in Detroit Race Riots," *New York Times*, June 22, 1943, p. 7.

39. Dominic J. Capeci and Martha Wilkerson, "The Detroit Rioters of 1943: A Reinterpretation," *Michigan Historical Review* 16, no. 1 (1990): 49–72.

40. Capeci and Wilkerson, *Layered Violence*, 33.

41. Capeci and Wilkerson, 37–39.

42. Capeci and Wilkerson, "The Detroit Rioters of 1943," 54.

43. Capeci and Wilkerson.

44. Richard Bak, *A Place for Summer: A Narrative History of Tiger Stadium* (Detroit: Wayne State University Press, 1998), 204.

45. Harold Draper, *The Truth About Gerald Smith: America's No. 1 Fascist*, Workers Party LA, 1945.

46. Richard Walter Thomas, *Life for Us Is What We Make It: Building Black Community in Detroit, 1915–1945* (Bloomington: Indiana University Press, 1992), 169.

47. Thomas, *Life for Us Is What We Make It*, 168.

48. Waston Spoelstra, "Through Gates of Ford Empire Pass Many Famous Athletes," *The Morning Herald* (Uniontown, PA), July 13, 1943.

49. Richard Rothschild, "Greatest 45 minutes Ever in Sports," *Sports Illustrated*, May 24, 2010, www.si.com/more-sports/2010/05/24/owens-recordday.

50. Jesse Owens, with Paul Neimark, *Jesse: The Man Who Outran Hitler* (New York: Fawcett, 1978), 101.

51. "Start Negro Housing," *Detroit Free Press*, November 21, 1943.

52. "National Roundup: Michigan," *People's Voice*, June 12, 1943.

53. Owens, *Jesse*, 137–38.

54. William J. Baker, *Jesse Owens: An American Life* (Urbana: University of Illinois Press, 2002), 166.

55. Baker, *Jesse Owens*, 167.

56. James Baldwin, *Notes of a Native Son* (Boston: Beacon Press, 1955), 85.

57. Baldwin, *Notes*, 94.

Twenty: June 22, 1938

1. This account is based on the film of the fight that is available on YouTube: "Joe Louis vs Max Schmeling II—June 22, 1938," Video, www.youtube.com /watch?v=6BLGdFQPh8c.

2. Quoted after David Margolick, *Beyond Glory: Joe Louis vs. Max Schmeling, and a World on the Brink* (New York: Vintage, 2010).

3. George Spandau, "Schmeling's *A Cultural Victory*," in *The Crisis*, vols. 43–44, ed. W.E.B. Du Bois (New York: Crisis Publishing Company, 1936), 301.

4. George Sullivan, *Knockout! A Photobiography of Boxer Joe Louis* (National Geographic Society, 2008), 43.

5. Kevin Boyle, *Arc of Justice: A Saga of Race, Civil Rights, and Murder in the Jazz Age* (New York: Henry Holt, 2007).

6. Dan Austin, "Meet the 5 Worst Mayors in Detroit History," *Detroit Free Press*, August 29, 2014.

7. "Bowles Wins by 7,800 Votes; Recount Likely," *Detroit Free Press*, November 6, 1929.

8. Rick Perlstein, "I Thought I Understood the American Right. Trump Proved Me Wrong," *New York Times Magazine*, April 11, 2017.

9. Allie Gross, "Michigan Has Long Been Fertile Ground for the Far Right," *Detroit Free Press*, August 17, 2017.

10. Tom Stanton, *Terror in the City of Champions: Murder, Baseball and the Secret Society That Shocked Depression-Era Detroit* (Guilford, CT: Lyons Press, 2016), 22–29.

11. Lawrence McCracken, "Candidate Reveals That Secret Bullet Club Made Threats Against Family," *Detroit Free Press*, March 5, 1935.

12. Stanton, *Terror in the City of Champions*, 128–34.

13. Joe Louis, Edna Rust, and Art Rust, *Joe Louis: My Life* (New York: Harcourt, 1978), 9.

14. Louis, Rust, and Rust, 15. The young Louis learned some important lessons at school. Talking about his friend Freddie Guinyard, he recalled, "The teacher had said, only to colored kids, that if they made good grades she would see to it that they were rewarded by getting a chance to shine shoes at J.L. Hudson's department store on weekends. Freddie jumped up and said, 'Why would you need to have good grades to shine shoes?' And they sent him straight home. It was the first time I started thinking about racial matters."

15. Louis, Rust, and Rust, 26.

16. Louis, Rust, and Rust, 35–36.

17. Noam Hassenfeld, "Hank Greenberg: Caught Between Baseball and His Religion," WBUR, September 22, 2017.

18. Dominic J. Capeci, "Black-Jewish Relations in Wartime Detroit: The Marsh, Loving, Wolf Surveys , nos. and the Race Riot of 1943," *Jewish Social Studies* 47 3–4 (1985): 221–42.

19. For example, a search of the *New York Times* for 1936 produces 239 references

to "Jesse Owens," but 352 to "Joe Louis." For 1937 the ratio is 38 to 394, and for 1938, 24 to 298.

20. Margolick, *Beyond Glory*, 325.

21. Margolick, 314–19.

22. Alan Gould, "Louis K.O's Schmeling in First, Flooring Maxie Three Times; Fight Lasts Only 2:04 Minutes," *Detroit Free Press*, June 23, 1938.

23. Margolick, *Beyond Glory*.

24. "A Pair With a Punch: How World-Class Boxer Max Schmeling Discovered His Love for Coca-Cola," *Coca-Cola Journey*, October 29, 2013, www.coca -colacompany.com/stories/00000142-05ea-dc23-a5c2-9fffccf20000. The story has been deleted, but the internet is forever, and it can still be accessed via the Wayback Machine at https://web.archive.org/web/20170502083824/www.coca-colacompany .com/stories/00000142-05ea-dc23-a5c2-9fffccf20000.

Twenty-One: April 18, 1936

1. Charles Avison, *Detroit: City of Champions* (Detroit: Diomedea Publishing, 2008). The governor's letter is reproduced on page 117.

2. Ironically, it was in his next fight, two months later, that he would be defeated by Max Schmeling. This would remain his only defeat until 1950.

3. Scott Ferkovich, *Motor City Champs: Mickey Cochrane and the 1934–1935 Detroit Tigers* (Jefferson, NC: McFarland, 2018), chapter 10.

4. John C. Skipper, *Charlie Gehringer: A Biography of the Hall of Fame Tigers Second Baseman* (Jefferson, NC: McFarland, 2008).

5. Charles Bevis, "Mickey Cochrane," in *Detroit the Unconquerable: The 1935 World Champion Tigers*, ed. Scott Ferkovich (Phoenix, AZ: Society for American Baseball Research, 2014), 38–41.

6. Gregory Wolf, "Schoolboy Rowe," in Ferkovich, *Detroit the Unconquerable*, 116–22.

7. The story of the regular season is told in Ferkovich, *Motor City Champs*. Chapter 11 deals with the start of the season, chapter 12 the first half up to the All Star Break, and then chapter 13 covers the second half of the season.

8. Ferkovich, *Motor City Champs*, chapter 16.

9. Richard Bak, *A Place for Summer: A Narrative History of Tiger Stadium* (Detroit: Wayne State University Press), 176–86.

10. On the failure of the Detroit banks see Darwyn H, Lumley, *Breaking the Banks in the Motor City: The Auto Industry, the 1933 Detroit Banking Crisis and the Start of the New Deal* (Jefferson, NC: McFarland, 2009).

11. On espionage see Sidney Fine, *Sit-Down: The General Motors Strike of 1936–1937* (Ann Arbor: University of Michigan Press, 1969), 37–42; on violence see Stephen Norwood, "Ford's Brass Knuckles: Harry Bennett, The Cult of Muscularity, and Anti-Labor Terror—1920–1945," *Labor History* 37, no. 3 (1996): 365–91; and on the role of the police see Nelson Lichtenstein, *Walter Reuther: The Most Dangerous Man in Detroit* (Urbana: University of Illinois Press, 1997), 99–101.

12. Wyndham Mortimer, *Organize! My Life as a Union Man* (Boston: Beacon Press, 1971), 104.

13. Mortimer, *Organize!*, 105.

14. Howard Zinn, "A People's History Of The United States: Chapter 15—Self-Help in Hard Times," *History Is A Weapon*, www.historyisaweapon.com/defcon1/zinnselhel15.html.

15. The complete story of the sit-down strike is recounted in Fine, *Sit-Down*.

16. Amy Wilson, "Harry Bennett: Henry Ford's Chief Thug Targets UAW, Later Threatens Family Peace," *Automotive News*, June 16, 2003.

17. "The Battle of the Overpass," *Detroit News*, August 6, 1997, blogs.detroitnews.com/history/1997/08/06/the-battle-of-the-overpass. See also Lichtenstein, *Walter Reuther*, 85–86.

18. See for example Beth Tompkins Bates, *The Making of Black Detroit in the Age of Henry Ford* (Chapel Hill: University of North Carolina Press, 2012), chapter 1, or August Meier and Elliott M. Rudwick, *Black Detroit and the Rise of the UAW* (Ann Arbor: University of Michigan Press, 2007), chapter 1.

19. Adolf Hitler, *Mein Kampf* (Boston: Houghton Mifflin, 1941), 930.

20. On Ford's anti-Semitism see David Lanier Lewis, *The Public Image of Henry Ford: An American Folk Hero and His Company* (Detroit: Wayne State University Press, 1976), chapter 9. See Bates, *The Making of Black Detroit*, 39–54, on rationalizing Ford's racial and political prejudices.

21. David M. Lewis-Colman, *Race Against Liberalism: Black Workers and the UAW in Detroit* (Urbana: University of Illinois Press, 2008), 14–24.

22. James Baldwin, "A Report from Occupied Territory," *The Nation*, July 11, 1966.

23. Bates, *The Making of Black Detroit*, 230–31. Schuyler is a fascinating character. He began life as a socialist and his most famous work is a bitter satire, the novel *Black No More*, in which scientists discover an operation that can turn skin white. Lampooning white and black alike, he had a sharp eye for hypocrisy. Yet after the war he became a virulent anti-communist, providing support for the McCarthy witch hunts, and in the 1960s he actively opposed the civil rights movement and campaigned for Barry Goldwater. See Oscar Renal Williams, *George S. Schuyler: Portrait of a Black Conservative* (Knoxville, TN: University of Tennessee Press, 2007).

24. Lichtenstein, *Walter Reuther*, 211.

25. "UAW Opens Drive on Jobs Bias," *Detroit Free Press*, November 22, 1952; Lewis-Colman, *Race Against Liberalism*, 54–55; "Senate Passes Watered Down FEPC Bill," *Detroit Free Press*, May 25, 1955.

26. Other projects with a nationalist leaning at this time include the America First Committee, established in 1940 as an advocacy campaign to keep the United States out of the war. Like Coughlin, the America First Committee was associated with anti-Semitism.

27. Michael Kazin, *The Populist Persuasion: An American History* (New York: Basic Books, 1995), 109.

28. Michael Beschloss, "Hank Greenberg's Triumph over Hate Speech," *New York Times*, July 25, 2014.

29. John Rosengren, *Hank Greenberg: The Hero of Heroes* (New York: New American Library, 2014), 115.

Twenty-Two: September 2, 1933

1. Jack Carveth, "20,000 See Gallant Sir Win Fair Grounds Inaugural," *Detroit Free Press*, September 3, 1933.

2. On the general decline of horseracing in the United States at the end of the nineteenth century, see Steven Riess, "The Cyclical History of Horse Racing: The USA's Oldest and (Sometimes) Most Popular Spectator Sport," *International Journal of the History of Sport* 31, nos. 1–2 (2014): 29–54, especially 37–38. On Michigan law see William Hamilton, "Horse Racing in Michigan—A Primer," Michigan House of Representatives Fiscal Agency, *Fiscal Focus*, June 2017, www.house.mi .gov/hfa/PDF/Agriculture/FiscalFocus_Horse_Racing_in_Michigan.pdf. The State of Michigan passed a law against lotteries in 1835, which was often taken to encompass horse race betting. Yet various forms of racing, especially trotting, were popular in and around Detroit, and this form of racing has survived in metro Detroit to the present day.

3. Hub M. George, "Horse Racing Bill Passes and Takes Immediate Effect," *Detroit Free Press*, June 17, 1933.

4. The data is from Hamilton, "Horse Racing in Michigan," 16.

5. Lewis H. Walter, "Seabiscuit Captures Feature by Nose as 28,000 Attend," *Detroit Free Press*, September 8, 1936. He took another prize less than three weeks later: Lewis H. Walter, "Seabiscuit and Sweep Like Share Fair Grounds Honors," *Detroit Free Press*, September 27, 1936.

6. Hamilton, "Horse Racing in Michigan."

7. JC Reindl and John Gallagher, "Northville Downs, Michigan's Last Horse Track, to Become Upscale Homes," *Detroit Free Press*, April 17, 2018.

8. W.J. Rorabaugh, *Prohibition: A Very Short Introduction* (New York: Oxford University Press, 2018). Michigan was the first state to vote to repeal on April 10, 1933.

9. Daniel Okrent, *Last Call: The Rise and Fall of Prohibition* (New York: Simon and Schuster, 2010), 257.

10. Lisa McGirr, *The War on Alcohol: Prohibition and the Rise of the American State* (New York: Norton, 2016), 49–54.

11. Okrent, *Last Call*, 256.

12. Okrent, 259.

13. "Blind pigs" were so called because savvy bar owners would charge entrance to see a blind pig, after which the patrons would pass into a second room where they were presented with a free drink.

14. Okrent, *Last Call*, 129.

15. Okrent, 260.

16. McGirr, *The War on Alcohol*, 140–41.

17. James Buccellato, Early Organized Crime in Detroit: Vice, Corruption and the Rise of the Mafia (Charleston, SC: History Press, 2015).

18. Okrent, *Last Call*, 321.

19. Paul Kavieff, *The Violent Years: Prohibition and the Detroit Mobs* (Fort Lee, NJ: Barricade Books, 2013), 33.

20. Immortalized in Elvis Presley's "Jailhouse Rock": "The whole rhythm section was the Purple Gang."

21. Paul Kavieff, *The Purple Gang: Organized Crime in Detroit, 1910–1946* (New Jersey: Barricade Books, 2013), chapter 1.

22. Kavieff, *The Purple Gang*, chapter 6.

23. Holly M. Karibo, *Sin City North: Sex, Drugs and Citizenship in the Detroit-Windsor Borderland* (Chapel Hill: University of North Carolina Press, 2015), 35.

24. Karibo, *Sin City North*, 36.

25. A good description of the numbers game is in Felicia Bridget George, "Numbers and Neighborhoods: Seeking and Selling the American Dream in Detroit One Bet at a Time" (PhD diss., Wayne State University, 2015).

26. "City Officials 'Pass Buck' on Vice, Charge," *Detroit Free Press*, July 11, 1926.

27. Okrent, *Last Call*, 260.

28. Kavieff, *The Purple Gang*, 99–108.

29. Karibo, *Sin City North*, 15–20. To this day young Detroiters between the ages of eighteen and twenty-one cross the river for the same reason.

30. Sidney Fine, *Frank Murphy*, vol. 1, *The Detroit Years* (Ann Arbor: University of Michigan Press, 1975), 246–47.

31. Beth Tompkins Bates, *The Making of Black Detroit in the Age of Henry Ford* (Chapel Hill: University of North Carolina Press, 2012), 146–47.

32. "Tells Food Need Here," *Detroit Free Press*, October 28, 1931.

33. Diane Bernard, "The Time a President Deported 1 Million Mexican Americans for Supposedly Stealing U.S. Jobs," *Washington Post*, August 13, 2018. A first wave of deportations had occurred in 1921, during the post–World War I recession. As the Great Depression set in, they resumed. See Zaragosa Vargas, *Proletarians of the North: A History of Mexican Industrial Workers in Detroit and the Midwest, 1917–1933* (Berkeley: University of California Press, 1993), 83, 176–77.

34. Maurice Sugar, *The Ford Hunger March* (Berkeley, CA: Meiklejohn Civil Liberties Institute, 1980), 30–39.

35. Fine, *Frank Murphy*, 408–9.

36. Fine, 257–96.

37. Greenberg, *The Story of My Life*, 140–41. He was not the only Detroit sports star to participate in prison exhibition games organized by Purple Gang members. In 1954, Gordie Howe and Ted Lindsay played a hockey game in the prison yard, with the Red Wings providing the equipment and constructing the temporary ice rink. Richard Bak, "Red Wings' 1954 Prison Game Featured Pros and Cons," *Vintage Detroit*, January 25, 2015, www.detroitathletic.com/blog/2015/01/25/red-wings -1954-prison-game-featured-pros-cons.

Twenty-Three: May 11, 1930

1. "Detroit Stars Win Two Games," *Detroit Free Press*, May 12, 1930.

2. "Cuban Nine Beats Stars in Overtime," *Detroit Free Press*, May 11, 1930.

3. Richard Bak, *Turkey Stearnes and the Detroit Stars: The Negro Leagues in Detroit, 1919–1933* (Detroit: Wayne State University Press, 1995), 189.

4. "Turkey Stearnes," National Baseball Hall of Fame, baseballhall.org/hall-of-famers/stearnes-turkey.

5. Bak, *Turkey Stearnes and the Detroit Stars*, 188.

6. Bak, *Turkey Stearnes*, 180.

7. Bak, *Turkey Stearnes*, 188.

8. Bak, *Turkey Stearnes*, 189.

9. Bak, *Turkey Stearnes*, 189–91.

10. "Night Game Draws Crowd," *Detroit Free Press*, June 28, 1930.

11. Bak, *Turkey Stearnes*, 191–95.

12. Bak, *Turkey Stearnes*, 195–97.

13. Norman L. Macht, "Does Baseball Deserve This Black Eye?," *Baseball Research Journal* 38, no. 1 (2009): 5–9.

14. Neil Lanctot, *Negro League Baseball: The Rise and Ruin of a Black Institution* (Philadelphia: University of Pennsylvania Press, 2004), 213.

15. Lawrence D. Hogan, *Shades of Glory: The Negro Leagues and the Story of African American Baseball* (Washington, DC: National Geographic Books, 2006), 195.

16. Hogan, *Shades of Glory*, 108.

17. Richard Bak, *Cobb Would Have Caught It: The Golden Age of Baseball in Detroit* (Detroit: Wayne State University Press, 1991), 99.

18. Bak, *Cobb Would Have Caught It*, 193.

19. "Lawyer Roxborough Dead," *Detroit Free Press*, August 19, 1908.

20. Greg Kowalski, *Wicked Hamtramck: Lust, Liquor and Lead* (Charleston, SC: History Press, 2010), 43–47, 57–64.

21. Bak, *Turkey Stearnes*, 195–99.

22. The story of this era is told in Lanctot, *Negro League Baseball*.

23. Bak, *Turkey Stearnes*, 205–7.

24. Richard Bak, *A Place for Summer: A Narrative History of Tiger Stadium* (Detroit: Wayne State University Press), 202–3.

25. Bak, *Turkey Stearnes*, 57–61.

26. Mark Ribowsky, *A Complete History of the Negro Leagues, 1884–1955* (Secaucus, NJ: Citadel Press, 1997), chapter 2.

27. Bak, *Turkey Stearnes and the Detroit Stars*, 55–59.

28. "Mayor Smith Welcomes Joint Annual Meeting of Eastern and Western Colored Leagues," *New York Amsterdam News*, January 19, 1927.

29. Young and Wheeler, *Hard Stuff*, 20.

30. Erdmann Doane Beynon, "The Voodoo Cult Among Negro Migrants in Detroit," *American Journal of Sociology* 43, no. 6 (1938), 894–907.

31. Born Elijah Poole in 1897, he moved his family from Georgia to Hamtramck in 1923. When Fard disappeared in 1934, Elijah Muhammad took over the Nation of Islam after a split with his co-religionists and moved to Chicago. "Elijah Muhammad," *Biography*, January 24, 2018, www.biography.com/political-figure/elijah -muhammad.

32. Bak, *Turkey Stearnes*, 184–87; Michael Lomax, *Black Baseball Entrepreneurs: The Negro National and Eastern Colored Leagues, 1902–31* (New York: Syracuse University Press, 2014), 401–3, 416–17.

33. Bak, *Cobb Would Have Caught It*, 136.

34. Bak, *Turkey Stearnes*, 5.

Twenty-Four: May 10, 1927

1. Harry Bullion, "Cobb in Auspicious Debut as Mackmen Turn Back Tigers," *Detroit Free Press*, May 11, 1927.

2. James Walker, *Crack of the Bat: A History of Baseball on the Radio* (University of Nebraska Press, 2015), 67–68.

3. Curt Smith, *Voices of the Game: The Acclaimed Chronicle of Baseball Radio and Television Broadcasting—From 1921 to the Present* (New York: Simon and Schuster, 1987), 34–37.

4. Matt Bohn, "'Good Afternoon, Boys and Girls': The 1935 Tigers on the Radio," in *Detroit the Unconquerable: The 1935 World Champion Tigers*, Scott Ferkovich, ed. (Phoenix, AZ: Society for American Baseball Research), 185–91.

5. "Ty Cobb," Baseball Reference, www.baseball-reference.com/players/c /cobbty01.shtml.

6. Al Stump, "A Money Player: Ty Cobb Was a Peach When It Came to Investments, Too," *Los Angeles Times*, July 12, 1991. In 2020 dollars, $85,000 is worth about $1.3 million. According to Spotrac, there are more than five hundred current MLB players with salaries in excess of $1.3 million.

7. Al Stump, *Cobb: A Biography* (Chapel Hill, NC: Algonquin Books, 1996), 284–86.

8. Stump, *Cobb*, 320.

9. Michael Jackman, "103 Years Ago, That Asshole Ty Cobb Attacked a Fan," *Detroit Metro Times*, May 15, 2017.

10. Stump, *Cobb*, 206–7.

11. Stump, 419.

12. Stump, 118–19.

13. Stump, 415.

14. Stump, 420.

15. Charles Leerhsen, *Ty Cobb: A Terrible Beauty* (New York: Simon and Schuster, 2015).

16. Leerhsen, *Ty Cobb*, 304.

17. Michael Bamberger, "Man of the Century Double Duty Radcliffe Nemesis of Ty Cobb, Close Friend of Satchel Paige, A Negro Leagues Legend Remains the Life of the Party as He Celebrates his 100th Birthday," *Sports Illustrated*, July 15, 2002.

18. Leerhsen, 151–53.

19. Leerhsen, 186–89.

20. A search of newspaper archives reveals hundreds of references to the incident published between September and November 1909, many of which are identical, but some of which vary significantly in detail. Not all mention the knife and not all mention the bellhop. However, none of them mention the race of the Euclid Hotel employees, and all refer to the victim as "Stanfield." In Stump's biography, however, he becomes "Stansfield," and both bellhop and nightwatchman are identified as black: Stump, 170–72.

21. Leerhsen, 302–4

22. Richard Bak, *Cobb Would Have Caught It: The Golden Age of Baseball in Detroit* (Detroit: Wayne State University Press, 1991), 170.

23. Kyle P. McNary, *Ted "Double Duty" Radcliffe: 36 Years of Pitching and Catching in Baseball's Negro Leagues* (Minneapolis: McNary Publishing, 1994), 45–46.

24. Karen Miller, *Managing Inequality: Northern Racial Liberalism in Interwar Detroit* (New York: New York University Press, 2015), 77–78.

25. Brent Staples, "How Italians Became White," *New York Times*, October 12, 2019. His column is partially based on Matthew Frye Jacobson's book, *Whiteness of a Different Color: European Immigrants and the Alchemy of Race* (Cambridge, MA: Harvard University Press, 1999).

26. The Italian consul Pasquale Corte wrote a harrowing contemporary account, preserved in the *New York Times*: "Signor Corte's Farewell," May 24, 1891.

Twenty-Five: July 12, 1921

1. "Auto Kills Son of Councilman," *Detroit Free Press*, July 13, 1921.

2. David Finkelman, "Frederick Winslow Taylor," in *The Automobile Industry, 1896–1920*, ed. George S. May (New York: Facts on File, 1990), 438–40.

3. Ford R. Bryan, *Henry's Lieutenants* (Detroit: Wayne State University Press, 2003). There is no evidence that Taylor worked directly with Ford, but Taylor's ideas were widely reported, and it seems certain that the Ford organization would have been aware of them.

4. Peter Collier and David Horowitz, *The Fords: An American Epic* (New York: Encounter Books, 2002), 39. These words were actually spoken under cross-examination in the George Selden patent case. Ford was accused of infringing a patent taken out in 1895, at a time when most producers were acknowledging the patent and paying licenses. Ford lost in the first instance but then won on appeal, with the court opining that the gasoline automobile was a "social invention" and therefore the patent did not apply.

5. "U.S. Automobile Production Figures," Wikipedia, https://en.wikipedia.org /wiki/U.S._Automobile_Production_Figures.

6. Steven Klepper, "The Capabilities of New Firms and the Evolution of the US Automobile Industry," *Industrial and Corporate Change* 11, no. 4 (2002): 645–66.

7. Bryan, *Henry's Lieutenants*, 69.

8. Charles E. Sorensen, *My Forty Years with Ford* (Detroit: Wayne State University Press, 2006), 36.

9. Harry Barnard, *Independent Man: The Life of Senator James Couzens* (Detroit: Wayne State University Press, 2002). On the early history of the company see chapters 7–12. Chapter 13 on the $5-a-day plan. Sorensen stated the plan actually originated with Ford, largely because Ford told him so, but historians consider this version less plausible. David Lanier Lewis, *The Public Image of Henry Ford: An American Folk Hero and His Company* (Detroit: Wayne State University Press, 1976), 69–73.

10. Michael Ballaban, "When Henry Ford's Benevolent Secret Police Ruled His Workers," *Jalopnik*, March 23, 2014.

11. Richard Snow, *I Invented the Modern Age: The Rise of Henry Ford* (New York: Scribner, 2013), 232.

12. Ford Motor Company, *Helpful Hints and Advice to Employees to Help Them Grasp the Opportunities Which Are Presented to Them by the Ford Profit-Sharing Plan* (Detroit: Ford Motor Company, 1915).

13. Snow, *I Invented the Modern Age*, 233.

14. Elizabeth S. Anderson, *Private Government: How Employers Rule Our Lives (And Why We Don't Talk About It)* (Princeton, NJ: Princeton University Press, 2017), xix. She mentions Ford's rules on page 47.

15. "Melting Pot Ceremony at Ford English School, July 4, 1917," The Henry Ford, www.thehenryford.org/collections-and-research/digital-collections/artifact /254569.

16. Bill Loomis, "1900–1930: The Years of Driving Dangerously," *Detroit News*, April 26, 2015.

17. "John A. Kronk," Find A Grave, www.findagrave.com/memorial/135056233 /john-a.-kronk. According to his obituary in the *Detroit Free Press* he was born in Detroit ("John Kronk Dies of Heart Attack," *Detroit Free Press*, February 24, 1954). Although the two sources disagree as to place, they agree that the date was April 19, 1883.

18. "John Kronk Dies of Heart Attack."

19. Daniel Amsterdam, *Roaring Metropolis: Businessmen's Campaign for a Civic Welfare State* (Philadelphia, University of Pennsylvania Press, 2016), 16–27.

20. He parted with the saloon even though he clearly liked to drink, a diversion he combined with a sense of humor. According to one tribute after he died, during elections he would go into a bar and start up a loud argument opposing the views of the local clientele, storming out once everyone was riled up, and declaring as he left, "If that isn't my attitude, my name is not . . . ," giving the name of an opposing candidate: James Ransom, "Pay Tribute to Council Dean," *Detroit Free Press*, February 28, 1954.

21. "John Kronk Dies of Heart Attack."

22. "D.U.R. Is Denied Fare Petition," *Detroit Free Press*, September 14, 1918.

23. Barnard, *Independent Man*, chapters 20–22.

24. Amsterdam, *Roaring Metropolis*, 58–59.

25. "City Building's Cost Is Shaved," *Detroit Free Press*, March 14, 1922.

26. "Kronk Is Honored by City Council," *Detroit Free Press*, January 6, 1926.

27. "Propose $900,000 Stadium For Athletics In Detroit," *Detroit Free Press*, December 22, 1921.

28. Genevieve Fox, "Recreation – A Part of the City's Job," *National Municipal Review* 10, no. 8 (1921): 423–27.

29. John H. Varnum, "Municipal Recreation Department Grows from $300-A-Year Start 25 Years Ago to Huge Undertaking Reaching Life of Every Citizen," *Detroit Free Press*, September 25, 1927; "Play Budget Is Explained," *Detroit Free Press*, January 5, 1930.

30. Forrester B. Washington, "Recreational Facilities for the Negro," *Annals of the American Academy of Political and Social Science* 140, no. 1 (1928), 272–82.

31. Richard Bak, *Joe Louis: The Great Black Hope* (Dallas, TX: Taylor Publishing, 1996), 26.

Twenty-Six: October 9, 1910

1. Rick Huhn, *The Chalmers Race: Ty Cobb, Napoleon Lajoie, and the Controversial 1910 Batting Title that Became a National Obsession* (Lincoln: University of Nebraska Press, 2014), 230.

2. For example, a walk is just as good a way to get to first base as a single, so any batter who gets more walks should be credited. This was the conceit behind the 2004 bestseller *Moneyball*, covering innovations credited with fundamentally changing the way that teams approach the game.

3. This is before the Black Sox Scandal of 1919 led the leagues to appoint a single, all-powerful MLB commissioner.

4. Rick Huhn, *The Chalmers Race*, 12–15.

5. Huhn, 40–44.

6. Huhn, 76–77.

7. Huhn, 99.

8. Huhn, 103–109.

9. Huhn, 109–11.

10. Huhn, 112–13.

11. E. A. Batchelor, "Unofficial Averages Make Lajoie Winner," *Detroit Free Press*, October 10, 1910.

12. Huhn, *The Chalmers Race*, 139–41.

13. Huhn, 141–42.

14. Huhn, 222–25.

15. Huhn, 156–57.

16. Kenneth Brevoort and Howard P. Marvel, "Successful Monopolization Through Predation: The National Cash Register Company," in *Antitrust Law and Economics*, ed. John B. Kirkwood (Bingley, UK: Emerald Group Publishing Limited, 2009), 85–125.

17. Walter A. Friedman, "John H. Patterson and the Sales Strategy of the National Cash Register Company, 1884 to 1922," *Business History Review* 72, no. 4 (1998), 552–84.

18. Huhn, *The Chalmers Race*, 10–12.

19. Brent D. Ryan and Daniel Campo, "Autopia's End: The Decline and Fall of Detroit's Automotive Manufacturing Landscape," *Journal of Planning History* 12, no. 2 (2013), 95–132. The mansion survives, and the architectural ensemble on Seminole and Iroquois Streets remains a spectacular monument to the wealth of that era.

20. See for example Hugh Chalmers, "Putting Sales Force into Advertising," 26–29; and Chalmers, "Advertising 'Copy,'" 42–43, 93, cited in Rob Schorman, "'This Astounding Car for $1,500': The Year Automobile Advertising Came of Age," *Enterprise & Society* 11, no. 3 (2010), 468–523.

21. Rob Schorman, "'This Astounding Car for $1,500': The Year Automobile Advertising Came of Age," *Enterprise & Society* 11, no. 3 (2010), 468–523.

22. Michael J. Seneca, *The Fairmount Park Motor Races, 1908–1911* (Jefferson, NC: McFarland, 2003), 65–94.

23. David Lanier Lewis, *The Public Image of Henry Ford: An American Folk Hero and His Company* (Detroit: Wayne State University Press, 1976), 72.

24. Hugh Chalmers, "1912 Prospects for Automobile Industry," *Scientific American* 105, no. 5 (1911): 109–10.

25. Donald Finlay Davis, *Conspicuous Production: Automobiles and Elites in Detroit, 1899–1933* (Philadelphia: Temple University Press, 1988), 101–3.

26. Davis, *Conspicuous Production*, 103–4.

27. Ken Voyles and Mary Rodrique, *The Enduring Legacy of the Detroit Athletic Club: Driving the Motor City* (Charleston, SC: History Press, 2012), 11.

28. Voyles and Mary Rodrique, 73.

29. Davis, *Conspicuous Production*, 90.

30. Davis, 154–56.

31. George S. May, *The Automobile Industry, 1896–1920* (New York: Facts on File, 1990), 76–79.

32. Ryan and Campo, "Autopia's End," 10.

33. "Hugh Chalmers Dies in East After Illness on Auto Tour," *Detroit Free Press*, June 3, 1932.

34. Charles K. Hyde, *Riding the Roller Coaster: A History of the Chrysler Corporation* (Detroit: Wayne State University Press, 2003), 19–20.

Twenty-Seven: October 10, 1901

1. Lawrence Goldstone, *Drive! Henry Ford, George Selden, and the Race to Invent the Auto Age* (New York: Random House, 2016), 105–7.

2. Peter Collier and David Horowitz, *The Fords: An American Epic* (New York: Encounter Books, 2002), 27.

3. "Alex Winton's Fast Mile," *Detroit Free Press*, October 11, 1901.

4. "Alex Winton's Fast Mile."

5. Goldstone, *Drive!*, 100.

6. David Lanier Lewis, *The Public Image of Henry Ford: An American Folk Hero and His Company* (Detroit: Wayne State University Press, 1976), 17.

7. Collier and Horowitz, *The Fords*, 27–28.

8. "Tom Cooper: Fastest Man in Detroit," *m-bike*, m-bike.org/2012/11/21/tom-cooper-fastest-man-in-detroit.

9. Goldstone, *Drive!*, 112–15.

10. "Oldfield Hero of Auto Races," *Detroit Free Press*, October 26, 1902.

11. Goldstone, *Drive!*, 116–18.

12. Lewis, *The Public Image of Henry Ford*, 25–26.

13. Lewis, 26–27. Ford did produce racing cars again in 1909 and did not formally announce an end to participation in competition until 1912. In 1935 the company resumed racing again.

14. James J. Flink, *America Adopts the Automobile, 1895–1910* (Cambridge, MA: MIT Press, 1970), 279–92.

15. Lewis, *The Public Image of Henry Ford*, 17.

16. (now 6520) Mack Av on Beltline RR—between Beaufait and Bellevue.

17. "Alex Winton's Fast Mile."

18. "Grosse Pointe, Michigan Harness Track 1894: Tuesday, July 17, 1894," *MI Harness*, www.mi-harness.net/Mich/grsptetrk.html.

19. "1853 Hamtramck: A Classic Race," MI Harness, www.mi-harness.net/Mich/1853.html.

20. "The Turf," *Detroit Free Press*, April 3, 1884; "American Trotting Association," *Detroit Free Press*, March 3, 1887.

21. Lewis, *The Public Image of Henry Ford*, 26.

22. Frank S. Cooke, "Famous Blue Ribbon Classics May Expire with the Local Driving Club," *Detroit Free Press*, February 17, 1918.

23. Dan Austin, "William Cotter Maybury Monument," *Historic Detroit*, www.historicdetroit.org/building/william-cotter-maybury-monument.

Twenty-Eight: October 24, 1887

1. Brian Martin, *The Detroit Wolverines: The Rise and Wreck of a National League Champion, 1881–1888* (Jefferson, NC: McFarland, 2017), 168.

2. Martin, *The Detroit Wolverines.*

3. Martin, 14–18.

4. Martin, 12–15.

5. There are many accounts of the beginnings of baseball—Harold Seymour's remains one of the best. Harold Seymour, *Baseball: The Early Years* (New York: Oxford University Press, 1960), chapters 1–8.

6. Martin, *The Detroit Wolverines*, chapter 2.

7. William G. Thompson was mayor between 1880 and 1883, and should not be confused with William B. Thompson, who had two stints as mayor, 1907–08 and 1911–12. William G. was a colorful character. Severely wounded at Chancellorsville in the Civil War, he enjoyed frequenting Detroit's many saloons and eventually died in 1904 after being knocked down by a bicycle. Melvin G. Holli and Peter d'Alroy Jones, *Biographical Dictionary of American Mayors, 1820–1980* (Westport, CT: Greenwood Press, 1981), 360–61.

8. Seymour, *Baseball*, 91–93.

9. Martin, *The Detroit Wolverines*, 43–50.

10. Martin, 53–56.

11. "Sporting Matters," *Detroit Free Press*, October 15, 1884.

12. Martin, *The Detroit Wolverines.*

13. Seymour, *Baseball*, chapter 12.

14. "Sporting Matters."

15. Martin, *The Detroit Wolverines*, chapter 8.

16. "Extend the Championship," *Detroit Free Press*, October 25, 1887.

17. Martin, *The Detroit Wolverines*, chapter 11.

18. Melvin Holli, *Reform in Detroit: Hazen S. Pingree and Urban Politics* (New York: Oxford University Press, 1969), 13–15. The following paragraphs are based on this book.

19. "H.S. Pingree for Mayor," *Plaindealer*, November 1, 1889.

20. Bill Loomis, "Hazen Pingree: Quite Possibly Detroit's Finest Mayor," *Detroit News*, January 6, 2013.

21. Loomis, "Hazen Pingree," 79. See also "The Pre-D.S.R. Years—Part II: The Streetcar Companies vs. Mayor Hazen Pingree (1890–1900)," Detroit Transit History, www.detroittransithistory.info/ThePingreeYears.html.

22. Holli, *Reform in Detroit*, chapters 5–6.

23. A stone memorial on Jefferson Avenue just east of the bridge to Belle Isle marks the spot where the last toll booth in the city stood.

24. Holli, *Reform in Detroit*, 57–59.

25. See Loomis, "Hazen Pingree," for these and other details.

26. Loomis, "Hazen Pingree," chapter 4.

27. Bak, *A Place for Summer: A Narrative History of Tiger Stadium* (Detroit: Wayne State University Press), 42–46.

Twenty-Nine: August 8, 1859

1. "Base Ball Match," *Detroit Free Press*, August 9, 1859.

2. "Base Ball Match."

3. John C. Schneider, *Detroit and the Problem of Order, 1830–1880: A Geography of Crime, Riot, and Policing* (Lincoln: University of Nebraska Press, 1980), 7.

4. Schneider, *Detroit and the Problem of Order*, 49.

5. Schneider, Tables 1-1 and 1-2, pp. 16–19.

6. Silas Farmer, *History of Detroit and Wayne County and Early Michigan: A Chronological Cyclopedia of the Past and Present* (1890; La Crosse, WI: Brookhaven Press, 2000), 360, 478.

7. "He Was the Champion," *Detroit Free Press*, March 14, 1896.

8. Farmer, *History of Detroit and Wayne County and Early Michigan*, 352.

9. Schneider, *Detroit and the Problem of Order*, 42.

10. Schneider, 36–40.

11. Schneider, 27.

12. Schneider, 23.

13. Schneider, chapter 3.

14. "Base Ball Match,"

15. Peter Morris, *Baseball Fever: Early Baseball in Michigan* (Ann Arbor: University of Michigan Press, 2003), 1.

16. Brian Martin, *The Detroit Wolverines: The Rise and Wreck of a National League Champion, 1881–1888* (Jefferson, NC: McFarland, 2017), 13–14.

17. Melvin Holli, *Reform in Detroit: Hazen S. Pingree and Urban Politics* (New York: Oxford University Press, 1969), 46.

18. Morris, *Baseball Fever*, 199.

19. Morris, 195–96.

20. James William Massie, *America: The Origin of Her Present Conflict; Her Prospect for the Slave, and Her Claim for Anti-slavery Sympathy* (London: John Snow, 1864), 309.

21. Massie, 66.

22. David Katzman, *Before the Ghetto: Black Detroit in the Nineteenth Century* (Urbana: University of Illinois Press, 1975), 46.

23. Farmer, *History of Detroit and Wayne County and Early Michigan*, 348.

24. Schneider, *Detroit and the Problem of Order*, 80–83.

Thirty: June 2, 1763

1. Francis Parkman, *The Conspiracy of Pontiac and the Indian War After the Conquest of Canada*, (London; New York: J.M. Dent; E.P. Dutton, 1851) 338–41.

2. A letter from Etherington dated June 12 was printed in George William Featherstonhaugh, *A canoe voyage up the Minnay Sotor; with an account of the lead*

and copper deposits in Wisconsin; of the gold region in the Cherokee country; and sketches of popular manners; &c. &c. &c. (London: Richard Bentley, 1846), 115–16.

3. Patty Loew, *Indian Nations of Wisconsin: Histories of Endurance and Renewal* (Madison: Wisconsin Historical Society Press, 2001). The alliance was recognized by the French settlers who arrived in the seventeenth century: Donald L. Fixico, "The Alliance of the Three Fires in Trade and War, 1630–1812," *Michigan Historical Review* 20, no. 2 (1994): 1–23.

4. Peter N. Moogk, *La Nouvelle France: The Making of French Canada—A Cultural History* (East Lansing: Michigan State University Press, 2000).

5. Jeremy Adelman and Stephen Aron, "From Borderlands to Borders: Empires, Nation-States, and the Peoples in Between in North American History," *American Historical Review* 104, no. 3 (1999): 814–41.

6. Fred Anderson, *The War That Made America: A Short History of the French and Indian War* (New York: Penguin, 2006).

7. Parkman, *The Conspiracy of Pontiac and the Indian War*, 167–68.

8. Parkman, *The Conspiracy of Pontiac and the Indian War*, 172–76, and Keith R. Widder, *Beyond Pontiac's Shadow: Michilimackinac and the Anglo-Indian War of 1763* (Lansing: Michigan State University Press, 2013), 96–98.

9. Alfred A. Cave, "The Delaware Prophet Neolin: A Reappraisal," *Ethnohistory* 46, no. 2 (1999): 265–90.

10. An account by an Ottawa written in 1887 suggests that he did not have the full support of his own people—Andrew J. Blackbird, *History of the Ottawa and Chippewa Indians of Michigan: A Grammar of Their Language, and Personal and Family History of the Author* (Ypsilanti, MI.: Ypsilantian Job Printing House, 1887), chapter 1.

11. Richard Middleton, "Pontiac: Local Warrior or Pan-Indian Leader?," *Michigan Historical Review* 32, no. 2 (2006): 1–32.

12. *The Siege of Detroit in 1763: The Journal of Pontiac's Conspiracy, and John Rutherford's Narrative of a Captivity*, ed. Milo Milton Quaife (Chicago: RR Donnelley, 1958), 21.

13. Quaife, *The Siege of Detroit in 1763*, 28–32.

14. Parkman, *The Conspiracy of Pontiac and the Indian War*, 305–21. "Bloody Run" is still marked on Google Maps.

15. Quaife, *Siege of Detroit in 1763*, 211.

16. Middleton, "Pontiac: Local Warrior or Pan-Indian Leader?," 30.

17. Parkman, *The Conspiracy of Pontiac and the Indian War*, chapter 31.

18. Linda Ball, "Early French Families of Detroit," *Michigan Roots*, January 6, 2014.

19. Jean Dodenhoff, "Grosse Pointe's First Settlers: From Whence Did They Come?," in *Tonnancour: Life in Grosse Pointe and Along the Shores of Lake St. Claire*, vol. 2, ed. Arthur M. Wood, www.gphistorical.org/pdf-files/tonnancour/settlers.pdf.

20. See Tiya Miles, *The Dawn of Detroit: A Chronicle of Slavery and Free-

dom in the City of the Straits (New York: The New Press, 2017).

21. Thomas Vennum, *American Indian Lacrosse: Little Brother of War* (Baltimore: Johns Hopkins University Press, 2008).

22. Indeed, according to descriptions by English settlers Native Americans also had their own version of football, which the English noted was much gentler to the one they had grown up with back home: William Wood, *Wood's New England Prospects* (Boston: Prince Society, 1865), part 2, chapter 7, p. 83.

23. Donald M. Fisher, *Lacrosse: A History of the Game* (Baltimore: Johns Hopkins University Press, 2002), chapter 1.

24. Miles, *Dawn of Detroit*, 1.

INDEX